Intellectual Property Law in Israel

Intellectual Property Law in Israel

Second Edition

Orit Fischman Afori, David Gilat,
Eran Bareket & Tamir Afori

The Assistants:

Sonia Shnyder
Chen Ben Dori-Alkan

This book was originally published as a monograph in the International Encyclopaedia of Laws/Intellectual Property Law.

General Editors: Roger Blanpain, Frank Hendrickx
Volume Editor: Hendrik Vanhees

Wolters Kluwer

Published by:
Kluwer Law International B.V.
PO Box 316
2400 AH Alphen aan den Rijn
The Netherlands
Website: www.wklawbusiness.com

Sold and distributed in North, Central and South America by:
Wolters Kluwer Legal & Regulatory U.S.
7201 McKinney Circle
Frederick, MD 21704
United States of America
Email: customer.service@wolterskluwer.com

Sold and distributed in all other countries by:
Turpin Distribution Services Ltd.
Stratton Business Park
Pegasus Drive, Biggleswade
Bedfordshire SG18 8TQ
United Kingdom
Email: kluwerlaw@turpin-distribution.com

ISBN 978-90-411-6858-0

This title is available on www.kluwerlawonline.com

The Authors

Prof. Orit Fischman Afori is the Dean of the School of Law, College of Management Academic Studies, Israel. Prof. Fischman Afori earned her degrees, LLB (*cum laude*) LLM (*cum laude*) and LLD, at the Hebrew University of Jerusalem, Israel. Her doctorate dissertation focused on derivative works in copyright law and was published as a book in Israel. Prof. Fischman Afori's main fields of research are intellectual property law in general and copyright law in particular. Her publications in the area of intellectual property law focus on copyright, industrial designs and cultural rights as human rights.

Prof. Fischman Afori publishes extensively in Israel, Europe and in the US. Prof. Fischman Afori is teaching various courses, including Corporate Law; Copyright Law; Introduction to Intellectual Property; and is directing various seminars in the intellectual property field. Prof. Fischman Afori conducted research as a visiting scholar at the School Of Law (Boalt Hall), University of California, Berkeley, US, in 2007, and at the Law Scholl, Cambridge University, UK, in 2013.

Prof. Fischman Afori's personal Author Page is at: https://www.colman.ac.il/en/node/4585.

David Gilat, Attorney-at-Law, Patent Attorney, is a Senior Partner at Gilat, Bareket & Co. – Reinhold Cohn Group. David earned his BSc (Chemistry) degree (1986) at the Hebrew University of Jerusalem, and his LLB degree (1991) at Tel Aviv University. David has extensive professional experience in all aspects of intellectual property, in particular patents, trademarks, designs, copyrights, distribution agreements and competition law, including litigation, transactions and general consulting on intellectual property issues. He has also served as a member of a committee for revising the patent law and appeared before Legislation Committees of the *Knesset* (Israel's parliament) in connection with legislation of amendments to the intellectual property laws. David is an adjunct professor at the Law Faculty of the Tel Aviv University, and occasionally lectures in the field of intellectual property in Israeli academic institutions and other forums. David served as a research fellow at the Max Planck Institute for Foreign and International Patent, Copyright and Competition Laws, in Munich, Germany (1992–1993).

He is the author of several publications including '*Experimental Use and Patents*', International Review of Industrial Property and Competition Law (IIC) Studies (Vol. 16, 1995), the Israel chapters of *Trademark Cancellation International Practice and Procedures Guide* of the *International Trademark Association (INTA);* the '*Brown Book*' (*Manual IP, Kluwer Law International*); '*Trademarks Throughout The World – Thomson Reuters*'; Expert Guides – Legal Media Group, as well as many articles and reports. David is a member of International Association for the Protection of Intellectual Property (AIPPI); Association Litteraire et Artistique Internationale (ALAI); International Trademark Association (INTA) (serves on the Publications Committee as a Contributing Author & Editor); Israel Bar Association (intellectual property committee); Israel Patent Attorney Association; Licensing Executives Society International (LES).

Eran Bareket, Attorney-at-Law, is a Senior Partner at Gilat, Bareket & Co. – Reinhold Cohn Group. Eran earned his LLB (*cum laude*) degree (1990) from Tel Aviv University. He is also an adjunct professor at the Centre of Law and Technology of the Haifa University Faculty of Law, where he teaches Patents Law and Patents Litigation to LLB and LLM students. Eran also serves as a special advisor for intellectual property matter to the Comptroller General of the Israeli Ministry of Finance.

Eran was also involved in the recent amendments of the Patents Law in the *Knesset* and is involved in the legislation of additional bills pending before the *Knesset*. In his private practice, Eran's main field of expertise is litigation and transactional work concerning intellectual property rights (patents, plant breeders' rights, copyright, trademarks and designs), unjust enrichment and competition law, as well as complex litigations, particularly those involving issues of technology. Eran is a member of the International Association for the Protection of Intellectual Property (AIPPI), Association Litteraire et Artistique Internationale (ALAI), International Trademark Association (INTA), Is Cham (Israel Chamber of Commerce China), the Israel Bar Association (member of the Intellectual Property Legislation Committee), and LES.

Tamir Afori, Attorney-at-Law, is a Senior Partner at Gilat, Bareket & Co. – Reinhold Cohn Group. Tamir earned his LLB degree at Haifa University (*cum laude*), and his LLM at the Hebrew University of Jerusalem, Israel. Tamir has been an adjunct professor at the Law Faculty of Tel Aviv University, and at the Law Faculty of Bar-Ilan University, and occasionally lectures in the field of intellectual property in academic institutions and other forums. He is the author of the book *'The Copyright Act'* (Nevo publishing house, 2012, Hebrew).

Tamir has extensive professional experience in all aspects of intellectual property. Until 2008, Tamir worked on intellectual property matters in the Israeli Ministry of Justice, and was responsible for, *inter alia*, the preparation and drafting of Israel's copyright act, the law for protection of integrated circuit, and many other statutory instruments. He has regularly appeared before Legislation Committees of the *Knesset* on behalf of the government, and has appeared before the Supreme Court in many of the precedential intellectual property cases during the last decade. Tamir was a member of the inter-ministerial committee for the determination of blank tape levy and the inter-ministerial committee for enforcement of intellectual property.

The Assistants

Sonia Shnyder earned her LLB degree from the Hebrew University of Jerusalem and her MA (English, *magna cum laude*) from Tel Aviv University. She is an attorney at Gilat, Bareket & Co. Her practice focuses on various aspects of intellectual property law (with an emphasis on trademarks, appellations of origin, commercial torts and patents), commercial law, company law, entertainment law and international transactions.

She regularly contributes articles, legal updates and reviews to leading international intellectual property publications and treatises, including *World Trademark Review*, *Trademarks Throughout the World* (Thomson Reuters), *Trademark Cancellation: International Practice and Procedures Guide* (INTA), *Patent Litigation* (European Lawyer), and *Manual of Industrial Property* (Kluwer). She authored the chapter on Israel in *E-Commerce and the Law of Digital Signatures* (Oceana, 2005) and co-authored the chapter in *World Intellectual Property Rights and Remedies – Laws with Commentary* (Oceana, 2003). She is a member of the Israel Bar.

Chen Ben Dori-Alkan is an associate at Gilat, Bareket & Co. Chen earned her LLB degree, her BSc.Med. degree and her MPH (Public Health) degree at the Hebrew University of Jerusalem, Israel. Chen handles various aspects of intellectual property law, with an emphasis on patents, trademarks and plant breeders' rights, as well as various aspects of commercial law, company law and international transactions. Chen was also involved in the recent amendments of the Patents Law in *Knesset* and is involved in the legislation of additional bills pending before the *Knesset*. She is a member of the Israel Bar Association.

The Authors

Table of Contents

List of Abbreviations

ACH	Additional Civil Hearing
ALA	Application for Leave to Appeal
CA	Civil Appeal
CC	Civil Case
Cr.A.	Criminal Appeal
HCJ	High Court of Justice
LCA	Leave to Appeal (Civil)
IPTO	The Israeli Patent Office
MA	Miscellaneous Appeal
MCA	Miscellaneous Civil Application
MCM	Miscellaneous Civil Motion
OM	Originating Motion
PBR	Plants Breeders' Rights
P.D.	Piskei Din (official Supreme Court decisions publication)*
P.M.	Psakim Mehoziim (Official District and Magistrate Court Decisions Publication)*
Sup. Ct.	Supreme Court
TA	Tel Aviv (District or Magistrate Court)

List of Abbreviations

Publication of Court Cases

Until the year 2008, Israeli court cases were published in officially printed publications. Supreme Court cases were published in *Piskei Din* (PD); District and Magistrate Court cases were published in *Psakim Mehoziim* (PM). Since the early nineties, court cases have been uploaded on a regular basis to various digital databases, such as *Dinim*, *Takdin* or *Nevo*, and to the official website of the Judicial Authority (www.court.gov.il). Reference to recent cases, therefore, may be made either by mentioning the serial number and classification of the case, and specific database in which the case was published or simply by noting the case is 'unpublished', although most cases appear in one of the digital databases.

General Introduction

§1. General Background

I. Geography

1. The State of Israel is located in the southwest of the Asian continent, between the Mediterranean Sea and the Arabian desert. The geographical borders of the State of Israel are the Mediterranean Sea in the West, Jordan in the East, Lebanon and Syria in the North, and Egypt in the South. Although the overall area of Israel is small, its views and climate are varied.

Israel comprises three principal climatic zones: in the central and northern portion of the State, the climate is Mediterranean, characterized by a hot summer and rainy winter. On the coastal plain, the summer is humid and the winter comfortable, whereas in the mountain areas the summer is dry and the winter cold. In the southern parts of the State, the climate is a desert climate, characterized by hot, dry weather and large differences in temperatures between night and day.

II. Cultural Composition

2. The population in Israel currently numbers about 8 million, 75% of whom are Jewish, 21% Arab (including Muslim Arabs and Christian Arabs) and the remaining 4% comprising Druze, non-Arab Christians, non-denominational and others. The rate of population growth differs among the different ethnic groups. The official languages of Israel are Hebrew and Arabic. Even so, given that Israel absorbs Jews from all parts of the world, there are a large number of spoken languages. English is frequently used before the Israeli Patent Office (IPTO) and is also used in litigation before the courts.

The population density in Israel is high, and the majority of the population lives in the centre of the country and along the coastline. The State of Israel has a strong economy and in 2011 joined the Organisation for Economic Co-operation and Development (OECD). Israel has relatively few natural resources and its economy is based primarily on what is known as 'human capital' that includes knowledge-rich industries (hi-tech, pharmaceutical drugs and security industries) and other branches of industry.

Among the numerous hi-tech industries in Israel, there is a high concentration of companies involved in hardware and software development, communications and natural sciences. Risk capital investment in these industries is particularly high, and this contributes to a keen awareness of the need for the protection of intellectual property. Israel is ranked very high on the world list with respect to the number of registered patents per capita.

III. Political System

3. The State of Israel is a parliamentary democracy. The head of State is the President, but he does not hold significant executive powers and his role is effectively symbolic. The executive authority is the *Knesset*. The *Knesset* consists of 120 members of *Knesset* and is elected in general, relative elections for a term of four years. Voting in the *Knesset* elections is for a list of candidates, composed by those political parties that are legally registered. The candidates on the list are graded – thus the higher up on the list the candidate appears, the greater are his chances of being elected to the *Knesset*. Every citizen votes for the party that he supports. As opposed to the European countries where divisions between parties are based primarily on their social-economic position, the political discourse in Israel focuses primarily on the political-security issue. The main political blocks in the *Knesset* are the left, the right, the centre, the Haredi (ultra-Orthodox) Jews and the Arabs.

The Israeli government is the executive branch. It is headed by the prime minister and its members are the ministers, whom the prime minister has the authority to appoint (with *Knesset* approval) and to dismiss. For a period of a few years a system of direct elections of the prime minister was introduced, the aim being to change the political system, but for various reasons this system was abolished. The President of the State imposes the task of forming the government upon the candidate recommended by the majority of the parties in the *Knesset*. In order to form the government, the prime minister must receive a vote of confidence from the majority of the *Knesset* members, and this generally compels him to form a coalition of a few parties, and to appoint the heads of the parties as ministers, and by so doing, to secure the support and confidence of the *Knesset*. At the same time, ministerial positions are occasionally filled by professionals in the relevant field and not by *Knesset* members. Since the nineties, most of the coalitions have been narrow, but on two occasions national unity governments have been set up, including a significant portion of the *Knesset* factions.

The legal system in Israel is based on the common law system, but also has its own distinctive and individual features. The sources of Israeli law reflect the history of the State of Israel. In 1917, the areas of *Eretz Yisrael* (the land of Israel), which had been under the control of the Ottoman Empire, were conquered by the British Empire. When the government of the British Mandate took effect in 1917, the common law system together with the English laws of equity was applied to the areas of *Eretz Yisrael* included in the Mandate. Gradually, Ottoman law was pushed to the sidelines and subsequently repealed. However, the English common law system was applied having consideration for 'the conditions of the country and its residents'. For example, already at the beginning of the British Mandate it was decided not to use the jury system used in England. In 1948, the State of Israel was established and so as not to leave the country in a legal vacuum with no operative system of law, it was determined that the English common law that had been in force on the eve of the establishment of the State would continue to apply apart from a number of exceptions, and that the *Knesset* which was to be established, would be fully authorized to enact laws that changed the applicable law.

Since the establishment of the State, the *Knesset* has enacted laws that replace the Mandate legislation in almost all areas of law, and the position today is that most areas of law are regulated by independent Israeli legislation. There are, however, a few outstanding pieces of British legislation that have remained in force, such as the Torts Ordinance, but these too have been transformed into a new Israeli version in the Hebrew language. Therefore, the only binding version of the laws is in Hebrew, and the translated versions of the laws are unofficial. This is the background against which we can understand the sources of legislation pertaining to intellectual property in Israel, which is based on the Mandate legislation. In 1967, a new Patents Law was enacted, which replaced the Mandate legislation from 1924. It was only in 2007 that a new Copyright Law was enacted, to replace the Mandate legislation. In the area of designs, modern legislation has yet to be enacted; hence, the legislation of 1924 is still in force, yet in a new Hebrew version. However, as of August 2015, a bill is pending before the *Knesset*, which once enacted will replace the 1924 designs legislation. The modern Israeli legislation is not always in accordance with the principles of the common law system, and in certain cases has preferred the principles of Continental law. An example of this is the Unjust Enrichment Law of 1979. The result is that the system of modern Israeli law has been constructed on the basis of mixture of traditions, with its own unique features.

The Israeli courts have interpreted the existing legislation in a manner that lends it a unique and independent character, even when coming to interpret Mandate law or even Ottoman law that remained in force. The use of laws from the common law States, primarily from England and the US, is purely for comparative purposes, and judicial rulings emanating from such jurisdictions have no binding status in Israel. As such, the sources of Israeli law are the legislative acts of the *Knesset* and of the secondary legislators, the precedents established by the Israeli courts, Mandate laws and Ottoman laws that are still in force, and the rules of international law to the extent that they are recognized by the domestic Israeli law. In addition to the above, according to Israeli law, Jewish law can also serve as a binding source.

In Israel, there is a network of civil courts consisting of three tiers of adjudication (Magistrates Courts, District Courts and the Supreme Court). The civil court system is supplemented by other tribunals with unique features, such as the religious courts, the labour courts and the military courts. The subject of the Israeli constitution is complex. To date, no Israeli constitution has been written, primarily by reason of disputes pertaining to the character of the State. The role of the constitution is fulfilled by the basic laws that have been enacted by the *Knesset* and which enjoy special status, and the ongoing rulings of the High Court of Justice. In reality, the written constitution has been substituted by the basic laws and the constitutional fundamental values, such as the freedom of speech, etc., all of which have received a protected and special status.

IV. Population Statistics

4. The Israeli population currently numbers 8 million people. The area of the State of Israel is 22,972 sq. km. The population density is extremely high, standing at 359 persons per sq. km. As of 2014, 40% of the Israeli population lived in the central area (which includes the Tel Aviv zone). As such, the population density in this area is even higher. The State of Israel absorbs immigration of Jews from all over the world. As of 2014, the Jewish population of Israel constituting 75% of the population consisted of 75% Jews born in Israel and 25% of Jewish immigrants. Among the native Israeli Jews, the division according to the father's origin is as follows: 39.5% the father is Israeli born, 8.5% the father was born in Asia, 10% the father was born in Africa and 14.5% the father is a native of Europe and America.

§2. Historical Background

5. The history of the State of Israel began with the renewal of Jewish immigration to *Eretz Yisrael* (Palestine at the time) for the purpose of creating a Jewish nation-State. In 1896, Benjamin Ze'ev Herzl published his book *'The Jewish State'* in which he outlined his vision. Herzl established the Zionist movement, with the aim of establishing a Jewish State. Following the establishment of the Zionist movement, Jews began immigrating to Israel in order to establish Jewish settlements; at that time, *Eretz Yisrael* was part of the Ottoman Empire. In 1917, the British Empire conquered the areas of the *Eretz Yisrael*, soon after which the Balfour Declaration was published, expressing the British Government's commitment to the idea of establishing a Jewish home in *Eretz Yisrael*. The period of British rule saw an increase in Jewish immigration to *Eretz Yisrael*, but the British authorities attempted to prevent it. The result was the development of a movement that rebelled against the British sovereign with the aim of enabling Jewish immigration to *Eretz Yisrael* to establish an independent State. From the very outset, the Jewish settlement was exposed to the opposition of the local Arab population, and so began the Israel-Palestinian dispute, which until today awaits its solution.

The Jewish Holocaust during the Second World War accelerated the recognition of the need for an independent State for the Jewish people, and indeed, in 1948 the State of Israel was established. Since the establishment of the State, a series of wars have been conducted against the neighbouring Arab States. In 1979, a peace agreement was signed with Egypt, and in 1994, a peace agreement was signed with Jordan.

Chapter 1. Copyright and Neighbouring Rights

§1. Sources: Legislation

I. Overview

6. The statutory source for copyright law in Israel is the Copyright Act of 2007 (the 'Act' or the 'Copyright Act'). The 2007 Act was passed on 19 November 2007 and came into force on 25 May 2008.[1]

Nevertheless, the Copyright Act of 1911 and the Copyright Ordinance, which had been in force in Israel since the period of the British mandate in the 1920s up through 2008, are still applicable for certain purposes. Generally, the previous law still applies for the purposes of determining initial ownership of works created, and assignments of rights that took place before 25 May 2008. In respect of acts of infringement that took place before that date, sections defining the liability and remedies are still applicable. Sections 3B–3E of the Copyright Ordinance, for the most part repealed by the 2007 Act, continue to apply to private copying of works on 'tapes'[2] and to its statutory compensation regime.

Section 3 of the Copyright Act provides that copyright shall not subsist in a work other than in accordance with the provisions of the Act. Thus, property rights in works of authorship are only those that are granted in the Copyright Act; there is no other statutory source for copyright-like protection, and there is no 'common law copyright'.

The Copyright Act covers works of authorship and sound recordings. It does not deal with the protection of performers and broadcasting organizations, which is governed by a separate act, the Performers and Broadcasters Rights Act of 1984 (as amended).

Secondary legislation includes regulations and orders promulgated by the Minister of Justice by virtue of his powers under primary legislation (specifically, regulations that define educational institutions and libraries for the purposes of sections 29 and 30 of the Act). The regulations promulgated under the Copyright Act of 1911 (specifically, section 72 of the Designs Rules of 1925, and various orders for the protection of foreign works) continue to be in effect notwithstanding the repeal of the 1911 Act itself, in accordance with the provisions of the Interpretation Act, 5741–1981.[3]

1. For a review of the new Copyright Act, see: Tamir Afori, *Copyright Act* (Nevo Publisher 2012) (*in Hebrew*).
2. The translation of s. 3A of the Ordinance available on the WIPO website makes use of the term 'recordable media'. It is our opinion that such translation of the underlying Hebrew term is inaccurate and that a more accurate translation of the term would be 'tapes'.
3. The Interpretation Act, s. 23.

II. International Conventions

7. Israel is party to several international treaties and agreements relating to copyright, including: the Berne Convention (as revised in Paris, 1971); the Universal Copyright Convention; the Agreement on Trade-Related Aspects of Intellectual Property Rights (TRIPS); the Convention for the Protection of Performers, Phonogram Producers and Broadcasting Organizations (Rome Convention); and the Marrakesh Treaty to Facilitate Access to Published Works for Persons Who Are Blind, Visually Impaired or Otherwise Print Disabled.

There are bilateral agreements that relate to intellectual property, including, *inter alia*, an exchange of letters with the US, a free trade agreement with the US, and an association agreement with the European Union (EU).

Israel has signed but has not yet adhered to the World Intellectual Property Organization (WIPO) Copyright Treaty and the WIPO Performances and Phonograms Treaty.

International obligations of Israel in the field of intellectual property are not self-executing. Thus, treaties do not have direct applicability in Israel unless and until implemented by legislation. On the one hand, treaties serve as the reason for statutory changes in the law, and on the other hand, as the source of authority for the Minister of Justice to enact 'orders' for the protection of foreign works.

III. Orders

8. The main statutory sources[4] for protection of foreign works are orders issued by the Minister of Justice, according to the various international obligations of the State of Israel.

The orders in force are:

- Copyright Order (Berne Convention), 1953.
- Copyright Order (United States), 1953.
- Copyright Order (International Convention), 1955.
- Copyright Order (Convention for Protection of Producers of Phonograms), 1978.
- Copyright Order (TRIPS Agreement), 1999.
- Performers and Broadcasters Rights Order (TRIPS Agreement), 1999.
- Copyright, Performers and Broadcasters Rights Order (Rome Convention), 2002.

The various orders apply the 'national treatment' regime according to the relevant treaties. Thus, the orders will usually grant the protection of the Copyright Act to works that have the relevant point of attachment to Member States of the treaty, such as personal qualification of the work's author (citizenship of or habitual residence in a Member State), or first publication of the work in a Member State.

4. See also the discussion of 'simultaneous publication', *infra*, at s. §3 'Conditions of Protection', s. III.

§2. Subject Matter of Protection

I. Different Categories of Protected Works

9. The Copyright Act protects literary, artistic, dramatic, and musical works and sound recordings.[5] The list of categories is a closed list, but every one of the categories is wide open, and may develop with time, using open-ended definitions that are phrased using the term 'including … '.[6]

Thus, the material test that set the threshold for copyright protection is 'originality', and the categorization is far less important.

Nevertheless, categorization may be significant with respect to the application of the different parts of the Copyright Act. Different categories may have different applicable rules with respect to the originality threshold (e.g., stronger 'creativity' test for useful art), the scope of protection (e.g., no public performance right to artistic works), permitted uses (e.g., permitted copying of certain types of artistic works located in public places), statutory licenses (e.g., license to produce phonogram copies of musical works) or moral rights (no moral right to computer programs).

Categorization may also influence the way courts use their discretion along the lines of the various sections of the Act, with respect to the 'substantial similarity' test, 'fair use' permitted acts, or 'reasonableness' test for moral right infringement, all of which will be addressed in the following sections of this treatise.

A. *Literary Work*

10. The Copyright Act defines a 'literary work' as including works expressed in writing, lectures, tables, compilations and also computer programs.

The core of the definition is in the term 'works expressed in writing'. The rest of the definition is intended for widening the normal meaning of the term to include tables, compilations and computer programs (which are not considered literary works in the normal meaning, see the text below), and lectures (which raise an issue of fixation, which is explained below).[7]

The term 'literary work' usually includes books, newspaper or scientific articles, poems, lyrics of songs, etc. It includes informational or functional texts, like teaching materials[8] or examination forms. It also includes purely commercial texts like the words of commercial advertisements, and even the writing on the packaging of a product or the product's customer instructions.

Except for being 'expressed in writing', there are no material conditions for a work to fall within the definition of literary work. Thus, subject to the originality test, any expression in writing may be eligible for copyright protection, without any need for literary quality.

5. As discussed below under 'neighbouring rights', the Performers and Broadcasters Rights Act protects the rights of performers and of broadcasters.
6. Such are the definitions of a literary work, artistic work and dramatic work. A musical work is not defined in the Copyright Act.
7. See s. §3 'Conditions of Protection', s. II below, which addresses the concept of 'fixation'.
8. CA 23/81 *Hershko et al. v. Averbuch et al.*, 42(3) P.D. 749 [1988].

For a text to be eligible for copyright protection, it needs to be longer than a few words. Usually, a few words such as titles or commercial slogans are not considered a literary work, but there may be cases in which the slogan or title was substantial enough to be protected as a 'substantial part' of another work from which it had been taken, as discussed below.[9]

B. Dramatic Work

11. The Copyright Act defines 'dramatic works' as including plays, cinematographic works, musical-dramatic works, choreography and pantomime. The basic idea of the definition is to include works that are visual and evolving by nature, and are intended to be seen by an audience (as a sequence of visible events, movements, etc., in progress). In other words, there is something happening in a way that is meant to attract the attention of viewers.

The definition of a 'cinematographic work' includes a television work and any work that is substantially similar to a cinematographic work or a television work. This definition makes 'cinema' a technology-neutral concept. Thus, not only traditional cinematographic works, but also television shows are protected. In a famous case regarding coverage of the Wimbledon tennis tournament, it was held that a televised version of a sports event is a protected dramatic work.[10]

It is worth noting that there is no distinct protection for a 'film' (or any other form of fixation) that embodies the cinematographic work; this is unlike the case of sound recordings, which are protected separately from the musical work they embody.

C. Musical Work

12. A musical work is not specifically defined in the Copyright Act. The records of the legislation hearings indicate that there was no effective way to define music, and that there was no need for a definition. The focus is on originality and fixation.

D. Artistic Works

1. Definition of an Artistic Work

13. The Copyright Act defines an 'artistic work' as including drawings, paintings, sculptures, engravings, lithography, maps, charts, architectural works, photographic works and works of artistic craftsmanship. Some of these examples are further defined and discussed below. The term 'artistic' does not always imply an artistic character. Some of the examples in the definition are purely informative or

9. See s. §6 'Scope of Rights', Part II below, which addresses the scope of protection of a work or of a substantial part thereof.
10. CA 2173/94 *Tele-Event Ltd v. Arutzei Zahav & Co. et al.*, 55(5) P.D. 529 [2001].

functional, such as maps or charts. It was held that even an advertisement sign can be an artistic work.[11]

2. Definition of a Photographic Work

14. A 'photographic work' is defined as including works produced by a process similar to photography, but excluding photographs that are part of a cinematographic work. This definition makes the protection of photography 'technology-neutral', thus allowing the law to evolve. It is clear that the definition covers digital photography.

There is no distinction in the Act between 'artistic', 'directed', or 'documentary' photography.[12] A photograph taken by a home camera is not differentiated from the work of a renowned artist. There may be a difference in the scope of protection to the content, due to the rule that denies protection to facts, which is discussed below. The last sentence of the definition excludes 'frames' of a cinematographic works. The protection of cinematographic work raises various problems, one of which is the problem of authorship/ownership. This last sentence makes it clear that frames of the cinematograph work are not protected separately from the dramatic work.

3. Work of Architecture

15. A 'work of architecture' is defined in the Copyright Act to include a building or other structure, as well as a model of such building or structure. An important part of the definition that appeared in the previous Act was omitted from the current definition: namely, the requirement of 'artistic character'. Thus, there are no special 'artistic' criteria for works of architecture; instead, the general 'originality' test applies.

4. Work of Artistic Craftsmanship

16. Works of artistic craftsmanship (sometimes referred to as works of applied art) are protected as any other artistic work, for the same term and by the same scope of protection. In a famous case regarding 'LEGO' blocks, the Supreme Court held that the 'originality' test for protection of this type of work is combined with an 'artistic' test[13] (also derived from the wording 'artistic' craftsmanship). Protectability of works of artistic craftsmanship raises a special problem regarding the interrelation of copyright law and design law. These issues are discussed elsewhere[14] in this chapter.

11. CA 360/83 *Strossky Ltd et al. v. Vitman Icecream Ltd et al.*, 40(3) P.D. 340 [1985].
12. CA 7774/09 *Weinberg v. Weishoff* [2012].
13. CA 513/89 *Interlego A/S v. Exin-Lines Bros S.A.*, 48(4) P.D. 133 [1996].
14. See s. §2.II below regarding the exclusion of works protectable as designs from copyright protection under s. 7 of the Copyright Act and s. §11 'Overlapping and Relation to Other Intellectual Property Rights' below.

5. Typography

17. There is no special rule regarding the typographical arrangement of published editions, and thus, the typographical arrangement may be protected only insofar as it is an original artistic work.[15] It is the author's view that only in very rare cases the preparatory work for print (such as text proofing, punctuation, pagination and paragraph design) may pass the 'originality' test required for copyright protection.

However, the work of typography (i.e., design of typefaces and fonts) is protected as an artistic work.[16]

II. Works Excluded of Protection

18. Ideas, concepts, facts. Under section 5 of the Copyright Act, copyright does not extend to ideas, methods of operation, mathematical concepts, facts or data, and daily news. The mode of expression of any of these is protectable by copyright. It is the author's view that the idea/expression rule does not exclude subject matter of protection, but rather defines the limits of protection for protected subject matter in such a way that allows the taking of an 'idea' or 'concept' as long as the original expression is not copied.

Official publications. Under section 6 of the Copyright Act, copyright protection does not apply to legislative publications (statutes, regulations) and to judicial decisions. Common commercial publications of analysed court decisions and revised texts of legislation are nevertheless protected as original derivative works.

Industrial designs. Under section 7 of the Copyright Act, copyright does not subsist in a design of goods, unless the design is not used and is not intended for use in industrial manufacture. The Design Rules, 1925, set a presumption in section 72 according to which a design is deemed to be used or intended for industrial manufacture where it is produced or intended to be produced in fifty articles or more.[17] The principal importance of this rule is that works of artistic craftsmanship (works of applied art) will not be protected by copyright if they are used industrially. The owner of the design must use industrial design registration in order to protect the design. In such a case, the term of protection and the scope of protection is substantially different from copyright protection, as described elsewhere in this chapter.[18]

15. Not as a literary work, which is the underlying substance of the typographical arrangement.
16. CC (Central Distr.) 5311-04-08 *The Estate of Zvi Narkis v. Microsoft Israel Ltd* [2010].
17. Section 72(a) of the Design Rules. An additional type of design deemed to be used or intended for use in industrial manufacture is a product sold in length as paper hangings, carpets, textiles and other similar products provided for in s. 72(b) of the Design Rules.
18. See the discussion in s. §11, *infra*.

III. Special Categories

A. Computer Programs

19. The Copyright Act defines a computer program to be 'in any form of expression'.[19] The previous legislation[20] protected a computer program whether in source code or object code (a definition derived from the relevant language of the TRIPS Agreement).

The Supreme Court held[21] that for the purpose of copyright protection, one may use the definition of a computer program in the Computers Act, 5755 – 1995, a statute that criminalizes certain acts of breaking into and interfering with a computer. The definition of a program in the Computers Act is that of:

> a set of instructions expressed in a computer-readable language which is capable of causing a computer to function/operate or to perform an operation/action and is embodied, recorded or marked in a device or article, via electronic, electromagnetic, electrochemical, electro-optical or other means, or is fixed or integrated with a computer.[22]

Preparatory Design Materials for a Computer Program. Preparatory design materials for a computer program are capable of protection as independent works, and if it is proven that there was a direct copying, it will be considered as copyright infringement. A more confusing question is whether a new program code developed via analysis of a previous program (reverse-engineering) would be considered infringement of the design material of the computer program.

The Supreme Court held that the preparatory design materials are a protected part of the computer program itself.[23] Article 5 of the Copyright Act, which was enacted after this ruling, states that copyright protection does not extend to an idea, process or method of operation. This change in the law, together with changes in US case law regarding this, led the Supreme Court to hint in a later case that it is not clear whether the previous rule still applies.[24]

It is likely to be a matter of degree, using the 'idea/expression' and the 'substantial similarity' tests. If the entire set of functions, including the essence of the user interface and input/output structures, is copied by writing a new program code, it would probably be a copyright infringement of the program itself, without the need to differentiate between the program and the preparatory design materials.

---

19. This definition follows the respective definition in WIPO Copyright Treaty (WCT).
20. The Copyright Ordinance, s. 2A.
21. CA 2392/99 *Ashraz Data Processing Ltd v. Transbeton Ltd*, 57(5) P.D. 255 [2003] (*Ashraz*) at 271.
22. The binding text of the statute is in Hebrew, and no official translation has been published to date. The above definition is our informal translation from Hebrew.
23. CA 139/89 *Harpaz et al. v. Achitov et al.*, 44(4) P.D. 16 [1990].
24. *Ashraz, supra.*

B. Compilations and Databases

20. Compilations and databases are protected as literary works. Article 1 of the Act defines a compilation as 'a compilation of works including an encyclopaedia or an anthology as well as a compilation of data including a database'.

It is important to note that the protection afforded to a database is for the originality in the selection of the material and its arrangement. This rule has two significant outcomes. First, there needs to be originality in the selection or the arrangement. Mere alphabetical listing of all of the relevant data (e.g., a telephone directory) will not be protected. However, a selection of recommended items, or the arrangement of items by some substantive criteria (e.g., the Yellow Pages) will be protected.

Infringement would be the taking of a substantial part of the original work. Copying specific items from the database would normally not be considered as taking the original part of the work since it is not a substantial taking of the selection nor of the arrangement, and the items are not themselves protected.

C. Sound Recordings

21. Sound recordings are protected within the Copyright Act, although the protection is different in character and in fact tends to be a 'neighbouring right' type of protection.

The definition of a sound recording covers a recording of sounds, excluding a recording of sounds in a cinematographic work. 'Recording', with respect to sounds, means preservation of sounds on media from which such sounds may be played back or copied.

The Act makes some of the fundamental principles that apply to works of authorship inapplicable to sound recordings. There is no moral right in a sound recording. Unlike works of authorship, there is no 'originality' requirement. The protection of sound recording includes copying, but does not include the making of a derivative work. The term of protection is fifty years. The applicable rules of international protection are different than those applicable to works of authorship.[25]

§3. CONDITIONS OF PROTECTION

22. The conditions for copyright protection are set forth in section 4 of the Copyright Act. In addition to the requirement that the subject matter is a work of one of the categories of protected works, the Act requires originality, fixation and a relation of the work to Israel. These three requirements are discussed below.

25. See the discussion of applicable rules of international protection in s. §3 'Conditions of Protection', s. III, *infra*.

I. Originality

23. The central and most important requirement for copyright protection is originality. Article 4, which sets the conditions for protection, grants copyright in 'original works which are literary works, artistic works, dramatic works or musical works, fixed in any form'.

Originality is not defined in the Copyright Act. The Supreme Court has addressed the question of originality several times, moving along the years from a 'labour' doctrine (minimum amount of work and effort) to 'intellectual creativity' doctrine (minimum intellectual contribution), and recently applying both of them, requiring both labour and creativity as a condition to copyright.[26] Thus, the current rule of originality[27] requires three layers of examination: first, the work has to have originated in the author, in the factual sense (i.e., not copied from another source); second, it has to be the fruit of minimal work and effort by the author; and third, it has to bear minimal creativity.

Over the years, the Supreme Court has found originality in tax calculation tables and forms,[28] in the televised version of a sports event,[29] and even in the reconstruction of writing on an ancient scroll.[30] However, the Supreme Court found no sufficient originality in 'Lego' blocks,[31] a plastic cabinet for communications equipment,[32] or football match schedules.[33]

As noted above, the requirement of originality does not apply to sound recordings.[34]

According to section 4(b) of the Act, originality of a compilation means the originality in the selection and arrangement of the works or of the data embodied therein. This rule, which reflects the wording of the TRIPS Agreement, is discussed above.[35]

II. Fixation

24. The Copyright Act protects original works that are literary works, artistic works, dramatic works or musical works, fixed in any form.[36]

The fixation rule has evidentiary purposes: it allows for more certainty regarding what the work is for the prospective user and for the courts.

26. CA 8485/08 *The FA Premier League Ltd v. Sport Gambling Regulation Council* [2010] (*Premier League 2010*) at para. 38.
27. CA 7996/11 *Safecom v. Raviv* [2013] at para. 15.
28. CA 136/71 *The State of Israel v. Achiman*, 26(2) P.D. 259 [1972].
29. CA94/2173 *Tele-Event Ltd v. Arutzei Zahav & Co.*, 55(5) P.D. 529 [2001].
30. CA 2790/93 *Eisenman v. Qimron et al.*, 54(3) P.D. 817 [2000].
31. CA 513/89 *Interlego A/S v. Exin-Lines Bros S.A.*, 48(4) P.D. 133 [1996].
32. CA03/3422 *Krone AG v. Inbar Plastic*, 59(4)P.D. 365 [2005].
33. *Premier League 2010.*
34. The Act, s. 4(a)(2).
35. See s. §2.II, *supra*, on the protection of databases.
36. The Copyright Act, s. 4(a)(1). In addition, the Act protects sound recordings, which are fixations of sounds.

It also has substantive significance: not every sound is a musical work; not every human gesture is a work of choreography. Originality (dealt with above) and fixation are substantive thresholds. The fixation may assist in delineating an idea from an expression. The fixation of a work is also a statement of the creator that 'this', the fixed expression, is his work.

Fixation does not raise practical problems with respect to artistic works, which are 'fixed' in nature. It may be significant regarding literary, musical or dramatic works.

For these types of works, fixation may set the boundary between a copyright work and a performance.

Thus, the playing of a tune that is not fixed will normally be protected as a performance. If it is fixed and contains original additions, one may argue that it is a derivative work.

III. Relation to Israel

25. Copyright protection under the Act is for works that have a certain relation to Israel as prescribed in section 8 of the Act ('local' works) or are protected under an order of the Minister of Justice according to section 9 ('foreign' works).

A. *'Local' Works*

26. The basic principles for the direct application of the Copyright Act, which are the principles that practically define the 'locality' of works, are derived from the 'points of attachment' that are applied in the relevant international agreements, the most significant of which are the rules of the Berne Convention.

Literary, artistic, dramatic or musical works are protected if:

(a) The work was first published in Israel, or first published in another country but simultaneously (within thirty days) in Israel. Publication is defined as the offering of copies of the work to the public. It does not include broadcasting or public performance.
(b) The author of the work is a national of Israel or has his habitual residence in Israel.

In addition to these two general rules, a cinematographic work is also protected if the producer of the work at the time of creation was domiciled or had headquarters in Israel.[37] An architectural work, as well as any other artistic work incorporated in a building or other structure, is protected if the architectural work (or the building incorporating the artistic work) is located in Israel.[38]

Copyright in a sound recording subsists if, at the time of its making, the individual producer of the sound recording was a national or domiciliary of Israel, or,

37. The Copyright Act, s. 8(b)(1).
38. The Copyright Act, s. 8(b)(2).

where the producer was a corporation, had headquarters in Israel.[39] In respect of sound recordings, certain rights (the right of reproduction, the right of making available to the public and the right of rental) also subsist where the sound recording was first published in Israel, or simultaneously (within thirty days) first published in Israel.[40]

The significance of the last rule is that broadcasting and public performance of foreign sound recordings is only covered by international agreements and not through simultaneous publication.[41] This is significant because the international protection of sound recordings is according to the Rome Convention and the TRIPS Agreement, which allow for material reciprocity, which is indeed reflected in the relevant orders.[42]

B. 'Foreign' Works

27. As explained above, copyright in a work may exist pursuant to a bilateral or a multilateral international treaty if implemented by an order of the Minister of Justice. The protection that the Minister is allowed to grant is up to the extent to which an Israeli work is protected, unless agreed otherwise in the treaty.

There are various orders of the Minister; each one of them implements the obligations in the various copyright treaties which Israel adhered to. In fact, due to the wide application of the Berne Convention, in most cases the Berne Order is applicable.[43]

IV. Formal Requirements

28. Under Israeli law, there are no formal requirements for copyright protection. A work is protected from its creation, without need for any special notice or registration. Moreover, there is no official copyright registry in Israel, not even a

---

39. The Copyright Act, s. 8(c).
40. The Copyright Act, s. 8(c).
41. Under the 1911 Act, it was held that foreign sound recordings that were simultaneously released in Israel (which was very often the case regarding international pop music) are eligible for protection without referring to the international regime of protection. Restrictive Practices Motion (Jerusalem) 3574/00 *IFPI v. Antitrust Commissioner* [2004] (*IFPI v. Antitrust Commissioner*), at 184.
42. TRIPs Order only grants 'reproduction' and 'rental' rights to phonograms. The Rome Order grants broadcasting and public performance on the basis of material reciprocity. The Copyright Order (US) is probably the most significant order to that issue because the US is the most significant country, which does not recognize public performance right to phonograms. A district court in Jerusalem in the case of *IFPI v. Antitrust Commissioner* (*supra*) expressed the view that this order protects US producers. It is the author's view that the order is far from being clear on that point, and that taking into account the wording of the new Copyright Act, which came to force after the IFPI case, it is likely that the opposite is true. It is yet to be seen how this issue will evolve when the question is directly raised in court.
43. According to the Copyright Order (Universal Copyright Treaty), it applies only to works for which the Berne order does not apply. In practice, almost all the works in the world are covered by the Berne Order, thus the Universal Copyright Treaty Order is applicable in rare cases only, and has not been used in Israeli courts for many years.

voluntary one. There is a duty to supply the national library with a copy of books (including phonograms and films) that were published in Israel, but that requirement is not connected in any way to copyright protection.

§4. Ownership

I. The Author

A. *Initial Ownership Is That of the Author*

29. Under section 33 of the Copyright Act, as under section 5 of the 1911 Act, the basic rule is that the author of a work is the initial owner of the copyright in it, except for those specific cases provided for in sections 34–36, which are discussed below.

The author is also presumed to be the initial owner of a commissioned work, unless otherwise agreed explicitly or implicitly with the commissioning party. Ownership in commissioned works is discussed below.

There is no definition of 'author' in the Copyright Act. In most cases, the author is simply the person who authored the work. Complications may arise where there is more than one person involved in the process.[44] Such is the case of a cinematographic work or a computer program. When authorship is vague, the matter is sometimes settled by an agreement. It is submitted that an agreement can allocate the rights to exploit the work, but cannot allocate the authorship status, which affects the term of protection and the moral rights.

According to Article 15 of the Berne Convention, the Copyright Act contains, in section 64(1), a rebuttable presumption of authorship, according to which the person, whose name (or the pseudonym of a person whose identity is publicly known) appears on the work in the usual manner as the author of the work, is indeed the author of the work and the owner of the copyright.

Under section 64(2) of the Act, for a work published anonymously or under a pseudonym of a person whose identity is not publicly known, the person indicated as the publisher of the work is presumed to be the owner of the copyright (not the author).[45] This section may also be applicable to cases where the anonymity of the authors is a part of normal authorship conditions, such as multi-author works of big corporations.

B. *Initial Owner of Copyright in a Sound Recording*

30. In accordance with section 33(2) of the Act, the initial owner of the right in a sound recording is the producer. The producer, as defined in the Copyright Act, is the person or corporate entity that is responsible for the arrangements that are necessary for the recording. This definition reflects a minor change from the previous

44. Joint authorship is discussed *infra* in s. II.
45. It should be noted that the presumption of ownership is not a presumption of authorship.

law, according to which the owner of the first fixation of the sounds was the owner of the copyright.

II. Joint Works: Works Created by Several Persons

A. Joint Work

31. Section 1 of the Act defines a joint work as a 'work created jointly by several authors, wherein it is not possible to discern each author's contribution to the work'.

A joint work will in most cases be co-owned by its joint authors, according to the general rule that the author is the initial owner of the work, and thus co-authorship results in co-ownership. It should be stressed that the ownership is not a part of the definition of a joint work and may vary, depending on the agreement (express or implied) between the authors. A work of joint authorship can very well be a commissioned work or a work of employees, and in these cases, the ownership will be determined by the relevant rules.

The concept of a joint work is mainly aimed at the calculation of the term of protection (see below), and/or the relation to Israel. These two are matters of 'status' and are not influenced by the ownership issues, which are basically contractual. Thus, it is the factual situation that will be considered and not the agreement between co-owners, with respect to the status of 'co-authorship'. For example, if one person writes the lyrics and another writes the melody, under an agreement of joint ownership, the song will not be considered as a joint work in Israel, but rather as two identifiably separate works which may be subject to an ownership agreement between the authors.

Co-ownership of a work can exist with respect to any work, including works that were created by a single author (e.g., assignment of the ownership to a number of assignees that will own the rights collectively, inheritance by a number of heirs, etc.).

Where there is no agreement between the co-owners of a work, then according to the general rules regarding the co-ownership of property, the share of each one of them in the work is equal.

The Copyright Act provides for no special rules regarding the use of a co-owned work. Where there is no agreement between the co-owners of a work, the general rules of property apply,[46] according to which each one of the co-owners has the right to 'reasonable use' of the property, subject to payment to the other co-owners. In appropriate cases, the co-owner can allow others to use the work, but granting an exclusive license to use the work will not be 'reasonable'.

In the case of an infringement by a third party, each one of the co-owners can sue the infringer, but the other co-owners must be added as parties to the proceedings.

46. CA *ACUM Ltd. v. EMI Music Publishing Ltd.* [2013], at para. 52.

B. Cinematic Works

32. No provision similar to that in respect of sound recordings has been made in respect of ownership in cinematographic works (which include television and other audio-visual works), and so the producer does not automatically become the first owner of copyright in a cinematic work and the rights in such work are defined by way of agreement. Typically, a producer commissions the services of the film director and the screenwriter, and the provisions governing the express or implied agreement in respect of a commissioned work will apply.[47]

III. Works Made for Hire (Including Commissioned Work)

33. The following sections deal with cases where a work was created by one person (the author) for another person (the commissioner). This includes works of employees, works commissioned by contract and works made for the State of Israel.

The basic principles are that the parties are free to determine the initial ownership by contract, and that the law sets rebuttable presumptions regarding the intention of the parties to typical contractual relations, which are employment contracts, commission contracts, and contracts of employment or commission for the government.

It should be stressed that the discussion below is all subject to the agreement by the parties. The agreement can be written or oral, express or implied.

A. Work of an Employee

34. In accordance with section 34 of the Act, the employer is the first owner of the copyright in a work made by an employee during the period of his service and for the purpose of his service, unless otherwise agreed. This wording is somewhat different from the wording of the English 1911 Act, which shifted the rights to the employer in works created by an employee 'in the course of his service'. The course of service is not necessarily identical to the purpose of the service.

It is important to note that the initial ownership of a work applies only to the copyright in the work, and not to the moral right in it. Moreover, the term of protection as well as the relation to Israel or to any Member State is determined by the actual author, and not the first owner; thus, the authorship of the employee is still important to many aspects of the Copyright Act.

As explained, the ownership of the employer is subject to the agreement between the parties. It is a common understanding of the law that employees of universities are the owners of the copyright (at least partially) in articles and books they write, even though there is no express contract in this regard in most universities in Israel.

47. See s. III *infra* for a discussion of commissioned works.

B. Commissioned Work

35. Under section 35(a) of the 2007 Act, the initial owner of the copyright (wholly or partially) in a commissioned work shall be the author, unless the commissioning party and the author agree otherwise, expressly or impliedly.

This statutory rule reflects several policy decisions of the legislator of the 2007 Act:

(1) The author is the initial owner unless it is proven that there is an express or implied agreement to the contrary. Thus, the burden to ensure the allocation of the rights is on the commissioning party.
(2) There is no need for an express agreement. An agreement to vest the copyright with the commissioning party can be implied from the circumstances, previous agreements, or even other agreements in the industry. Thus, if it is common in a specific industry that the commissioning party is the owner, it may be regarded as an implied agreement between the parties even without any specific express arrangement between them, not even orally. The answer may be the same even if the parties made an agreement regarding all other aspects of job, but ignored the copyright issue.
(3) There is no need for a written document. As opposed to the rule regarding transfer of copyright, an oral agreement is enough for the vesting of the initial ownership with the commissioning party.

In the specific case of a commissioned portrait or a commissioned photograph of a family event or of another private event, the initial owner of the copyright therein shall be the commissioning party, as provided in section 35(b) of the Act.

C. Government Works

36. Unless agreed otherwise, the State is the initial owner of a work made by, or commissioned for, the State or by an employee of the State in consequence of his service and during the period of his service, as provided in section 36 of the Copyright Act. A 'State Employee' is defined for the purposes of this section to include soldiers, policemen and any other person who holds a position according to a statute in a State entity or institution.

In comparison to other 'non-government' commissioned works, the rights of the State are safeguarded in two aspects: first, commissioned works are presumed to belong to the State, unlike the general rule of commissioned works (which is discussed above); and second, works of government employees belong to the State in accordance with the 'consequence of service' rule, which is probably wider than the 'purpose of service' rule which applies to other employee inventions.

It is worth noting that Israeli legislation and court decisions are not copyrighted at all as discussed above.[48]

48. See s. §2 'Subject Matter of Protection', s. II (Works Excluded of Protection) *supra*.

The term of protection to works initially owned by the State is fifty years only.

The State is bound by a twofold set of norms. While it is an owner of property according to general property legislation, it is also bound by administrative law, including freedom of information law, and many other rules that may oblige the State not to enforce its copyright in the manner a private owner would have enforced his.

IV. Works Created before the Entry into Force of the Copyright Act 2007

37. The ownership of works created before the 2007 Act came into effect continues to be determined in accordance with the provisions of the Copyright Act of 1911.[49]

The initial ownership has always been vested in the author of a work as a general rule, but several substantive changes have been made to the exceptions to that rule. These exceptions will be concisely described in this section.

Under the previous Act, commissioned works were under a complicated legal regime.

The 'title' to the work was initially in the hands of the author unless and until assigned in writing to the commissioning party. Only in the cases of 'plates' or some other listed types of works that are intended for reproduction of copies, the initial copyright may be in the commissioner if the plate was ordered and paid for.

Notwithstanding the 'title' of the work, in some cases, according to common law rules that were rather vague, the commissioning party had equitable rights in the work, which were enforceable between it and the author even without a written agreement.

Works of employees were defined in a somewhat different manner: 'in the course of service', as opposed to 'during the service and to the purpose of the service' in the new Act. There has not been much jurisprudence regarding the works of employees, neither before nor after the coming into force of the new Act, so it is not yet clear whether this difference in the wording is significant.

Under the 1911 Act, special rules applied to works of journalist employees. The use of a work for a purpose other than the publishing of the work in a newspaper required the consent of the employee. This rule is not exactly an 'ownership' rule, but rather a 'veto' right of the author.

Under the 1911 Act, ownership in a photograph belonged to the owner of the 'negative', rather than the author.

A. *Choice of Law Regarding Ownership*

38. The Israeli Copyright Act leaves it to the parties to agree upon the initial ownership. Thus, if the contract between the parties is made under the laws of another country, it is 'the law of the contract' that will apply to the question of copyright ownership.

49. Copyright Act 2007, s. 78(i).

If the parties did not make any contract, but the general rules of choice of law regarding contracts point to the law of another country, it may well be regarded as a part of their contractual relations, and thus the rules of initial ownership in that country shall apply.

For example, the US rules of work made for hire may apply in Israel to determine the ownership of a work created by a US author who is an employee of a US employer. In one case, an Israeli court held that the plaintiff (a Russian Federation publisher) is the owner of the work of a Russian author under the Russian law.[50]

§5. Transfer

I. Assignment of Copyright

39. In accordance with section 37(a) of the Act, copyright may be assigned by contract or by operation of law. Transfer by operation of law may occur, for example, on the death, or bankruptcy of the copyright owner.

The Act further provides, in section 37(b), that assignment of the copyright may refer to the copyright in whole or in part, and it can be limited to a certain territory, period of time, or to specific acts with respect to the work. Thus, copyright is divisible. Different persons can hold identified portions of the right.

A contract for the assignment of copyright requires a written document.[51] The requirement of a document is probative (evidentiary) rather than substantive. It reflects the need for some level of certainty with respect to the ownership of these highly abstract rights. It is the author's view that the purpose of the requirement will usually be for proving ownership against a third party, and not between the two parties to an assignment agreement.

It should be noted that moral rights cannot be assigned.[52]

Assignments made prior to the commencement of the 2007 Act continue to be governed by the Copyright Act 1911,[53] but it seems that there are no substantive differences between the two.

II. Licenses

A. General

40. The owner of a copyright may grant an exclusive license or non-exclusive license with respect to the copyright.[54]

50. CC (Rishon Lezion Mag.) 3226/07 *ZAO Kommersant Publishing House Ltd v. Vesti 1992 Ltd et al.* [2010].
51. The Copyright Act, s. 37(c).
52. The Copyright Act, s. 45(b).
53. The Copyright Act, s. 78(f).
54. The Copyright Act, s. 37(a).

As in the case of transfer, the grant of a license may refer to the copyright in whole or in part, and it can be limited to a certain territory, a period of time, or to specific acts with respect to the work.[55]

Licenses granted prior to the commencement of the 2007 Act continue to be governed by the Copyright Act 1911.[56] There seem to be only small differences in the law regarding licenses. The most significant change is the express grant of power to the exclusive licensee to sue for infringement.

B. Exclusive License

41. A contract for the grant of an exclusive license in the copyright requires a written document.[57] An exclusive licensee has a proprietary right; he can sue for infringement, and thus the grant of such license is dealt with similarly to the transfer of the right. An 'exclusive license' is defined as a license which grants its holder the exclusive right to do any acts reserved for the copyright owner, as specified by the license, while restricting the owner of the copyright from doing those acts or from permitting others to perform those acts.[58]

A license that does not comply with the above definition is not an exclusive license, and therefore will not give the licensee the power to sue for an infringement.

C. Non-exclusive License

42. A non-exclusive license is, in fact, a permission to use the work in a manner that falls within the exploitation rights of the owner (which are discussed in detail below).

As opposed to the transfer of right and to the grant of an exclusive license, a mere license to use the work does not require a written document. A permission to use the work may be granted orally, or even impliedly.

The permission to use the work may be given subject to various terms, above all payment of license fees to the right's owner. The terms and conditions to the use of the work are subject to contract laws, including consumer protection law and standard agreement law. In the absence of an express statutory provision, it is yet to be seen whether the license terms of use of a copyright work can restrict the use of the work by the licensee in a manner that exceeds the statutory property rights of the licensor or derogates from the statutorily permitted uses as defined in the Copyright Act.

---

55. The Copyright Act, s. 37(b).
56. The Copyright Act, s. 78(f).
57. The Copyright Act, s. 37(c).
58. The Copyright Act, s. 37(d).

III. Collective Rights Management

43. Collective rights management is well established in Israel, but is subject to competition law and not to copyright law. The principal Collective rights Management Organizations (CMOs) in Israel are ACUM (Composers, Authors and Publishers Society of Israel, Ltd);[59] *IFPI Israel* (International Federation of the Phonographic Industry), *Eilam* – the collecting society of Israeli musicians,[60] which represents performing musicians, *Eshkolot* – the Israeli Artists Society for Performers' Rights Limited, which represents performing artists, *Tali* – Royalties Society of Cinema and Television Creators Ltd,[61] which represents directors and screenwriters, and *PIL* – the Israeli Federation of Independent Record Producers Ltd,[62] which represents several smaller local recording companies.

Three of the above collecting societies – ACUM, IFPI Israel and PIL – are subject to detailed antitrust arrangements prescribed by the Commissioner for Restrictive Trade Practices under the Restrictive Trade Practices Act, 5748 – 1988. The terms under which these three collective societies were allowed to operate include procedures for the courts regarding the setting of royalty rates in cases of controversy between the relevant society and a user of the works.

In the case of ACUM, the Supreme Court decided that ACUM's executive board must include a certain number of directors on behalf of the public, due to the dual nature of the collective society, which is a private entity that serves public purposes.[63]

As for TALI, a recent amendment to the Israeli Cinema Law 5759-1999 obliges the Commissioner for Restrictive Trade Practices to allow an individual (i.e., not corporations) who created or owns an Israeli Cinematographic Work (as defined therein) to manage its rights via a collecting society.[64] It should be noted that the amendment was enacted in parallel to proceedings held before the Israeli Restrictive Trade Practices Tribunal, which are still pending with regard to the terms of TALI's activity.

§6. Scope of Rights

I. Moral Rights

A. General

44. Moral right in respect of a work is the right of attribution[65] and the right to the integrity of the work.[66] Moral rights subsist in artistic, dramatic, musical and

59. http://www.acum.org.il/.
60. http://eilam.org.il/.
61. http://www.tali-rights.org.il/.
62. http://www.pil.org.il/.
63. CA *ACUM Ltd. v. EMI Music Publishing Ltd.* [2013].
64. The Cinema Law 5759-1999, s. 12(c).
65. The Act, s. 46(1).
66. The Copyright Act, s. 46(2).

literary works.[67] Moral right does not subsist in computer programs[68] and in sound recordings.

The moral right is personal and cannot be transferred; it subsists even if the author never owned the copyright in the work (i.e., economic rights) or has assigned it.[69] Thus, an employee is entitled to moral right even if the initial copyright is vested in the employer. Similarly, where an author assigned his copyright, the moral right nevertheless remains with him. In appropriate cases, the author can sue the owner of the copyright for infringement of the moral right (e.g., the owner published copies of the work without attribution of the work to the author).

Moral rights cannot be assigned, even if the author so desires; thus, an assignee of the copyright cannot ask the author to assign the moral right, and there is no possibility that the owner will have the right to sue third parties for moral right infringement.

The author may permit a use of the work that prejudices his moral right. He may waive the moral right partly or entirely. There is no formal rule regarding the permission or waiver, and thus it seems that it may be done orally or even impliedly, like any other contract under Israeli law.

The permission or waiver is subject to general rules of contract law, including consumer protection law, standard agreements law and general rules regarding the nullity of contract that are illegal or against public order. It is not clear yet whether a complete waiver of moral right in certain cases would be considered to be against public policy. It is the author's view that at least in the case of employee authors and commissioned works, such waiver may well be reasonable.[70]

The duration of the moral right in a work is for the same term as the copyright (exploitation right), that is, in most cases, seventy years after the death of the author. Due to its personal nature, the moral right is not a part of the estate and cannot be transferred or sold. After the death of the author, the moral right is being enforced by his natural heirs (spouse, descendants), acting to safeguard the honour of the deceased author and of his work.

B. Right of Attribution

45. The right of attribution is the right of the author to have his name identified with the work to the extent and in the manner appropriate in the circumstances. It has been held that the relation of an author to his work is like the relation of a parent to his child,[71] and that the law is meant to protect this special relation.

As can be seen from the text, it is not an automatic right to have all works attributed to the author in all circumstances; the right is limited to 'the extent and in the manner appropriate'. The extent and manner may relate to the means of attribution,

67. The Act, s. 45(a).
68. The Act, s. 45(a).
69. The Copyright Act, s. 45(b).
70. See Orit Fischman Afori, *Employees' Moral Rights: The Israeli Solution to an Ongoing Dilemma*, 30 Eur. Intell. Prop. Rev. 521 (2008).
71. CA 2790/93 *Eisenman v. Qimron et al.*, 54(3) P.D. 817 [2000].

the size and location of the name on the work, etc., and may also relate to the attribution itself. Thus, it has to be shown that the specific author, of the specific work, regarding the specific use of the work, has a right of attribution. For example, a commercial advertisement that was created by a graphic designer, or by a music composer, will not bear their names, and it seems that attribution of such a work is way above the appropriate extent. Appropriateness is a term that needs to be developed by the courts on a case-by-case basis.

Under the previous Act, the right of attribution was to the extent and manner 'customary', thus pointing to the customs in the industry. It is the author's view that the 'customary' manner will in most cases also be 'appropriate'.

Employee authors usually have lower expectations to claim authorship. Works that have to be attributed to the author on a physical copy that is sold to the public do not necessarily have to be attributed when performed in public.

The appropriate extent and manner of the attribution right can be agreed upon by contract. It is common to see this kind of terms in production contracts relating to movies or music.

C. Right to Integrity of the Work

46. The right to integrity is the right to prevent distortion, mutilation, modification or other derogatory acts, which are prejudicial to the author's honour or reputation.

Distortion of a work may occur where the work is published with a change that is prejudicial to the author. Thus, for example, it is distortion of the work to reproduce a verse from a poem with altered wording that negatively affects the work. Change to a work of architecture may infringe the author's moral right. A substantial portion of the lawsuits brought in respect of moral right infringement in Israel has related to changes made to works of architecture.

Distortion or mutilation may also occur through inaction. For example, if a work situated in a public space is neglected to an extent that it starts disintegrating, such neglect may be deemed to injure the author's moral right.

A prejudicial act may occur also where the work is presented without change but within a prejudicial context, for example, if an artistic work is displayed in a commercial context prejudicial to the author or a literary work is published in connection with an extremist political group with a racist agenda or the like.[72]

The provision regarding the author's moral right to the integrity of the work must be read in conjunction with section 50 of the Act, which provides that an act which constitutes an injury to the moral right but is reasonable in the circumstances of the case shall not be deemed infringement of the moral right. Section 50 is intended to balance the author's interests against the interests of whoever possesses a copy of the work or the economic rights in the work and needs to perform certain acts in respect of the work in order to further his legitimate interests, such as, for example,

---

72. Joshua Weisman, *The Personal Right in Copyright Law*, 7 Mechkarey Mishpat 51 (1989) (*in Hebrew*).

the owner of a building who needs to make changes to it in order to conform to his needs, notwithstanding the potential prejudice to the architect's moral right.

The Act prescribes a number of considerations that may be weighed to determine where a prejudicial act is reasonable: the character of the copyright work, the nature and purpose of the derogatory act, whether the work was created in the course of employment or under a commission, practice in the industry, and the need for the derogatory act versus the damage to the author.[73]

II. Exploitation Rights

A. General: Nature of Exploitation Rights

47. Copyright is a property right. It is defined as the exclusive right to do (or authorize others to do) certain acts with the work. It is not a right to get paid for uses of the work; it is a right to control these uses.

The power to permit or to forbid a use of the work is in most cases exercised by the copyright owner by asking for payment in return for the permission to use the work. Still, the payment is not a part of copyright law; it is the contractual consequence of the proprietary power to permit the use.

Copyright comprises a specific list of uses of a protected work. For copyright to be invoked, the use has to be one of the specific uses enumerated in section 11 of the 2007 Copyright Act. The uses protected by copyright are copying, first publication, broadcasting, public performance (other than in respect of an artistic work), making available to the public, the making of a derivative work (other than in respect of recordings) and rental (solely in respect of recordings, cinematic works and computer programs).[74]

To come within the scope of copyright, the specific use has to be in relation to the category of works which is enumerated in section 11. For example, rental right only applies to certain types of works. It does not apply to books or to artistic works. If a person commercially rents to the public copies of artistic works or books, this is not an infringement of copyright simply because rental of books and artistic works is not within the scope of copyright protection.

The list of specific uses, and the relevant categories of works which are covered, are exhaustive lists. Any other use of the work is not restricted by copyright.

The exclusive right vested in the copyright owner is to do acts in relation to the work or a substantial part thereof. The expression 'substantial part' of the work reflects an expansion of the scope of protection. The provision means that the copyright owner not only has the right to control the use of the work in its entirety, but also the use of a significant extract from his work (e.g., a chapter from a book or a verse from a poem). Moreover, the copyright owner has the right to control the use of a substantial part of the work in an abstract sense, for example, in a case where there was no literal copying of a certain portion of the work but the principal plot

73. The Copyright Act, s. 50(c).

74. These rights are discussed in more depth below.

and the characters were copied. Such a case would also be deemed to constitute use of a substantial part of the work.

The question as to what part of a work is to be considered 'substantial' for this purpose may be examined quantitatively or qualitatively, leaving broad discretion to the court.

B. Reproduction Right

48. For all types of works, the owner has the exclusive right to reproduce the work.[75] The reproduction right consists of the right to 'the making of a copy of the work, in any material form' including storage of a work through electronic means or any other technological means, making a three-dimensional copy of a two-dimensional work, making a two-dimensional copy of a three-dimensional work, and making a temporary copy of a work.[76]

C. Right of First Publication

49. For an unpublished work, the owner has the exclusive right to publish it.[77] Publication of a work is defined in section 1 of the Act as 'publishing a reasonable quantity of copies of the work to the public, taking into consideration the character of the work, with the consent of its author, but not including a public performance or broadcast of the work, or the public display of an "artistic work"'.

The right of first publication is not a distribution right. It is a limited right that only relates to works that have not been previously published. Thus, after the first publication of a work, any person may 'publish' copies of the work without infringing the copyright. The publication of unauthorized copies is dealt with separately in the law, as discussed below.[78]

D. Right of Public Performance

50. The right of public performance is defined as 'the aural playing or staging of [a work] publicly, either directly or through use of a device'.[79] As can be seen, the core of the definition is 'publicly', and this term is not further defined in the Copyright Act.

The exact scope of the right of public performance is thus determined by the courts on a case-by-case basis. It has been held that the playing of music (live or recorded) in restaurants, cafés, stores, gyms and even hairdresser salons, constitutes public performance. A hotel would be deemed to engage in public performance by

75. The Copyright Act, s. 11(1).
76. The Act, s. 12.
77. The Act, s. 11(2).
78. See the discussion of indirect infringement of copyright at s. §9 'Infringement and Remedies'.
79. The Act, s. 13.

having a television in its lobby, whereas equipping a hotel room with a television is less likely to be deemed 'public'. It follows from case law that two central criteria that would affect the determination as to whether the performance of a work would be deemed to be public are whether the performance is made to a random audience and whether it is made for a commercial purpose.

A public performance of a work may be direct or indirect. Thus, a person who plays radio music to the public through speakers would be engaging in public performance, which requires permission from the owner of the content played, even though such person has no control over and cannot choose the content played to his customers.

The right of public performance of musical works and sound recordings is administered in Israel by collecting societies, usually under 'blanket licenses'.

The issue of public performance usually arises in Israel in connection with musical works and sound recordings; in recent years, lawsuits have also been brought by owners of television content in respect of public performance, in particular by owners of rights in sports broadcasts against owners of restaurants and pubs who displayed the broadcasts on giant screens.

E. Right to Create Derivative Works

51. The copyright owner has the exclusive right to make derivative works and to exercise, in respect of such derivative works, the exclusive rights constituting copyright.[80]

The right to make a derivative work is the right to make an original work, which is substantially based upon the initial copyrighted work, such as translation or arrangement.[81] Translations and arrangements are only examples. Derivative work is defined in a flexible and open manner. It may include the dramatization of a story, the musical variation of a previous work and many other examples.

The right of the copyright owner to exercise the rights in respect of the derivative work that derived from his work means that any person that wants to exploit the derivative work needs permission from both the owner of the derivative work and the owner of the underlying work. For example, if a film producer wants to use a theatrical work, that is itself based on a previous novel, he will have to get permission from both the owner of the theatre play and the owner of the original novel. Similarly, the use of a translation of a work will require the permission of both the owner of the translation (the derivative work) and the owner of the work in the original language (the underlying work). The consent of each one of them can be given by the other, if so agreed between them. It is very common that the owner of the derivative work gets, in advance, the permission of the owner of the underlying work to perform the necessary acts for the exploitation of the derivative work. But this is done by contract law, just like the exploitation of any other of the rights.

---

80. The Act, s. 11(6). For a review of the scope of the right to create derivative works, see: Orit Fischman Afori, *The Right to Prepare Derivative Works in Copyright Law* (Nevo pub. 2005) (*in Hebrew*).
81. The Act, s. 16.

The right to make derivative works does not apply to sound recordings. This exception reflects the different nature of the right in a sound recording. Whereas writing a story which is substantially based on a previous story is part of the copyright in the literary work, producing a new recording of a work, which sounds exactly like a previous sound recording of that work, is not restricted by copyright in the sound recording.

F. Right to Broadcasting

52. The owner has the exclusive right to broadcast the work.[82] Broadcast of a work is defined in the Act as the transmission to the public, by wire or wireless means, of sounds, images or a combination thereof, contained in a work. The term 'wire or wireless' practically covers any form of transmission of sounds or images to the public, including all customary broadcasting methods, cable TV, and also internet streaming and similar technologies.

The transmission of a work is considered broadcasting only if it is done 'to the public'. If one person is transmitting a work to another specific person, this transmission will not be considered 'to the public'. Thus, transmission of a TV programme from an antenna on a roof to a TV set inside the house is not considered broadcasting; but if the same antenna is connected to houses circumstantially amounting to 'public', it will be considered a broadcast. Thus, the term 'public' is the core of the definition. While there is no significant case law regarding the 'public' element of broadcasting, it is the author's view that the same considerations used for interpreting 'public' in public performance, would typically apply: namely, a random audience and a commercial character of the broadcast.

It is not necessary that the person who broadcasts the work will have any control over the content of what is being broadcast. Thus, it was held that a cable TV operator that retransmitted broadcasts that were received from other countries was nevertheless doing an act of broadcasting that required the permission of the owners of the content.[83]

G. Making Available to the Public

53. The copyright owner has the exclusive right to make the work available to the public.[84] Making a work available to the public is defined as the doing of an act in relation to a work that permits members of the public to access the work from a place and at a time of their choosing.[85] [the language should remain "chosen by them", this is a text from the WIPO treaty]

82. The Act, s. 11(4).
83. CA94/2173 *Tele-Event Ltd v. Arutzei Zahav & Co.*, 55(5) P.D. 529 [2001]; ACH 6407/01 *Arutzei Zahav & Co. v. Tele-Event Ltd* [2004].
84. The Act, s. 11(5).
85. The Act, s. 15.

Making a work available at a time and from a place chosen by members of the public is in practice uploading the work to an internet site. The right of making available was included in the new Copyright Act in order to meet the requirement of the WIPO Copyright Treaty in this regard. Whereas public performance and broadcasting were already covered by Israeli law, it seemed necessary to add a right that will cover a situation in which the work is not simultaneously shown or transmitted to the public, but rather being handled in a way that allows members of the public to access the work at different times.

It is yet to be seen who is considered to be the person responsible for the act of making available: whether it is only the person who 'uploads' the work, or maybe it is also the person who operates the platforms that enable members of the public to access the work.

H. Rental Right

54. In respect of sound recordings, cinematographic works and computer programs, copyright includes rental,[86] defined as the rental of physical copies of a work to the public for a commercial purpose.[87]

The act of rental is not defined for itself in the Act. According to the Rental and Lending Act, 5731-1971, rental is defined as the right to hold and use an asset temporarily for consideration.

The rental right is thus rather limited and requires the fulfilment of these cumulative terms and conditions:

(1) The right only applies to phonograms, cinematic works and computer programs.
(2) The right applies to rental and not to lending (without payment); lending of works is not part of the copyright.
(3) The rental right applies only to rental 'to the public'. A one-time act of renting a copy of the work by one person to another is not covered by the rental right.
(4) The right applies only to rental for a commercial purpose.

Renting by a public institution not acting for commercial purposes is not covered by copyright. In this respect, the Supreme Court held in the matter of *NMC v. The Municipality of Holon*[88] that the lending/renting of records by a municipal library is not within the scope of renting for a commercial purpose. In the wake of the *NMC* decision, section 17(b) clarified that public libraries and libraries of educational institutions that lend copies of works do not act 'for commercial purposes'.

The right of rental does not include the rental of a computer program or sound recording, which constitutes an integral part of another object where such other object is the primary object of the rental.[89] By way of example, the rental of a motor

86. The Act, s. 11(7).
87. The Act, s. 17(a).
88. CA 326/00 *Municipality of Holon v. NMC Music Ltd et al.*, 57(3) P.D. 658 [2003].
89. The Act, s. 17(a).

vehicle that includes computer programs as integral parts thereof is not deemed to be rental of the programs.

§7. Limitations or Exemptions to the Scope of Copyright Protection

55. While broadly defining the rights which are conferred by copyright in respect of a work, the Act sets forth a number of limitations and exceptions to the scope of the rights.

Sections 20 through 30 of the Copyright Act set forth specific exceptions, which permit using the works for the statutorily permitted purposes and on the conditions set forth in the Act. Section 19 provides for a general exception of permissible 'fair use' of protected works.

In addition, as discussed below,[90] the Communications Act (Bezeq and Broadcasts), 5742-1982, provides for an exception to copyright protection in respect of retransmission of works as part of mandatory transmission of broadcasts by cable or satellite operators.

I. Fair Use

56. Fair use of a work, formerly permitted as 'fair dealing' for an exhaustive list of purposes, is defined under section 19(a)of the Copyright Act of 2007 as an open-ended exemption, for purposes 'such as' the purposes enumerated therein.[91] The purposes expressly enumerated in section 19(a) of the Act are private study, research, criticism, news reporting, quotation, and instruction and examination by an educational institution. With the possible application of the rule to purposes 'such as' these list of purposes, the principal test as to the permissibility of a given use is the 'fairness' of the use, and in effect the enumeration of the purposes in the section does not represent a significant restriction on whether the use will be recognized as fair use, as long as the use is 'fair' and has at least some proximity to any of the enumerated purposes.[92]

Whether a use made of copyrighted material falls within the scope of 'fairness' is determined with regard to these four factors: (1) purpose and character of the use that has been made, (2) the character of the work used, (3) the scope of the use in relation to the work in its entirety, and (4) the impact of the use on the value of the work and its potential market.[93]

It remains to be seen how the doctrine of fair use will be applied by Israeli courts;[94] the following principles may, however, be inferred from earlier case law, including cases that made use of the fairness criteria under the old law.

90. See the discussion at s. §10 'Neighbouring Rights', s. I *infra*.
91. See Orit Fischman Afori, *An Open Standard 'Fair Use' Doctrine: A Welcome Israeli Initiative*, 30 Eur. Intell. Prop. Rev. 85 (2008).
92. See Niva Elkin-Koren, *Creating Rights – Essays on the New Copyright Act in Israel* 327 (Michael Birnhack & Guy Pessach eds, Nevo Publisher 2009) (*in Hebrew*).
93. The Copyright Act, s. 19(b).
94. So far the issue of fair use under the new Act came before the Supreme Court in a few cases:

If a work was used for a commercial purpose, then it may be a consideration towards not recognizing such use as being fair.[95] Another consideration as to the fairness of the use, in addition to the four factors mentioned in the Act, is the indication of the author's name. It has been held that a person who published the work without crediting the author cannot be deemed to have made fair use.[96]

The four factors to be taken into account for determining fairness are clearly and deliberately influenced by the US copyright legislation, and it is very likely that the interpretation and application of these factors in US courts will influence Israeli courts in the future, at least until some judicial experience is gained in Israeli courts regarding fair use.[97]

Fair use affects the copyright markets not only through court judgments, but in various other ways. In the field of higher education, legislation of fair use led to adoption of 'best practices' regarding the use of book excerpts for educational purposes, which were later on accepted and agreed as part of a mediation with book publishers.[98]

II. Specific Permitted Uses

A. *Use in Legal or Administrative Proceedings*

57. The Act, in section 20, makes it permissible to use a work in legal or administrative proceedings, including for the purpose of reporting on such proceedings, to

---

In CA 5977/07 *The Hebrew University of Jerusalem v. Schoken Publishing House Ltd et al.* [2011], the Supreme Court noted that fair use is the principal tool for realizing public goals/role of higher education institutions; copying of an entire book will seldom be recognized as fair use;

In CA 9183/09 *The Football Association Premier League Ltd v. Anonymous* [2012] it was held that a website that contained links in order to allow members of the public to watch live football games was not making 'fair use'; the reasons were (1) the fact that the website gained income from commercials and/or received donations; (2) the character of the sports broadcasts and the copyright therein as the main source for the sports organizations; (3) the scope of use, as the website enabled its users to watch the games in their entirety; and (4) the fact that internet broadcasting is damaging the value and the potential market of the work;

In CA 7996/11 *Safecom Ltd. v. Raviv* [2013], it was held that reproduction of a technical illustration of electrical circuit belonging to another, in the framework of a patent application, is not Fair Use of that work.

95. CC (Tel Aviv Distr.) 2221/91 *The Walt Disney Co. v. Geva*, 5753(1) P.M. (3) [1992]; CA 8393/96 *The National Lottery et al. v. The Roy Export Establishment Company*, 54 (1) P.D. 577 [2000].
96. CA 2790/93 *Eisenman v. Qimron et al.*, 54(3) P.D. 817 [2000].
97. See Neil Netanel, *Creating Rights – Essays on the New Copyright Act in Israel* 377 (Michael Birnhack & Guy Pessach eds, Nevo Publisher 2009) (*in Hebrew*).
98. The Hebrew University, one of Israel's leading universities, was sued by two book publishers arguing that the university's practice of copying chapters from books for the benefit of students violates the publishers' copyright. Mediation between the parties resulted in a compromise, which received the court's approval, according to which the use of up to 20% of a book's pages for the benefit of the students of a course is to be considered fair use of the copyright material. This agreement is valid until 2017, when it will be renegotiated.

the extent justified in light of the purpose for which the use is being made. For example, copying a document written by the defendant for the purpose of using it as evidence in court to prove that a certain act was done by the defendant cannot be deemed an infringement of the defendant's copyright.

It appears that this section also gives license to governmental authorities to copy documents for the purpose of conducting relevant administrative proceedings. For example, if a governmental authority makes copies of a document submitted to it in order to consult with others, such copying will not constitute copyright infringement.

B. Publicly Accessible Works

58. The Act, in section 21, permits copying of works made accessible for public inspection by law, provided that such copying is consistent with the purpose for which the work was made accessible and to an extent justified in light of that purpose.

C. Incidental Inclusion in a Photographic or Cinematic Work or in a Sound Recording

59. The Act in section 22 permits incidental inclusion of a copyrighted work in a photographic work, a cinematographic work or a sound recording; a musical work, including its lyrics, or a sound recording of such work are not regarded incidentally included if included deliberately.

D. Broadcast or Reproduction of Works Situated in Public Places

60. The Act in section 23 makes it lawful to broadcast or reproduce works of architecture, sculptures and works of applied art permanently situated in a public place, by photographing, drawing or visually representing them in a similar way.

E. Temporary Copying of Computer Programs for Backup

61. The Act permits, in section 24, the holder of an authorized copy of a computer program, to copy the program for back-up purposes,[99] or, if necessary for using the program, for purposes of maintenance of such authorized copy or of a computer system; copying is also permitted in order to provide service to the holder of an authorized copy.[100] An authorized copy is a copy made by the copyright owner or licensed by it.[101]

99. The Act, s. 24(a).
100. The Act, s. 24(b).
101. The Act, s. 24(e).

The holder of an authorized copy of a computer program is allowed to copy the program or to make a derivative work for a limited number of purposes: to make the intended use of such program (including error correction and ensuring its interoperability);[102] to ensure data security;[103] to obtain information to ensure interoperability of independently developed computer system or program with such program;[104] all such use is permitted to the extent necessary for the permitted purposes.[105] Copying or making derivative works for such purposes is not a permitted use if the information was readily available without doing so, or if such information is transmitted to a third party for a different purpose or is used to make a different computer program.[106]

F. Copying for Broadcast

62. The Act, in section 25, permits a person permitted to broadcast a work to record it for broadcasting purposes (with such recording to be subsequently destroyed).

G. Transient Copying

63. The Act further permits, in section 26, transient copying for the purpose of transmission of a work between two parties through a communications network, by an intermediary entity, or for the purpose of enabling any other lawful use of the work, provided that said copy does not have significant economic value in itself.

H. Additional Artistic Work Made by the Author

64. The Act allows, in section 27, the author of a copyrighted artistic work to create a new artistic work involving partial copying of the earlier work even where the author does not own the copyright in the earlier work, as long as the new work neither repeats the essence of the earlier work nor imitates it.

I. Renovation and Reconstruction of Buildings

65. For the purpose of renovating or reconstructing a building, it is permitted to use the architectural work, which is the building or its model, as well as the

102. The Act, s. 24(c)(1).
103. The Act, s. 24(c)(2).
104. The Act, s. 24(c)(3).
105. The Act, s. 24(c).
106. The Act, s. 24(d).

drawings and plans used for its construction with the consent of their copyright owner.[107]

J. *Public Performance in an Educational Institution*

66. The Act permits public performances of copyrighted works by staff or students of educational institutions in the course of such institutions' educational activity, where the audience is limited to staff, students, students' relatives or others directly connected to such an institution; a cinematographic work may only be screened for teaching or examination purposes.[108]

K. *Permitted Uses in Libraries and Archives*

67. The Act, in section 30, allows public libraries and archives (qualifying libraries and archives are to be prescribed by orders of the Minister of Justice) to make reserve or replacement (but not additional) copies of the works whose copies are in their permanent collection, on the condition that additional copies of these works cannot be purchased on reasonable terms in reasonable time. Libraries and archives are further permitted to make a copy at the request of a person who would be permitted by law to make such a copy for himself.

L. *Permitted Use in Retransmission of Local Broadcasts by Cable and Satellite Television Operators*

68. An additional permitted use exempted from copyright infringement is retransmission by cable or satellite television operators of local television and radio broadcasts. The operators of cable and satellite services are obliged to retransmit these broadcasts for the benefit of the viewers, and these mandatory retransmissions are exempt from any royalties or copyright claims.

M. *Creating an Accessible Format Copy of a Work for Persons with Disabilities*

69. Section 28A of the Act, which was enacted in view of the Marrakesh Treaty,[109] allows specific entities and persons to perform an act with respect to a protected work for the purpose of making it accessible for use by a person with

107. The Act, s. 28.
108. The Act, s. 29.
109. Marrakesh Treaty to Facilitate Access to Published Works for Persons Who Are Blind, Visually Impaired or Otherwise Print Disabled.

disabilities (e.g., reproducing a book in Braille or recording an audio version of a book).

Said permission applies only to an entity or a person that is:

(1) an organization that is: (a) a non-profit organization, one of the main goals or activities of which is the education or training of persons with disabilities, the provision of welfare services to such persons or the making available of information for them; (b) a government ministry; (c) an educational institution determined by the minister according to a separate section in the law; provided that it be noted on each accessible copy that reproducing or transferring the accessible copy in a manner contradictory to the Act (namely, not to a disabled person or to another organization as described herein) constitutes copyright infringement;
(2) a disabled person or a person operating on his behalf, provided that the act is done for the private use of the disabled person; or
(3) an entity that has a duty under law to perform adjustments in the work to make it accessible, provided that the act performed with respect to the work is done within the scope and to the extent required by the relevant law and that the accessible copy include the same condition mentioned in (1) above. Additional conditions for said permitted act are:
    (a) the entity or person carrying out said act has legal access to a copy of the work;
    (b) the changes in the work are no greater than those which are necessary to make it accessible; and
    (c) there are no accessible copies of the work available on reasonable terms, taking into account price, location and available quantity of accessible copies.

III. Permitted Uses Subject to Remuneration (Statutory License)

70. The Act permits, in section 32, copying of previously recorded musical works onto sound recordings by way of a statutory license subject to giving prior notice to the copyright owner and to the payment of royalties. This statutory license corresponds with section 19 of the 1911 Act and reflects Article 13 of the Berne Convention.

Recording or copying a work on recordable media (other than media intended for computer use) for private non-commercial use is permitted, with royalties payable by the government on sales of recordable media[110] to the collecting societies.[111]

110. See the discussion *supra* in s. §1 'Sources'.

111. Copyright Ordinance 1924, s. 3B–3E, surviving in accordance with the Copyright Act, s. 69.

§8. DURATION OF PROTECTION

I. Duration of Copyright

A. *Local Works*

1. General: Joint Works – Anonymous Works

71. As a general rule, copyright in a work subsists for the lifetime of its author and for seventy years after his death,[112] for all kinds of literary, artistic, dramatic or musical works.

Copyright in a joint work subsists for the lifetime of its longest surviving joint author and for seventy years after his death.[113] Copyright in an anonymous work, where the author's name neither appears on the work nor is commonly known, shall subsist for a period of seventy years from the first publication date, or, if not published within seventy years from the date of its creation, for the period of seventy years from the date of its creation; however, where the author's identity becomes publicly known during the period of copyright, the general rule of lifetime plus seventy years shall apply.[114]

Photographs, formerly protectable for a shorter period (fifty years from the making of a negative), in accordance with Article 21 of the 1911 Act, enjoy the same period of protection as other works under the 2007 Act.

All the periods of protection are extended until the end of the calendar year in which the date of expiration took place.[115]

It should be noted that the term of protection for works of employees, or for commissioned works, is calculated according to the life of the actual author, notwithstanding the initial ownership that may be vested in the employer or the commissioning party.

2. Government-Owned Works

72. One exception to these general rules is the term of protection for government works. Copyright in a work in which the State of Israel is the first owner of the copyright (in accordance with the provisions of the Act governing the determination of ownership reviewed above) lasts for a period of fifty years from the date of the creation of the work.[116]

112. The Act, s. 38.
113. The Act, s. 39.
114. The Act, s. 40.
115. The Act, s. 43.
116. The Act, s. 42.

3. Sound Recordings

73. The duration of copyright in a sound recording is for a period of fifty years from the date of its making.[117]

4. Works Prior to the 2007 Act

74. In general, works created prior to the 2007 Act coming into force (May 2008) enjoy the new period of protection. Works of photography created before that date will be protected according to the previous legal regime, i.e., for fifty years only.[118] There are slight variations in the wording regarding the term of protection for sound recordings and for works made for the government.

B. Foreign Works

75. As a general rule, foreign works are protected in Israel on the same terms and for the same period of time as local works, subject to the rule of the shorter term prescribed by section 44 of the Act. In accordance with section 44, a foreign work that is protected in Israel merely because of its publication in Israel (i.e., not because its author is a citizen or a resident of Israel) is protected for a period of time not exceeding the duration of copyright protection in its 'country of origin' as defined in the Copyright Act, which is in turn based on the definition and criteria in the Berne Convention.

II. Duration of Moral Right

76. Under the Act, moral rights of an author subsist for the entire duration of copyright in his work.[119]

This means that moral rights will usually be protected for the life of the author and seventy years after his death.

§9. Infringement and Remedies

I. Infringement

A. General

77. The Act provides a definition for copyright infringement and the infringement of an author's moral rights. Copyright infringement, as well as the

117. The Act, s. 41.
118. The Act, s. 78(i).
119. The Act, s. 45(a).

infringement of an author's moral right, is a civil tort governed by the provisions of the Civil Wrongs Ordinance [New Version].[120] Thus, all general rules of tort law apply, including rules of liability and rules related to remedies.

B. Infringement of Copyright

1. Direct Infringement

78. Under the Act,[121] copyright infringement consists of doing, or authorizing another to do, without consent of the copyright owner, any of the acts that fall within the scope of a copyright owner's exclusive right, unless the act falls within the permitted uses provided for in the Act.

2. Indirect Infringement: Trading in Infringing Copies

79. The Act further provides for indirect infringement, defined as follows in section 48 of the Act:

> A person who does one of the foregoing acts with respect to an infringing copy of a work, infringes the copyright, if at the time such act was done he knows, or he should have known, that said copy is an infringing copy:
>
> (1) Sells or lets for rental said infringing copy, including offering or displaying for sale or rental.
> (2) Possesses said infringing copy for a commercial purpose.
> (3) Distributes said infringing copy on a commercial scale.
> (4) Exhibits said infringing copy to the public in a commercial manner.
> (5) Imports into Israel said infringing copy that is not for personal use as provided for in section 129 of the Customs Ordinance.

This section imposes liability on persons who trade in infringing copies, where they did not make such copies themselves. It is often hard to find the actual maker of infringing copies, which are often made outside Israel. Imposing liability on traders who sell or hold for commercial purposes infringing copies of copyrighted works permits enforcing copyright also in those cases where the identity of the original maker of the infringing copies is unknown.

The required state of mind, namely actual or constructive knowledge, imposes liability on intermediaries who trade in infringing copies even where they deny knowledge of the fact that the copies are infringing. The courts infer that such intermediaries knew or ought to have known of the infringement based on the overall circumstances such as undocumented purchases from suspect/dubious sellers, purchase at prices radically lower than the usual price, and so on.

---

120. The Act, s. 52.
121. The Act, s. 47.

3. Indirect Infringement: Public Performance in Places of Public Entertainment

80. It is an indirect infringement to permit, for profit, a place of public entertainment (defined as a 'place used for entertainment and cultural performances' and specifically including catering halls, outdoor function areas, restaurants, coffee shops and clubs) to be used by another person for an infringing public performance of a copyrighted work.[122]

This section is regularly used by collecting societies to enforce the performing right royalty claims on restaurants and wedding halls, when the performance itself is done by someone else (very often by independent DJs). Whenever the owner of the venue claims he did not publicly perform any work, this section makes him liable for authorizing his venue to be used by the person who actually performed the works.

4. Contributory Infringement

81. The Supreme Court in Israel held in the *Hebrew University* matter[123] that the doctrine of contributory infringement, adopted via section 12 of the Civil Wrongs Ordinance, which addresses the liability of persons joining, aiding or abetting /inducing the direct tortfeasor, applies to copyright infringement, provided that three conditions are met: commitment of a direct infringement, the contributory infringer's actual knowledge of the infringement, and real and significant contribution to the commitment of the direct infringement.

While the knowledge has to be actual rather than constructive, so as to enable the contributory infringer, typically an intermediary entity, to prevent infringement, it need not have specific knowledge of every infringing copy, and general knowledge of the infringing activity suffices.[124]

Contribution to the direct infringement is examined in accordance with the circumstances of each case, having regard, *inter alia,* to the contributory infringer's actions, including actions taken to encourage the infringement, the degree of its involvement in the events that led to the infringement, and its ability to effectively prevent the infringement through reasonable means.

Thus, it was held that the Hebrew University is not liable to the infringement committed by a student who copied and distributed the infringing copies of a book.

With respect to 'internet intermediaries', it was held by the Supreme Court in *Premier League* that a website that invited its users to watch football games via infringing links met the conditions of contributory infringement.[125] In another case, a district court held,[126] based on the *Hebrew University* precedent, that a website operator can be liable for infringements committed by third-party users of the web-

122. The Act, s. 49.

123. CA 5977/07 *The Hebrew University of Jerusalem v. Schoken Publishing House Ltd et al.* [2011] (*Hebrew University*).

124. *Ibid.*

125. *Premier League* [2012], *supra.*

126. CC 567-08-09 *(Central Distr.) 'ALICE' Association for the Protection of Cinematographic Works (1993) Ltd et al. v. Rotter.net Ltd* [2011].

site, if he has sufficient knowledge of the infringement and a significant contribution to it. It was held that in the usual case, if a website operator that allows the publication of 'links' by its users implements a policy of 'notice and take down' of infringing links (i.e., links that lead to infringing copies of copyright material on other websites), it will normally be enough to keep him out of the risk of liability as a contributory infringer. Nevertheless, if the website seems to focus on infringing activity, then a notice-and-take-down policy will not suffice, and the operator will be deemed to have known about the infringement that his site has contributed to.

In a different case, the Supreme Court held that the selling of devices which intercept and decode encrypted transmissions did not amount to either indirect or contributory infringement since the viewing of the transmitted work by using said device did not amount to a direct infringement;[127] the Court did note, however, that such selling may amount to unjust enrichment, and returned the case to the first instance in order for it to reconsider the case on such grounds.

C. *Infringement of Moral Right*

1. Direct Infringement of Moral Right

82. Under the Act, it is an infringement of an author's moral right to do in respect of a work an act prejudicing the author's moral right as set forth by the Act – that is, to prejudice the author's right to adequate attribution or to the integrity of his work.[128]

However, an act prejudicing the integrity of an author's work in contravention of section 46(2) of the Act is not deemed infringement of the moral right if it is reasonable in the circumstances of the case.[129] For the purpose of determining whether an act prejudicing the work's integrity falls within the defence of a reasonable act, the court may, in accordance with section 50(c) of the Act, have regard to the nature of the copyrighted work in question, to the nature of the prejudicial act and its purpose, to the question of whether the work was created by an employee as part of his work or was commissioned, to what is customary in the specific industry, and to the need to make the act in question versus the injury that it caused to the author.

A typical case in which an act prejudicial to the work is likely to be deemed reasonable is the case of a work of architecture. If, for example, the owner of a property needs to demolish part of the building in order to build another building or to renovate the existing building to conform to the changing needs, it would be unreasonable to prevent the owner from making use of the building to meet new needs because of the architect's moral right. The balancing formula set forth by the Act permits weighing the owner's needs against the strength of the injury to the architect's moral right.

---

127. CA 5097/11 *Telran Communications (1986) Ltd. v. Charlton Ltd.* [2013].
128. The Act, s. 50(a).
129. The Act, s. 50(b). The reasonableness exception may be described as defining the scope of the moral right.

2. Indirect/Secondary Infringement of Moral Right

83. In accordance with section 51 of the Act, it is indirect infringement of moral right to sell or to rent (or offer or display for sale or rent), or to possess for a commercial purpose, or to distribute on a commercial scale, or to exhibit to the public in a commercial manner, a copy of a work that infringes the right to integrity, where the person doing so knows or should have known at the time of doing so that such copy infringes the right to integrity. The reason for the existence of indirect infringement of moral right of integrity is basically similar to the reason for the existence of indirect infringement of copyright: It allows for the enforcement of the moral right even if the identity of the main infringer is unknown, and even after the infringing materials are no longer in the possession of the main infringer.

There is no indirect infringement of the right to attribution. That is, a person selling or distributing copies of a work that do not bear the author's name is not liable for the infringement of the moral right, and so liability for non-attribution is limited to the person who committed the direct infringement.

Indirect infringement of moral right does not apply to buildings and structures. The reason for the exception is a practical one, as a building is different in its nature from other works; a modification of the building that is deemed to injure the author of the architectural work may result in direct infringement of the author's moral right, but such acts as displaying the modified building to the public, or selling or renting such building, cannot reasonably incur indirect liability.

D. Who May Sue?

84. Action for copyright infringement may be brought by the owner of copyright or by the exclusive licensee; the plaintiff is obligated to join as a party all persons entitled to bring an action for copyright, i.e., co-owners or exclusive licensees, but may be exempted from such duty by the court.[130]

Action for the infringement of moral right may be brought by the author, or, if the infringement occurred after the author's death, by the author's relatives, namely the author's spouse, descendant, parent or sibling.[131]

II. Civil Remedies

A. General

85. Remedies for copyright or moral right infringement consist of injunctions, damages/compensation and several other remedies discussed below. The framework for the law of remedies is the Civil Wrongs Ordinance, which provides the general rules for affording damages and injunctions in Israeli law. There are certain

130. The Act, s. 54.
131. The Act, s. 55.

specific rules (additional remedies and exceptions to remedies) that are set within the Copyright Act. The general and specific rules will be discussed below.

B. Injunction

86. Under section 53 of the Act, a plaintiff in a copyright infringement action is entitled to injunctive relief unless the court finds that there exist reasons that justify denying the claimant from receiving the injunctive relief. According to the legislative history, reasons that may justify denying injunctive relief may be based on public interest, such as freedom of expression considerations and competition considerations. It is yet to be seen how this section will be applied by the courts.[132]

The author's right to injunctive relief for the infringement of his moral right is not specifically dealt with within the Copyright Act and is thus subject to the general provisions of the Civil Wrongs Ordinance, which give wide discretion to the court. In most cases, the court will use its discretion to grant an injunction.

Where a building or another structure already under construction infringes, or upon completion will infringe, copyright or moral right, the plaintiff is not entitled to an injunction against the continuance of the construction.[133]

The Supreme Court noted in *obiter dictum* that where a photographic work of historical importance is concerned, the owner of the work may not be entitled to an injunction, and may only receive damages for the infringement.[134]

In a recent decision, the Tel Aviv District Court held that Israeli courts may order Internet Service Providers to block their clients' access to infringing internet sites, even though there is no law expressly authorizing the courts to do so.[135]

C. Damages

1. Actual Damages

87. A plaintiff in a copyright action may be entitled to pecuniary and non-pecuniary damages under various heads of damage to compensate for the actually incurred damage as a result of the copyright infringement or as a result of the infringement of moral rights. Pecuniary damages may be awarded to compensate for injury/damage suffered by the copyright owner, for loss of his profits, and for restitution of the infringer's profits, all as long as the cumulative damages do not result in double compensation. Non-pecuniary damages may be awarded, including for

132. For a review of such considerations, see: Orit Fischman Afori, *Creating Rights – Essays on the New Copyright Act in Israel* 529 (Michael Birnhack & Guy Pessach eds, Nevo Publisher 2009) (*in Hebrew*).
133. The Act, s. 59.
134. CA 7774/09 *Weinberg v. Weishoff* [2012].
135. CC (Tel Aviv) 33227-11-13 *NMC United Entertainment Ltd. et al. v. Bloomberg Inc. et al.* [2015].

mental anguish,[136] although non-pecuniary damages would be more difficult to prove.

Because actual damage for copyright infringement is often hard to prove, the courts may award damages at large (by way of global assessment).[137] The Supreme Court in the *Hershko* case gave regard, in awarding damages at large, to the scale of the infringement (large quantities of copies of the infringing work distributed over a long period of time), the commercial success of the infringing work, the damage caused by the infringing work to the commercial success (or potential for success) of the copyrighted work, and the mental anguish caused to the author as a result of the distortion of his work and injury to his lifetime enterprise.[138]

2. Compensation without Proof of Damage (Statutory Damages)

88. As a substitute to the right to recover actual damages, the Act provides for the court's discretion to award the plaintiff compensation without proof of damage/injury.[139] Damages without proof are available both for the infringement of copyright and for the infringement of moral right, in the amount of up to ISL 100,000 for each infringement.

For the purpose of statutory damages, the Act provides that infringements carried out as part of a single set of activities (may consist of separate but related acts that combine into the same overall infringing activity) shall be deemed to constitute a single infringement.[140] The Supreme Court interpreted the provision of the earlier law[141] regarding statutory damages as relating to each type of infringement, rather than to each occurrence, or act, of infringement (such as each performance or each copy).[142]

The Act sets forth a non-exhaustive list of considerations that may be weighed by the court in determining the entitlement to damages without proof, and their amount: the scope, duration and gravity of the infringement, the actual injury to the plaintiff and benefit to the defendant, as assessed by the court, as well as the character of the defendant's activity, the relationship between the parties and the defendant's good faith.[143]

3. No Damages for Innocent Infringement

89. An innocent infringer is exempted from damages, provided he neither knew nor should have known that copyright subsisted in the work.[144] This exception

136. CA 4500/90 *Hershko et al. v. Averbuch et al.*, 49(1) P.D. 419 [1995] (*Hershko*) at 432.
137. *Hershko*; CA 528/73 *Ettinger v. Almagor*, 29 (2) P.D. 116 [1975].
138. *Hershko*, at 434.
139. The Act, s. 56 (a).
140. The Act, s. 56(c).
141. The Ordinance, s. 3A.
142. CA 592/88 *Sagi et al. v. Estate of Abraham Ninio et al.*, 46(2) P.D. 254 [1992].
143. The Act, s. 56(b).
144. The Act, s. 58.

relates to cases in which it could be reasonably assumed that there is no copyright at all in the used object, such as works that seem to be in the public domain, or works that seem to be non-original. It does not apply to cases in which the defendant has been wrong (even in good faith) regarding the identity of the owner of the copyright in the work or regarding the legal character of the defendant's act.[145]

D. *Other Remedies*

1. Accounting

90. A detailed accounting ['detailed report of the infringement'] may be ordered both in respect of the infringement of copyright and in respect of the infringement of moral right.[146] Case law indicates that such an order will be granted only if the plaintiff shows *prima facie* evidence for the infringement. The remedy of an accounting order is not limited to an accounting of profits but also obligates the defendant to provide details regarding the infringement committed, which may enable the plaintiff to bring further claims.

2. Disposition of Infringing Copies: Order for Destruction, Order for Delivery-Up

91. In a copyright infringement action, the court may order the destruction or other disposition of the infringing copies, the transfer of the ownership of the infringing copies to the plaintiff at his request (subject to payment to the defendant prescribed by the court if the plaintiff is likely to make use of the infringing copies).[147]

Where destruction or transfer is requested, the plaintiff must notify the police and the claims of the police must be heard.[148]

Destruction or transfer of ownership may also be ordered in respect of infringing copies in the possession of non-infringing third parties, unless they are protected by the market overt provision of the Sales Act, 5728-1968. The market overt protection applies to a third party who purchased and received possession of the infringing copy in good faith from a trader in the ordinary course of business; a market overt purchaser is, however, barred from trading in such infringing copies.[149]

145. CA 2312/02 *Drook v. Danziger*, [2005].
146. The Act, s. 57.
147. The Act, s. 60(a).
148. The Act, s. 60(b)).
149. The Act, s. 60(c), the Sales Act, s. 34.

3. No Destruction Order for Infringing Buildings

92. Where a building or another structure already under construction infringes, or upon completion will infringe, copyright or moral right, the plaintiff is not entitled to a demolition order.[150]

III. Criminal Offences and Sanctions

93. Copyright infringement in certain circumstances incurs criminal liability. It is an offence to make, or to import into Israel, an infringing copy for the purpose of trading therein,[151] and a person doing so is liable to up to five years of imprisonment or to a fine of up to ISL 2,260,000 (approximately euros (EUR) 450,000).[152]

It is an offence to engage in the sale, rental or distribution of infringing copies, or to sell, rent or distribute infringing copies on a commercial scale, or possess infringing copies for the purpose of trading therein[153] and a person doing so is liable to up to three years imprisonment or a fine of up to ISL 1,582,000.[154]

It is also an offence to make or possess an object designed for the making of infringing copies where such copies are made for trading therein,[155] and a person doing so is liable to up to one year's imprisonment or a fine of up to ISL 452,000.[156]

A. *Offence by a Corporation*

94. The Act provides that an offence committed by a corporation incurs a double fine.[157] The Act imposes personal liability on corporate officers for offences committed by the corporation or its employees, unless it is shown that the officer took all possible action to prevent the offence.[158]

IV. Proceedings Involving Customs

95. The copyright owner may by way of written notice to the Director of Customs request that allegedly infringing copies of his work be detained and treated as goods prohibited for importation under the Customs Ordinance.[159] For the purpose of such detention, the copyright owner must provide the Director of Customs with

150. The Act, s. 59.
151. The Act, s. 61(a) and (b).
152. The Act, s. 62(a)(1) and (2).
153. The Act, s. 61(c), (d), (e).
154. The Act, s. 62(b)(1), (2) and (3).
155. The Act, s. 61 (f).
156. The Act, s. 62(c).
157. The Act, s. 62(d).
158. The Act, s. 63.
159. The Act, s. 65(a).

preliminary evidence regarding the infringement, and a personal guarantee in the amount prescribed by the Director of Customs to cover all expenses connected with detaining the goods, or in order to compensate for any damage caused by the detention, should it turn out to be unjustified.[160] However, there is no detention of infringing copies imported for personal use as defined in section 129 of the Customs Ordinance.[161]

§10. Neighbouring Rights

I. General: Performers and Broadcasters Rights

96. The rights of performers and broadcasters are governed by the Performers' and Broadcasters' Rights Act, 5744-1984 (hereinafter the '*Performers Rights Act*').

II. Scope

A. *Performers' Rights*

97. Section 2 of the Performers Rights Act mandates that certain acts in respect of a performance require the performer's consent. A performer is defined as a person who performs through acting, singing, playing an instrument, dancing or in another manner, a literary, artistic, dramatic or musical work.[162] A performance is defined as 'the performance of a literary, artistic, dramatic or musical work by a performer'.[163] The acts requiring the performer's consent are recording, copying, broadcasting and commercial distribution, as discussed below.

1. The Right to Control Recording

98. Recording requires consent of the performer.[164] Recording is defined in section 1 as the preservation of a performance by any means allowing the performance to be seen, heard or copied.

2. The Right to Control Copying

99. In accordance with section 2(2) of the Performers Rights Act, copying requires the consent of the performer; however, copying is permitted where the recording was made with the performer's consent, and the recording was copied for

160. The Act, s. 65((d).
161. The Act, s. 65(e).
162. The Performers Rights Act, s. 1.
163. The Performers Rights Act, s. 1.
164. The Performers Rights Act, s. 2(1).

the same purpose for which the performer's consent was given. Thus, where a performer consented to the recording of his performance for the making of a commercial record, his consent is not required for any further making of copies by the record company. Of course, such consent may be required if it was so agreed when the initial consent to the recording was given (e.g., a recording contract).

3. The Right to Control Broadcasting

100. In accordance with section 2(3) of the Performers Rights Act, a performer's consent is required for broadcasting a performance. Broadcast is defined as transmission or distribution to the public – by wire, wireless or any other means – of sounds and images or of a combination of sounds and images.[165]

Consent is not required for a broadcast of the performance by specified governmental broadcasting entities (the Broadcasting Authority, Educational Television Channel and the Israel Defense Forces (IDF) Channel) of a recorded performance (or a copy thereof) where the performer had agreed to the recording and there is an agreement between the recorder and the broadcaster regarding the use of the performance.[166]

Furthermore, consent is not required for a rebroadcast made with the consent of the original broadcaster;[167] a rebroadcast is defined as a simultaneous broadcast of another's broadcast.[168]

Due to the addition of section III, A (see below), it is not clear whether the consent of the performer is needed for the broadcast of his recorded performance. In practice, the performers are collecting royalties from all broadcasters through collecting societies.

4. The Right to Control Distribution

101. The performer's consent is required for the sale, lending, rental, distribution, importation or possession for purposes of commerce, of a recording (or a copy thereof), if the recording or the copy was made without the performer's consent.[169]

5. Performer's Right to Royalties

102. A performer is entitled to 'equitable royalties' for the playing or performance of his performance, payable to a collecting society.[170]

165. The Performers Rights Act, s. 1.
166. The Performers Rights Act, s. 2(3)(a).
167. The Performers Rights Act, s. 2(3)(b).
168. The Performers Rights Act, s. 1.
169. The Performers Rights Act, s. 2(4).
170. The Performers Rights Act, s. 3A.

Collecting societies have not been formally recognized, but in practice, the management of performers' royalties in Israel is done by two separate bodies, which collaborate for the purpose of collection of royalties: (i) *Eilam* – Israeli musicians performing right society;[171] and (ii) *Eshcolot* – royalty association of Israel artists.

6. Employee Performer

103. The rights of an employee performer in respect of a performance that took place in the course of and in consequence of his employment are owned by the employer during the first fifteen years of the term of the performers rights and owned by the performer during the rest of the period, unless otherwise provided by agreement.[172]

7. Performer's Moral Right

104. The performer's moral right is provided for in section 4A of the Act. In accordance with this section, the performer has a right of attribution and a right to the integrity of his work.

The right of attribution consists of having the performer's name stated with every performance by him and on every recording or copy thereof, to a customary extent and degree.

The right to integrity means that a performance, or a copy thereof, should not undergo falsification, damage or other change, or that no act is done to denigrate the performance in a manner liable to injure the performer's honour or reputation.

B. Broadcasters' Rights

105. The Performers Rights Act accords protection to a broadcaster within the scope of its definition in the Act. The Act defines a 'broadcaster' as 'a person who makes a radio or television broadcast by lawful authorization';[173] a 'broadcast' is defined[174] as transmission or distribution to the public – by wire, wireless or any other means – of sounds and images or of a combination of sounds and images.

Under section 4A1 of the Performers Rights Act, a broadcaster's consent is required for recording broadcasts, copying, broadcasting or commercially distributing recorded broadcasts, and for making rebroadcasts. Most of these rights have little application in practice, because recording and dealing with recorded copies of broadcasts is not common. The broadcaster's consent is not required for rebroadcasts which the rebroadcaster is obligated to transmit pursuant to the Telecommunications (Bezeq and Broadcasts) Act[175] (i.e., rebroadcasts by operators

171. http://eilam.org.il/?page_id=66.
172. The Performers Rights Act, s. 11.
173. The Performers Rights Act, s. 1.
174. The Performers Rights Act, s. 1.
175. The Performers Rights Act, s. 4A1(5).

of cable and satellite services). Acts that involve retransmission of broadcasts by digital means such as internet streaming are indeed covered by the Act and may be controlled by the broadcaster.

III. Conditions for Protection

106. The Performers Rights Act does not make its protection conditional upon meeting any formal criteria (such as registration or marking). In respect of broadcasters' rights, the Performers Rights Act sets forth two conditions: the first being that a broadcaster fall within the scope of the statutory definition, namely that it broadcast in accordance with a lawful authorization;[176] the second is a negative condition, in that the protection of the Performers Right Act for broadcasters shall not apply to a broadcast performed in violation of a copyright or of performers' rights.[177]

Time of making a performance or a broadcast. As to performers' rights, the Performers Rights Act applies to performances made after its entry into force, namely after 1984.[178]

As to broadcasters' rights, there is no express provision in the Performers Rights Act in this regard, and the application of the Act to broadcasters' rights may in principle be limited to broadcasts made after 1996, when the Act that formerly dealt solely with performers' rights was amended to add broadcasters' rights.

Place of making a performance or a broadcast. The Performers Rights Act applies to performances and broadcasts made in Israel and also to performances and broadcasts made outside of Israel, with the protection in Israel of the latter being prescribed by order of the Minister of Justice.[179] The Performers and Broadcasters Rights Order (TRIPS Agreement), 1999, made some of the performers' rights under the Performers Rights Act applicable to performances made in accordance with the criteria set forth in the TRIPS Agreement.[180]

The Copyright, Performers and Broadcasters Rights Order (Rome Convention), 2002, also made certain performers' rights under the Performers Rights Act applicable to performances meeting the criteria of the Rome Convention.[181]

---

176. The Performers Rights Act, s. 1.
177. The Performers Rights Act, s. 4B.
178. The Performers Rights Act, s. 14.
179. The Performers Rights Act, s. 13 and 4D.
180. The Performers and Broadcasters Rights Order (TRIPS Agreement), 1999, ss. 1 and 2 apply the provisions of the Performers Rights Act regarding the right to control recording, copying and commercial distribution and rental in respect of a performance made in a WTO Member State. The same sections partially apply the provision regarding the right to control broadcasting, in respect of real-time broadcasts of a live performance made in a WTO Member State, but excluding rebroadcasts.
181. The Copyright, Performers and Broadcasters Rights Order (Rome Convention), 2002, s. 2 (a live performance which meets any of the following requirements: (i) takes place in another State signatory to the Rome Convention; (ii) is incorporated in a phonogram protected in Israel under the Rome Convention Order; (iii) is carried by a broadcast which is protected by the Rome Convention Order).

Such rights made applicable are only those rights prescribed in the Rome Convention and the TRIPS Agreement, accordingly. These rights are a performer's rights in respect of the recording and broadcast of a live performance.[182] Thus, a performer's right to royalties in respect of a public performance and broadcasting of a recorded performance does not extend to performances made outside Israel.

As to broadcasters' rights, the TRIPS Order did not make the Performers Rights Act applicable to broadcasts made outside Israel. The Copyright, Performers and Broadcasters Rights Order (Rome Convention), 2002, made certain broadcasters rights under the Performers Rights Act apply to broadcasts meeting the criteria of the Rome Conventions, namely broadcasts made from the territory of a signatory to the Rome Convention by a foreign broadcasting organization headquartered in the territory of a signatory of the Rome Convention. Under the Order,[183] such foreign broadcasters will enjoy the protection of broadcaster's rights under section 4A1 of the Performers Rights Act as to controlling its broadcasts (the exception of mandatory rebroadcasts not being applicable).

Broadcast content is very often protected by copyright, so foreign broadcasting entities may invoke copyright for the protection of the content of their broadcasts in Israel.

A. *Exception to Performers' and Broadcasters' Rights*

107. In accordance with section 4 of the Performers Rights Act, the performer's consent is not required in cases of fair distribution or use, for purposes of private study or non-profit instruction, or for research, criticism, survey or a journalistic summary.

In accordance with section 4C of the Performers Rights Act, the broadcaster's consent is not required in cases of private use or fair use, 'fair use' being defined as adequate use for private study, for non-profit instruction, for research, or for criticism.

108. Similar to the Copyright Act, the Performers Rights Act was also amended in order to allow for the creation of accessible copy recordings. In accordance with section 4A(d) and 4C1(a) of the Performers Rights Act, an act with respect to a performance or a fixation of a performance or a reproduction of the fixation of a performance, which would otherwise be perceived as infringing, is permitted if such an act was done with respect to a performance, a fixation or a reproduction that is not adequately accessible to a person with disabilities due to his disability, and for

182. Section 2 of the Copyright, Performers and Broadcasters Rights Order (Rome Convention), 2002, makes applicable to such foreign performances the provisions of the Performers Rights Act regarding the right to control recording, copying and commercial distribution and rental, and partially applies the provision regarding the right to control broadcasting, in respect of real-time broadcasts of a live performance or unauthorized fixation thereof, but excluding rebroadcasts.
183. The Copyright, Performers and Broadcasters Rights Order (Rome Convention), 2002, s. 4.

the purpose of making an accessible copy of same, provided that the conditions set forth in paragraph 28A of the Copyright Act, *mutatis mutandis*, are fulfilled.

B. *Term of Protection*

109. The protection of the Performers Rights Act in respect of a performer's rights applies for fifty years from the end of the year in which the original performance took place,[184] and in respect of a broadcaster's rights, for twenty-five years from the end of the year in which the original broadcast was made.[185]

C. *Infringement of Performer's Rights*

110. Infringement of performers' or broadcasters' rights is the making of an act that, under the Performers Rights Act, requires consent without obtaining such consent.

In addition, there may occur an infringement of a performer's moral right,[186] or the infringement of the right to receive royalties via a collecting society. Such infringements are different in their nature in that they do not relate to a property right.

D. *Remedies*

111. Section 5 of the Performers Act provides that infringement of a performer's right under the Performers Act entitles the performer to the same civil remedies, *mutatis mutandis*, that are available for infringement of copyright.[187]

In addition, the court may order that a recording be seized (and disposed of as directed by the court) and that the distribution of such recording or its copies be prohibited;[188] a seizure order may be directed against a non-party.[189]

E. *Criminal Penalties*

112. Section 6(a) of the Performers Rights Act provides for criminal liability and penalties, based on the language of the parallel provisions of the Copyright Act. Concisely, it is a criminal offence to make an infringing copy of a performance or a broadcast, for the purpose of trading therewith, and it is an offence to knowingly deal, commercially, with infringing copies of broadcasts or performances.

---

184. The Performers Rights Act, s. 10.
185. The Performers Rights Act, s. 10A.
186. The Performers Rights Act, s. 4A(c).
187. See s. §9 'Infringement and Remedies', *supra*.
188. The Performers Rights Act, s. 8.
189. The Performers Rights Act, s. 9.

§11. OVERLAPPING AND RELATION TO OTHER INTELLECTUAL PROPERTY LAWS

I. Copyright and Industrial Designs

113. Under the Act, copyright does not subsist in a design that is used or intended for use in industrial manufacture.[190] The Design Rules, in section 72, define industrial manufacture as thc making of fifty articles or more.

II. Copyright and Trademarks

114. Subject matter protectable by copyright may be eligible for trademark protection if the trademark protection criteria are met; trademark registration (or eligibility for trademark registration) of a work meeting the criteria of copyright protection does not preclude copyright protection. A genuine use of a trademark for the purpose of informing the public regarding the sale of the trademark goods may be permitted with regard to the underlying copyright as well.

190. The Copyright Act, s. 7.

Chapter 2. Patents

§1. Sources: Legislation

I. Legislation

115. The patent system in Israel is governed by the Patents Law, 5727-1967 (the 'Patents Law' or the 'Law'), and the Regulations thereunder, as amended from time to time. The Patents Law has replaced the patents-related provisions of the Patents and Designs Ordinance of 1924 that dates back to the times of the British mandate over Palestine. The practice and procedures of the Israel Patent Office (IPTO) are regulated primarily by the Patents Regulations (Office Practice, Procedures, Documents and Fees), 5728-1968 (the 'Patents Regulations'), the Patents Regulations (Extension of Patent Term – Application for Order, Opposition and Cancellation Procedure), 5758-1998 (the 'PTE Regulations'), and the Patents Regulations (Implementation of the Patent Cooperation Treaty), 5756-1996 (the 'PCT Regulations').

II. Conventions

116. The international conventions pertaining to patents to which Israel is a party have been implemented in the provisions of the Patents Law and the Regulations thereunder.

Israel is a party to the Patent Cooperation Treaty (PCT) since 1996. Applications for the grant of an Israeli patent may, therefore, be made as national patent applications or as national phase applications of PCT applications.[191] The IPTO also serves as a Receiving Office of the PCT,[192] as well as an International Search Authority (ISA) and international agency for preliminary examination[193], in respect of international applications that are submitted by Israeli citizens, Israeli residents or bodies corporate incorporated in Israel, in accordance with the Convention of Cooperation on Patents.

As Israel is a signatory to the Paris Convention for the Protection of Industrial Property and a member of the World Trade Organization (WTO), priority can be claimed from a prior patent application submitted in another Paris Convention Member State or a WTO Member State;[194] conversely, priority from an Israeli application may be claimed in other Paris Convention or WTO Member States.

As a signatory to the Budapest Treaty on the International Recognition of the Deposit of Microorganisms for the Purposes of Patent Procedure, Israel allows the deposit of biological materials.

191. The Law, s. 48A et seq.; the PCT Regulations.
192. The Law, s. 48B.
193. The Law, s. 48I.
194. The Law, s. 10.

Israel is party to several bilateral agreements calling for cooperation between the IPTO and other national patent offices.[195]

§2. PATENTABLE SUBJECT MATTER

I. Patentable Invention

117. A patentable invention is defined in section 3 of the Patents Law as 'an invention, whether a product or a process in any field of technology, which is new and useful, can be used industrially and which involves an inventive step'. Thus, in addition to the requirements of novelty, inventive step, utility and susceptibility to industrial application, all discussed in section §3 'Conditions of Patentability' below, the Law delimits the scope of patentable inventions to *inventions*, whether products or processes, in any area of technology.

By contrast to earlier statutory law, the Patents Law, by deliberate choice of the legislator, does not define an 'invention' so as to leave open the determination of what innovative discovery may be eligible for protection; it was the legislative intent not to impose unwarranted limits on patentability of future discoveries showing inventiveness in such form as may evolve with the development of science in the future.[196]

A. *'Whether a Product or a Process'*

118. The provision of section 3 of the Law, which relates to the invention 'whether a product or a process', may be interpreted either as an exhaustive definition or as a non-exhaustive reference. Taking the view that this is an exhaustive definition, the Registrar of Patents has expressed a position that claims directed to use *per se* are not allowable because such claims do not define a product or a process. Accordingly, the Circular Letter MN 30 of 17 August 2004 (the 'Circular Letter MN 30') provides by way of an example that a claim such as 'use of X as a paint' is not allowable.[197] Such position is not devoid of conceptual difficulties; allowable

---

195. As at August 2015, the IPTO is party to Prosecution Highway Programs (permanent or pilot) with the following foreign offices:

> Patent Prosecution Highway Program (PPH) between the Israel Patent Office (IPTO) and the Canadian Intellectual Property Office (CIPO); Patent Prosecution Highway Program between the Israel Patent Office (IPTO) and the United States Patent and Trademark Office (USPTO); Patent Prosecution Highway Pilot Program between the Israel Patent Office (IPTO) and the Danish Patent and Trademark Office (DKPTO); Patent Prosecution Highway (PPH) Pilot Program between the Israel Patent Office (IPTO) and the European Patent Office (EPO); Patent Prosecution Highway Pilot Program between the Israel Patent Office (IPTO) and the Japan Patent Office (JPO); Patent Prosecution Highway Pilot Program between the Israel Patent Office (IPTO) and the National Board of Patents and Registration of Finland (NBPR).

196. Bill 637, Patents Law, 5725-1965, 20 Jan. 1965.
197. Circular Letter MN 30, s. 2.

claims are discussed at more length in section §3 'Conditions of Patentability', section IV. It may be noted in this context that the provisions of the Law that address Patent Term Extension (PTE) define the 'basic patent', *inter alia*, as a patent that protects the 'use of a material',[198] so that, on the face of it, interpretation of section 3 of the Patents Law as allowing 'use' claims may also be tenable.

B. *'In Any Field of Technology': Discoveries, Business Methods, Computer-Implemented Inventions*

119. To be patentable, an invention must be 'in any field of technology'. In this context, the Practice Guidelines for Patent Examination published by the IPTO[199] (the '*Practice Guidelines*') provide that the determination as to whether an invention is in a field of technology will be made based on the requirement that the performance of such invention, whether a product or a process, must involve a concrete technological process.[200] In this regard, the Practice Guidelines follow and seek to implement the 1994 district court appellate decision in the matter of *United Technologies Corporation* concerning a software-related invention,[201] to date the highest jurisdiction that ruled on the issue.

Although the Patents Law does not contain any express exclusion provision in this regard, scientific discoveries and mathematic formulae, rules for playing games and mental processes as such[202] are considered by the IPTO abstract ideas or processes that are not 'in an area of technology', whether performed manually or by a computer.[203]

Methods of doing business. Although not expressly excluded by the Patents Law, the IPTO held that methods of doing business *per se* are deemed not to relate to any area of technology and therefore to be ineligible for patent protection.[204] However,

198. Section 64A of the Law defines a 'basic patent' as follows: the patent that protects any material whatsoever, including a process for the production of a material, use of a material, a medical preparation that incorporates a material, a process for the production of a medical preparation that incorporates a material or medical equipment that requires a license in Israel […].
199. Available at http://www.justice.gov.il/MOJHeb/RashamHaptentim/Ptentim/Bhina/ (last revised on 15 Mar. 2012).
200. Practice Guidelines, Appendix B, s. 7.2.
201. MA 23/94 *United Technologies Corporation v. Registrar of Patents*, 26 Dinim Mechozi (8) 729 [1994] (*UTC*) (appeal from the Patent Registrar's refusal of a system of helicopter engine control designed to minimize fuel consumption during cruise mode, comprising mechanical measuring components and digital fuel control software; the District Court held that a software-related invention in which the novelty resided in the software must be examined in its entirety, without isolating the software element. The invention was held to be a process that causes through the use of software a new result (saving of fuel consumption), and deemed patentable subject matter on appeal).
202. Cf. EPC, Art. 52(2).
203. Practice Guidelines, Appendix B, s. 7.3; MA (TA) 501/80 *Rosenthal v. Registrar of Patents*, 5744 (3) P.M. 441 [1980] (*Rosenthal*) (the appellate court affirmed the Registrar's refusal of a patent for a method of tool compensation for numerical calculation machines, held to be an unpatentable calculation method); also discussed in Application for patent No. 131733 in the name of *Eli Tamir* [2006] (*Tamir*).
204. *Tamir*, at 33 (method of sales promotion through sale of coupons held to be a business method and thus not patentable); *Compearls Ltd v. Mobydom Ltd*, Application for cancellation of Patent 118898

the Practice Guidelines do not rule out the possibility that a business method, or other methods not patentable *per se*, may be patentable if combined with additional technological means and viewed as a whole, as discussed below. These decisions and enunciation of policy were not yet reviewed by the appellate courts.

Computer-implemented and software-implemented inventions. The issue of patentability of computer-implemented inventions, addressed in certain earlier decisions of the courts and the Registrar of Patents[205] prompted subsequent reconsideration of the IPTO examination policy, as reflected in the current Practice Guidelines.

Following the *UTC* ruling of the district court, in order to determine whether the invention is in an area of technology, an examiner must examine the invention as a whole without dissecting it into hardware and software elements, to ascertain whether the invention, as a whole, makes a contribution that possesses a concrete technological character compared to prior art, on a case-by-case basis.[206] A software-implemented invention may be eligible for patent protection if it possesses a technological character.

Under the Practice Guidelines, the examination of a concrete technological character of a software-implemented invention may use such auxiliary tests as whether the execution of the invention affects physical features beyond the regular operation of an integrated computer system and whether it causes the computer to operate in a new manner or creates previously non-existent interoperability between components of a computer system.[207]

It may be noted that software code may be entitled to protection by copyright as a 'literary work', in accordance with section 1 of the Copyright Act, discussed in Chapter 1 'Copyright and Neighbouring Rights', *supra*.

II. Statutory Exclusions

120. The Law in section 7 specifically excludes certain categories of subject matter from the scope of patentability: methods of medical treatment of the human body, new varieties of plants and of animals and microorganisms derived from nature are not patentable.

[2008] (the invention held to be a business method for reporting and reservation of parking slots involving the use of a computerized database and thus not eligible); *Mordechai Teicher*, Patent Application no. 171773 (Administrative appeal on an Examiner decision) [2012] (an invention of an apparatus and method for managing social games was found to lack patentable subject matter, because the effect caused by the invention is on human relationships and thus is not a technological effect. The Registrar also noted that in general, games and interpersonal relations cannot be the subject of a patent, since they especially involve an abstract thought process).

205. *Rosenthal*; *Tamir* at 42 et seq. (addressing patentability of a computer-implemented business method); *Elbit Systems Ltd v. Biosense Inc.*, Opposition to patent applications 125755, 126864 [2009] (*dictum* regarding patentability of software-related inventions, proposing that use of software or computer should be disregarded when patentability is analysed).

206. Practice Guidelines, Appendix B, ss 7.3 and 7.4.

207. Practice Guidelines, Appendix B, s. 7.4.

A. Medical Treatment Methods

121. Under section 7(1) of the Law, methods of medical treatment of the human body are not patentable.[208] The Circular Letter MN 30 accordingly provides that claims relating to medical treatment, such as 'use of X in the treatment of disease Y' are not allowed.[209]

The statutory exception applies to therapeutic treatment but not to diagnostic methods, which are not excluded.[210] Veterinary treatment methods are also patentable.[211]

New use of known materials for treatment may, however, be patented, as the courts acknowledged the patentability of both first and second indications.[212] In addition, the Supreme Court in Israel allowed, incidentally to addressing other issues, a new medical use of a compound as product-for-purpose claims.[213]

The Circular Letter MN 30 accordingly provides that Swiss-type claims[214] must meet the criteria of eligibility, *inter alia*, under section 7;[215] it further provides that claims of a type 'Compound X for use as a medicament' are allowable.[216]

In contradistinction to the European Patent Convention (EPC) 2000[217] amendment to Article 54(5) of the EPC in Europe, which, while expressly allowing second medical use claims, was held to make Swiss-type claims (for use in manufacturing) no longer allowable,[218] Swiss-type claims remain allowable in Israel.

An IPTO decision, affirmed on appeal by the District Court,[219] held that a claim directed to a new dosage regimen is in principle allowable.[220]

208. The Law, s. 7.
209. Circular Letter MN 30, s. 6.
210. Cf. EPC, Art. 52(4) of the EPC.
211. Cf. EPC, Art. 52(4) of the EPC.
212. CA 244/72 *Plantex Ltd et al. v. The Wellcome Foundation*, 27(2) P.D. 29 [1973] (*Plantex*); MiscA (TA Distr.) 93/477 *The Wellcome Foundation Ltd v. Registrar of Patents* [1993]; LCA 5293/93 *The Wellcome Foundation Ltd v. Registrar of Patents* [1993]; *Teva Pharmaceutical Industries et al. v. Merck & Co., Inc.*, Opposition to the patent application 153109 [2010].
213. *Sanofi* at 732 (the patent at issue claimed 'pharmaceutical compositions for treatment of … , comprising … ').
214. Such as 'use of X in the manufacture/preparation of Y', allowable subject to meeting other criteria of patentability (Circular Letter MN 30, s. 3).
215. Circular Letter MN 30, s. 4.
216. Circular Letter MN 30, s. 5.
217. The 2000 Amendments to the EPC.
218. Decision G 2/08.
219. MCA (Jer. Distr.) 35096-09-10 *Merck Sharp & Dohme Corp. v. Unipharm Ltd et al.* [2012]. An application for leave to appeal to the Supreme Court was dismissed, without addressing this issue (ALA 6837/12 *Merck Sharp & Dohme Corp. v. Unipharm Ltd et al* [2013]).
220. *Teva Pharmaceutical Industries et al. v. Merck & Co., Inc.*, Opposition to the Patent Application 153109 [2010] (on the facts of the case, the new dosage regimen was held to lack novelty and to lack an inventive step); the District Court in the appellate decision, where the issue of the medical treatment exception to patentability was not raised, reiterated the Registrar's analysis of this issue without criticism.

B. New Plant and Animal Varieties: Microorganisms

122. Section 7(2) of the Patents Law provides that no patent shall be granted for '*new varieties of plants or animals, except microbiological organisms not derived from nature*'.

Plant varieties *per se* may, however, if eligible, be subject to registration and protection under the Plant Breeders Rights Law, 5733 – 1973, discussed in Chapter 5 'Plant Variety Protection', *infra*. In addition, inventions having a technological effect, such as, for example, genetically modified plants, may be patentable.

Microorganisms derived from nature are unpatentable.[221] Microorganisms not derived from nature are patentable.

III. Inventions Contrary to Public Policy

123. Unlike the law before the enactment of the Patents Law, there is no express exclusion in the Patents Law to patentability of inventions that are contrary to public policy. Such exclusion existed in the Patents Ordinance but was deliberately omitted by the legislator of the Patents Law. Nevertheless, it is reasonable to suppose that in extreme cases the public policy provision of the Contracts (General Part) Law, 5733-1973,[222] may be invoked, which in accordance with another provision of the Contracts Law may be applied to any legal act.

§3. CONDITIONS OF PATENTABILITY

I. Conditions of Patentability: General

124. The conditions of patentability, set forth in section 3 of the Patents Law,[223] are that the invention must be: (i) new; (ii) useful; (iii) susceptible of industrial application and that it must; (iv) involve an inventive step. In addition to these substantive requirements of novelty, inventive step, utility and susceptibility of industrial application,[224] an invention must be sufficiently described in the patent application to enable its execution, as prescribed by section 12 of the Law, and the patent claims must reasonably arise from the specification, as prescribed by section 13 of the Law.[225]

The burden of proof that an invention meets the requirements of novelty or other patentability requirements rests upon the applicant during prosecution[226] and during pre-grant opposition proceedings,[227] whereas during revocation or infringement

221. The Law, s. 7(2).
222. Contracts (General Part) Law, 5733-1973, ss 30 and 61(b).
223. Cited in s. §2 'Patentable Subject Matter', *supra*.
224. Discussed *infra* in s. II of this s. §3.
225. Discussed *infra* in s. III of this s. §3.
226. *Unipharm Ltd v. Bayer AG*, Opposition to patent application 71871 [1994] (*Bayer*) at 101–102.
227. The *Bayer* matter at 101–102; CA 665/84 *Sanofi Ltd v. Unipharm Ltd et al.*, 41(4) P.D. 729 [1987] (*Sanofi*) at 737 (*a propos* the utility requirement).

proceedings the burden rests upon the party attacking the validity of the patent – namely, the applicant for revocation or the defendant in an infringement action, respectively.[228] A possible change in the law may be inferred from the *Merck v. Teva* ruling of the Supreme Court,[229] which suggested that in the opposition proceedings the burden is on the opponent to show that the invention is not eligible for patent protection. In fact, even before the *Merck* ruling, in pre-grant oppositions, the opponent commences bringing evidence and such order of adducing evidence was rationalized by the reason that the opponent needs to overcome the shift of a secondary burden of proof that stems from the act of acceptance of the patent application.

II. Patentability of an Invention

A. *Novelty*

1. Statutory Definition of Novelty-Destroying Disclosure

125. Novelty, as required in section 3 of the Law, is defined in section 4 of the Law as follows:

> An invention is deemed new if it was not published,[230] in Israel or abroad, before the application date –
>
> (1) by written, visual, audible or any other description, in a manner that enables a skilled person to carry it out according to the particulars of the description;
> (2) by exploitation or exhibition, in a manner that enables a skilled person to carry it out according to the particulars thus made known.

Under section 4, the novelty requirement is universal, so that novelty is destroyed by disclosure anywhere in the world and in any language.

To be novelty-negating, a disclosure must be: (i) a disclosure of the invention, (ii) made publicly, (iii) made by way of description or by way of exploitation or display, and (iv) such that it enables a skilled person to carry out the invention.

2. What Constitutes Prior Art for Purpose of Examining Novelty?

126. Disclosure must describe the entire invention. Agreeing with the reasoning of the UK Court of Appeal in *General Tire & Rubber Co. v. Firestone Tyre &*

228. CA 345/87 *Hughes Aircraft Company v. State of Israel et al.*, 44(4) P.D. 45 [1990] (*Hughes*) at 102; CA 47/87 *Chesem Reliable Protection Systems Ltd v. Bachri*, 45 (5) P.D. 194 [1991] (*Chesem*) at 196; *Sanofi* at 737 (a propos the utility requirement).
229. LCA 6025/05 *Merck & Co. Inc. v. Teva Pharmaceutical Industries Ltd* [2011] at 22.
230. While the English translation of the Patents Law makes use of the term 'published', we propose that a more accurate translation of the binding Hebrew version would be 'made available to the public'.

Rubber Co. Ltd,[231] the *Hughes* court held that for a prior publication to anticipate the invention, a signpost on the road to the invention, would not suffice and the inventor must be shown to have planted his flag at the precise destination.[232] A novelty-destroying publication of the invention must thus be a single publication that contains all the elements of the invention, as distinguished from a 'mosaic' of publications.[233] The rule against 'mosaic' does not apply where one publication cites or refers back to another publication.[234]

The rule that a novelty-destroying disclosure must contain all the elements of the invention is to an extent qualified by a subsequent Supreme Court decision in the *Snitovsky*[235] matter, which held that a disclosure may be novelty-destroying when it contains the essence of the invention, even if it lacks a certain element which is not essential (i.e., the Court applied the infringement test). The *Snitovsky* ruling appears to set a somewhat unwarranted exception to the rule requiring that a novelty-destroying publication must disclose all elements of the invention; in the author's opinion, the infringement test of the essence of the invention is more appropriate in the examination of inventive step than in the examination of novelty. However, the *Snitovsky* ruling in this regard remains in force and was applied by district courts.[236]

Substance over form. Whether a publication discloses an invention is determined by having regard to the substance of the publication, rather than its form. Thus, a novelty-destroying publication that describes the invention substantively may differ from the language of the specification in its wording and terminology; conversely, similarity of language in itself is not sufficient to make a prior publication novelty-destroying if the patent differs from the prior art publication substantively.[237]

Mode of disclosure; made available to the public. It has been held in case law that the requirement that a novelty-destroying publication be made available to the public means that whoever was exposed to the invention was free to make use of it without restriction; a secrecy restriction may be inferred from the circumstances even though there was no express secrecy undertaking.[238] Where a publication was made publicly available, it need not be proved that any person was actually exposed

---

231. *General Tire & Rubber Co. v. Firestone Tyre & Rubber Co. Ltd* [1972] R.P.C. 457 (C.A.).
232. The Supreme Court in *Hughes* at 103, cited the English Court of Appeals in *General Tire* at 486 'To anticipate the proprietor's claim the prior publication must contain clear and unmistakable directions to do what the proprietor claims to have invented … . A signpost, however clear, upon the road to the proprietor's invention will not suffice. The prior inventor must be clearly shown to have planted his flag at the precise destination before the proprietor.'
233. *Hughes* at 103; CA 4867/92 *Snitovsky v. Taamas Ltd et al.*, 50(2) P.D. 509 [1996] (*Snitovsky*) at 515; CA 314/77 *L. M. Lipski v. Manor*, 32(1) P.D. 205 [1977] at 207.
234. *Hughes* at 103.
235. *Snitovsky* at 516–517 citing CA 75/55 *'Donag-Or' Ltd v. Aktiebolaget Sievert & Fornander*, 10 P.D. 1990 [1956] at 1993.
236. For example, MA 1168/04 (TA Distr.) *SmithKline Beecham Plc v. Unipharm Ltd* [2005], CC (TA Distr.) 1179/00 *Anna Lotan Ltd v. Belmon Nurit Ltd* [2007].
237. *Hughes* at 104.
238. LCA 2012/95, 3608/95 *Krone AG v. Inbar Reinforced Plastic*, 51(3) P.D. 548 [1997] at 558 (disclosed documents contained a confidentiality warning, the defendant unsuccessfully alleged trade usage to disregard such warning; the Supreme Court has observed in a *dictum* that confidentiality obligation may be inferred from the circumstances of disclosure).

to it and it suffices that such publication was accessible (e.g., in a public library);[239] publications in foreign languages constitute part of the prior art for the purpose of assessment of the novelty of an invention.[240]

Unpublished patent applications are not prior art. Differently from the law in other jurisdictions, such as the EPC Member States,[241] under which novelty may be destroyed by an unpublished earlier application for the same invention, there is no similar provision in Israeli law. Previously filed patent applications not yet published cannot be cited as prior art publication for the purpose of examining novelty.[242] The precedence of patent applications is provided for in section 9 of the Patents Law, which sets the first-to-file principle.

Inherent disclosure. The concept of inherent disclosure, or inevitable result, according to which the invention is deemed non-novel if the execution of the prior publication inevitably results in the claimed invention, even if not described therein, has been to an extent recognized in the decisions of lower instances[243] and is in line with the leading Supreme Court *Hughes* judgment.[244]

3. Disclosure through Use

127. As provided in section 4 of Law cited above, novelty may be destroyed through the use (exploitation) or display (exhibition) of the invention in public. In order to negate novelty, such display must allow the person exposed to the invention to understand it, i.e., it must be enabling.[245]

Experimental and demonstration use. By way of an exception, the courts have been willing to rule that experimental use does not destroy novelty. Nevertheless, experimental use, or use for testing purposes, made in public for such purposes as demonstrating product quality to prospective customers destroy novelty.[246] Working an invention in public, where it could not be determined whether experimental

239. CC (TA Distr.) 1003/51 *Park Davis & Co. v. Abic Chemical Laboratories Ltd*, 5 P.M. 348 [1952] at 373 (a publication catalogued in a scientific institute's library accessible to the public constituted prior art).
240. *Gisser v. Compucraft Ltd*, Application for cancellation of Patent 123976 [2008] (foreign patents published and accessible online in a foreign language constitute prior art).
241. EPC, Art. 54(3).
242. Examination Guidelines, 23.1/F/, ss 1.3.3.2 and 4.
243. *Unipharm Ltd v. Eli Lilly and Company*, Opposition to Patent Application 115314 [2004] at para. 44 (the decision was affirmed on appeal at MA (TA Distr.) 1086/04 *Unipharm Ltd v. Eli Lilly & Company* [2007]). See also *FMS Enterprises Migun Ltd v. DSM IP Assets BV*, opposition to patent application No. 142789, 17 Oct. 2013 where it was held that for showing so-called inherent disclosure one should be able to clearly convince that an element of the claim is necessarily found in the prior publication, and that such element can be identified by a person of average skill in the art.
244. *Hughes* at 105.
245. See *infra* s. 4 of s. II of this s. §3 Conditions of Patentability.
246. CC 1563/91 (TA Distr.) *Kleiman Meteor Net and Metal Products Factory v. Gil-Gad (1982) Ltd* [1993] (*Kleiman*) (use of the invention on model farms for the purpose of demonstrating its efficacy to prospective customers (not purely experimental use) was deemed novelty-destroying use in the sense of s. 4).

use was possible other than in public, was not held, in interim proceedings, to destroy novelty.[247]

Prior secret use. Prior use that is not made in public does not negate novelty and is not considered to be part of the prior art.[248]

4. Novelty-Destroying Disclosure Must Be Enabling

128. Under section 4 of the Law, a disclosure negating novelty, whether through description or use, should be such as to enable the invention to be carried out by a person skilled in the art; a mere general description, from which it cannot be ascertained how to work the invention, does not suffice.[249] Use of the invention in public in a manner that does not allow a person skilled in the art to understand the working of the invention does not destroy novelty.[250]

A publication will destroy novelty even if some trial and error is required, provided it does not require undue experimentation; the Supreme Court has held that trial and error not involving undue experimentation would not prejudice sufficiency of disclosure in the patent specification;[251] the same rule would seem to hold in respect of enabling prior art in the context of novelty.

5. Assessing Novelty

129. It is permitted to read prior printed publications in the light of the knowledge possessed by persons skilled in the art, as long as essential elements are not read into the prior publication.[252]

In order to examine whether prior publication negates novelty, courts have also used the so-called infringement test which has been enunciated by the epigram '*That which infringes if later would anticipate if earlier*'.[253]

In the *Unipharm v. SKB* matter,[254] the Supreme Court held that a prior publication which contained a description of a free base (*rosiglitazone*), but did not describe the process of preparation of an acidic salt (*rosiglitazone maleate*) claimed in a subsequent patent as a preferred compound due to its improved features, was held not to destroy novelty of the acidic salt, even though the prior patent claimed pharmaceutically acceptable salts of the free base.

---

247. LA 375/84 *Meitam (1981) Ltd v. Narkis Health Equipment* [1984] (unpublished).
248. Prior user's right to continue its use is discussed in s. §7 'Limitations and Exceptions to the Scope of Patent Protection', s. II.
249. *Hughes* at 103.
250. CA 141/88 *Shemi et al. v. Monson et al.*, Dinim Supreme 54, 736 [1989], at para. 5.
251. *Hughes* at 117; CA 804/89 *Lanplast (1974) Ltd et al. v. Berkman et al.*, 46 (2) P.D. 295 [1992] (*Lanplast)* at 306; *Sanofi* at 750–751.
252. *Hughes* at 104.
253. *Lipsky* at 211; *Hughes* at 104–105.
254. CA 8802/06 *Unipharm Ltd v. SmithKline Beecham Plc et al.* [2011] (*SmithKline Beecham*).

The discovery of a new advantage of a known product or method does not meet the requirement of novelty where the claim is for the product *per se*.[255]

6. Statutory Exceptions: Grace Periods for Specific Circumstances of Disclosure

130. In Israel, there is no *general* grace period for an inventor's own publication. The Law provides in section 6 that, in certain circumstances, an invention owner is entitled to a grace period during which the prior publication, by himself or by another, will not be deemed novelty-destroying.

Unauthorized disclosure. Section 6(1) of the Law provides for a grace period in the event where the publication was made without the owner's consent of the material obtained from him (or his predecessor in title).[256] The grace period is for the owner to file 'within a reasonable time' after the publication comes to his knowledge.

Unlike in certain other jurisdictions, e.g., the EPC requirement of filing within six months,[257] no specific period is prescribed in Israel for applying for a patent in case of such unauthorized disclosure; the requirement is merely that a patent should be applied for within reasonable time after the owner becomes aware of the publication.

Publication at a recognized exhibition. According to section 6(2) of the Patents Law, a grace period of six months is provided for where the invention was either: (i) published by the owner by way of display, description or use at a recognized industrial or agricultural exhibition and subject to prior notice to the Registrar; or (ii) published by way of use during a recognized exhibition without the owner's consent.[258] The Law and the Regulations thereunder do not define what constitutes a recognized exhibition.

Inventor's publication before a scientific society or in its transactions. In addition, section 6(3)[259] provides for a grace period of six months where the publication

---

255. Application 150511, *Unipharm Ltd v. The Procter & Gamble Co.* [2011] at para. 43. See also *Lanplast*, at 310.

256. The Law, s. 6: The right of the owner of an invention to be granted a patent shall not be affected by publication said in s. 4 – (1) if it is proved that the matter published was obtained from him, the owner of the invention or his predecessor in title, and was published without his consent, and if the patent application was filed within a reasonable time after the publication became known to the applicant; […].

257. EPC, Art. 55.

258. The Law, s. 6: The right of the owner of an invention to be granted a patent shall not be affected by publication said in s. 4 – […] (2) (a) the publication was by the owner of the invention or his predecessor in title in one of the following ways: (i) display at an industrial or agricultural exhibition in Israel or at a recognized exhibition in one of the Member States, of which official notice was given to the Registrar before its opening; (ii) publication of a description of the invention at the time of a said exhibition; (iii) use of the invention for the purposes of the exhibition and at the place of the exhibition; (b) the publication was by use of the invention, even without its owner's consent, at the time of the exhibition, at the place of the exhibition or outside it, on condition that the patent application was submitted within six months after the exhibition opened; […].

259. The Law, s. 6: The right of the owner of an invention to be granted a patent shall not be affected by publication said in s. 4 – […](3) publication was by way of a lecture by the inventor before a scientific society or by publication of the lecture in official transactions of the society, on condition

of the invention was made by way of the inventor's lecture given before a learned society or published in its transactions, subject to prior notice to the Registrar. This exception, arising from the then UK law[260] is, to the authors' knowledge, rather rare; importantly, it is limited to obtaining a grace period in the IPTO but cannot protect an invention from being deemed disclosed in other jurisdictions.[261]

B. Inventive Step

131. Besides novelty and as prescribed by section 3 of the Law, a patentable invention should demonstrate an inventive step. An inventive step is defined in section 5 of the Patents Law as:

> a step which does not, to an average skilled person, appear obvious in the light of information published before the application date in ways said in section 4.

The requirement of an inventive step is broader than that of novelty and derives from the rationale that, to warrant patent monopoly to the exclusion of competitors, the product or process must be not merely novel and not yet known to the public, but also must demonstrate an actual contribution to the field.[262]

1. Assessing the Inventive Step

132. As required by the statutory provision of section 5 of Law, an inventive step is examined through the eyes of an averaged skilled person in the relevant art. A person skilled in the art for the purpose of examining an inventive step is a fictitious entity and may also be a team of professionals rather than a single person.[263] A skilled person is a person skilled in the relevant art but acting without any inventive capacity.[264]

The existence of an inventive step – that is, obviousness to an average skilled person – is not an issue of fact but an issue of law, determined by the court on the basis of the facts proved to it, *inter alia*, by witness testimony, in accordance with the objective standard of an average skilled person.[265]

---

that the Registrar was given notice of the lecture before it was delivered and that the patent application is filed within six months after the aforesaid publication.

260. The British Patents and Designs Ordinance, s. 20A, that preceded the Patents Law; cf. UK Patents Act, 1949, s. 51(2)(d).

261. See M. Noam, *Inventors' Lectures before a Learned Society in Light of the Patents Law – Caution, Trap!* (*in Hebrew*), 14 Mishpatim 317 (1986).

262. *Hughes* at 108.

263. *Hughes* at 108–109.

264. *Chesem* at 197.

265. CA 433/82 *Bachri et al. v. Padalon et al.*, 39 (3) P.D. 533 [1985] (*Bachri*) at 537–538; CA 528/61 *Greenwald v. SeeBee Ltd*, 16 P.D. 2490 [1962] at 2493; CA 4867/92 *Snitovsky v. Tamas Ltd et al.*, 50(2) P.D. 509 [1996] at 516; *Chesem* at 197.

Analysis of prior art should refrain from use of hindsight.[266]

Combination of prior art sources. The existence of inventive step is examined against all available prior art in its entirety, where prior art negating the inventive step may be contained in multiple sources; however, the act of combination of sources into a general picture must be obvious to a skilled person not possessing inventive capacity.[267] If combining prior art references is not obvious to a skilled person, it represents an inventive step. Although the IPTO held that combining prior art references will be considered obvious if prior art contained 'teaching, suggestion or motivation' to combine,[268] it is submitted that this test is not the sole test for inventiveness.[269]

Degree of inventiveness. The threshold of inventiveness need not be high; an inventive step has been held not to require a significant advance, so that a 'modest inventive step' would suffice.[270]

Obvious to try. The IPTO has held that an invention is obvious when it is shown that it was obvious for the person skilled in the art to try the invention and such person also believed that it has reasonable chances of success.[271]

Auxiliary tests. Auxiliary tests, or secondary considerations, that may be applied in examining the inventive step are the long-felt need test, the commercial success test, the acclaim of the invention when received (surprise, etc.) and the tribute of imitation by competitors.[272] Such considerations, or tests, are not determinative but merely auxiliary.[273]

What constitutes prior art for purposes of examining an inventive step. The mode of publication of information that renders it 'prior' art is the same as for novelty, that is, by way of an enabling description, use or demonstration.[274] The Supreme Court left open the issue whether, in assessing inventive step, a prior art publication must be such that an average skilled person would have access to it (e.g., a prior publication in a language that is not widely used may arguably be outside the scope of the relevant prior art).[275] Patent applications not yet laid open for public inspection are not citable as publications for the purpose of examining the inventive step.[276]

---

266. *Hughes* at 109–110; *Chesem* at 197; also, e.g., *Trima Israeli Pharmaceutical Products Maabarot Ltd v. G. D. Searle & Co.*, Opposition to patent application 136532 [2008] at para. 58.
267. *Hughes* at 108, *Snitovsky* at 15; *Chesem* at 197, *Lipsky* at 209.
268. *Elbit Electro-Optical Systems Elop Ltd v. Thales S.A.*, Opposition to Application for Patent 128468 [2008], at para. 37; *Ogi Systems Ltd v. Sarin Technologies Ltd*, Opposition to Application for Patent 138347 [2008], at para. 49.
269. Cf. *KSR International Co. v. Teleflex, Inc.*, 550 U.S. 398 (2007).
270. *Hughes* at 109.
271. *FMS Enterprises Migun Ltd v. DSM IP Assets B.V.*, Opposition to patent application 14278 [2015]. See also MCA (Jer. Distr.) 35096-09-10 *Merck Sharp & Dohme Corp. v. Unipharm Ltd et al.* [2012], and ALA 6837/12 *Merck Sharp & Dohme Corp. v. Unipharm Ltd et al* [2013]. Notably, the decision of the appellate courts did not specifically address the requirement of expectation for reasonable chances of success.
272. *Hughes* at 111–112.
273. *Hughes* at 111; *Bachri* at 540 (commercial success not a determinative consideration).
274. The Law, s. 4.
275. *Bachri* at 537.
276. Examination Guidelines, 23.1/G, s. 14.2.

Results of failure to identify the prior art's problem. In one case, the Supreme Court noted, in passing and as *obiter dicta*, that failure to identify the prior art and the problem to be solved by the invention renders the attempt to argue 'inventive step' perplexing task.[277]

Inventive step not required for patents of addition. A patent of addition may be granted over an improvement or modification of to the invention subject of the main patent even in the absence of inventive step (discussed below at section III).[278]

No petty patents or utility models. In Israel, there are no petty patents or utility models but only patents of utility.

III. Patents of Addition

133. Israeli law recognizes the possibility of obtaining patents of addition for inventions, which represent non-inventive modification of earlier inventions owned by the same proprietor.[279]

Under section 44(a) of the Law, a patent owner may apply to have a later patent application, for an invention which is an improvement or modification of the invention for which he already holds his existing patent, issued as a patent of addition. Similarly, in terms section 44(c) of the Law, an applicant who submitted several applications may request that the patent for one of them be granted as a main patent and the patents for the others as patents of addition to such main patent.[280]

A patent of addition need not involve an inventive step beyond the invention covered by the main patent or by any patent of addition to such main patent.[281] A patent of addition cannot be obtained if the application for it is submitted before the date of the application for the main patent.[282]

Grant of a patent of addition serves as conclusive evidence that the subject matter of that patent is an improvement or modification of the main patent and that it is fit to be a patent of addition.[283]

A. *Utility and Susceptibility of Industrial Application*

134. Section 3 of the Patents Law that defines a patentable invention also provides that a patentable invention should be useful, and that it should be susceptible of industrial application.

The usefulness (utility) requirement may be analysed under two types of tests. The first type of a test, derived from English law, is whether the result promised by the specification is achieved by following the teaching of the specification; if not,

277. ALA 7337/12 *Cohen v. John Deere Water Ltd* [2013].
278. The Law, s. 44(b).
279. The Law, ss 44 et seq.
280. Literal reading of s. 44 of the Law suggests that it is not possible to transform a granted patent to a patent of addition.
281. The Law, s. 44(b).
282. The Law, s. 45.
283. The Law, s. 46.

the invention lacks utility.[284] In the *Sanofi* matter, it was held that a credible promise as to utility suffices for filing an application; the achievement of the promise is an issue for subsequent opposition, revocation and infringement proceedings.[285] It was further held that utility of a pharmaceutical preparation need not be proved by clinical data, provided the asserted utility is not unbelievable on the face of it amid skilled persons, and that the standard of proof is lower than that required by the US Food and Drug Administration (FDA) as to the efficacy of a pharmaceutical, i.e., does not require clinical data.[286] The approach that the achievement of the promise contained in the specification suffices to establish utility was adopted in a subsequent decision of the Registrar of Patents.[287]

A different test, not widely adopted in Israeli jurisprudence, derives from the US case of *Brenner v. Manson*,[288] and requires that an invention must have a specific useful purpose beyond general/basic scientific knowledge.[289] This notion of utility may also be based upon the requirement for industrial application of the invention in view of the perception expressed in footnote 5 to Article 27 of the TRIPS Agreement, where the concept of usefulness and susceptibility of industrial application are deemed synonymous. It is to be noted that in the Patents Law the requirement of susceptibility of industrial application is a remnant of the older version of the Law which did not include the requirement 'in any field of technology' but contained a requirement of susceptibility to application in industry or agriculture.

IV. Requirements of a Patent Specification

A. *Sufficiency of Description/Enablement*

135. Section 12(a) of the Law provides, *inter alia*, for the requirement of sufficiency of description:

> The specification shall include a title by which the invention can be identified, its description with drawings that may be necessary, and also a description of the manner in which the invention can be performed, enabling a skilled person to perform it.

One of the leading authorities on sufficiency of description is the Supreme Court ruling in *Hughes*, which clarified that the requirement of sufficiency of description set forth in section 12 is intended to serve the informational purpose of patent law, namely to convey to the public the scope of the invention and the mode of working it, so as not to discourage research and to permit the public to benefit from the invention after the expiry of the patent. It is also intended to ensure that at the time

284. *Sanofi* at 733.
285. *Sanofi* at 737, 743.
286. *Sanofi* at 741–743.
287. *Tircovot Brome Ltd v. Great Lakes Chemical Corporation*, Opposition to application for grant of patent 115188, [2009] at para. 42.
288. *Brenner v. Manson*, 383 U.S. 519 (1966).
289. Applied in CC 21/83 *Eckerstein v. Alumim*, 5449(3) P.M. 197.

of the application the inventor is in possession of the invention for which the patent is sought (similarly to the written description requirement of 35 U.S.C. § 112) and thus to prevent speculative applications.[290]

1. Examination of Sufficiency

136. Sufficiency of description is examined against all relevant art as available to a notional average skilled person, or team, defined in accordance with the nature and complexity of the relevant technological field, as is done in examination of an inventive step.[291] The specification must permit the invention to be carried out without undue experimentation, although a reasonable degree of trial and error is permissible.[292]

In the matter of *Donag-Or*,[293] the Supreme Court held that sufficiency of description is an issue of fact that the court must decide according to the facts proved to it.

In the *Abic*[294] matter, the Supreme Court affirmed the district court ruling according to which a patent specification that teaches an invention that was said to have a synergistic effect is enabled where such effect is stated to be an advantage of the invention, and that the specification need not necessarily include experimental data proving the promised result.

Disclosure of best mode not required. The Law does not require that the specification disclose the best mode for carrying out the invention.[295] In light of the US patent reform following which non-disclosure of the best mode is no longer a ground for invalidity, it does not appear to the Authors that the chances are high that the best mode requirement might be introduced in Israel through the conduit of the duty of good faith.

Deposit of biological materials. As Israel is a member of the Budapest Convention for the International Recognition of Living Matter for Patent Proceedings, section 12(b) of the Law further provides in respect of inventions concerning biological materials or processes for their production, as follows:

> For purposes of subsection (a), if the subject of the invention is a biological material or a process for the production of a biological material or an invention that involves the use of a biological material, and if the biological material was deposited with a deposit institution, then part of the description of the invention or of the manner of its performance may consist of referral to that deposit, all in a manner and on conditions to be prescribed by the Minister of Justice with approval by the *Knesset* Constitution, Law and Justice Committee.

290. *Hughes* at 115–116.
291. *Hughes* at 116, *Sanofi* at 750.
292. *Hughes* at 117, *Sanofi* at 750.
293. CA 75/55 *'Donag-Or' Ltd v. Aktiebolaget Sievert & Fornander*, 10 P.D. 1990 [1956] at 1997.
294. LA 547/86 *Vitamed Ltd v. Abic Ltd* [1986] (unpublished) at para. 4.
295. CC 1512/93 (TA Distr.) *The Wellcome Foundation Ltd et al. v. Teva Pharmaceutical Industries Ltd* [1995]. (*Quaere* whether the best mode requirement applies in Israel in the absence of statutory provisions.)

'Biological material' is defined in section 12(b) as a 'biological material not easily available to the public, which cannot be described in a manner that will enable a skilled person to perform the invention, on condition that the biological material can be duplicated or reproduced, either independently or in a host animal or plant cell'.

B. Allowable Claims: Clarity, Fair Basis, Special Types of Claims

137. Section 13(a) of the Law requires that patent claims should define the invention and should reasonably arise from the specification, in the following language:

> The specifications shall end with a claim or claims that define the invention, on condition that each said claim reasonably arise out of the subject described in the specification.

1. Defining the Invention Unambiguously

138. As the statutory requirement is interpreted in case law, the claim must define the invention clearly and with precision, delimiting the boundaries of the patent holder's exclusive right.[296] Regulation 20(b)(3) of the Patents Regulations provides that the claims must define the invention 'clearly and concisely'. Accordingly, ambiguity is a ground for revocation of the patent or for cancelling the claim.[297] Ambiguity is interpreted having regard to the language of the claims, as these would be read by skilled addressees.[298]

2. Fair Basis: Covetous Claims Are Not Allowed

139. The other aspect provided for in section 13(a) is that a claim should reasonably arise from the description. The purpose of the fair basis requirement is that the proprietor should not be granted unwarranted protection for what is not disclosed in the specification.

Before the enactment of the Patents Law, it was held in the *American Cyanamid* matter,[299] in which the Supreme Court drew upon English law to interpret the statute preceding the Patents Law, that deliberately covetous claims may cause a refusal of amendment. However, the language of section 185 of the Patents Law suggests that where 'the claims in the specification of the original patent were not worded in

296. *Hughes* at 68.

297. *Innovia Telecoms Ltd v. Media Online Services Inc.*, Opposition to patent application 124617 [2006] (*Innovia*), at para. 37.

298. *Innovia* at para. 37; CA 25/65 *LePetit S.p.A. v. American Cyanamid Company* 20 (1) P.D. 495 [1966] 495 at 498.

299. CA 245/60 *American Cyanamid Company v. LePetit S.p.A.*, 18 P.D. 788 [1962] at 804.

good faith or were not worded clearly' the only sanction is denial of damages for the infringement of an amended patent.

3. Claim Types

140. As is evident from section 3 of the Patents Law, Product Claims and Method/Process Claims are expressly allowed by the Law. Additional types of claims have been found allowable over the years.

Product Claims. A Product Claim protects the product *per se*. It is sufficient to show one use for a new product, in order to claim the product *per se*, without limitation for a particular use. DNA sequences (molecules) are allowable as product claims, with the following qualifications, enunciated in Circular Letter MN 64 of 2008: the biological activity of the claimed biological sequence must be described in the specification but need not be claimed; however, claims directed to a larger sequence that includes the specified sequence (worded as 'containing', 'including', etc.) of a specified sequence, are not allowed unless limited to a specified activity of the claimed sequence; conversely, claims to a specified sequence are allowed without such limitation. Claims directed to portions, derivatives and homologues of a specified sequence will be allowed only if limited to an activity identical with that of the specified sequence.

Method (Process) Claims. As noted above, a claim for an invention that is a process (or method) must recite the steps, which form the process or the method. In accordance with section 50(a) of the Law, a patent granted for a process also protects the direct product of the patented process.

In an invention claiming a production process, the burden of proof in an infringement action may shift, in accordance with section 50(b) of the Law, to the defendant to show that the accused product is obtained through a process different from the patented process. Such shift may occur where the proprietor shows that the accused product is identical to the patented product, provided that: (1) the patent holder is unable through reasonable efforts to determine the production process that was actually used to produce the identical product; (2) there is a substantial likelihood that the identical product was produced by the patented process.[300] Where the court found that the point of novelty of the invention lies not in the process, but in the specific mixture of materials used in the process and the temperature of its burning, the court held that the proprietor may not avail itself of the benefit of the presumption of section 50(b).[301]

Functional claims. Functional claims, namely claims defining a product by its function and not by its structure, were found allowable in the *Hughes* case.[302]

300. Cf. Art. 34(1)(b) of the TRIPS Agreement.

301. C.A. 2626/11 *Hassin Esh Industries ltd. v. Koniel Antonio (Israel) Ltd.* [2013].

302. *Hughes* at 79. It was also held that, to avoid overreaching and vague claims, such claim must clearly define the protected result and the patent specification must disclose sufficient information permitting a skilled person to determine whether or not he comes within the scope of the patent claims without making any but simple experiments that do not require inventiveness.

Section 13(b) of the Law as amended[303] after the *Hughes* judgment now reads as follows:

> It is permissible to express in the claim any of the basic elements of the invention as a means or a step for the performance of a certain act, and it is not necessary to specify the structure, the material or the acts required for the performance of that act; a claim expressed as aforesaid shall be deemed to include particulars of the relevant structure, material or acts, as described in the specifications.

The bill preceding the enactment of the amendment clarified that section 13(b) was intended to clarify that a claim can be expressed as means or step towards a specified act, namely what function the invention is intended to attain.[304] Accordingly, it may be argued that such functional claims are now restricted to the structures disclosed in the specification (and their equivalents).[305]

The Supreme Court in *Hughes* further held that a claim directed to the attainment of a new and non-obvious result may be broadly worded, whereas a claim directed to the achievement of a known result will be too wide if it claims any method of attaining it.[306]

Product-by-Process Claims. Product-by-Process Claims are allowable. However, it seems that such claims will be regarded as process claims, rather than as product claims.[307]

New use of a known product. The leading authority on patentability of use of a known product for a new purpose is the Supreme Court ruling in the *Lanplast* matter,[308] in which the Supreme Court, reiterating the established principle that discoveries are not patentable, held that for a discovery to become a patentable invention it must propose a practical act which would result in a 'new product, new process, new result, or new combination'.[309] To be allowed, a new use must be innovative in comparison to the known use of such product or process and not merely analogous to it.[310] The innovation may lie either in the idea itself of such new use or in the method of implementing such new use or both.[311] Note, however, that the

303. Amendment 2 to the Patents Law, 1995.

304. Government bill 2215, Patents Law (Amendment No. 2), 1993.

305. Cf. 35 U.S.C. § 112(6).

306. *Hughes* at 80.

307. Misc. A (TA Distr.) 1016/06 *Merck & Co., Inc. v. Unipharm Ltd.* The district court held on appeal that the Registrar properly held that where the active ingredients, their reaction and therapeutic action were known, the applicant's contribution was formulating the preparation and its 'product-by-process' claim consisted of the process of manufacturing the preparation.

308. *Lanplast* at 309 et seq. (in an action for the infringement of a patent for a method of producing a multipurpose screen board suitable for screening images and for writing and for such screen board). On the facts of the case, the new use was held to be patentable as it was not claimed by itself but as a process, was not analogous to the prior use and was not obvious (313).

309. *Lanplast* at 310.

310. *Lanplast* at 310 and 313.

311. *Lanplast* at 311 and 313.

Court in *Lanplast* held that, to be patentable, a new use must be claimed as a process or a product.[312] It may further be noted that the mere discovery of a novel advantage of a known product would not by itself be considered a novel invention.

In the *Sanofi* matter,[313] the Supreme Court allowed, without discussion, a purpose-bound claim for a new use of a known pharmaceutical composition (a new property of a known composition which permitted its use for a different indication).[314]

In practice, product-for-purpose type claims as well as Swiss-type claims are allowed.

As a matter of practice, a patent for use of a known pharmaceutical material for a new purpose may be obtained.

The Circular Letter MN 30 clarifies that Swiss-type claims, such as 'use of X in the manufacture/preparation of Y',[315] are allowable as falling within the scope of a patentable invention under section 3, provided that other requirements of patentability – including specifically the requirement of allowed subject matter – are met.[316]

The Circular Letter MN 30 further clarifies that such claims as 'Product X for use in Y' and 'Compound X for use as a medicament' are allowable as long as other criteria of patentability are met.[317] The Practice Guidelines clarify that 'use claims' *per se*, as claims that ascribe a certain use to a substance or compound, do not define a product or process and are therefore not allowable; claims worded in accordance with the provisions of Circular Letter MN 30 are allowable.[318]

Omnibus claims. Under the Circular Letter 008/2011 of December 2011, omnibus claims (which do not expressly specify the technical features claimed) will not be allowed (either as dependent or independent claims) due to the vagueness of the claimed protection. This notice completes the pendulum cycle that started with omnibus claims being widely used, continued with a previous policy enunciation by the IPTO that prohibited independent omnibus claims (but allowed dependent ones) and now prohibits such claims altogether.

Selection patents. In its ruling in the 2011 *SmithKline Beecham* matter,[319] the Supreme Court expressed doubt that the concept of a selection patent, adopted from English law as court-made law before the Patents Law was enacted, continues to apply following the enactment of the Law, as the Law sets forth patentability criteria without providing for selection patents. The Court did not resolve the question because the concept of a selection patent was held to be by definition inapplicable to the patent at hand.

312. *Lanplast* at 311 and 313.
313. The *Sanofi* matter (appeal from refusal in opposition proceedings of a patent application claiming a known chemical compound for treatment of neuro-psychic disturbances, on the basis of inutility and insufficiency of description).
314. In *Sanofi*, which focused on utility and sufficiency of description, the issue of patentability of a new purpose of a known compound was not contested.
315. Circular Letter MN 30, s. 3.
316. Circular Latter MN 30, s. 4.
317. Circular Letter MN 30, s. 5.
318. The Guidelines, Appendix A, s. 4.
319. The *SmithKline Beecham* matter of 2011.

§4. FORMALITIES (PROCEDURE FOR GRANT AND OBTAINING PROTECTION)

I. Patent Application: Filing Requirements

A. The Application

141. First-to-File. Israel is a first-to-file jurisdiction in that whoever first validly files a patent application has a superior right.[320]

142. Electronic Submission. As of 2015, any body corporate (except security entities) and professional representing any person or body corporate (except security entities) must submit new patent applications, and all notifications and documents only electronically, through a designated submission site.[321] Exempted unrepresented individuals and security entities may make submissions on paper.

143. International Applications: National phase application must be submitted within thirty months of their application date.[322] In addition, in the *Mindcake* case,[323] it was held that in Israel, the test regarding the examination of the application to extend the date of entry into the national phase is the 'due care' test, and not the 'unintentional circumstances' test.

144. Other provisions. A patent application must be filed by the owner of the invention.[324] Where the applicant is not the inventor, the manner of acquiring ownership in the invention should be indicated.[325]

The application is filed with the Patent Office and must consist of an application form, which among other details includes the name of the applicant and address for service in Israel, and a specification of the invention.[326]

A specification must include the title of the invention in English and Hebrew, a description of the invention, accompanied with drawings as necessary, and a description of the manner of carrying out the invention which permits that it be carried out by a person of the art (the enablement requirement is discussed in section §3 'Conditions of Patentability' above).[327] The specification must conclude with a claim or claims reasonably arising from the description[328] (the fair basis requirement is discussed in section §3 above).

Where an invention involves biological material deposited with a recognized international depositary institution, as discussed above, the specification of the invention or its mode of performance may make reference to such deposit.[329]

320. The Law, s. 9.
321. The Patents Regulations, regulation 10A.
322. The Law, s. 48D.
323. ALA 2341/13 *Mindcake LLc v. The Register of Patents* [2013].
324. Ownership of the invention is discussed in s. §5 'Ownership'.
325. The Law, s. 11(b).
326. The Law, s. 11(a).
327. The Law, s. 12(a).
328. The Law, s. 13(a).
329. The Law, s. 13(b).

A patent is to be granted for a single invention.[330] An application that claims more than one invention will be divided.[331]

B. Claiming Priority

145. Priority may be claimed from a prior application in a WTO or Paris Convention member country, which was filed within twelve months prior to the application in Israel.[332] Priority must be claimed within two months of the filing in Israel.[333] Priority may also be claimed from multiple prior applications,[334] from a part of a prior application[335] or in respect of a part of the Israeli application.[336]

For the applicant to claim priority, the Registrar must *prima facie* conclude that the invention subject of the Israeli application is identical in substance to the invention described in the prior application.[337]

Under section 164 of the Law, the Registrar may extend the time for filing an application in Israel beyond the twelve-month period from the prior application, only if satisfied that the failure to file resulted from circumstances beyond the control of the applicant and his representative.[338] The Registrar may extend the two-month period for claiming priority only if the application has not yet been accepted and if he is satisfied that the failure to claim resulted from an innocent mistake.[339]

C. Filing Date and Publication of the Fact of Filing

146. An application, even defective as to form, is considered filed, and the date of filing is considered the application date, unless the application fails on the face of it to disclose an invention or fails to list the applicant or if the prescribed fee has not been paid in full, in which case it is considered filed only after such defects are remedied.[340]

The filing date is critical both as regards examining prior art for patentability purposes and as regards the first-to-file principle.

Where the patent application undergoes amendment, it may be antedated.[341]

The name of the invention, the name of the applicant and the application date, including details of the priority if claimed, are published online as soon as possible

330. The Law, s. 8.
331. Division of applications is discussed below at greater length at s. II.F.
332. The Law, s. 10(a)(1).
333. The Law, s. 10(a)(2).
334. The Law, s. 10(b).
335. The Law, s. 10(c).
336. The Law, s. 10(d).
337. The Law, s. 10(a)(4).
338. The Law, s. 164(1).
339. The Law, s. 164(2).
340. The Law, s. 15.
341. Amendments are discussed at greater length at s. II.G *infra*.

after the application was submitted to the Patent Office.[342] If priority is claimed after the fact of filing the application has been published, the fact of filing the application is published again with the priority details.[343] The file of the application maintained by the IPTO remains confidential and sealed, until early publication after eighteen months (see immediately below).

D. *Early Publication*

147. Since 2012, the Registrar publishes online, upon eighteen months of the earlier of the filing date or the priority date if claimed, the patent application and all documents pertaining to it (its file wrapper). A PCT application shall be so published within forty-five days of the filing of the national phase application in Israel.[344]

The applicant will be given notice prior to publication, so as to permit him to withdraw his application before it is laid open to public inspection.[345]

If the patent is subsequently granted, the proprietor will be entitled to damages (equal to reasonable royalties) for infringements that occurred after early publication and before the publication of acceptance of the application.[346] This basis for damages may be narrower than the basis for calculating damages for infringement that occurred after the publication of acceptance of the application.[347]

II. Examination, Pre-grant Oppositions and Grant

A. *Examination*

1. Regular Examination and Acceptance

148. The Patent Office examines the application for the patentability of the invention (discussed in section §2 'Patentable Subject Matter' and section §3 'Conditions of Patentability' above) and its compliance with the formal requirements;[348] the examination need not, however, include an examination of whether novelty was destroyed through display or use of the invention.[349] If satisfied upon examination that the requirements of the patentability of the invention and the form of the application are met, the examiner will accept the application.[350]

---

342. The Law, s. 16(a).
343. The Law, s. 16(b).
344. The Law, s. 16A.
345. See the Registrar's Notice of 25 Jul. 2012.
346. See s. §9 'Infringement and Remedies', at Part VI.B.
347. *Ibid.*
348. The Law, s. 17(a)(1) and (2).
349. The Law, s. 17(b).
350. The Law, s. 17(a1).

2. Modified Examination

149. The applicant may request modified examination under section 17(c) of the Law so that a patent will be granted not on the basis of full substantive examination in Israel but rather based on a corresponding foreign patent granted in certain jurisdictions[351] or favourable examination of an accepted corresponding application in such jurisdictions. Under the modified examination route, the Israeli application is deemed on the basis of such correspondence to conform to the requirements of patentability (novelty, inventive step, unity of invention, enablement and fair basis). The conditions for modified examination under section 17(c) are that the Israeli application and the corresponding application are for the same invention and the Israeli application's claims are identical to (but may be fewer than) those of the corresponding patent, and they share a common priority (i.e., the Israeli application claimed priority from the corresponding application or *vice versa*, or both claimed priority from another application). The applicant must submit a copy of the translated claims of the corresponding patent and description and drawing identical to those of the corresponding patent or meeting the Israeli sufficiency requirements of section 12 of the Law.

Such application may nevertheless be refused acceptance under the modified route and examined substantively if the Registrar or the supervisor of examiners concludes in the course of examination that the requirements of eligibility for modified examination are not met or that another special reason exists for refusing acceptance.[352] In addition, the question of whether an invention embodies patentable subject matter is examined substantively even under the modified examination route, in particular concerning software and 'method of doing business' patents.

Under section 17(e) of the Law, the applicant must notify the Registrar of opposition proceedings in respect of the corresponding application and of revocation proceedings in respect of the corresponding patent. Breach of the duty to make disclosure under this section may constitute a ground for revoking the patent.

3. Accelerated Examination

150. As of January 2013, a significant reform of the Patents Law provisions concerning acceleration of examination took place (until then this issue was provided for in the Patents Regulations[353]).

Acceleration at the request of applicant. According to section 19A of the Law, an applicant may request accelerated examination on 'any reasonable grounds', including in particular the applicant's advanced age or medical condition, examination results in other countries on conditions prescribed by the Registrar (e.g., under the Patent Prosecution Highway), unauthorized third-party exploitation of the invention or reasonable apprehension thereof, unreasonable delay in commencement of

351. The Law, s. 17(c)(1), Circular Letters MN 65 and 75 (Australia, Austria, US, Germany, Denmark, UK, Russian Federation, Japan, EPO, Norway, Canada, Sweden).
352. The Law, s. 17(d).
353. The Patents Regulations, s. 35.

examination, public good, or special circumstances that would justify acceleration. Extensions at the applicant's request will terminate the accelerated status unless circumstances beyond his and his representative's control are shown.

Acceleration at the request of a third party. Accelerated examination may also be requested by a third party, a possibility that was not available before. The grounds for such request include postponement of a development programme of such third party due to prolonged examination of the application, unreasonable delay in commencement of examination, public good or special circumstances that would justify acceleration. In an accelerated examination under such third-party request, the applicant will not be granted extensions unless circumstances beyond his and his representative's control are shown.

B. *Office Actions Regarding Defects*

151. If the Registrar or an examiner finds that an invention is not patentable or that the application does not comply with the requirements therefor, he shall inform the applicant of the grounds of non-patentability or the defects of the application.[354] The applicant may then within the four months' timeframe prescribed by Regulations[355] remove or correct the objection grounds or defects; otherwise, the Registrar shall refuse to accept the application.[356] According to the IPTO policy, an applicant is entitled to extensions that do not exceed fifteen months cumulatively.[357]

C. *Postponement of Examination Due to Unpublished Third-Party Application*

152. If an invention is found not to be patentable (wholly or partially) due to the existence of an earlier third-party application which has not yet been published, the Registrar or an examiner may direct that the examination of the later application be postponed until after the publication of the earlier application, and must do so at the request of the later applicant.[358]

D. *Duty of Disclosure During Examination*

153. According to section 18 of the Law, and as a manner of assistance in the examination process, the examiner is required, and as done in practice, to order the applicant to provide a list of documents relied upon by patent authorities abroad in the examination of a patent application on the same invention as well as publications made before the application date known to the applicant and directly relating

354. The Law, s. 20.
355. The Patents Regulations, s. 42.
356. The Law, s. 21.
357. Circular Letter 005/2011 'Policy of granting extensions in a patent application' as updated, of 28 Aug. 2012.
358. The Law, s. 19.

to the invention.[359] The examiner may also require copies of said documents and publications referred to by said documents.[360]

Accordingly, under section 36 of the Patents Regulations, the examiner will require the applicant, within four months before the commencement of the substantive examination, to submit, within four months of the request, such documents and publications, as well as a list of countries in which the patent application for the same invention was filed.[361]

Furthermore, an external search may be commissioned,[362] although in practice such searches are conducted by the examiner.

The applicant is under further duty to keep the Patent Office informed of any change that comes to his knowledge, or to the knowledge of his representative, in the list of any documents or publications he has been required to submit, until the acceptance of the application.[363]

Non-compliance with such duty of disclosure, that is, delivery of a misleading particular in response to a documentary request or knowingly failing to inform the Patent Office of a significant change in the list of publications and documents, exposes the applicant, and subsequently the patent owner, to sanctions of revocation of a patent, refusal of the patent application, grant of a license to a third party or abridgement of the patent term, as well as a fine.[364]

E. Third-Party Observations

154. Section 18(b)(3) of the Law, introduced in 2012, allows third parties to submit to the IPTO, within a prescribed time period, lists and copies of prior art publications that were relied upon by patent authorities abroad in the examination of a patent application on the same invention, publications made before the application date (even if unknown to the applicant) and directly relating to the invention and documents referred to by said documents. This right may be exercised by third parties within two months of the applicant's response to the examiner's documentary request under section 18 and the examiner may consider such materials provided by third parties. This period is non-extendible.[365]

F. Division of Applications

155. Voluntary division. In accordance with section 24(a) of the Law, at any time before acceptance, the applicant may request division of his application into several applications.

359. The Law, s. 18(a)(1)-(2) and s. 18(b)(1).
360. s. 18(a)(3)-(4) of the Law.
361. See also Circular Letter 11/2012 of January 2014.
362. The Law, s. 18(a)(5).
363. The Law, s. 18A.
364. The Law, s. 18C.
365. The Law, s. 164(a).

Non-voluntary division. In accordance with section 24(b) of the Law, where the application includes more than one invention, the Registrar may, as long as he has not accepted the application, direct the applicant to divide his application.

As a result of a policy change of the IPTO in 2016,[366] made pursuant to a decision in the matter of *Genentech*'s application,[367] the filing of a division of a divisional application is allowed.

As noted, it is not possible to file a divisional application after the publication of acceptance of its parent application.

A divisional application receives the same date as the application from which it was divided.[368]

Where the applicant has an earlier application pending, the Registrar may direct that the applicant's application, the applicant's earlier application (as long as its acceptance was not yet published) or both, be divided, or that some of the claims in each application be struck, at the applicant's choice, if the two applications prejudiced each other's patentability.[369]

Where an opposition has been filed against a parent application when one or more divisional applications thereof are still pending, the opponent is entitled to request a stay of proceedings of the opposition until publication of acceptance of the last remaining divisional application.[370]In practice, the IPTO tends to favour a stay, a policy which is not without difficulty.

G. *Amendment of Patent Application*

156. Amendment before acceptance. The applicant may, at any time before the application is accepted, amend the specification either in consequence of an office action advising of defects or at his own initiative.[371] If substantive amendments were made in the specification, then the Registrar may prescribe, for the purpose of examining novelty, inventive step and first-to-file rights, that, where such amendments may be distinguished from the existing specification, the date of the amendments shall be the date on which they were submitted, and where they cannot be so distinguished, that the date of the entire application shall be the date on which the amendments were submitted.[372]

Amendment after acceptance. Following the acceptance of the application, the applicant may amend the specification in the same manner as if he were a patent owner (see paragraph 163 below).[373]

366. The Registrar's Notice regarding cancellation of Circular Letter M.N. 81, dated January 25, 2016.
367. Application for patent No. 234696 in the name of *Genentech Inc.* [2016]
368. The Law, s. 24(c).
369. The Law, s. 24(b1)(2).
370. Until 2012, such stay was the rule of default and the patent applicant was entitled to request lifting the automatic stay. This practice was changed in 2012, but oppositions stayed before 2012 remain stayed, unless a lift of the stay is requested (see Circular Letter MN 23).
371. The Law, s. 22.
372. The Law, s. 23.
373. The Law, s. 29.

H. *Registrar's Review of Examiners' Decisions*

157. A decision or act of an examiner may be brought for a hearing before the Registrar.[374]

I. *Refusal of Acceptance: Reconsideration and Appeal*

158. Upon refusal, the Registrar may at the applicant's request reconsider the refusal in an *ex parte* proceeding before the Registrar in the presence of the examiner, which should be brought within twelve months from the refusal of acceptance.[375] This twelve-month period may be extended.[376]

The Registrar's final decision to refuse is subject to appeal by right within two months of the decision.[377]

Case law has also recognized the Registrar's administrative authority to cancel acceptance where acceptance was improper,[378] e.g., in cases of error, bad faith, failure to disclose information, and so forth.

J. *Publication of Acceptance: Pre-grant Opposition*

1. Publication of Acceptance

159. The decision to accept the application is published for oppositions, by way of a notice of acceptance in the online publication of the *Patents Journal*.[379] The publication of acceptance includes the name of the invention and its category, the applicant's name and address for service in Israel, the application date, priority details if a priority right was claimed, and any other relevant particulars that the Registrar deems necessary to include in the publication.[380] Acceptance of the application shall be conclusive evidence that it contains only one invention and that it complied with the requirements in respect of the form of the application, the specification and the drawings.[381]

Pursuant to the acceptance of the patent application, the application may no longer be divided into several [divisional] applications (see paragraph 155 above). The applicant may request to amend the specification solely for purposes of clarification, elimination of a mistake or in order to limit the claims (see paragraph 163

374. The Law, s. 161.
375. The Law, s. 21A.
376. Circular letter 26/2014 of May 2014 stipulates that a request to reconsider the refusal may be filed after twelve months with an official fee for the *ex post* extension and with an affidavit detailing the reasons why the request was not filed within twelve months.
377. The Law, s. 174(a); the Regulations, s. 191.
378. *Omrix Biopharmaceuticals Ltd v. CSL Behring Gmbh*, Opposition to registration of patent 157360 (cancellation of acceptance) [2012].
379. The Law, s. 26(a).
380. The Law, s. 26(b).
381. The Law, s. 28.

below); and the remedies, to which the applicant may be entitled for the period after the publication of the acceptance and before the grant, are identical to those awarded post-grant (see paragraph 234 below).

2. Opposition Procedure

160. In Israel, oppositions are pre-grant, and any person may oppose the grant of a patent within three months following the publication of the application, by way of a notice of opposition.[382] The three-month period for lodging an opposition is non-extendible.[383] The opposition proceeding is conducted in a manner similar to a litigation proceeding, consisting of the phases of pleadings, exchange of evidence and oral arguments.

Grounds of opposition. The Patents Law provides for the following grounds for opposition:

(1) there exists a reason for which the Registrar was entitled to refuse acceptance of the patent application;[384]
(2) the invention is not patentable in light of novelty-destroying prior use or display (these are not necessarily part of the examination by the Patent Office);[385]
(3) the opponent, and not the applicant, is the owner of the invention.[386]

With regard to the opposition grounds, it may be inferred from case law dealing with revocation of patents and invalidity defences in infringement cases,[387] which held that the opposition grounds may be relied upon for attacking the patent by any person due to the public interest in preventing registration of ineligible patents, that in light of such public interest the list of opposition grounds set forth in the statute should be considered non-exhaustive.

Burden of proof in opposition proceedings. The burden of proof in opposition proceedings rests on the applicant.[388] However, a possible change in the law may be inferred from the 2011 *Merck v. Teva* ruling of the Supreme Court,[389] which suggested that in the opposition proceedings the burden is on the opponent to show that the invention is not eligible for patent protection.

382. The Law, s. 30.
383. The Law, s. 164(a).
384. The Law, s. 31(1).
385. The Law, s. 31(2). This is addressed as a separate ground due to the absence of the examiner's duty to examine non-eligibility as a result of public display or exploitation.
386. The Law, s. 31(3).
387. CA 217/86 *Schechter v. Abmatz Ltd*, 44 (2) P.D. 847 [1990]; CA (TA Distr.) 3032/06 *Kamil v. Bezeq International Ltd* [2007].
388. *Sanofi* at 737 (regarding usefulness); *Bayer* at para. 17 (regarding other eligibility criteria); *Abbott Laboratories v. Teva Pharmaceutical Industries*, Opposition to patent application 127833 [2007] at para. 25.
389. ALA 6025/05 *Merck & Co. Inc. v. Teva Pharmaceutical Industries Ltd* [2011], at 22.

Outcome of opposition. The Registrar may allow or dismiss the opposition, in whole or in part, or divide the application.[390] Upon dismissal of an opposition the Registrar may maintain the opposed application as filed or in an amended form, as requested by the applicant. The Registrar may also decide *sua sponte* that a patent may be granted in an amended form.[391]

If the opposition relied on the grounds of ownership, then the opponent may request that the patent be granted to him, and the Registrar may – in addition to any other relief – grant the patent to the person who proved that he is the owner of the invention. In proceedings under this section, the Registrar may join any person whom the Registrar believes to have an interest in the matter.[392]

Supplementary Examination. Where an opposition was withdrawn, the Registrar may refuse to grant the patent if, in the course of the opposition, he discovered material according to which the application should not have been accepted.[393]

Appeal. The Registrar's final decision in opposition proceedings is subject to appeal by right within two months of the decision.[394]

Further Evidence in Appeal Proceedings. As held by the Supreme Court in the *Gabai* (2014)[395] case, the criteria for allowing further evidence to be adduced in an appeal of a decision of the Registrar of Patents are more flexible than the rigid criteria generally applicable in civil appeals.

Deference. Courts tend to refrain from interfering with the decisions of the Registrar of Patents, as the latter is deemed a highly professional and expert tribunal.[396]

K. Pre-grant Cancellation of Application by Applicant

161. The applicant may cancel his patent application up to the grant of the patent; however, the Registrar may in certain circumstances disallow such cancellation if satisfied that the application was cancelled improperly, e.g., where the application was made on behalf of co-owners of an invention and the applicant sought to cancel the application without knowledge of the other owners, the Registrar may disallow cancellation and leave the application pending.[397]

L. Grant

162. If no opposition is filed, or if an opposition is finally dismissed without an appeal being duly notified to the Registrar, the patent shall be granted to the owner

390. The Law, s. 32. During the course of the opposition, the Registrar may also exercise the power to demand additional disclosure of information pursuant to s. 18 of the Law (see para. 153 above).
391. ALA 11194/04 *Polivid Partnership v. Givati* [2005].
392. The Law, s. 33.
393. The Law, s. 34.
394. The Law, s. 174(a); the Regulations, s. 191.
395. ALA 5041/13 *Gabai et al v. Aminach Furniture and Matrices Industry Ltd.* [2014].
396. The *Gabai* [2014] case, *supra*.
397. The Law, s. 21B.

of the invention at that time, unless the Registrar exercises its power to conduct supplementary examination (see paragraph 160 above) and renders a decision to refuse a patent *sua sponte* based on materials that came to his knowledge in the course of opposition.[398] If an appeal is filed from the Registrar's decision to deny the opposition, and an appropriate notice in this regard was timely filed with the Patent Office, the grant will be stayed pending the appeal .[399]

III. Amendment of Patents

A. *Permitted Purposes and Scope of Amendment*

163. Permitted purposes. In accordance with section 65 of the Law, a patent owner may request the amendment of the specification for a limited number of purposes: for the purpose of clarification, for the purpose of elimination of mistake or for the purpose of limiting the claims.[400] The list of permitted purposes of an amendment set forth in section 65 is exhaustive.

Under section 66, which sets forth cumulative conditions for an allowable amendment,[401] the Registrar shall permit an amendment if it is satisfied that it will not broaden the scope of claims in the specification nor add anything to the specification not initially included in it, in substance.[402] An amendment expanding the scope of claims or extending the specification to include matters not originally included will not be allowed.

Permitted scope. The Patents Regulations require that an application for permission to amend a patent specification must specify the requested amendment and the purpose of such amendment[403] and must clearly indicate the requested amendment, as distinct from the earlier version.[404]

According to case law, an application to amend should expressly, accurately and clearly state, in respect of each claim, how the requested amendment meets any one (or more) of the three purposes set forth in section 65; the applicant should also specify why the requested amendment does not broaden the scope of the claims and does not add elements not originally mentioned (in substance) in the specification, and should supply specific references to the original specification or claims on which the requested amendment relies.[405]

The patent specification may be amended by adding an element to the claims (an independent claim), where such element had been mentioned, in substance, in the

398. The Law, s. 34.
399. The Law, s. 35.
400. The Law, ss 65 et seq.
401. Opposition to amendment of specification in patent 149567, *Schwartz Pharma AG v. Teva Pharmaceutical Industries Ltd* [2010] (*Schwarz*).
402. The Law, s. 66.
403. The Patents Regulations, regulation 95(a).
404. The Patents Regulations, regulation 95(b).
405. *Schwartz.*

specification (i.e., in the description part of the specification or in the drawings) even if not mentioned in the original claims.[406]

An element mentioned in the specification cannot be added to the claims if such amendment would result in a broadened scope of the claims (for example, a narrower claim of 'anaphylactic-like reactions' was not allowed to be amended to 'hypersensitivity reactions' despite the presence of the term in the description).[407]

It has been held that claims cannot be amended to include new independent claims, as such amendment does not conform to the purposes set forth in section 65 of the Law.[408] This holding has not yet been reviewed by the courts.

The elements in the amendment must have been disclosed in substance in the original specification; such elements need not be the essence of the invention.[409]

In addition to amendments according to section 65 and 66 of the Law, it is possible to correct clerical errors (Section 69).

B. Procedure

164. Opposition to amendment. Notice that an amendment was allowed is published online.[410] In accordance with section 67 of the Law, the decision to allow amendment is subject to opposition by any person within three months. The grounds for opposing an amendment are that there exists a reason for which the Registrar was not authorized to allow the amendment, or that the amendment does not achieve the purpose for which it was requested.[411]

Registration of amendment. If no opposition to the amendment is submitted, or if the opposition is rejected by the Registrar or by final judgment, or if permission to amend the specification was given by the court in court proceedings under paragraph 195 (discussed below), the Registrar shall enter the amendment in the Register, and from the date of the entry the amended specification shall be treated as if it had been accepted in that form from the outset.[412] Registration of the amendment serves as conclusive evidence that the amendment is permissible in that it does not broaden the scope of the claims nor add anything not originally included in the specification, as required under section 66, unless the registration was obtained fraudulently.[413]

---

406. *Unipharm Ltd v. Merck& Co., Inc.*, Opposition to application to register patent 101537[2003] (*Merck 2003*); *Unipharm Ltd v. Bristol-Myers Squibb Company*, Opposition to application to register patent 105879[2003] (*Bristol-Myers 2003*).
407. *Bristol-Myers 2003.*
408. *Schwartz.*
409. *Merck 2003.*
410. The Law, s. 66.
411. The Law, s. 68.
412. The Law, s. 71. See, however, s. 185 of the Law, discussed in para. 234 below.
413. The Law, s. 72.

C. Amendment during Contentious Proceedings

1. Amendment during Contentious Proceedings before the Registrar

165. If the amendment is requested while the patent application is subject to oppositions, or during a pending opposition proceeding, Regulation 102 of the Patents Regulations, which is *lex specialis* to section 67 of the Law, provides that the opponent may oppose the application to amend within two months.[414] Similarly, during a pending revocation proceeding, the applicant for revocation may oppose the proprietor's application to amend within two months.[415]

If the opponent (or revocation applicant) agrees to the requested amendment, the Registrar suspends the opposition (or revocation) proceedings until the amendment is effectuated.[416] If the opponent opposes the requested amendment, the Registrar hears the opposition to the amendment in the presence of the parties to the opposition proceedings.[417] If the Registrar grants the application for the amendment, it suspends the opposition (or revocation) proceedings until completion of the amendment proceedings, and the opposition (or revocation application) is deemed to have been filed in respect of the specification as amended.[418]

Where opposition to the grant of permission to amend is filed while opposition proceedings against the grant of the patent are pending, the Registrar shall deal with the oppositions simultaneously unless the parties have requested that it proceed otherwise and the Registrar is satisfied that it is reasonable to do so.[419] The procedure under Regulation 102 may be opted out of if the parties have agreed that the amendment application shall be heard after the decision on the opposition and it appears to the Registrar that the amendment should *prima facie* be permitted; if it has been so agreed: (1) the Registrar shall deal with the opposition as if the amendment had been accepted; (2) the Registrar shall publish the fact of the amendment application after the decision on the opposition.[420]

The Registrar has power to maintain an opposed patent application, in an amended form, without resorting to the amendment proceedings described above. Thus, in the *Givati* matter,[421] the Supreme Court recognized the Registrar's power and discretion to amend a patent *sua sponte* in revocation proceedings where it is fair to do so, interpreting the Registrar's power to revoke a patent under section 73B as including the power to revoke partially.

414. The Patents Regulations, regulations 102(c) and 108; *Sano Bruno's Enterprises Ltd v. Colgate Palmolive Company*, Opposition to Amendment of Accepted Application 102433, [2006] (*Colgate*).
415. *Colgate*.
416. The Patents Regulations, regulations 102(b) and 108.
417. The Patents Regulations, regulation 102(c).
418. The Patents Regulations, regulation 102(d) and 108.
419. The Patents Regulations, regulation 102(e).
420. The Patents Regulations, regulation 102(f).
421. ALA /11194/04 *Polivid Partnership v. Givati* [2005].

2. Amendment during Court Proceedings

166. By the Registrar. An application to amend, which is filed during the pendency of court proceedings for the infringement or for the revocation of the patent, requires court permission for the Registrar to entertain it.[422] If, however, court proceedings for infringement of a patent are instituted after an application to amend was filed, the Registrar shall continue to hear the application unless the court otherwise orders.[423]

If the court permits the Registrar to hear an application for amendment of a patent which is the subject of a court action, it may stay the court proceedings pending before it in respect of such patent, for such period and on such conditions as it shall prescribe; each party may apply to the court to alter or cancel the stay order.[424]

By the court. Under section 190, in any proceedings under the Patents Law, the court may, on the application by the patent holder, order the specification to be amended for the purposes stated in section 65 (for the purpose of clarification, for the purpose of elimination of error or for the purpose of limiting the claims) or to correct a clerical error, under section 69.

IV. Restrictions on the Registrar's Acts in Respect of Certain Inventions and on the Right to File Abroad

167. Restrictive orders in respect of Israeli applications. Special restrictions may apply to applications for inventions bearing on national security or nuclear energy. Under section 94 of the Law, where the Minister of Defence deems it necessary for national security, he has the power, after consultation with the Minister of Justice, to order the Registrar to refrain from, or postpone, performing any act under the Patents Law in respect of a particular application, and the power to prohibit or restrict the publication or release of information concerning a particular application. Under section 99 of the Law, where the designated government minister finds that an invention subject of a patent application is important for developing the use of nuclear energy in Israel, or that the publication of an invention is liable to damage nuclear research in Israel, he has the power, after consultation with the Minister of Justice, to order the Registrar to refrain from, or postpone, performing any act under the Patents Law in respect of a particular application, and the power to prohibit or restrict the publication or release of information concerning a particular application.

Restriction on filing abroad. Under section 98 of the Law, an Israeli national or resident and any other person owing a duty of loyalty to the State is restricted from filing abroad an application for an invention of military value or related to national security, unless he receives permission from the Minister of Defence or unless he first filed in Israel and the Minister of Defence did not issue a restrictive order in

422. The Law, s. 70(a).
423. The Law, s. 70(c).
424. The Law, s. 191.

respect of the Israeli application within six months of the date of the patent application, or if such order lapsed. Under section 103 of the Law, an Israeli national or resident and any other person owing a duty of loyalty to the State is restricted from filing abroad an application relating to nuclear energy, unless he receives permission from the designated government minister or unless he first filed in Israel and no restrictive order in respect of the Israeli application was issued within six months of the date of the patent application, or of such order lapsed.

Compensation for restriction of activities. If a restrictive order in respect of inventions pertaining to national security or nuclear energy was made under section 94 or 99 of the Law or if a permit to file abroad in respect of such inventions was not granted under section 98 or 103 of the Law, the owner of the invention is entitled to compensation from the State in the amount agreed by the parties or, absent an agreement, as determined by the Compensation and Royalties Committee[425] established under the Patents Law.[426]

Restrictions of State Employees: State employees, soldiers and other persons owing an enhanced duty of notification to the State under section 137 of the Law[427] are restricted from filing applications for patent or other protection abroad without prior permission from the State or unless there was no determination within six months of the notification that the invention belongs to the State.

§5. Ownership and Transfer

I. Ownership of the Invention and of the Patent

A. *Right to Patent Belongs to the Owner of the Invention*

168. Under Israeli law, only the owner of a patentable invention may apply for a patent.[428] In the event that the applicant is not the inventor, he is required to disclose how he acquired title.[429] An applicant is presumed to be the owner of the invention as long as the contrary has not been proved.[430]

B. *Owner of the Invention*

169. Such owner need not be the inventor; the 'owner of an invention' as defined in section 1 of the Patents Law is the inventor or whoever is entitled to the invention by virtue of operation of law or by assignment or by agreement.

Rights in an invention (and subsequently in a patent) may be assigned, as discussed below, and may devolve by operation of law – for example, through

425. The Law, s. 107.
426. The Law, s. 109. The Committee comprises a Supreme Court judge, the Registrar of Patents and a university professor.
427. Discussed in s. §5 'Ownership', Part E 'Service Inventions'.
428. The Law, s. 2.
429. The Law, s. 11(b).
430. The Law, s. 76.

succession or as service inventions.[431] It is not settled whether a person's declaration that he transfers to another the ownership of future inventions constitutes a contractual undertaking to transfer in the future or an actual assignment of property rights that becomes effective upon creation of the invention.

C. Owner of the Patent

170. Owner of the patent is defined in section 1 of the Law as the person registered in the Register as the person to whom a patent was granted or to whom ownership of a patent has passed. Therefore, where a patent infringement suit is contemplated, the plaintiff must first of all record his ownership.[432]

D. A Non-owner Inventor's Right to Have His Name Indicated

171. It is not a requirement that the patent application identify the name of the inventor. However, an inventor (or his successors) may request in the prescribed manner that his name be indicated in the specification, the Register and the patent certificate.[433] Where the inventor is not the owner of the invention, notice of the request is given to the applicant or patent owner, and if opposition proceedings are pending, to any other parties of the opposition proceedings. The Registrar decides the request after hearing the parties.[434] Indication of the inventor's name as such does not by itself confer rights in the invention.[435] A waiver of the right to be named as an inventor is unenforceable.[436]

The law does not provide a definition for the term 'inventor' and as a result, the term was developed through case law. The questions involved in determining inventorship seldom came before the courts and was never addressed by the Supreme Court. In 2011, the Tel Aviv District Court[437] referred to precedents used in US courts and in the UK House of Lords,[438] and held that a person who was engaged in developing a novel device but did not contribute to the mental process of conceiving the invention (as distinguished from its reduction to practice) would not be deemed an inventor for the purposes of the Patents Law.

431. The Law, s. 82.
432. See CA 520/80, 635/80 *Rosenberg et al. v. Rubinstein et al.*, 38 (1) P.D. 85 [1984] at 105.
433. The Law, s. 39.
434. The Law, ss 40–41.
435. The Law, s. 43.
436. The Law, s. 42.
437. RA (TA) 49328-10-10 *SHL Telemedicine International Ltd v. Oren* [2011].
438. *Inter alia, Murdock Webbing Company, Inc. v. Dalloz safety, Inc.*, 213 F.Supp. 2d 95, 95 (2002); *Edison v. Foote*, 1871 C.D. 80; *Burroughts Wellcome Co. v. Barr Laboratories Inc.*, 40 F.3d 1223 (1994); *Oren Tavory v. NTP., Inc.*, 297 Fed. Appx. 976 (2008); *Ethicon v. US Surgical Corporation*, 135 F.3d 1456, 1460 (1998).

II. Joint Ownership

A. *Joint Ownership of an Invention or a Patent*

172. An invention,[439] and subsequently a patent,[440] may be co-owned by joint owners. Co-owners of an invention or a patent are deemed to own it in equal shares unless a written agreement between them or the law provides differently.[441] Even though each of the joint owners owns a share in the patent in its entirety, ownership between the joint owners is in non-specific shares and cannot be divided according to the patent claims (in the same manner as joint ownership under section 27 of the Land Law, 5729-1969, cannot be divided into specific shares).

B. *Co-filing of a Patent Application*

173. Accordingly, an application may be filed by co-applicants.[442] In the event of a dispute between co-applicants that delays the prosecution, the Registrar may act on the initiative of some of the co-applicants but shall not cancel the application unless all of the co-applicants agree.[443]

C. *Exploitation by Joint Owners*

174. Exploitation right. Each of the joint owners of a patent has the right to exploit the patented invention in a reasonable manner unless the joint owners have otherwise agreed in a written agreement or unless the law provides otherwise.[444] In the event that exploitation by any of the joint owners as permitted by the Patents Law prevents such exploitation by another joint owner, the non-exploiting joint owners may, at their option, demand of the exploiting owner a royalty or profit sharing.[445] However, a co-owner cannot grant a license for the exploitation of a jointly owned patent unless there is consent of all the joint owners, or unless such license has been approved by a court order under section 81 of the Law.[446]

Judicial intervention in exploitation by joint owners. Under section 81 of the Law, upon application of one or more of the joint owners of a patent, the court may order the other joint owners to do certain acts for the exploitation of the patent or of any right therein or to grant a license thereunder, or may issue orders to them as to any other matter relating to the patent, and the Court may authorize one of the applicants to do the act in place of the respondents. The court will not grant an order contrary to any of the conditions of a written agreement between the joint owners of the patent.

439. The Law, s. 77(a).
440. The Law, s. 77(a).
441. The Law, s. 77(b).
442. See s. 25 of the Law regarding joint filing.
443. The Law, s. 25.
444. The Law, s. 78.
445. The Law, s. 78.
446. The Law, s. 88(a).

D. Assignment of a Joint Owner's Share

175. Each of the joint owners of a patent may transfer ownership of his share without the consent of the other owners, unless the parties agreed otherwise between them and the fact of the agreement was entered in the Register.[447]

E. Purchase of Patented Product from a Joint Owner

176. If a person in good faith acquires from one of the joint owners a product for which there is a jointly owned patent, or a product produced by a process protected by said patent, then he shall be treated like a person who acquired the product from a sole patent holder.[448]

F. A Joint Owner's Right to Sue for Infringement

177. A co-owner of a jointly owned patent may bring an action for infringement by himself, without being required to obtain consent of the other joint owner(s).[449] Co-owners who do not join such action as co-plaintiffs must be joined by the plaintiff as co-defendants but if such joined defendants do not take part in the proceedings, they shall not be liable to pay attorney fees.[450]

III. Transfer of Ownership

178. Rights in an invention or patent may be either transferred in writing or may devolve by operation of law.[451]

A. Assignment

1. Requirements for a Valid Assignment

179. Rights in an invention or in a patent may be assigned in writing.[452] The writing requirement is evidentiary.[453] The assignment shall have effect towards third parties only upon its recordal in the Register in accordance with the Patents Law.[454]

447. The Law, s. 80.
448. The Law, s. 79.
449. The Law, s. 178(b).
450. The Law, s. 178(c).
451. The Law, s. 82.
452. The Law, s. 82.
453. CA 520/80, 635/80 *Rosenberg et al. v. Rubinstein et al.*, 38 (1) P.D. 85 [1984] at 101; affirmed AH 2/84 *Rosenberg et al. v. Rubinstein et al.*, 38(3) P.D. 689 [1984].
454. The Law, s. 83.

The transferee of the rights in an invention subject of a patent application or in a patent may apply for the recordal of the transfer.[455]

The Patents Law does not set a limit for the time to record and assignment nor does it provide that late recordal of an assignment may prevent the collection of damages for the period during which the assignment was not recorded. However, the Patent Office might refuse to record an assignment with retroactive effect to the date of assignment.

2. Assignment by a Joint Owner

180. As noted above, each of the co-owners of a jointly owned patent may transfer his share without need for consent of the co-owners, unless they had previously agreed otherwise and such agreement had been recorded with the Registrar.[456]

B. Operation of Law

181. Ownership of inventions may be transferred by operation of law, including of foreign law, e.g., in the cases of succession or merger of companies. Transfer through operation of law includes succession and service inventions. The law governing service inventions is discussed below at Part E.

C. Licenses

1. The Grant of a License

182. The proprietor, or the owner of the invention for which a patent application was made, may license the invention by way of an exclusive or a non-exclusive license.[457] An exclusive license is a license that confers on the exclusive licensee the exclusive right to prevent exploitation of the invention in Israel as if he were the patent holder, including from the proprietor himself.[458] Accordingly, a license that does not prevent the proprietor from exploiting the invention will not be deemed an exclusive license. A non-exclusive license confers the right to exploit the invention subject of the patent, to the extent and on the conditions prescribed in the license.[459] As will be mentioned below, an exclusive licensee may initiate an infringement action, whereas a non-exclusive licensee may not.

455. The Law, s. 169.
456. The Law, s. 80.
457. The Law, s. 84.
458. The Law, s. 85.
459. The Law, s. 86.

2. Recordal Is a Condition of Validity towards Third Parties

183. A license, whether exclusive or non-exclusive, must be in writing.[460] To be valid against third parties, a license is to be recorded with the Patents Registrar.[461] It was accordingly held by a district court that a patent holder cannot rely on the fact of non-recordal of a license in a suit against a third-party user who received permission from the unrecorded licensee, as an unrecorded license is valid toward parties thereto.[462]

The licensee of the rights in an invention subject of a patent application or in a patent may apply for the recordal.

In the *Albad* matter,[463] the district court, affirmed by the Supreme Court,[464] refused to enjoin, at the request of the patent applicant, a licensee from submitting an opposition to the patent application. Although the court left it open for the Patent Office to decide on the issue of estoppels (and the case was not finally ruled upon as the parties settled), the district court's remarks regarding the applicability of estoppel indicate an unwillingness to estop the licensee from attacking the validity of the patent, in light of the public interest in preventing registration of unmeritorious patents.

3. License to Exploit a Jointly Owned Patent

184. For jointly owned patents, the grant of a license requires the consent of all joint owners, unless such license has been approved by a court order under section 81.[465]

D. Pledge

185. Rights in a patent may be pledged.[466] In order to be effective, a pledge must be registered in the Patents Register within a prescribed timeframe.[467] Where the pledgor is a company, the pledge must also be registered by the Registrar of Companies.[468]

To create a pledge over the rights in an invention or in a patent application, in the absence of a provision in the Patents Law regarding such pledge, such pledge must be registered in the Pledges Register under the Pledge Law, 5727-1967. However, as reflected in the Circular Letter 10/2012 of July 2012 (and the Circular Letter it replaced), the IPTO practice is to allow for registration of pledges over patent applications as well.

460. The Law, s. 84.
461. The Law, s. 87.
462. CC (TA Distr.) 1028/92 Motion 8698/92 *Biogen Inc. v. General Technologies (Israel) Ltd* [1993].
463. OM (TA Distr.) 517/03 MCA 8295/03 *Apfel and Havlin v. Al-bad Mesuot Itzhak Ltd* [2003].
464. LCA 4221/03 *Apfel and Havlin v. Al-bad Mesuot Itzhak Ltd* [2003].
465. The Law, s. 88(a).
466. The Law, s. 89.
467. The Law, s. 90.
468. The Companies Ordinance [New Version], 5743-1983, s. 178(a)(6).

E. Service Invention

1. Service Invention and Its Ownership

a. Statutory Definition and Default Ownership

186. Under the Patent Law, an invention made by an employee as a result of his service and during the period of his service belongs to the employer unless there is a different agreement in this regard. This is a default arrangement which leaves the parties room to agree otherwise (subject of course to limitations that may apply by virtue of the general contract and labour laws). The employer may also waive, within six months, its right to the invention upon receiving notice, which the employee is obligated to give; the employee may also state in such notice that absent a contrary answer from the employer within six months, the invention will be the employee's property.[469] Failure to respond to such an adverse notification will vest ownership of the invention with the employee.

b. Determining Whether an Invention Is a Service Invention

187. The cumulative conditions required by section 132 of the Law for establishing a service invention, were reiterated and interpreted in the *Yissum*[470] decision of the Registrar as follows:

(a) the subject should be an invention (to differentiate, for example, from discovery) but no determination is required as to whether it is eligible for patent protection;
(b) there exists an employer-employee relationship;
(c) the employee must arrive at his invention:
  – in consequence of his service with the employer; and
  – during the service with the employer.
(d) no agreement exists between the employer and the employee to the contrary.

Existence of an invention. Section 132 requires the existence of an 'invention' during the service; a mere idea which has not crystallized and took tangible shape

469. Section 132 of the Law: (a) An invention by an employee, arrived at in consequence of his service and during the period of his service (hereinafter: referred to as 'service invention') shall, in the absence of an agreement to the contrary between him and his employer, become the property of the employer, unless the employer renounces the invention within six months from the day on which notification under s. 131 is delivered to him. (b) If, in his notification under s. 131, the employee stated that – in the absence of a contrary reply from the employer within six months after delivery of the employee's notification – the invention will become the employee's property, and if the employer made no contrary aforesaid reply, then the invention shall not become the employer's property.

470. *Yissum Research and Development Company of the Hebrew University of Jerusalem Ltd v. Dr Benenson et al.*, Application for patent 50065 (ownership dispute) [1979] (*Yissum*) at paras 21–22. The Yissum holding was approved by the IPTO in the *Anonymous* case (infra n. 454), but the issue was left open in the later appeal proceedings.

as an invention would not be deemed a service invention.[471] This means that if conception of the invention occurred before or after the period of service, the fact that certain development efforts occurred during the service may be insufficient to render the invention a service invention. The *Yissum* decision held that section 132 requires the existence of an 'invention' but such invention need not necessarily be *patentable* as a condition for the application of section 132. In view of the vagueness of the term 'invention', such interpretation creates uncertainty regarding the scope of application of section 132 of the Law and blurs the line between the Patents Law and the trade secrets legislation.

Employment relationship. It must be established that the inventor was an employee of the employer, namely that an employer-employee relationship existed. However, for the purpose of service inventions, the courts have departed from the criteria of labour law formerly followed[472] in such cases and may also find that a person who is not an employee in the sense of labour law is nevertheless an employee for purposes of a service invention.[473]

In consequence and during the service. Israeli courts have interpreted section 132 as requiring two cumulative elements: (1) that the invention be invented in consequence of the employee's service with the employer; and (2) that the invention be invented during the period of the employee's service with the employer.[474] The 'period of employment' is usually taken to mean that as long as the employer-employee relationship exists, it is within the employment period.[475] The 'in consequence of' element has been interpreted to require a causal connection between the invention and the service. In the past, a 'loose' connection between the invention and the employment was sometimes deemed sufficient to establish this element.[476] In a recent case,[477] the Supreme Court, affirming the district court decision in an appeal from the Registrar's decision, agreed with the district court that such approach may be open for reconsideration.[478] All the instances in that case agreed that an employee need not be employed in an R&D position in order for his invention to be a service invention, where the invention was within the scope of his duties even if not essential to them. Among relevant factors to consider is whether the employee's invention was affected by secret information belonging to the employer and known to the employee in consequence of his duties and his fiduciary relationship with the employer.[479]

---

471. O.M. (TA Distr.) 729/80 *Dolev et al. v. Amgar et al.*, 43(1) P.M. 99 [1982] at 102–103.
472. See *Yissum*.
473. CC 1767/00 (TA Distr.) *Roni Cohen v. Z.A.G. Industries Ltd* [2006]at paras 12–13 (affirmed on appeal at CA 5186/06 *Roni Cohen v. Z.A.G. Industries Ltd* [2007], this issue was not raised at appeal); see also Y. Tzur, *Legal Aspects Relating to Service Inventions*, 34 Hapraklit 185 (1981) (*Tzur*).
474. For example, *Yissum* at 21, 24.
475. Tzur, at 190.
476. *Yissum* at 27.
477. *Anonymous v. The State of Israel*, Application for registration of patent (determination of service invention), [2010]; appellate district court decision (unpublished); LCA 783/12 *Anonymous v. The State of Israel* [2012].
478. In a *dictum*, the district court ruled, and the Supreme Court agreed, that the invention was made in consequence of the employment even under more stringent criteria.
479. CA 8730/96 *Fried v. Israel Aerospace Industry Ltd*, 55(3) P.D. 49 [2000] at 67, *Deutch* at 542.

Absent agreement to the contrary. Contractual arrangements between the employee and the employer as to the ownership of an invention may supersede the default arrangement under sections 131 and 132 of the Patents Law.

2. Employee's Notification Duty

188. To bring an employee's inventions – whether or not these fall within the scope of service inventions – to the employer's knowledge, the employee is under a duty of giving the employer prompt written notice of having made an invention *either* as a result of his employment or during the period of employment as well as of any patent application he submits.[480] That is, notice must be given during the period of employment even if the invention is not in the course of employment. Special and more stringent notice obligations apply under the Law to State employees, soldiers, policemen, employees of State, enterprises and people receiving pay from the State, who, *inter alia*, must also give notice of inventions within the scope of their functions if made within six months of termination of service and before a patent application is submitted;[481] furthermore, as noted above, State employees are restricted in filing patent applications abroad.[482] Special duties apply to State employees under the Government Service Regulations where applicable.

3. Employee's Entitlement to Remuneration for Service Invention

189. Entitlement and determination. The employee whose invention is, as a service invention, deemed to be the employer's property may, under section 134 of the Law, be entitled to remuneration, whether under an existing agreement with the employer, or as decided by the Compensation and Royalties Committee established under the Patents Law (the '*Committee*').[483] Section 134 of the Law provides that where 'there is no agreement that prescribes whether, to what extent, and on what conditions the employee is entitled to remuneration for a service invention', the entitlement to remuneration and its amount are determined by the Committee.

a. Contractual Waiver of Right to Remuneration

190. In a series of decisions between 2012 and 2014, the Committee handed down contradictory rulings on the validity of a contractual waiver of an employee's right to remuneration for service inventions.

---

480. The Law, s. 131: An employee must notify his employer in writing of any invention he made in consequence of his service or during the period of his service, as soon as possible after he invented it, and also of any patent application submitted by him.
481. The Law, s. 137.
482. The Law, s. 138.
483. See s. §4 'Formalities', s. IV, *supra*, regarding the composition of the Committee.

In *Barazani v. ISCAR Ltd.*,[484] the most recent decision, the Committee held that the provision of section 134 is not inalienable and that the inventor's right for remuneration for an invention does not constitute a social right stemming from labour relations. The Committee further held that an employee who explicitly waived his right to remuneration will not be entitled to argue before the Committee for a right to remuneration according to section 134 of the Law. This decision reversed the Committee's previous *obiter dictum*,[485] which was indirectly upheld by the Supreme Court,[486] according to which section 134 of the Law allows for both an interpretation permitting a waiver and an interpretation that the right to remuneration is an inalienable right that cannot be waived.

Determining remuneration amount. Under the Law, in determining remuneration the Committee is to take into account: (1) the capacity in which the employee was employed; (2) the nature of the connection between the invention and the employee's work; (3) the employee's initiative in making the invention; (4) the possibilities of exploiting the invention and its actual exploitation; and (5) the employee's reasonable expenses to secure protection for the invention in Israel.[487] There is a paucity of published decisions awarding remuneration for service inventions, as such matters are typically heard *in camera* and often end in a settlement.

§6. Scope of Exclusive Rights

I. Patent Is a Negative Right

191. The patent confers a negative right to prevent unlawful exploitation;[488] it does not confer rights to exploit any invention. The right of a proprietor is anchored in section 49(a) of the Patents Law, which provides:

484. *Barazani v. ISCAR Ltd.*, Application to determine remuneration for service invention [2014] (‘*Barazani*’). Petition to the Supreme Court for Judicial review refused (HCJ 4353/14) *Barazani v. ISCAR Ltd.* [2015].
485. *Actelis Networks v. Ilani*, Application to determine remuneration for service invention [2010]. In *Actelis*, the Committee held that contractual language made it unnecessary to rule on this aspect of the interpretation of s. 134, as it was limited to the employee's assignment to the employer of all proprietary rights but did not address the right to remuneration, which the Committee held was personal rather than proprietary. Because a waiver of the right to remuneration was not explicitly provided for in the agreement, the Committee concluded that the right was not waived.
486. LCA 3564/12 *Dr Bayer v. Plurality Ltd (in liquidation) et al.* [2012]. In *Plurality*, an employee sought leave from the district court (overseeing the liquidation of the company) to bring action against the company before the Committee to determine compensation for his service invention; the Supreme Court held that the district court erred in refusing to grant leave to bring action before the committee (on the grounds that the agreement between the parties expressly ruled out additional remuneration for inventions). The Supreme Court held that, as the right to remuneration may possibly be inalienable, the Committee has (possibly exclusive) jurisdiction to entertain the claim of an employee whose contract with the employer denied his right to compensation. One may argue, however, that the *Bayer* decision was limited only to the ‘*competence*’ issue, namely, that the Supreme Court held that the question of inalienability of the right for remuneration may be decided only by the Committee and not by the district court.
487. The Law, s. 135.
488. HJC 280/60 *Abic Chemical Laboratories Ltd v. Authority for Importation of Pharmaceuticals*, 15(2) P.D. 1323 [1961] at 1334.

> A patent holder is entitled to prevent any other person from exploiting the invention for which the patent has been granted without his permission or unlawfully, either in the manner defined in the claims or in a similar manner which – in the light of what is defined by those claims – involves the essence of the invention which is the subject matter of the patent (hereafter: 'infringement').

Section 49(b) accordingly clarifies that:

> The grant of a patent does not constitute permission to exploit any invention unlawfully or in a manner that constitutes violation of rights existing under any law.

The proprietor's right to prevent unauthorized or unlawful 'exploitation of the invention' is further explained by the definition of such term in section 1 of the Patents Law as follows:

(1) in respect of an invention that is a product – any act that is one of the following: production, use, offer for sale, sale, or import for purposes of one of the said acts;
(2) in respect of an invention that is a process – use of the process, and in respect of a product directly derived from the process – any act that is one of the following: production, use, offer for sale, sale, or import for purposes of one of the said acts.

The aforesaid definition of 'exploitation of the invention' has certain statutory exceptions, such as certain non-commercial and experimental acts, discussed in section §7 'Limitations and Exceptions to the Scope of Patent Protection; Compulsory Licenses' below.

The scope of the proprietor's right to exclude is further explained in section §9 'Infringement', below.

II. Territoriality of Patent Rights

192. As a general rule, the Patents Law applies only to acts carried out in the territory of the State of Israel.[489]

An exception to the territoriality rule arises from the conjunction of the provisions of section 1, which expressly includes importation within the scope of exploitation, and the provision of section 50 of the Law regarding direct products of a

489. CA 148/64 *Hochman v. Gershon Paglin and Sons*, 18(3) P.D. 640 [1964] at 644–645; HCJ 5379/00 *Bristol-Myers Squibb Company et al. v. Minister of Health*, 55(4) P.D. 447 [2001] at 468 (the general principle of territoriality of patent rights does not necessarily mean national exhaustion); LCA 8831/05 *Harar v. Dialit Ltd* [2006] at para. 6 (the Supreme Court reversed a district court's grant of an interim injunction insofar as it related to acts performed abroad, ruling that a design right – like a patent right – is a territorial right limited to the territory of the State of Israel).

patented process; accordingly, importation into Israel of a product made abroad by a process protected by patent in Israel constitutes infringement.[490]

In the *Orbotech v. Camtech* matter, where a patent infringement occurred at the product development stage and once developed the product (the infringing component) was outsourced for manufacturing by the defendant's foreign subsidiary outside the jurisdiction, the district court granted an interim injunction both against the Israeli company and against its foreign subsidiary, while noting in an *obiter dictum* that the definition of 'exploiting the invention', while it did not explicitly include exportation, was broad enough to include acts of commercial nature that prejudiced the proprietor's right to exclusively exploit its invention in Israel.[491]

In the *Harar* matter,[492] an application for injunction against an allegedly infringing activity that occurred outside of Israel was refused. The Supreme Court held that Israeli intellectual property laws (in the case at hand, the Designs Ordinance) do not have ex-territorial effect and also expressed doubts concerning the possibility of applying a foreign intellectual property law in a case pending before an Israeli court. The fact that the activity abroad was a continuation of an infringement in Israel was not found material.

In the *Beecham* matter,[493] a foreign manufacturer was found to infringe in Israel as a joint tortfeasor together with the local distributor of its products. The foreign manufacturer's activities were also found to constitute 'marketing' and hence unauthorized 'exploitation of the invention'.

III. Parallel Importation and Exhaustion of Rights

193. Following its amendment in 1998, the Patents Law specifically stipulates that the importation of patented goods falls within the scope of exploitation of an invention;[494] however, the Law does not specifically address unauthorized parallel importation of patented products manufactured abroad under authorization of the patent holder and so far the issue has not been conclusively resolved in Israeli law.[495]

In the *Bristol-Myers*[496] matter, in which Bristol-Myers petitioned the Supreme Court sitting as the High Court of Justice against government Regulation facilitating

490. CA 436/77 *Ikapharm Ltd v. Gradstan Ltd*, 33(1) P.D. 260 [1978] (interim injunction against importation of a pharmaceutical product affirmed where the defendant failed to rebut the presumption of s. 50(b) that the imported product was produced by the patented process; the decision handed down even before 'importation' was expressly included in the definition of exploitation in s. 1 of the Patents Law).
491. MCA 814/05 (Jer. Distr.) CC 7076/05 *Orbotech Ltd v. Camtech Ltd* [2005] (*Orbotech*) at para. 37 (the decision withstood appeal; the particular issue was not raised before the appellate court).
492. LCA 8831/05 *Harar v. Dialit Ltd* (Sup. Ct.) [2006].
493. CA 817/77 *Beecham Group Ltd v. Bristol-Myers Co.*, 33 (3) P.D. 757 [1979].
494. The Law, s. 1 as amended in 1998.
495. HCJ 5379/00 *Bristol-Myers Squibb Company et al. v. Minister of Health et al.*, 55(4) P.D. 447 [2001] (*Bristol-Myers*).
496. *Bristol-Myers* at 468–470.

marketing approval of pharmaceuticals imported by parallel importers,[497] the Supreme Court held that the considerations of the Ministry of Health are not to be affected by the risk of violation of private intellectual property rights, so that issues of infringement should be decided by courts in the framework of civil actions for intellectual property infringement. The Supreme Court left open the question whether the doctrine of national or international exhaustion applies; in a *dictum*, the Court appeared to favour the principle of international exhaustion of patent rights; subsequently the *Bristol-Myers* case has been interpreted as adopting the international exhaustion doctrine in patents.[498]

Interestingly, it was held by the district courts that an exclusive licensee – i.e., a licensee holding a recorded exclusive license to exploit the patent in Israel – has the right to prevent parallel imports by a third party.[499] Thus, regardless of whether the principle of international exhaustion applies in Israel or not, it seems that the issuance of an exclusive license with respect to an Israeli patent could possibly exempt such patent from the applicability of said doctrine. The case law has not yet directly addressed the right of the proprietor to prevent parallel imports.

§7. LIMITATIONS AND EXCEPTIONS TO THE SCOPE OF PATENT PROTECTION: COMPULSORY LICENSES

I. Non-commercial and Experimental Use

194. Section 1 excludes from the definition of 'exploitation of an invention' (addressed in section §6 'Scope of Exclusive Rights' above): (i) non-commercial acts; (ii) experimental acts aimed at improving the invention or developing another invention; (iii) experimental acts towards obtaining regulatory licenses after the lapse of the patent.

A. *Non-commercial Acts*

195. An act that is 'not on a commercial scale and is not commercial in character' is outside the statutory definition of exploitation.[500] In the *Wellcome* matter, the district court noted the cumulative nature of the non-commercial scale and non-commercial character conditions. Thus, while private use or pure research would fall within the scope of this exception, acts such as manufacture of non-commercial quantities as samples for potential customers or large-scale distribution of an

497. Parallel import of pharmaceuticals, by certain medical institutions, has been specifically envisaged in the Pharmacists Ordinance [New Version], 5741-1981, s. 47C and the Pharmacists Regulations (Medical Preparations), 5746-1986.

498. For example, CC (Haifa Distr.) 1089/05 *Dyson Ltd et al. v. Shalom Ltd et al.* [2007] (in the context of industrial designs).

499. CC(TA Distr.) 1182/95 *Yu Zheng v. S. Agami Ltd* [1999], and CC(TA Distr.) 1242/97 *S.D.R. Import Marketing Ltd v. Cohen Hadad Trade Ltd* [1999], discussed in the *Bristol* case at 466–467.

500. The Law, s. 1.

infringing product for free would be regarded as 'exploitation' and, if done unlawfully or without consent, would be deemed infringement.[501]

B. Experimental Acts towards Improving the Invention or Making Another Invention

196. Excluded by section 1 from the definition of exploitation is 'an experimental act in connection with the invention, the objective of which is to improve the invention or to develop another invention'.

In the district court case of *Genzyme*,[502] it was held that clinical trials with respect to improvements on a patented medicine would fall within the scope of this exception.

However, in another district court case (the *Orbotech* matter), it was held that experimental acts, whether for research and development purposes, or for obtaining regulatory approvals to be used after the patent lapses, cannot serve as disguise for activities of commercial character intended to penetrate the market and prepare marketing channels.[503]

This experimental use exception in the Patents Law is worded rather broadly compared to other jurisdictions. While in the US this type of the experimental use exception is very narrow and is limited to non-commercial use to satisfy curiosity[504] and does not refer to use towards improving the invention, and in Europe the exception of experimental acts to explore the unknown is limited to experiments relating to the subject matter of the invention,[505] the statutory language of section 1 in Israel possibly implies an even broader exception. Thus, in the *Genzyme* matter,[506] the district court dismissed the argument that the experimental use statutory exception should be limited to 'experimenting on' the invention (as distinguished from 'experimenting with' the invention). In addition, while the court in the *Orbotech* matter held that commercial motivations may exclude the application of the experimental use exception, the court in the *Genzyme* matter held that it does not. It is yet to be seen how the courts in Israel would continue to interpret the section.

---

501. CC (TA Distr.) 1512/93 *The Wellcome Foundation Limited et al. v. Teva Pharmaceutical Industries Ltd* [1995] at para. 5 (in its analysis, the district court cited D. Gilat, *Experimental Use and Patents*, 16 IIC Studies 1 (1995)). Similarly, in the *Kleiman* matter of 1993, where the issue was that of novelty, the district court held that the use of the invention on model farms for the purpose of demonstrating its efficacy to prospective customers was not commercial in its scale but commercial in its character, and thus constituted 'exploitation' in the sense of s. 1 of the Law.
502. CC 1102/05 (TA Distr.) MCA 19682/05 *Transkaryotic Therapies Inc. v. Genzyme Corporation* [2006] (*Genzyme*).
503. The *Orbotech* matter at para. 40.
504. *Roche Products Inc. v. Bolar Pharmaceutical Co.*, 733 F.2d 858 (Fed. Cir. 1984).
505. For example, s. 60(5)(b) of the UK Patents Act of 1977, interpreted at *Monsanto Co. v. Stauffer Chemical Co. and another* [1985] RPC 515; see also *Klinische Versuche (Clinical Trials) I* [1997] RPC 623 and *Klinische Versuche (Clinical Trials) II* [1998] RPC 423 regarding the German Patents Act 1981.
506. The *Genzyme* matter.

C. Experimental Acts Aiming at Obtaining Regulatory Approvals

197. A *Bolar*-type exception allowing for experimental use for the purpose of obtaining regulatory approval was enacted in 1998, simultaneously with provisions regarding patent term extension for pharmaceutical patents.[507] This exception in section 1 excludes from the definition of exploitation experimental acts performed in accordance with section 54A, which provides as follows:

> An experimental act, which is part of an effort to obtain a license to market the product after the patent has lapsed, does not constitute 'exploitation of an invention', if the following two conditions are met:
>
> (1) the effort to obtain a license is made in order to obtain a license in Israel or in a country, in which an experimental act on a patent protected invention for the purpose of obtaining a license is permitted before the patent lapses;
>
> (2) any product produced under the terms of this section is not used – both while the patent is in effect or thereafter – for any purpose other than obtaining a license as aforesaid;
>
> for purposes of this section, 'license' – certification, permit or any other document required under law in order to market the product.

Section 54A applies to all products that require a 'license', namely, marketing authorization, and not only to pharmaceutical products. Notably, section 54A applies to agrochemical inventions, although such inventions do not benefit from the patent term extension provisions of the Law.[508]

The exception of section 54A would not apply where the product for which regulatory approval was sought would be used for other purposes, such as sale or stockpiling. Nor would the statutory exception of section 54A apply in the event that such products are used for obtaining regulatory approval outside of Israel in countries where *Bolar*-type experimental use is not allowed.

It appears from the language of section 54A that if the party invoking the section 54A exception violates the conditions of section 54A, all such experimentation will constitute infringement.

However, in the *Genzyme*[509] matter, the Tel Aviv District Court took a rather broad view of the scope of the exception under section 54A, holding that development of generic and innovative drugs in reliance on patented drugs, including conducting clinical trials, in Israel was in itself an interest that section 54A aimed to promote. The court further held that the performance of exempted acts does not by itself point to future infringement or constitute bad faith, and therefore did not amount to infringement. This holding was made without addressing the question, arising from the statutory condition, of whether or not the experiments were supposed to be submitted for regulatory approval in countries that did not provide for

---

507. Amendment No. 3 of the Patents Law of 1998, Bill No. 2651 of 27 Oct. 1997, Bill No. 2664 of 12 Dec. 1997.

508. Discussed *infra* at s. §8 'Duration of Protection', s. II 'Extensions of Patent Term'.

509. The *Genzyme* matter.

a *Bolar*-type exemption in their laws. Furthermore, the *Genzyme* court did not address a situation of local manufacturing of the drug, but merely the conducting of clinical trials.

II. Prior User Rights

198. The patent holder's exclusive right does not bar rights based on prior exploitation, in accordance with section 53 of the Law. Under section 53, a prior user of the invention who, on the filing date or the date of the priority application, made good faith use or made actual preparations in good faith for the use of an invention, in Israel, is allowed to continue exploiting the invention without consideration.[510] Such exploitation right cannot be transferred and cannot devolve upon another, other than as part of the business in which the invention is being used.[511]

Similarly, a person who, after the patent lapse was published, commenced use or made actual preparations for the use of the patented invention, in Israel, is allowed to continue exploiting the invention without consideration even after the patent is restored.[512] Such exploitation right cannot be transferred and cannot devolve upon another, other than as part of the business in which the invention is being used.[513]

III. Compulsory Licenses

A. Compulsory License in Case of Abuse of Monopoly

199. The statutory provisions of the Patents Law dealing with compulsory licenses underwent significant change when Israel acceded to the TRIPS Agreement. In the past, compulsory licenses could be easily obtained, especially in the field of pharmaceuticals, under the rubric of public health.[514] However, after Israel's accession to the TRIPS Agreement, the relevant provisions were considerably narrowed in the framework of the TRIPS Law,[515] which entered into force in 2000 (e.g., exploitation by the patent holder is not only by manufacturing but also by importation). Thus, while the Israeli pharmaceutical companies made considerable use of such provisions in the past, since 2000 there has been no precedent defining what constitutes an abuse of monopoly under the amended Law.

Under section 117 of the Law, three years after the patent grant (or four years after the filing of the patent application, if later), the Registrar has the power to grant a third-party applicant a compulsory license where he is satisfied that the patent

510. The Law, s. 53.
511. The Law, s. 54.
512. The Law, s. 63.
513. The Law, s. 64.
514. Section 120 of the Law before its cancellation in 1999 provided for the Registrar's broad powers to grant compulsory licenses in the field of medical and pharmaceutical patents for reasons of public health.
515. The Law for the Amendment of Intellectual Property Laws (in accordance with the Provisions of the TRIPS Agreement), 5760-1999.

holder abuses his monopoly. The patent holder is deemed to admit to an abuse of monopoly if he fails to respond to the Registrar's request of notification as to whether he exploits the invention by way of production or importation.[516] An abuse of monopoly is deemed to exist if, in respect of a patented product or patented process, the patent holder fails to provide a reasonable justification for a situation where demand in Israel is not satisfied in its entirety on reasonable terms, or where the conditions imposed by the patent holder on the supply of the product or on the grant of a license for its production or use are not fair in the circumstances, arise primarily out of the existence of the patent and fail to take account of the public interest.[517]

Entertaining an application for a compulsory license due to abuse of monopoly, the Registrar shall, *inter alia*, have regard to: (1) the applicant's ability to remedy the defect; (2) the public interest, which generally requires that inventions that can be exploited in Israel by way of production or importation should be so exploited to the greatest extent possible under existing circumstances and without delay; (3) the right to reasonable remuneration given the nature of the invention; (4) protection of the rights of any person who exploits the invention in Israel, by way of production or by way of import, and of persons engaged in developing that invention; (5) the nature of the invention, the time elapsed since the patent grant, and the steps taken by the patent holder or by his representative for the exploitation of the invention in Israel by way of production or by way of import.[518] A compulsory license is granted predominantly for the supply of the domestic market.[519]

B. Compulsory License to Permit Exploiting a Later Patent

200. A compulsory license to exploit an earlier patent may be granted to the owner of a later patent, which cannot be exploited without infringing such earlier patent, to the extent necessary for the exploitation of the later invention, provided that the later invention involves an important technical advance of considerable economic significance in relation to the earlier invention.[520]

C. Conditions for Grant of Compulsory Licenses in Case of Abuse of Monopoly or to Permit Exploitation of Later Patent

201. Compulsory licenses are non-exclusive and may be subject to conditions, including appropriate royalties;[521] they are not transferable other than together with

516. The Law, s. 118.
517. The Law, s. 119.
518. The Law, s. 122.
519. The Law, s. 123.
520. The Law, s. 121.
521. The Law, s. 126.

that part of the enterprise or the goodwill that is connected to the use of the patent.[522] The conditions may include the terms on which the license will terminate or will be revoked.[523] The proprietor may apply for a reconsideration of the compulsory license due to a change of circumstances or a violation of its terms by the licensee.[524]

D. Compulsory License under Section 18C Due to Non-disclosure

202. Under section 18C of the Law, the court or the Registrar have the power to grant a license to a third party to exploit the patent in the event the patent holder breached his duty of disclosure at the examination stage by providing misleading particulars or knowingly withholding information regarding a substantive change in the list of publications and documents.[525] The terms of such license are to be agreed upon by the parties, and in the absence of agreement, are prescribed by the court or the Registrar.

IV. Right of the State to Exploit Certain Inventions

203. As a general rule, a patent is effective against the State.[526] However, section 104 of the Law grants the State a right to permit, by way of a ministerial permit, the exploitation of an invention by a governmental department or agency (or by a person under contract with the State)[527] if the designated governmental minister[528] finds it necessary in the interests of national security or the maintenance of essential supplies and services.

Such exploitation by the State, if permitted, entitles the owner of the invention (or the patent owner or the exclusive licensee, as the case may be) to royalties from the State as agreed by the owner or, absent an agreement, as determined by the Compensation and Royalties Committee.[529] In determining the amount of royalties, the Compensation and Royalties Committee must have regard to the scope and character of the permitted exploitation, and may take into account royalties payable under licenses that have similar terms to those of the permit.[530]

522. The Law, s. 126A.
523. The Law, s. 126(1).
524. The Law, s. 127.
525. The Law, s. 18C(1)(b).
526. The Law, s. 51.
527. The Law, s. 105.
528. The Law, s. 112. Regarding the Committee, see s. §5 'Ownership', Part E 'Service Inventions', *supra*.
529. The Law, s. 108.
530. The Law, s. 110.

§8. Duration of Protection: Maintaining and Termination of Patent Protection

I. Term, Maintenance and Restoration

A. Term, Maintenance and Lapse of Regular Patents

204. Term. Patents are granted for the term of twenty years from the date of filing the application[531] or, under the PCT, from the PCT filing date in Israel.[532]

Maintenance and lapse. The continued validity of a patent is subject to the timely payment of maintenance fees.[533] A grace period of six months is provided for.[534] Failure to pay maintenance fees results in the lapse of the patent.[535]

Contractual extension of patent term is impermissible. In the *Blas v. Kibbutz Dan*[536] matter, the Supreme Court held that the provisions of a license requiring the payment of royalties after the patent ceased to be in effect were invalid and unenforceable due to considerations of public policy, citing *inter alia* the US case of *Lear, Inc v. Adkins.*[537]

B. Term of Patents of Addition

205. Patents of addition remain in force for the duration of the parent patent, without maintenance fees.[538]

If a main patent in respect of which a patent of addition exists was cancelled at the owner's request or due to public interest and the patent of addition was not cancelled together with it, then the patent of addition may, at the owner's request, become an independent patent and will remain in effect until the end of the period during which the main patent would have been in effect, subject to payment of maintenance fees.[539]

C. Restoration of a Lapsed Patent

206. A patent lapsed through non-payment of maintenance fees may be restored, by application to the Registrar, upon payment of increased fees,[540] if the Registrar is satisfied that the non-payment occurred through a reasonable cause; such application must be submitted promptly after the omission became known to the patent

531. The Law, s. 52.
532. The Law, s. 48C.
533. The Law, s. 56.
534. The Law, s. 57.
535. The Law, s. 58.
536. CA 427/86 *Blas v. Kibbutz 'Dan'*. 43(3) P.D. 323 [1989].
537. 395 U.S. 653 (1969).
538. The Law, s. 47.
539. The Law, s. 48(a).
540. The Law, s. 59.

holder or his representative.[541] Such application is advertised and can be opposed.[542]

Restoration of a patent may be retroactive.[543] In a provision similar to the protection of a prior user, the Law provides for continued protection of a third party which commenced exploiting in Israel the patented invention after the lapse of the patent was advertised, or made actual preparations for such exploitation.[544]

D. Patent Term Adjustment Not Available

207. The Patents Law does not provide for patent term adjustments.[545]

II. Extensions of Patent Term

A. General

208. Patent term extensions (PTE or Extension Orders) of up to a maximum five years may be requested with respect to patents for inventions in the field of pharmaceuticals and medical devices, to compensate the patent holder for regulatory review activities delaying commercial exploitation of the pharmaceutical or medical device.

The PTE provisions, anchored in section 64(A)-(Q) of the Patents Law, were introduced in 1998 to create balance with the *Bolar*-type provision of section 54A of the Law that permitted generic manufacturers to experiment with the patented invention during the term of the patent by exempting preparatory activities conducted for obtaining regulatory authorization of products in Israel or in any other country where such activity is permitted as well. Unlike the *Bolar*-type exemption, the Israeli PTE provisions do not cover agrochemical products nor veterinary products registered by the Ministry of Agriculture; however, veterinary products registered by the Ministry of Health can provide a basis for such an extension. In addition, the Patents Law does not provide for extensions for paediatric indications.

On 27 January 2014, new PTE provisions within the Patents Law were enacted following a memorandum of understanding between the Israeli government and the US Trade Representative (USTR) dated 2010 ('*2014 Amendment*'). These provisions overhauled the Israeli PTE regime in many aspects, the implications and ramifications of which have yet to be determined.

541. The Law, s. 60.
542. The Law, s. 61.
543. CA 319/85 *Ackstein v. Alumim Bnei Akiva Group for Cooperative Agricultural Settlement Ltd*, 39 (4) P.D. 602 [1985].
544. The Law, s. 63.
545. Cf. 35 U.S.C. § 154.

B. Eligibility for a Patent Term Extension Order

209. Basic Patents eligible for patent term extension. Under section 64D of the Law, to be eligible for a patent term extension a patent (a Basic Patent in the language of the Law) must relate to a *Substance*, defined in the Law as 'the active ingredient of a pharmaceutical preparation or the salts, esters, hydrates, or crystalline forms of such ingredient, or to a medical device'. Namely, a patent is eligible if it includes claims directed to a Substance *per se*, or to the process of its manufacture or its use, or to a pharmaceutical preparation that contains a Substance or the process of manufacture of such preparation, or a medical device.

Conditions for the grant of an Extension Order. The Patent Office will issue an Extension Order only if the following conditions are met: (i) the Basic Patent is in force and it includes claims directed as aforesaid; (ii) with respect to a pharmaceutical preparation, a pharmaceutical preparation containing a Substance is registered in the Israeli Register of Pharmaceuticals (hereinafter the *'Register of Pharmaceuticals'*) maintained by the Israeli Ministry of Health; (iii) the registration in the Register of Pharmaceuticals is the first registration that enables use of the Substance in Israel for medical purposes; (iv) no prior Extension Order was granted in respect of the Basic Patent or in respect of the Substance; (v) if a marketing authorization was issued in the United States – an Extension Order to the US Reference Patent[546] in the US was also granted and has not yet expired; and (vi) if a marketing approval was issued in a Recognized European Country[547] – an Extension Order of the Reference Patent[548] in that country was also granted and has not yet expired;

546. A Reference Patent is defined in the Law as any patent in any Recognized Country that protects the Substance, the process of manufacture of the Substance or the use of the Substance, the pharmaceutical preparation that contains the Substance, the process of manufacture of a pharmaceutical preparation containing the Substance, or the medical device that is claimed in a basic patent in Israel, whether or not such patent corresponds to the basic patent. The list of Recognized Countries includes the US, Italy, the UK, Germany, Spain, and France. Notably, the definition of a 'Reference Patent' is broader than a 'corresponding patent'.
547. The definition of a Recognized European Country was introduced in the 2014 Amendment to include all countries listed in part B of the addendum of the Patents Law, namely, Italy, the United Kingdom, Germany, Spain and France.
548. A 'Reference Patent Extension Order' was introduced in the recent amendment, and reads as follows:

> *an order or approval which provides for an extension, by one or more days, of a Reference Patent's term, with respect to a medical preparation that contains the substance or with respect to medical device protected by the Reference Patent, to which one of the following provisions applies:*
>
> (1) *It was issued in the United States of America (Patent Term Extension) and the term thereof was determined by an authorized entity according to the part of the examination period for the purpose of granting the first Marketing Authorization by the authority authorized to grant marketing authorizations, which commenced after the grant of the Reference Patent, after the deduction of the terms in respect of which it was determined that the extension order applicant did not act with due diligence in the course of the said examination period and with the addition of half the term of the clinical trials for a medical preparation or medical equipment protected by the Reference Patent;*

In the decision of *Kirin-Amgen*,[549] the District Court ruled that if the US Reference Patent was *not granted* a US *Extension Order*, the Israeli Basic Patent will consequently not be entitled to an Extension Order since it does not comply with the conditions for the grant of an Extension Order (namely, condition indicated in paragraph 209(v)-(vi) above). If the Registrar finds that all of the foregoing conditions have been met, the Registrar will issue the Extension Order, provided that: (i) an application for an Extension Order was filed in good faith; and (2) the scope of protection pursuant to the Extension Order does not extend beyond the scope of protection provided by the Basic Patent.

1. 'First Registration as Pharmaceutical for Medical Purposes'

210. Second indications and formulation patents. Where a pharmaceutical preparation containing a certain Substance was previously registered with the Ministry of Health, additional patents claiming new medical uses of the compound or new formulations of the compound will not be eligible for patent term extension because such applications will fail to meet the requirement of first registration of the pharmaceutical preparation. However, where the Substance was not previously registered in Israel, a later patent claiming a formulation invention or second medical use invention may be eligible for an Extension Order.

Enantiomers. It was decided by the Supreme Court in the *Lundbeck*[550] case that a patent claiming only a specific enantiomer was not eligible for an Extension Order on the basis of a pharmaceutical whose active pharmaceutical ingredient is the enantiomer, in view of an earlier registration of a pharmaceutical whose Active Pharmaceutical Ingredient (API) was the racemic mixture, which was deemed to have 'contained' the enantiomer. In other words, the registration of the earlier pharmaceutical was held to be the first registration of the enantiomer 'contained' in the racemic mixture.

Combination drugs. With respect to applications for Extension Orders for patents directed to combinations of Substances, in one case, affirmed on appeal,[551] an application for an Extension Order based on a combination pharmaceutical was refused,

---

(2) *It was granted by a Recognized European Country (Supplementary Protection Certificate) and the term thereof was determined in view of the period which had elapsed from the date of the application's filing for a Reference Patent until the date of the receipt of the first marketing authorization, after the deduction of five years;*

(3) *It was granted by a Recognized Country and was intended to temporarily extend the term of the Reference Patent until a decision on the grant of an order pursuant to clauses (1) or (2) or until an earlier date prescribed therein (hereinafter: Temporary Order);*

549. Application for Extension Order for Patent 110669 in the name of Kirin-Amgen, Inc [2012]; M.A. 41839-10-12 *Kirin-Amgen, Inc v. The Registrar of Patents* [2015].

550. Application for Extension Order for Patent 90465 in the name of H. Lundbeck [2009]; M.A. 223/09 *H. Lundbeck v. Unipharm Ltd et al.* [Jer. Distr., 2009]; ALA 5267/09 *H. Lundbeck v. Unipharm Ltd et al.* [2010].

551. The Registrar's decision was upheld upon appeal by the District Court and an application for leave to appeal to the Supreme Court was refused (formally on other grounds). See Application for an Extension Order for IL Patent No. 97219 in the name of *Novartis* [2005]; M.A. 1063/06 *Novartis*

where both Substances of the combination were previously registered with the Ministry of Health; the combination in and of itself was not deemed to constitute a 'new Substance' in and of itself. It therefore appears that a patent for a combination drug may be ineligible for patent term extension if both Substances were previously separately registered in the Register of Pharmaceuticals.

The outcome may well be different where one Substance of the combination was previously registered with the Ministry of Health and the other Substance was not registered. A patent for a combination drug may be subject to patent term extension if at least one of the Substances comprised in the combination had not previously been registered (even if the other Substances in the combination are already registered).

In the decision of *Guardasil*,[552] the Registrar ruled that a combination patent of several active ingredients might be a basis for filing an application for an Extension Order for a patent claiming *one* of said active ingredients. In other words, a patent claiming an active ingredient 'A' may be extended on the basis of a registration of a pharmaceutical which includes the active ingredient 'A', either by itself or in combination with other active ingredients.

One Substance per patent. Only one Extension Order may be issued with respect to one patent, even where the patent claims two Substances (and a patent may receive only one Extension Order).

Veterinary products. In one decision, the IPTO held that a patent relating to a veterinary product is eligible for an Extension Order only if the product is registered by the Ministry of Health, but not if registered by the Ministry of Agriculture.[553] In another decision, the Jerusalem District Court reversed the IPTO refusal of an application for an Extension Order that was based on the registration of a pharmaceutical containing the Substance (Circadin) whose medical use on humans was the first, where a previous veterinary drug containing the same Substance was already registered in the Register of Pharmaceuticals, and held that a prior registration in one field (veterinary medicine) did not preclude the grant of an Extension Order in the other field (human medicine).[554] Following the District Court's decision, the Registrar ordered that a notice of the intention to grant an Extension Order be published for opposition for an abbreviated period, and a temporary Extension Order be granted at the end of the opposition period or the end of the opposition proceeding.[555] Subsequently, an opposition to the grant of a PTE was

AG v. Manufacturers Association *of Israel* [TA Distr., 2007]; ALA 2890/07 *Novartis AG v. The Registrar of Patents* [Sup. Ct., 2009].

552. Application for Extension Order for Patent 117459 in the name of *MERCK SHARP & DOHME CORP.* [2015].

553. Application for Extension Order for Patent No. 108419 in the name of Kilvelner [27 Oct. 2002].

554. Application for Extension Order for Patent 103411 in the name of Neurim Pharmaceuticals Ltd (9 May 2012) (extension order refused, as the registration of the veterinary drug was deemed the first registration allowing medical use of the Substance); reversed by MCA (Jer. Distr.) 13281-06-12 *Neurim Pharmaceuticals (1991) Ltd v. Registrar of Patents* [Nevo, 27 Sep. 2012]; the appellate decision applied in Application for Extension Order for Patent No. 103411 in the name of Neurim Pharmaceuticals Ltd. [Nevo, 30 Sep. 2012].

555. Application for Extension Order for Patent No. 103411 in the name of Neurim Pharmaceuticals Ltd. [Nevo, 30 Sep. 2012].

dismissed by the Registrar, and the Registrar's decision was upheld by the District Court.[556]

Medical devices. A PTE can be granted to a patent claiming a medical device if the registration of the medical device is required by law. The Patents Law does not specify the date on which a PTE application based on a medical device should be filed (the deadline is specified only for pharmaceutical preparations). In a decision of the Registrar issued before the 2014 Amendment, it was ruled that the ninety-day period to file a PTE application based on a pharmaceutical preparation was to be applied by analogy to PTE applications based on medical devices.[557]

Furthermore, the language of the Patents Law with respect to, *inter alia*, the conditions to grant a PTE on the basis of a medical device and the scope of protection during the extension is somewhat ambiguous. The implementation of the PTE provisions mentioned above on extensions based on medical devices have yet to be developed in decisions of the IPTO and courts.

C. Calculation of the Duration of Extension Orders

211. The method for calculating the duration of an Israeli Extension Order is complicated and unique as it depends on the duration of Extension Orders granted abroad.

Method for calculating the extension term. The first step of calculation of the PTE's duration performed as a dual step calculation: The Extension Order shall in principle have a term equal to the shortest term of the Reference Patent Extension Orders granted in the Recognized States, namely, the *shortest* extension granted to a Reference Patent in one of the Recognized Countries; however, the Israeli PTE Order shall expire no later than the date on which, in any one of the Recognized Countries wherein a marketing authorization was issued, any Reference Patent Extension Order has expired[558] or any Reference Patent was revoked.

The duration of the PTE order may also be reduced,[559] based on two additional conditions:

(i) The cumulative duration of the Basic Patent and the term of extension must not exceed fourteen years from the *first date* of marketing authorization of the pharmaceutical preparation containing the Substance or of the medical device in *any one of* the Recognized Countries.
(ii) The duration of the PTE Order may not exceed five years.

556. Decision in the opposition to the grant of an Extension Order to Patent No. 103411 *Unipahrm Ltd v. Neurim Pharmaceuticals Ltd.* [Nevo, 3 Mar. 2013]; MCA (Jer. Distr.) 20857-04-13 *Unipharm Ltd. v. Neurim Pharmaceuticals Ltd.* [Nevo, 19 Jan. 2014].

557. A request to extend the term of protection of Patent No. 217056 in the name of Advanced Bio-Technologies Inc. (Nevo, 29 Dec. 2013).

558. Expiry is defined as one of the following events: (1) shortening, revocation or cancellation of a Reference Patent Extension Order; or (2) Revocation of a Reference Patent. This does not include a substitution of a temporary extension order with a permanent one.

559. If reduced to zero, the PTE request will be refused.

Identifying the Reference Patent(s). In the case of *Novartis*,[560] the proprietor argued that for the sake of the calculation of the duration of the extension, the Registrar should take into consideration only one of the two European Reference Patents for which SPCs have been granted.[561] The Registrar rejected this argument and ruled that since any of the European Reference Patents may be relied upon for the purpose of meeting the conditions for grant of a PTE order,[562] all European Reference Patents should also be taken into consideration for the sake of calculation of the duration of the Israeli Basic Patent.

The term of the Extension Order commences upon the expiry of the patent's regular twenty-year period.

The massive reduction of the list of Recognized Countries in the framework of the 2014 Amendment provided that in many cases a longer extension of term will be granted in Israel, in comparison to the provisions of the law prior to said amendment.

Calculation where marketing authorization was obtained only in Israel. Different provisions apply to an Extension Order based on the registration of a pharmaceutical registered only in Israel, but this seldom occurs.

Additional ground for expiration. In addition, an Extension Order will expire upon the occurrence of any of the following: failure to make timely payment of maintenance fees (reinstatement is possible; see below); revocation of the registration of the pharmaceutical preparation in the Register of Pharmaceuticals on which the Extension Order was based; the Basic Patent is revoked or is amended in such manner that it no longer claims the Substance, its process of manufacture, its use, the pharmaceutical preparation containing the Substance, or the medical device.

D. *Scope of Protection*

212. An Extension Order entitles the proprietor of the Basic Patent (and arguably, also the exclusive licensee) to prevent during the term of extension any person from marketing or manufacturing for the purpose of marketing, without the patent proprietor's permission, a medical device or a pharmaceutical preparation that contains the Substance, to the extent that the Substance, the process of manufacture or use thereof, the pharmaceutical preparation, or the process of its manufacture (and arguably a medical device) is claimed in the Basic Patent.

If the Extension Order is infringed during the term of extension, the proprietor of the Basic Patent and an exclusive licensee are entitled to all remedies available for patent infringement, namely injunctions and damages.

560. A request to grant an extension order for Patent No. 113403 in the name of *Novartis AG* [Nevo, 25 Jul. 2013].

561. In the circumstances of that case, two SPCs were granted based on the same pharmaceutical preparation [for EP678503 and EP1303478].

562. See s. II above.

E. Procedure in Respect of Extension Orders

213. Right to file. An application for an Extension Order may be filed by the proprietor, a patent applicant or by an exclusive licensee of a patent. Where a patent is jointly owned, each joint proprietor may apply for an Extension Order. If the proprietor, any of the joint proprietors, or the exclusive licensee does not join in the filing of the application for an Extension Order as an applicant, the applicant must join such party as a respondent to the application.

Time for filing. An application for an Extension Order must be filed with the IPTO within ninety days from the date of *registration of the first pharmaceutical* comprising the Substance that is claimed in the patent whose term is to be extended. Heed must be paid to the fact that the act of registration of a drug in the Register of Pharmaceuticals precedes the receipt of a marketing authorization and is not equivalent to it. Registration in itself does not allow marketing of a pharmaceutical in Israel, and marketing authorization may be granted some time after registration, provided that additional requirements are met. The ninety-day period, however, commences upon registration rather than issuance of marketing authorization. The PTE application must be filed with the IPTO within the ninety days even if the patent application is still pending at the time.

The ninety days granted to file a PTE application *cannot be extended.*[563] Therefore, failure to observe this provision will likely result in a loss of rights.

Examination. The examination procedure was amended significantly in the 2014 Amendment, providing for an expedited examination procedure and the rapid issuance of decisions to grant Extension Orders in Israel.

The examination of an application for Extension Order filed with respect to granted patents must commence within sixty days from the date of its filing. If the application for Extension Order was filed before the Basic Patent was granted, the examination of the Basic Patent application is accelerated. Examination of the patent application commences within thirty days after the filing date of the application for Extension Order, and is to be completed as soon as possible.[564] The examination of the application for a Patent Extension Order will commence only after the grant of the Basic Patent.

If anything is missing or if there is a defect in the application for an Extension Order, the Registrar will inform the applicant accordingly and the applicant will complete what is missing or amend the defect within two months of the date of the notice; if the applicant does not complete what is missing or amend the defect within said period, the Registrar shall reject the application for Extension Order. The two-month period may be extended *only once* during the examination of an application for a patent extension order.

563. Section 164 of the Patents Law stipulates that the Registrar has the power to extend any deadline brought forth in the Patents Law, except for certain deadlines, one of which is the ninety-day period granted to file a PTE application.

564. The Registrar may set stricter schedules to comply with this requirement. In addition, if no citations or publications according to s. 18 of the Patents Law (relating to the patent applicant's duty of disclosure; see s. §4.II.D 'Duty of Disclosure during Examination' above) were provided, these should be filed together with the PTE application.

The Registrar has to complete the examination of the application for Extension Order within sixty days from the date of the commencement of the examination or from the date on which the applicant completed what is missing or amended the defect as stated above, whichever is later.

If the Registrar is informed or becomes aware that the conditions to grant an Extension Order are met, it will publish the intent to grant an Extension Order and its duration,[565] within sixty days from the completion of the examination. If the Registrar is informed or becomes aware that the conditions to grant an Extension Order are *not* met, it will publish the decision to refuse the application for Extension Order within sixty days from the completion of the examination.

Applications for Extension Orders are examined under the premise that examination and subsequent publication for opposition will be completed prior to the twenty-year expiration date of the Basic Patent (and the IPTO is authorized to shorten any statutory deadline to meet with the goal). In a decision rendered by the Patents Registrar prior to the 2014 Amendment, it was decided that third parties lack standing and are not entitled to interfere in the examination of applications for Extension Orders.[566] The right of third parties to be heard may be exercised only by way of lodging an opposition to the application for an Extension Order, if the application is accepted.

Bifurcated examination. If all of the conditions for the grant of an Israeli Extension Order are met, except for the condition of a Reference Patent Extension Order being granted in a Reference Country that issued a marketing authorization for the pertinent pharmaceutical preparation,[567] then the Registrar will bifurcate the examination of the application for Extension Order.

In such cases, the Registrar will publish, within sixty days of the conclusion of the examination's first stage, a notice of intent to grant an Extension Order and its duration,[568] subject to the condition that the Reference Patent Extension Order(s) is granted during the Basic Patent's term. Any person may lodge an opposition to such first notice of intent to grant an Extension Order. However, even if the opposition is dismissed, the Extension Order will not be granted until after the grant of the Reference Patent Extension Order and completion of the examination of the application for an Extension Order and the dismissal of an additional opposition, if filed.

Where the examination was bifurcated, the Applicant has to notify the Registrar of the grant or refusal of the Reference Patent Extension Orders within ninety days of their grant or refusal. The ninety days granted to notify the Registrar *cannot be*

565. The duration of extension will be determined according to the information before the Registrar at this stage.

566. Third-party request to grant a decision in Applications for Extension Orders for Patent Nos. 122910, 126431 and 110977, *Manufacturers Association of Israel v. Novartis AG et al.* [26 Dec. 2010].

567. See s. II above.

568. The duration of extension will be determined according to the information before the Registrar at this stage.

extended.[569] Therefore, failure to observe this provision may result in a loss of rights.

If the Registrar is informed or becomes aware that no Reference Patent Extension Orders will be granted before the expiry of the Basic Patent, or if the applicant fails to notify him of said rejections, no Extension Order will be granted and the Registrar will publish said rejection within sixty days after the expiry to the Basic Patent or at the end of the ninety-day term, whichever is later.[570]

Acceptance, oppositions and grants. Where, following examination of the application for an Extension Order, the IPTO decides to accept the application, namely, it intends to grant an Extension Order, the IPTO publishes the intent so that third parties may file a *pre-grant* opposition to it.

If an opposition is initiated by a third party, the IPTO hears the opposition as a small-scale litigation that includes the filing of pleadings, evidence (such as affidavits), cross-examination and summations. If an opposition is not filed within three months from the publication of the intent, or if the opposition is dismissed, the IPTO grants the Extension Order.

Temporary extensions. Several decisions issued by the Patents Registrar and District Court before the 2014 Amendment enabled the grant of temporary extensions of term for Israeli Basic Patents in certain circumstances.[571]

It is unclear at this stage, after the legislation of the 2014 Amendment, under which conditions and in which circumstances a temporary extension would be granted. The influence and effects of this recent law on the issuance of temporary extensions is yet to be determined.

Appeal. The decision of the IPTO not to grant an Extension Order following examination of an application for an Extension Order and the decision of the IPTO to allow or dismiss an opposition to an application for an Extension Order may be appealed by right to the District Courts of Jerusalem or Tel Aviv.

Revocation of Extension Orders. Any person may file with the Patent Office an application for revocation of a granted Extension Order or an application to amend the term of extension of a granted Extension Order. The IPTO will revoke or amend the Extension Order if it finds that there exists a ground for opposition to the grant of the Extension Order or to its term of extension.

Reinstatement. An Extension Order expired due to failure to pay maintenance fees may be reinstated following the procedure applicable for reinstatement of patents that expired for the same reason. A request for reinstatement of an Extension Order must be filed as soon as possible after discovery of its expiry. As in the case

569. Section 164 of the Patents Law stipulates that the Registrar has the power to extend a deadline brought forth in the Patents Law except for certain deadlines, one of which is the ninety-day period granted to notify the Registrar of the grant or refusal of the Reference Patent Extension Orders.

570. Section 64 E(e)4 of the Patents Law.

571. For example, the *Neurim* case (where a temporary extension was issued since the opposition proceeding could not have been finalized before the expiry of the Basic Patent); the *BTG* case (where a temporary extension was issued in the absence of a permanent order to the US Reference Patent); a request for an Extension Order for IL Patent No. 83148 in the name of Roche Diagnostics GmbH (13 Jun. 2007) (where a temporary extension order was issued to a basic patent that was nearing expiry, until the temporary extension granted to the Reference Patent in the US became permanent.)

with respect to reinstatement of patents, a third party who commenced exploitation of an invention protected by an Extension Order after its expiry and before its reinstatement, may acquire prior user rights and is entitled to continue such exploitation.

III. Revocation of Patent or Shortening of Patent Term

A. *Revocation or Cancellation at the Request of the Patent Owner*

1. Procedure for the Owner's Request

214. Under section 73 of the Law, a patent holder may apply to the Registrar that he revoke or cancel a patent granted to him. Such application is advertised and may be opposed; absent an opposition or if the opposition is not successful, the Registrar shall revoke or cancel the patent as requested.

If the patent holder applies for revocation or cancellation while proceedings on the patent are pending in court, the Registrar shall decide whether to revoke or cancel the patent.[572]

2. Effect of Revocation or Cancellation at Owner's Request

215. Where a patent has been revoked at the owner's application, revocation will have retroactive effect in that the patent will be deemed not to have been granted.[573] Where the patent is cancelled at the owner's application, it will be deemed cancelled from the date of the cancellation application.[574]

B. *Revocation of Patent at the Request of a Third Party*

1. Procedure and Grounds for Third-Party Request

216. Under section 73B of the Law, the Registrar may, on application by any person who is not the patent holder, revoke a patent, if it found that there are grounds on which it was possible to oppose granting the patent. Grounds on which a patent grant may be opposed, as discussed above at section §4 'Formalities', are that: (i) there exists a reason for which the Registrar was entitled to refuse acceptance of the patent application;[575] (ii) that the invention is not patentable in light of a novelty-destroying prior use or display (these objections are not necessarily part

572. The Law, s. 78(f).
573. The Law, s. 73A(a).
574. The Law, s. 73A(b).
575. The Law, s. 31(1).

of the examination by the Patent Office);[576] or that the opponent and not the applicant was the owner of the invention.[577]

Under section 75 of the Law, a final revocation order obtained by the third party shall go into effect thirty days after the time for submitting appeal against it; however, if an appeal against it was submitted, then the court may postpone or set conditions for its coming into effect.[578]

2. Effect of Revocation at Third-Party Request

217. A patent finally revoked at the request of the third party is treated as if it had not been granted.[579]

In the *Blas v. Kibbutz Dan*[580] matter, the Supreme Court, while holding that under the applicable previous law, which did not provide for retroactivity of revocation, a licensee cannot recover royalties paid under a patent that turns out to be invalid, left open the question whether such rule would change after the enactment of section 75 of the Law, which provides for retroactive effect of a revocation.

C. Cancellation in the Public Interest due to Abuse of Monopoly

218. The Registrar may cancel a patent for which a compulsory license was granted, if satisfied that the granting of the license did not suffice to prevent the abuse of the monopoly which was the ground for granting the license. An application for such cancellation may be made, two years after the grant of the license, only by a person qualified to receive a compulsory license.[581]

Such cancellation goes into effect sixty days after the cancellation decision unless the court delays it pending appeal.[582]

These provisions were never applied.

D. Cancellation of Patent or Shortening of Patent Term Due to Breach of Duty of Disclosure

219. Under section 18C of the Law, the court or the Registrar has the power to cancel a granted patent or shorten its term in the event the patent holder breached his duty of disclosure at the examination stage by providing misleading particulars

576. The Law, s. 31(2).
577. The Law, s. 31(3).
578. The Law, s. 75(a).
579. The Law, s. 75(b).
580. CA 427/86 *Blas v. Kibbutz 'Dan'*. 43(3) P.D. 323 [1989] at 334–337 (the licensee argued against payment of royalties to the patent holder where the patent was revoked at the request of an unrelated third party for lack of novelty, not contested by the proprietor).
581. The Law, s. 129.
582. The Law, s. 130.

or knowingly withholding information regarding a substantive change in the list of publications and documents.[583]

E. Revocation by Court in Infringement Proceedings

220. Section 182 of the Law provides that, where the court in an infringement action accepts a defence relying on any grounds of opposition to the grant of a patent, it shall order the patent to be revoked in whole or in part, as the case may be.

A patent finally revoked in the course of infringement proceedings under section 182 is treated as if it had not been granted.[584]

F. Proceedings before Registrar during Pendency of Court Proceedings

221. If the patent owner files an application for revocation or cancellation, or a third party applies for revocation, while infringement or revocation proceedings are pending in court, then the Registrar shall hear it only with the court's permission.[585] If court proceedings for infringement commenced after an application for cancellation or revocation was filed, the Registrar shall continue to hear the application unless the court orders otherwise.[586] If the court permits the Registrar to hear an application for revocation of a patent the subject of a court action, it may stay the court proceedings before it concerning such patent, and each party may request the court to vary or cancel the stay order.[587]

§9. Infringement and Remedies

I. What Constitutes Infringement?

A. Definition of Infringement

222. As discussed above in section §6 'Scope of Exclusive Rights', infringement is defined in section 49(a) of the Patents Law as exploiting the patented invention without the proprietor's permission or unlawfully, either in the manner defined in the claims or in a similar manner which – in the light of what is defined by those claims – involves the essence of the patented invention.

583. The Law, s. 18C(1)(a) and (c). The patent was, for example, cancelled due to non-disclosure in contravention of the ongoing obligation imposed by s. 18C in CC 14/92 (Nazareth Distr.) *Plasson Maagan Michael Industries Ltd v. Freddi Priant et al.* [1993], at paras 26–27.

584. The Law, s. 75(b).

585. The Law, s. 74(a).

586. The Law, s. 74(c).

587. The Law, s. 191.

B. Infringement by Taking the 'Essence of the Invention'

223. In accordance with section 49(a) of the Patents Law, infringement is not limited to 'literal' infringement, but it is also infringement to take the 'essence of the invention'.[588]

The Supreme Court in *Hughes* cited with approval a district court decision in *Sapsha,*[589] which equated the taking of the essence, or substance, of the invention with the UK 'pith and marrow' test and held that literal infringement where the infringer will simply and openly perform exactly what is defined in the claims is very rare, and normally it is expected that an infringer would disguise the infringement by changing its product. However, if the changes are immaterial, such infringer will be deemed to have taken the 'pith and marrow' of the invention.[590] While defining the metes and bounds of the 'essence of the invention' doctrine, the Supreme Court in *Hughes* referred both to the UK doctrine of variations[591] and to the US doctrine of equivalents.

As the test for determining whether infringement took place, the *Hughes* court adopted the function-way-result test as enunciated in the US case of *Graver Tank.*[592] Thus, infringement may be found where the accused product performs 'substantially the same function in substantially the same way to obtain the same result' as the claimed invention.

It is to be noted that the *Hughes* authority does not necessarily require that the function-way-result test should be performed as element-by-element comparison, and the test has been applied also through comparison of the accused product to the invention as a whole.[593]

Furthermore, the Supreme Court in *Hughes* adopted the approach as pronounced by Lord Diplock in the UK *Catnic* case,[594] that a patent may be either infringed or not, and the distinction between literal copying and non-literal taking of the essence under section 49(a) is not meant to constitute two separate causes of action for infringement.

It has been held that the issue of the scope of the invention and what constitutes 'the essence of the invention' is an issue of law to be determined by the court[595] and not an issue of fact determined through expert testimony.

C. Claim Construction

224. Given the statutory definition of infringement as exploitation of the invention (in the manner defined by the patent claims or in a similar manner involving the essence of the invention in light of said claims), the scope of patent protection

588. See also *Hughes* at 69.
589. CC 2051/69 (TA Distr.) *Intco Installations et al. v. Sapsha*, 79 P.M. 240 [1972] at 248.
590. *Hughes* at 71.
591. *Hughes* at 71.
592. *Hughes* at 72; *Graver Tank & Mfg. Co., Inc. et al. v. Linde Air Products Co.*, 339 U.S. 605 [1950].
593. Cf. *Hughes* at 71–73.
594. *Catnic Components Ltd v. Hill & Smith Ltd* (1982) R.P.C. 183.
595. *Hughes* at 69.

for an invention is delineated by patent claims. The claims form the basis for determining whether an accused act amounts to infringement and therefore great importance is attached to claim construction.

The Supreme Court in *Hughes* held that proper patent construction requires reading the patent document as a whole, rather than the claims in isolation.[596] The Supreme Court further held that the patent claims must be given purposive, rather than strictly literal, construction. Claim construction is aimed at ascertaining the intention of the inventor expressed in the document, as perceived by a technical professional against the background of professional knowledge that existed on the determining date.[597] Certain flexibility is allowed in giving meaning to terms and expression in the claims in accordance with the meaning ascribed by the inventor in the specification.[598] The *Hughes* court also noted the need for caution due to the nature of the instrument as conferring monopoly.

Where a claim is unclear, it was held by the Supreme Court in the *Car Security* matter that a series of ancillary tests may be applied for determining claim construction, as follows. A greater degree of innovation and pioneering would afford greater liberality of construction, whereas a more modest inventive step would warrant a narrower reading of the claims.[599] While the starting point of analysis is that the scope of the claims is identical with the scope of the invention, the court must recognize that in some cases the inventor deliberately narrowed the scope of the claimed monopoly so as not to cover the entire invention that could potentially be patented.[600] Where the language of the claims is ambiguous without a justified reason (e.g., the complexity or novelty of the field), a narrow reading of the claims would be preferred according to the rule of interpretation against the author of the document.[601] A justified reason for ambiguous language may arise from such factors as the relative complexity of the field of the invention or objective difficulties in wording the invention (such as limitations on terminology).[602]

At times, when the meaning of the terms is not ascertainable from the patent document itself, interpretation may be assisted by external documents, such as correspondence with the Patent Offices, to ascertain the intention of the inventor. Nonetheless, it does not follow that the principle of file wrapper estoppel has been adopted, and its applicability under Israeli law was left open.[603] The IPTO held[604] that even if file wrapper estoppel were to be applied, it would not apply to actions taken before foreign patent offices.

596. *Hughes* at 65, also CA 407/89 *Tzuk Or Ltd v. Car Security Ltd*, 48(5) 661 [1994] (*Car Security*) at 684.
597. *Hughes* at 65, *Car Security* at 678.
598. *Hughes* at 65–66, *Lanplast* at 302.
599. *Car Security* at 691.
600. *Car Security* at 687, 690.
601. *Car Security* at 691.
602. *Car Security* at 691.
603. *Lanplast* at 303.
604. *FMS Enterprises Migun Ltd v. DSM IP Assets B.V.*, Opposition to patent application 142789 [2015].

D. *Without Permission or Unlawfully*

225. Statutory exceptions from the scope of 'exploitation of the invention' are discussed in section §7 'Limitations and Exceptions to the Scope of Patent Protection; Compulsory Licenses' above.

E. *Indirect Infringement*

226. While the Patents Law expressly provides only for the liability of a direct infringer and does not include explicit rules regarding indirect infringement, the Israeli Supreme Court, in several decisions, has determined that the concept of indirect patent infringement applies under Israeli law,[605] so that liability may be imposed on persons who collaborate with the infringer by facilitating the infringement or inducing it.

1. Accessory Liability: Inducing and Abetting Infringement

227. While the liability for indirect patent infringement may in principle be anchored in the general provisions of the Civil Wrongs Ordinance [New Version], 5728-1968 (the 'Civil Wrongs Ordinance'), which address the liability of persons abetting or inducing the commitment of a tort as joint tortfeasors, these provisions would not, in many cases, be applicable to infringement under the Patents Law, since the accessory liability for facilitating or inducing infringement requires both a showing of direct infringement and concerted action between the accessory and the direct infringer; hence, the applicability of the accessory liability doctrine is narrower than that of the contributory infringement doctrine.[606]

2. Contributory Infringement

228. Contributory infringement as an independent cause of action was established in 2001 as court-made law, in the judgment of the Supreme Court in the *Rav Bariach*[607] matter, where the Court held that the contributory infringement concept applies in Israel. Under the doctrine of contributory infringement, liability may be found also where no connection between the direct infringer and the contributory infringer is shown. In the *Rav Bariach* case, the indirect infringer was selling two out of three components of a patented invention defined in the claims, hence not directly infringing the patent. The Court set the following requirements for determining contributory infringement: (1) the components used by the indirect

605. CA 1636/98 *Rav Bariach Ltd v. Havashush Car Accessories Trading House (1987) Ltd*, 55 (5) P.D. 337 [2001] (*Rav Bariach*).
606. *Rav Bariach* at 352.
607. *Rav Bariach* at 353.

infringer formed a substantial part of the patented invention; (2) the indirect infringer knew, or should have known, that the components would be used for infringing the patent; and (3) the components were not 'staple commercial products' suitable for a substantial non-infringing use. It is not clear from the *Rav Bariach* ruling whether a showing of direct infringement is a precondition for establishing contributory infringement.[608]

II. Right of Action

A. *Who Can Sue?*

229. The right to bring an action for infringement is given to the patent holder or the exclusive licensee.[609] Where the proprietor has not joined the action brought by the exclusive licensee as a plaintiff, or *vice versa*, he must be joined as a defendant.[610] Similarly, where the patent is owned by several owners, each of the joint owners may bring an action, provided that the other joint owners are joined to the action either as plaintiffs or as defendants.[611]

B. *Only Post-grant Actions Are Possible*

230. Under section 179 of the Patents Law, an action for infringement shall not be brought until the patent has been granted; but once an action for infringement has been brought, the Court may grant relief for a pre-grant infringement committed after the date of publication under section 16A.[612] Attempts have been made to rely on the Unjust Enrichment Law in order to seek injunctions after the acceptance of a patent application while it was under opposition. In accordance with the Unjust Enrichment Law,[613] equitable remedy thereunder may be granted where there are no special provisions to that effect in another law. In 2011, the Supreme Court ruled in the *Merck* matter[614] that the Unjust Enrichment Law was not applicable in this regard, because the provisions of section 179 of the Patents Law represent an exhaustive arrangement, which deliberately omits the possibility of pre-grant actions and therefore rules out the application of the Unjust Enrichment Law.

608. *Rav Bariach* at 355 at para. 35 (refers to the commission of direct infringement as a precondition under US law and determines that in this case there was direct infringement as well).
609. The Law, s. 178.
610. The Law, s. 178.
611. The Law, s. 178.
612. The Law, s. 179 as amended in 2012.
613. The Unjust Enrichment Law, s. 6(a).
614. LCA 6025/05 *Merck & Co. Inc. et al. v. Teva Pharmaceutical Industries Ltd et al.* [2011] at paras 33–34.

III. Evidence

231. The burden of proof regarding infringement rests with the plaintiff (proprietor). The burden of proof regarding invalidity of the patent rests with the defendant.[615]

232. A district court held that a plaintiff must bring evidence of infringement before the defendant brings its own evidence. Where the plaintiff failed to do so fresh evidence on infringement it filed within its evidence in reply was removed from the court's file.[616]

IV. Defences

233. The defendant in an infringement action may claim in defence that the plaintiff's patent is invalid or claim that the accused use is not infringing.

Defence of invalidity. In accordance with section 182 of the Law, it is a good defence in an infringement action to raise any ground on which the grant of the patent could have been opposed. If the defence is accepted, the patent will be ordered wholly or partially revoked.[617] The foregoing enunciation of defences is not exhaustive.[618]

Where the infringement action relates to a patent extended by a patent term extension order, it is a good defence to raise any ground on which the extension order may be cancelled or shortened; if the defence is successful, the extension order will be cancelled or shortened.[619]

Activity not an infringement. A defendant may argue that its activity does not fall within the patent claims or within the scope of activities statutorily defined as 'exploitation'. Furthermore, certain use constituting 'exploitation' and falling within the patent claims may be excepted as permissible use (discussed above in section §7 'Limitations and Exceptions to the Scope of Patent Protection').

V. Application to Amend during Infringement Proceedings

234. In the context of infringement proceedings in court, the patent holder may apply to have the patent specification amended (for allowable amendments, see the discussion in section §4 'Formalities', section III above).

615. CA 7623/10 *Hydro Noa (unregistered partnership) v. San Hitech Ltd* [2014] at s. 12.
616. CC (TA Distr.) 53424-12-10 *Aerotel Ltd v. Cellcom Israel Ltd et al.* [2015].
617. The Law, s. 182(a).
618. CA (TA Distr.) 3032/06 *Kamil v. Bezeq International Ltd* [2007]; CC (Tel Aviv Distr.) 2284/83 *Hydroplane Engineering Ltd v. Naan Metal Factory*, 5744(2) P.M. 133 [1983].
619. The Law, s. 182(a1) and (a2).

VI. Remedies

A. Final Remedies

235. Under section 183(a) of the Patents Law, a plaintiff is entitled to relief by way of an injunction and damages.

Injunction. Permanent injunction is the central remedy that follows from the essence of a patent holder's right conferred by the patent, namely the right to prevent exploitation by others. Nonetheless it is within the discretion of the court whether an order for permanent injunction is appropriate upon the facts of the case.

Compensation. Compensation, according to section 183(b) of the Law, is to be determined having regard to the infringement and the plaintiff's situation as a result of the infringement, including such factors as the direct damage to the plaintiff, the extent of infringement, the profits derived by the infringer and reasonable royalties. In the *Beecham Group Limited v. Bristol Myers Company* decision,[620] the Supreme Court treated the list of considerations in section 183(b) as a non-exhaustive list and emphasized that the method by which damages are to be calculated in a given case is discretionary. In the *Ein Tal* decision[621] of 2005, the Supreme Court cited additional factors that may be considered when assessing damages, which include the 'type' of the product sold (whether it is sold as an independent unit or together with other products). After holding that damage had been inflicted and that there was a causal connection between the infringement and the damage, the court ruled that in assessing the damages it ought to take into consideration also the loss of sales of products that accompany the patented product. Thus, ancillary damages, whether consequential or pure economic loss, may be obtained provided that the loss is duly proved through evidence showing causal connection between the infringement and the claimed ancillary damages.

Infringement prior to patent expiry with post-expiry effect. Where the infringement took place before patent expiry, and consequently a springboard effect is shown, damages caused by the defendant's early entry to the market after expiry that are attributable to the springboard effect may in principle be obtained.

Order for accounts; damages by assessment. An accounting may be ordered for the purpose of calculation of damages but will not be binding on the court.[622] Alternatively, compensation may be awarded by way of judicial assessment (damages at large).[623]

Compensation without proof of damage. The Law contains no express provision for awarding compensation for patent infringement without proof of damage. Following a Supreme Court decision which noted, in an *obiter dictum*, that it was possible to award compensation for design infringement without proof of damage, even though the awarding of such damages is not anchored in statute,[624] a 2013 district

620. CA 817/77 *Beecham Group Ltd v. Bristol-Myers Co.*, 33 (3) P.D. 757 [1979].
621. CA 3400/03 *Rubinstein et al. v. Ein Tal (1983) Ltd et al.*, 59(6) P.D. 490 [2005] (*Ein Tal 2005*).
622. The Law, s. 183(d).
623. *Ein Tal 2005* at 503–504.
624. CA 3853/11 *Ronit National Flags Ltd. et al. v. Shatan et al.* [2013]

court decision awarded compensation without proof of damage for patent infringement, drawing inspiration from statutory damages provisions in other IP laws;[625] however, its ruling in this respect was overturned by the Supreme Court and the case was remanded to the lower court for determining damages by assessment.[626] (In an unrelated 2014 decision, the Supreme Court held that it was not possible to award compensation without proof of damage for trademark infringement, absent express statutory authority to do so.[627]) It thus appears that the Supreme Court views compensation without proof of damage as inappropriate for patent infringement cases, absent an express provision therefor in the statute and given the compensatory, rather than punitive, principle of compensation in patent law.

Punitive damages. Where infringement continued after a cease-and-desist warning by the proprietor or the exclusive licensee, compensation may in the court's discretion comprise, in addition to an award of actual damages, also punitive damages in an amount not exceeding the actual damages, so that entire compensation in such case may reach double the amount of actual damages.[628]

Damages where the patent was partially cancelled or amended. A partial revocation of a patent does not by itself rule out damages; however, damages may be refused if the claims in the original patent were formulated in bad faith or vaguely.[629] Where a patent is amended subsequent to the filing of an infringement action, the court may in determining damages disregard the amendment if the claims in the original patent were formulated in bad faith or vaguely.[630]

The court may also refrain from awarding damages in the case of a lapsed patent that was reinstated, in respect of the infringement between the original deadline for maintenance fees and their actual payment.[631]

Additional remedies. Additional remedies may be granted, such as a receivership order, delivery-up, recall, destruction or other remedy deemed appropriate by the court.

B. Remedies for Pre-grant Exploitation

236. Section 179 of the Law, as amended in 2012, provides that once an action for infringement has been brought, which can only be done after the patent has been granted, the court may award damages for the exploitation of the invention made between the early publication of the application under section 16A and its actual grant. Compensation in respect of infringement that occurred after early publication of the application (under section 16A) and before publication of acceptance of the patent application (under section 26) is limited to damages in the amount of reasonable royalties. For the period between the publication of the acceptance of a patent

625. CC (TA Distr.) 1133-09-10 *Twitoplast Ltd. v. Tavig - Israel Gruber Ltd. et al.* [2013]
626. CA 7201/13 *Tavig - Israel Gruber Ltd. Et al. v. Twitoplast Ltd.* [2015]
627. CA 7629/12 *Swissa et al. v. Tommy Hilfiger Licensing LLC et al.* [2014] (see the discussion in the Trademarks chapter *infra*).
628. The Law, s. 183(c).
629. The Law, s. 184.
630. The Law, s. 185.
631. The Law, s. 186.

application and grant of the patent thereon, any type of compensation may be awarded at the discretion of the court.

C. *Interim Relief*

237. Pending the judgment in the case-in-chief, a plaintiff may seek preliminary relief, such as, for example, preliminary injunctions, receivership orders, *Anton Piller*-type search-and-seizure orders and attachment orders.

Preliminary relief, anchored in the Civil Procedure Rules, 5744 – 1984 (*Civil Procedure Rules*), retains characteristics of equitable remedies. Therefore, interim relief must be petitioned for in good faith, and the court considers whether granting the relief is just and appropriate in the circumstances.[632] Thus, for example, failure by the party seeking the preliminary relief to disclose to the court an important fact, particularly in an *ex parte* application, may by itself cause the denial of the motion for interlocutory injunction.[633] The plaintiff should also bring the petition for relief in a timely manner; excessive delay – depending on the circumstances – may amount to *laches* and cause the denial of the motion.

Generally, a motion for an interim injunction must demonstrate the urgency and importance of intervention by the court at an early stage of the proceedings, in order to preserve the status quo until the judgment and to prevent irreparable harm. Particularly, a party seeking interlocutory relief needs to show a *prima facie* likelihood of success in the case-in-chief and that the balance of convenience tilts in his favour.

The court may grant *ex parte* relief where the court is satisfied on the basis of *prima facie* reliable evidence that there exists a reasonable apprehension that delay of the hearing until an *inter partes* hearing will render the order moot or cause severe harm to the petitioner.[634] An *inter partes* hearing must be held within fourteen days of the grant of an *ex parte* order.[635]

Anton Piller-type order. An *Anton Piller*-type search-and-seizure order may be granted where the court is convinced by *prima facie* reliable evidence that a real apprehension exists that the respondent or anyone on its behalf is about to suppress or destroy evidence or objects requisite for the trial of the claim and that the trial of the claim will be substantially impeded as a result.[636] The court must exercise extra caution when issuing an order *ex parte*. The entry into the premises of the defendant is made by an independent receiver who acts as an officer of the court, in order to prevent abuse of the order by the plaintiff, who might otherwise become exposed to sensitive information of a competitor.

In preliminary injunction proceedings, the court will normally rely on the registration of a patent as evidence of its validity; the assumption of validity is based on

---

632. The Civil Procedure Rules, Rule 362.

633. See, for example, CC (TA Distr.) 18514-12-13 *Magnetica Interactive Ltd v. Ambrosia Supherb Ltd* [2014] (the applicant licensee's failure to disclose the fact of refusal of an identical patent application by the USPTO was taken into consideration in the court's decision to refuse interim relief).

634. The Civil Procedure Rules, Rule 366.

635. The Civil Procedure Rules, Rule 367.

636. The Civil Procedure Rules, Rule 387A.

the fact that the patent was granted following an examination. The defendant's ability to put the validity of a patent at issue, as an exception to the assumption of validity, is limited to cases where it can bring convincing evidence, such as prior art publication that, *prima facie* and without need for thorough inquiry, demonstrates the invalidity.[637]

D. Post-expiry Injunction

238. The law is not settled on the question of whether a post-expiry injunction may be granted where the defendant infringed prior to patent expiry in order to increase sales immediately on expiry of the patent, i.e., obtain a springboard into the market, for example, by stockpiling products ready for launch. There are conflicting district court rulings on this subject.[638] In one case,[639] the court noted that, in principle, a court may award, as a remedy for patent infringement, a post-expiry injunction, while in another,[640] the district court was against the grant of a post-expiry injunction prohibiting the use of information gathered during infringement (and indicated that the appropriate remedy would be damages).

VII. Declaratory Judgment of Non-infringement

239. In accordance with section 187 of the Law, a person intending to exploit any product or process may – if it first approached the patent holder for a declaration of non-infringement, without success – apply to the court for a declaratory judgment according to which the intended exploitation does not constitute an infringement of the specific patent. Respondents in such application are the patent holder and the exclusive licensee. In an application for such declaratory judgment, the applicant cannot make the argument that the patent is invalid, and the grant or refusal of the declaration shall not be decisive on the question of the patent's validity.

§10. Overlapping and Relation to Other Intellectual Property Rights

I. Patents and Trade Secrets

240. In principle, an invention can be protected as a trade secret as long as it is not published, including during the pendency of a patent application until its

637. LCA 11964/04 *Zafi Profil Chen (1983) Ltd v. Azoulay et al.*, 59(3) P.D. 350 [2005], LCA 920/05 *Hassin Esh Industries Ltd v. Cunial Antonio (Israel) Ltd* [2005].
638. CC 1512/93 (TA Distr.) *The Wellcome Foundation Ltd v. Teva Pharmaceutical Industries Ltd et al.* [1994] and CC 881/94 (TA Distr.) *Eli Lilly and Company v. Teva Pharmaceutical Industries Ltd et al.* [1998].
639. CC 881/94 (TA Distr.) *Eli Lilly & Co. v. Teva Pharmaceutical Indus. Ltd*, Takdin-Dist. (98) 3 1586.
640. CC 1512/93 (TA Distr.) *The Wellcome Foundation Ltd v. Teva Pharmaceutical Industries Ltd*, Dinim-Dist. 26(8) 658.

publication,[641] which as of 2012 occurs within eighteen months of the filing or the priority date (see section 147). Thus, if a patent application is abandoned or rejected before its publication, it should in principle be possible to maintain its protection as a trade secret. Once the application is published, even if no patent is eventually granted or the patent is subsequently found to be invalid, there is no protection as a trade secret for the content disclosed in the specification.[642]

There is also an opinion that the provisions of section 132 of the Patents Law regarding the ownership of service inventions[643] also apply to trade secrets. This is because section 132 refers to 'inventions' and is not limited to 'patentable inventions', let alone patents.

II. Patents and Copyright

241. Copyright protection[644] may be afforded to the form of expression of a patented invention and the susceptibility of an invention for patent protection does not preclude protection under the Copyright Act of certain aspects of the invention and *vice versa.*

III. Patents and Plant Breeders Rights

242. Section 7(2) of the Patents Law excludes plant varieties from patentable subject matter. In Israel, there is protection for the rights of plant breeders in new varieties of plants under the Plants Breeders Rights Law, 5733 – 1973, discussed in detail in Chapter 5 'Plant Variety Protection'.

An Israeli invention was the subject of prolonged litigation before the various instances of the European Patent Office, which revolved around the relations and boundaries between Plants Breeders' Rights (PBR) and patents. Israeli corresponding patent[645] was granted without opposition, and no proceeding was held in respect of section 7(2) of the Patents Law, which has to date remained absent from being addressed in the IPTO.

IV. Patents and Trademarks/Passing Off

243. In principle, copying of functional features of a product is not protectable by the tort of passing off.[646] In one of the leading cases on passing off, the *Amichai*

641. Discussed in s. §4 'Formalities'.
642. Miguel Deutch, *Commercial Torts and Trade Secrets* (2002), at 465.
643. See s. §5 'Ownership and Transfer', *supra.*
644. See Ch. 1 'Copyright and Neighbouring Rights'.
645. IL131509.
646. CA 18/86 *Phoenicia Israeli Glass Works Ltd v. Les Verreries de Saint Gobain*, 45(3) P.D. 224 [1991] at 236.

Trade[647] matter, the Supreme Court, while upholding in the circumstances of the case protection under the tort of passing off (discussed at greater length in Chapter 3 'Trademarks') for a sandal formerly protected by a patent that lapsed (as the Court found that the copied features were not functional), left open the issue as to whether the existence of a lapsed patent for a product is relevant for passing off protection as evidence of the functionality of the product.

As to the possibility of trademark protection for products protected or protectable by patents, the Supreme Court held in the *Storck*[648] and *Ein Gedi*[649] cases that, given the different rationale and duration of patent protection and that of trademarks, functional products *per se* cannot be protected through trademarks, so as not to deprive the public in perpetuity of the useful features.[650]

V. Patents and Unjust Enrichment

244. The Unjust Enrichment Law, 5739 – 1979 applies to provide for restitution where no specific provision exists to that effect in another statute. In the leading case of *A.S.I.R.*, discussed in detail in Chapter 6 'Unjust Enrichment', the majority opinion of the Supreme Court was that the laws of unjust enrichment may apply alongside the laws of intellectual property.[651] Thus, even when a patent was not applied for, alternative protection for innovative inventions may be available under the Unjust Enrichment Law. However, the duration of protection would be shorter,[652] and protection may be available only upon showing that the elements of such cause of action exist.

Multiple causes of action, and reliance on the laws of unjust enrichment in particular, should not result in double recovery.[653]

As discussed at greater length in section §9 'Infringement and Remedies', in the 2011 *Merck* matter,[654] the Supreme Court held that, given a different arrangement in the Patents Law as *lex specialis* (which envisages only post-grant actions), interim injunctive relief cannot be obtained under the Unjust Enrichment Law to protect an invention subject of a pending patent application. A statutory provision limiting causes of actions in respect of inventions to actions in respect of valid patents has been proposed but so far not been enacted.

647. CA 4030/02 *Amichai Trade Ltd v. Source Vagabond Systems Ltd*, 58 (5) P.D. 632 [2004] at 637–638.
648. CA 11487/03 *August Storck KG et al. v. Alpha Intuit Foodstuffs Ltd et al.* [2008].
649. CA 3776/06 *Ein Gedi Cosmetics v. Registrar of Trademarks* [2008].
650. In the *Cyber* matter – *Application to register trademark 218060 (RADIO ISRAEL) in the name of Cyber Guy Enterprise and Marketing Ltd* [2010] – it was observed that a patent holder will not be able to extend patent protection after the lapse of a patent by way of registering a trademark depicting the patented product.
651. LCA 5798/94 et al. *A.S.I.R. Import Manufacture and Distribution Ltd v. Forum Accessories and Consumer Goods Ltd*, 52(4) P.D. 289 [1998] at 422–425.
652. CA 3894/03 *Deutsch v. Israflowers Ltd*, 2012 (110) Dinim Supr. 379 [2012].
653. For example, CA 2634/09 *Rotenberg v. Elgo Irrigation Ltd* [2011].
654. LCA 6025/05 *Merck & Co. Inc. et al. v. Teva Pharmaceutical Industries Ltd et al.* [2011] at paras 33–34.

Chapter 3. Trademarks

§1. Sources: Legislation

I. General Overview

245. The law of trademarks in Israel takes its origin in the British legislation dating from the time of the British civil administration of Palestine between 1920 and 1948, ratified by the League of Nations mandate. Trademark protection comprehends civil liability for infringement and criminal liability for counterfeiting, false marking and other fraudulent activities.

Civil liability. The protection of registered trademarks and of unregistered well-known trademarks in Israel is governed primarily by the Trade Marks Ordinance [New Version], 5732 – 1972 (the 'Trade Marks Ordinance' or the 'Ordinance'), which imposes civil liability for unlawful use of registered marks and of marks shown to be well known. Several other statutes provide additional sources of liability in tort. Unregistered trademarks may also be entitled to protection under the tort of passing off codified in the Commercial Torts Law, 5759 – 1999 (the 'Commercial Torts Law'). Further protection may be afforded under the doctrine of unjust enrichment codified in the Unjust Enrichment Law, 5739 – 1979 (the 'Unjust Enrichment Law'), which may be invoked to prevent unfair use of another trader's goodwill, and under the tort of consumer deception proscribed in the Consumer Protection Law, 5741 – 1981 (the 'Consumer Protection Law').

Criminal liability. Certain types of fraudulent conduct, such as counterfeiting trademarks and falsely marking goods, give rise to criminal liability under the Trade Marks Ordinance, under the Merchandise Marks Ordinance, 1929 (the 'Merchandise Marks Ordinance') and under the Consumer Protection Law.

II. Specific Acts of Legislation

A. *The Trade Marks Ordinance and Trade Marks Regulations*

246. The primary act of legislation applicable to trademarks is the Trade Marks Ordinance, a revised version of the formerly applicable British Trade Marks Ordinance no. 35 of 1938, which in turn was based on the British Trade Marks Law of 1905. The so-called New Version of the Trade Marks Ordinance was determined by a parliamentary committee of the Israeli legislature in accordance with statutorily prescribed procedure.[655] Since its adoption, the Trade Marks Ordinance has been

655. The new (Hebrew) version was adopted by the Constitution, Legislation and Law Committee in accordance with the Law and Administration Ordinance, 5708-1948, s. 16. As a principle of interpretation, the governing version of a law is the language in which the law was issued (the Interpretation Law, 5741-1981, s. 24). However, where a new version of a pre-1948 English-language statute is adopted by the Constitution, Legislation and Law Committee in accordance with s. 16 of the Law and Administration Ordinance, 5708-1948, which defines the scope of its powers and the procedure to be followed, such version prevails (the Interpretation Law, 5741-1981, s. 24).

amended by several legislative acts enacted by the *Knesset* through a full-fledged legislative process.

The Trade Marks Ordinance governs the registration, validity and maintenance of trademarks[656] and defines the scope of exclusive rights conferred by a registered trademark as well as by unregistered well-known trademarks.[657] The Ordinance addresses the civil tort of trademark infringement[658] and imposes criminal liability for certain activities such as unauthorized, or counterfeit, marking of goods.[659] Offences under the Trade Marks Ordinance may also be prosecuted by way of criminal proceedings brought by an aggrieved private person.[660]

The amendments made over the years to the Trade Marks Ordinance have been primarily designed to bring Israel's law into conformity with the international treaties to which Israel has acceded over the years. Thus, following Israel's accession to the TRIPS Agreement in 1999 the Trade Marks Ordinance was amended to reflect Israel's undertakings thereunder.[661]

In 2005[662] and in 2007,[663] the Trade Marks Ordinance was amended to reflect Israel's accession to the Protocol relating to the Madrid Agreement Concerning the International Registration of Marks (the 'Madrid Protocol'); such amendments went into full effect on 1 September 2010. The prominent changes are the mechanism for processing international applications and a change of the initial registration and renewal terms. In 2010, the Trade Marks Ordinance was further amended[664] to change the channels of appellate review under the Ordinance in line with the ongoing comprehensive judicial reform.

Procedural aspects of various issues relating to, e.g., trademark prosecution, maintenance and removal from the register, are governed by the Trade Marks Regulations, 1940. The Trade Marks Regulations (Implementation of the Madrid Protocol), 5767 – 2007, set forth the procedure for processing international applications originating in or designating Israel.

In addition, the Trademarks Registrar issues from time to time Circular Letters on issues of procedure, which serve as administrative guidelines.[665]

B. Other Applicable Acts of Legislation

247. The Commercial Torts Law. Regardless of registration, trademarks may be entitled to protection under the tort of passing off codified in section 1 of the

656. The Trade Marks Ordinance, Chs 2, 3, 4, 5 and 6.
657. The Trade Marks Ordinance, Ch. 7.
658. The Trade Marks Ordinance, Ch. 9.
659. The Trade Marks Ordinance, Ch. 10.
660. The Criminal Procedure Law [Consolidated Version], 5742-1982, s. 68; the Trade Marks Ordinance, s. 60.
661. The Law for the Amendment of Intellectual Property Laws: Modifications to Implement the Provisions of the TRIPS Agreement, 5760-1999.
662. By way of the Law for the Amendment of the Trade Marks Ordinance (No. 5), 5763-2005.
663. By way of the Law for the Amendment of the Trade Marks Ordinance (No. 6), 5767-2007.
664. By way of the Law for the Amendment of the Trade Marks Ordinance (No. 7), 5770-2010.
665. Circular Letter No. 001/2011 of 28 Aug. 2012.

Commercial Torts Law.[666] The Commercial Torts Law provides for a number of remedies specific to this Law; subject to the provisions of the Commercial Torts Law, the principles of the Civil Wrongs Ordinance [New Version][667] (the '*Civil Wrongs Ordinance*') apply to commercial torts under the Commercial Torts Law.[668] If the requirements for a passing off action[669] are met, such action may offer protection to the owner of a mark that is not protected under the Trade Marks Ordinance due to its being unregistered or unregistrable. Certain torts under the Civil Wrongs Ordinance, such as injurious falsehood, may be invoked in appropriate circumstances to supplement trademark protection.[670]

The Unjust Enrichment Law. Additional protection for trademarks, regardless of their registration, may be available under the doctrine of unjust enrichment codified in the Unjust Enrichment Law, which may be invoked to prevent unfair use of another trader's goodwill.[671]

The Consumer Protection Law. The Consumer Protection Law makes deceptive practices, including misrepresentation as to the name, commercial appellation or sponsorship of a product or service, as well as misrepresentation as to the manufacturer or importer of a product or the provider of a service,[672] a civil wrong actionable under the Civil Wrongs Ordinance[673] and imposes criminal liability for it.[674] The civil action under the Consumer Protection Law is available not only to an aggrieved consumer[675] but also to an aggrieved trader.[676] Certain offences under the Consumer Protection Law in respect of labelling of goods may also be prosecuted by way of criminal proceedings brought by an aggrieved private person.[677]

The Merchandise Marks Ordinance and the Civil Wrongs Ordinance. The Merchandise Marks Ordinance (an amended British ordinance) provides for criminal liability for designating goods by a false trade description or counterfeit trademark.[678] A person aggrieved by offences under the Merchandise Marks Ordinance in respect of false description of goods may bring a private criminal complaint.[679]

---

666. The Commercial Torts Law, s. 1; formerly anchored in the Civil Wrongs Ordinance [New Version], s. 59.
667. A new version of a British ordinance of 1947 adopted in 1968.
668. The Commercial Torts Law, s. 11.
669. Discussed in s. §11 'Overlapping and Relation to Other Intellectual Property Rights', s. II.A 'Passing Off', *infra*.
670. The Civil Wrongs Ordinance, s. 58.
671. The Unjust Enrichment Law, s. 1. Discussed in s. §11 'Overlapping and Relation to Other Intellectual Property Rights', *infra*.
672. The Consumer Protection Law, s. 2(a).
673. The Consumer Protection Law, s. 31(a).
674. The Consumer Protection Law, s. 23(a)(1).
675. The Consumer Protection Law, s. 31(a1).
676. The Consumer Protection Law, s. 31(a1). Discussed in s. §11 'Overlapping and Relation to Other Intellectual Property Rights', *infra*.
677. The Criminal Procedure Law [Consolidated Version], 5742-1982, s. 68.
678. The Merchandise Marks Ordinance, ss 1 and 3.
679. The Criminal Procedure Law [Consolidated Version], 5742-1982, s. 68; the Merchandise Marks Ordinance, s. 3.

In conjunction with the tort of breach of statutory duty under the Civil Wrongs Ordinance,[680] the Merchandise Marks Ordinance may be invoked as the basis for civil liability. It has been noted, however, by the Supreme Court[681] that the provisions of the Merchandise Marks Ordinance form the criminal facet of the tort of passing off so that the protection under the former coincides with that of the latter.

The Customs Ordinance. The Customs Ordinance [New Version] (the 'Customs Ordinance') (a 1957 new version of the British Ordinance No. 11 of 1929, as amended) empowers the Customs Commissioner to detain goods suspected of trademark infringement, subject to a procedure of notifying, and requesting indemnification guarantee from, the trademark owner.[682] The trademark owner may initiate the exercise of such power by notice to the Customs authorities.[683]

III. Trademark Jurisprudence

248. An important source of law alongside statutory provisions in the area of trademarks is jurisprudence.[684] The body of case law comprises the decisions of the Registrar of Trade Marks (the 'Registrar') appointed by the Minister of Justice and the courts of various instances.

Only case law handed down by the Supreme Court, which sits as the Court of Appeals over the district courts,[685] is binding as precedent.[686] District courts have first-instance jurisdiction over infringement claims[687] and appellate jurisdiction over the decisions of the Registrar;[688] their decisions as well as those of the Registrar have suggestive, but not precedential value; however, the decisions of district courts guide magistrates' courts.[689]

Israeli courts have traditionally drawn upon English jurisprudence, especially in the interpretation of statutes originating with the British administration, and have been willing to draw inspiration from relevant sources of comparative law, *inter alia*, from the practice in the US and other common law countries and the practice in the EU.

680. The Civil Wrongs Ordinance, s. 63.
681. CA 490/85 *Jericho Salts Ltd v. Dead Sea Enterprises Ltd*, 41(4) P.D. 401 [1987].
682. The Customs Ordinance, s. 200A.
683. Discussed in s. §10 'Infringement and Remedies', *infra*.
684. The Foundations of Law, 5740-1980, s. 1.
685. The Courts Law [Consolidated Version], 5744-1984, s. 41; the Trade Marks Ordinance, s. 63C. Until 1 Sep. 2010, the Supreme Court had parallel first-instance jurisdiction in certain proceedings under the Trade Marks Ordinance and was the Court of First Appeal.
686. The Basic Law: The Judicature, s. 20(b).
687. The Courts Law [Consolidated Version], 5744-1984, s. 40(4).
688. The Trade Marks Ordinance, ss 19 (refusal of application), 25 (opposition), 29 (rival claims), 30(b) (concurrent use), 36(b) (amendment of registration at proprietor's request), 37(b) (alteration of the mark at proprietor's request), 38(b) (rectification of the register at third-party request), 41(e) (cancellation), 45(b) (amendment of registration as to goods/classes), 49(b) (registration of transfer), 53 (registration of authorization).
689. The Basic Law: The Judicature, s. 20.

§2. Subject Matter of Protection

I. Signs Which May Serve as Trademarks

249. Definition of a mark. A 'mark' is defined in the Trade Marks Ordinance as 'letters, numerals, words, devices or other signs, or combinations thereof, whether two-dimensional or three-dimensional'.[690] The definition of a mark under the Trade Marks Ordinance is broad enough to allow for registration of various graphic marks, including stylized or non-stylized words, letters, numerals and pictorial devices, alone or in combination, and leaves room for the registration of 'other signs'. Three-dimensional marks are eligible for registration, provided they meet other registrability criteria.

Script and language of a mark. Marks may be registered in any language.[691]

Other signs: sounds, scents, flavours. The term 'other signs' in the definition of a 'mark' in the Trade Marks Ordinance seems to open the gate for the registration of non-traditional trademarks. The term 'other signs' has been interpreted to include sound marks, registrable in the form of a sequence of music notes or other notation of sound, such as sound frequencies.[692] Registrability of scents and flavours has not yet been addressed in case law.

II. Different Categories of Marks

A. Trademark and Service Mark

250. Israeli law recognizes trademarks, which are used, or intended to be used, by a person in relation to goods that he manufactures or deals in,[693] and service marks used, or intended to be used by a person in relation to a service provided by him.[694] Service marks are treated like trademarks, and statutory provisions applicable to trademarks are deemed to apply to service marks with requisite changes.[695]

B. Collective Marks

251. The Trade Marks Ordinance recognizes collective marks and regards them as trademarks or service marks.[696] A collective mark is a trademark or service mark

690. The Trade Marks Ordinance, s. 1.
691. The Registrar may require that any application with wording in languages other than Hebrew or Arabic be accompanied with translation (the Trade Marks Regulations, s. 21).
692. E. Seligsohn, *The Law of Trade Marks and Neighbouring Laws* 6–7 (Tel Aviv 1972) (*Seligsohn*). Sound marks have indeed been registered upon the presentation of musical notation of the mark and a deposit of a sample recording.
693. The Trade Marks Ordinance, s. 1.
694. The Trade Marks Ordinance, s. 1.
695. The Trade Marks Ordinance, s. 2.
696. The Trade Marks Ordinance, s. 3.

that belongs to an association of persons who have an interest in the goods or service covered by the mark and who use or intend to use the mark in respect of such goods or service.[697] A collective mark would be registered if the Registrar is satisfied that the mark is intended for use by members of the association of persons concerned and that such association exercises control over the use of the mark by its members.[698] Use of a collective mark by a member of the association is attributed to the association.[699] The transfer of a collective mark requires the permission of the Registrar.[700]

C. Certification Mark

252. Israeli law allows for the protection of certification marks and regards them as trademarks or service marks.[701] A certification mark is defined as a mark intended to be used by a person other than a person carrying on a business, to certify the origin of goods in which he has an interest, their components, mode of manufacture, quality or other characteristics, or to certify the nature, quality or type of a service in which he has an interest.[702]

A certification mark would be registered if the Registrar is satisfied that the proprietor of the mark is competent to certify the characteristics designated by the mark.[703] A certification mark need not be distinctive in order to be registered.[704]

The transfer of a certification mark requires the permission of the Registrar.[705]

§3. Conditions for Protection

I. Overview of Protection under the Trade Marks Ordinance

253. Protection through registration. Protection under the laws of trademarks is afforded, primarily, to registered trademarks. Marks may be registered directly as national marks or through pursuance of the national stage of an international application. Except for well-known marks, non-registered trademarks may be protected under other causes of action, in particular the tort of passing off.

Protection of unregistered marks under the Trade Marks Ordinance. Under the Ordinance as amended in 1999 so as to accommodate the provisions of the TRIPS

697. The Trade Marks Ordinance, s. 1.
698. The Trade Marks Ordinance, s. 15(a).
699. The Trade Marks Ordinance, s. 15(b).
700. The Trade Marks Ordinance, s. 15(c).
701. The Trade Marks Ordinance, s. 3.
702. The Trade Marks Ordinance, s. 1.
703. The Trade Marks Ordinance, s. 14(a).
704. The Trade Marks Ordinance, s. 14(b).
705. The Trade Marks Ordinance, s. 14(c).

Agreement, well-known marks may be protected to an extent also absent registration.[706]

II. Eligibility for Registration

A. Overview of Criteria of Eligibility for Registration

254. Marks Eligible for Registration – General. In order to be eligible for registration, a mark must satisfy the requirements set forth below:

- *The mark must function, or be intended to function, as a trademark.* To constitute a registrable trademark, a mark (as defined) must be used, or intended to be used, by a person 'in relation to goods he manufactures or deals in', and for service marks, 'in relation to a service he renders'.[707] The mark must be a sign capable of serving as a mark.[708]
- *The mark must possess a distinctive character,* that is, must be capable of distinguishing the goods or services of the owner of the mark from the goods or services of third parties.[709] Specific grounds of refusal define certain categories of marks as inherently non-distinctive and therefore non-registrable unless shown to have acquired a distinctive character through use (secondary meaning).
- *Registration of a mark may be refused on either absolute or relative grounds.* Israeli law recognizes absolute grounds for refusal of registration based on policy considerations and relative grounds for refusal that address the mark's potential conflict with the rights of third parties.

The foregoing fundamental requirements are discussed in more depth below.

Conditions for telle quelle registration. Conditions for *telle quelle* registration in accordance with Article 6 *quinques* of the Paris Convention, are less restrictive, as discussed below.

B. Function as a Trademark

255. The mark must function, or be intended to function, as a trademark. To constitute a registrable trademark, a mark (as defined) must be used, or intended to be used, by a person '*in relation to goods he manufactures or deals in*', and for service marks, '*in relation to a service he renders*'.[710] The Trade Marks Office has

706. The Trade Marks Ordinance, s. 11(13), 11(14) and 11(6) (discussed below in s. E 'Relative Grounds for Refusing Registration') and s. 46a(a), further discussed in s. §6 'Scope of Exclusive Rights' and s. §10 'Infringement and Remedies', *infra.*
707. The Trade Marks Ordinance, s. 1.
708. See s. §2, *supra,* for a discussion of signs capable of serving as marks.
709. The Trade Marks Ordinance, s. 8(a).
710. The Trade Marks Ordinance, s. 1.

interpreted the statutory definition of a trademark as requiring that a mark is eligible for registration only if intended for '*business or commercial activity*'.[711] Use is not a precondition for registration and intention to use the mark in the future suffices.[712]

C. Distinctive Character

1. Inherent Distinctiveness and Secondary Meaning

256. Requirement of distinctive character. A mark is not eligible for registration unless it is distinctive – that is, adapted to distinguish the goods of the proprietor of the mark from those of other persons.[713] Distinctiveness is determined having regard to the type of goods or services for which the mark is requested. A mark may be deemed inherently distinctive or may be shown to have acquired distinctiveness (secondary meaning) through use.[714] The greater the inherent distinctiveness the smaller is the quantum of evidence required to show secondary meaning, and *vice versa.*[715]

Where a mark is applied for in a specified colour or several colours, the limitation as to colour will be taken into account in the determination of the mark's distinctiveness.[716]

Assessing inherent distinctiveness. In determining whether a mark is inherently distinctive, the courts have regard to the location of the mark on the so-called 'spectrum of distinctiveness', extending from a generic mark to arbitrary or fanciful marks with the intermediate range being descriptive and suggestive marks, respectively.[717]

Arbitrary and fanciful names are considered inherently distinctive.[718] Suggestive names, which hint at the relevant goods without describing them, require some mental effort on the part of the consumer to connect the mark with the goods and are for the most part also deemed inherently distinctive.[719] Descriptive names, which describe features or components of the relevant goods or services, are considered non-distinctive and therefore not eligible for registration unless shown to have

711. Circular Letter MG 37 of 2 Jan. 2005.
712. HCJ 144/85 *Klil Metal Indus. Ltd v. Registrar of Patents, Trademarks and Designs, Mifromal Jerusalem Ltd*, 42(1) P.D. 309 [1988] (the '*Klil*' matter); HCJ 296/85, 319/85 *Sia Siak Howe v. Registrar of Patents, Trademarks and Designs*, 40(4) P.D.770 [1986].
713. The Trade Marks Ordinance s. 8(a).
714. The Trade Marks Ordinance, s. 8(b).
715. The *Klil* matter.
716. The Trade Marks Ordinance, s. 9. If a mark is registered without limitation as to colour, it will be deemed registered for all colours (the Ordinance, s. 9).
717. CA 5792/99 *Religious Jewish Media & Education (1997) Ltd – 'Mishpaha' [Family] Newspaper v. SBC Advertising, Marketing and Promotion Ltd – 'Mishpaha Tova' [Good Family] Newspaper*, 55(3) P.D. 933 [2001] (the '*Good Family*' matter).
718. The *Good Family* matter.
719. The *Good Family* matter at 944; CA 4116/06 *Gateway Inc. v. Passcall Advanced Technologies Ltd* [2007] (*Gateway*) at para. 14.

acquired distinctiveness through use.[720] The distinction between generic names and descriptive names is at times difficult to make. Generic names are names which are devoid of any distinctiveness and some may be deemed altogether incapable of acquiring secondary meaning and thus not registrable.[721] In *Adidas*,[722] it was held that secondary meaning acquired by a mark does not supersede the inherent distinctiveness, and both inherent and acquired distinctiveness are assessed when determining confusing similarity.

Showing secondary meaning. A mark that lacks inherent distinctiveness may be registrable if it is shown to have acquired distinctiveness through use.[723] Secondary meaning should be shown in the sense of association of the product with the source in the mind of the general consumer.[724] Secondary meaning is proven having regard to such criteria as the duration and extent of use, the extent of advertising and the proprietor's effort in creating the association of the product with the proprietor; types of evidence and weight attributed to each such criterion vary depending on the circumstances of each case.[725] The showing of extensive sales and advertising does not avail if those have failed to bring about such association.[726] Surveys, although not obligatory, are considered a most efficient tool for showing goodwill.[727]

Loss of distinctive character (genericide). A mark may lose its distinctive character through use by others either as a trademark or in a generic manner.[728] Great caution must be exerted when making a determination of a loss of distinctiveness.[729]

2. Specific Categories of Marks as to Distinctiveness

257. A mark is regarded as distinctive unless it falls within any of the statutory categories of inherently non-distinctive marks, which are registrable only upon

720. The *Good Family* matter at 944; the *Gateway* matter at para. 14; upon proof of distinctive character acquired through exclusive use, a descriptive term is registrable (HCJ 44/49 *Kay Daumit Inc. v. General Registrar*, 4 P.D. 109 [1950] ('LUSTRE-CRÈME for shampoo, refused)).
721. The *Klil* matter; the *Good Family* matter at 944–945 [2001]; CA 3559/02 *Toto Gold Subscribers Club Ltd v. Sports Lottery Council*, P.D. 59(1) 873 (the *Toto* matter) at 890–891.
722. CA 563/11 *Adidas Salomon AG v. Jalal Yassin* [2012] (*Adidas 2012*), an additional hearing refused by the Supreme Court in ACH 6658/12 *Adidas Salomon AG v. Jalal Yassin* [2014] (*Adidas 2014*).
723. The Trade Marks Ordinance, s. 8(b).
724. The *Klil* matter; CA 941/05 *Winemakers Cooperative Association of Rishon Lezion and Zichron Yaakov Wineries v. Hakerem Company Ltd* (unpublished) [2006] (the '*Tirosh*' matter) (in an infringement context, a dictionary Hebrew word (tirosh) for 'grape juice' was held to be ineligible for registration because descriptive for the product under 11(10) and not proven to have acquired a secondary meaning, in the sense of unambiguous association of the product with the source, in the mind of the consumer public, despite a showing of extensive sales and advertising).
725. The *'Toto'* matter at 890–891; the *Tirosh* matter.
726. CA 18/86 *Phoenicia Israeli Glass Works Ltd v. Les Verreries de Saint Gobain*, P.D. 45 (3) 224 [1991] (*Phoenicia*); the *Toto* matter at 890.
727. CA 8778/04 *Yotveta Dairies Ltd v. Tnuva Cooperative Center for Marketing Agricultural Produce in Israel Ltd* [2007] (*Yotveta*); CA 4410/06 *NRG Energy International Ltd v. Texaco Inc.* [2010].
728. HCJ 450/80 *Al Addin v. Registrar of Trade Marks*, 35(2) P.D. 187 [1980].
729. The *Yotveta* matter.

showing a secondary meaning, or within a category of not inherently distinctive marks evolved through jurisprudence.

a. Mark Comprising Words Commonly Used in the Trade

258. The Ordinance provides in section 11(10) that a mark 'consisting of numerals, letters, or words which are in common use in trade to distinguish or describe goods or classes of goods or which bear direct reference to their character or quality' is not capable of registration, unless the mark is shown to have acquired distinctiveness through use.[730]

Similarly, simple geometrical figures, pictorial devices or colour combinations would be considered *prima facie* unregistrable as it is conceived that such elements should remain open to the trade.[731] Registration of such marks becomes possible upon the acquisition of a secondary meaning through use.[732]

Marks that should remain open to the trade include descriptive names (such as indispensable or natural names for goods or their characteristics),[733] as well as ordinary laudatory epithets (as opposed to unusual, or unusually used, laudatory words).[734]

b. Geographical Names

259. A mark whose ordinary meaning is geographical is not inherently distinctive but may be registered upon proof of acquired distinctiveness, or if presented in special, stylized form.[735] The limitation is intended to prevent any trader from monopolizing a geographical name. The bar to registering a mark comprising a geographical name under section 11(11) has been held to be inapplicable where the choice of the geographical name for the specific goods was arbitrary, and the relevant geographical name had no reputation in relation to the goods in question.[736] The metes and bounds of this limitation are unclear, as the Supreme Court has failed to distinguish between the limitation in section 11(10) and the provision of section 11(6A) which bars from registration marks containing a misleading geographical indication, as per Article 22 of the TRIPS Agreement (see below). This redundancy,

730. The Trade Marks Ordinance, s. 11(10).
731. E. Seligsohn, *The Law of Trade Marks and Neighbouring Laws* (Tel Aviv 1972), at 21.
732. HCJ 44/49 *Kay Daumit Inc. v. General Registrar*, 4 P.D. 109 [1950] (actual exclusive use resulting in acquired distinctiveness permits registration of a word directly relating to the character or quality of goods); the *Good Family* matter at 944; *Gateway* at para. 14.
733. HCJ 296/86 *Philip Morris Inc. v. Moorgate Tobacco Co. Ltd*, P.D. 41(1) 485 [1987].
734. Seligsohn at 22; HCJ 305/63 *Tambour Colours Ltd v. Registrar of Trade Marks*, 18 P.D. 561 [1964] (refusal to register SUPERLAC affirmed). Ordinary laudatory terms are interpreted to fall within the scope of s. 11(10).
735. The Trade Marks Ordinance, s. 11(11): 'a mark whose ordinary signification is geographical (…), unless represented in a special manner or unless having a distinctive character within the meaning of section 8(b) or 9'.
736. CA 10959/05 *Tea Board v. Delta Lingerie SA* (unpublished) [2006]; ACH 10639/06 *Tea Board India v. Delta Lingerie S.A.* (unpublished)[2008].

although acknowledged by the Supreme Court in a later decision,[737] was left unresolved.

c. Mark That Is a Surname

260. A non-stylized mark, the ordinary meaning of which is a surname, is not inherently distinctive but may be registered upon proof of acquired distinctiveness.[738]

d. Colour Shades as a Mark

261. Trademarks consisting solely of a colour shade are deemed to be inherently non-distinctive; however, upon proof of acquired distinctiveness, a mark consisting solely of colour may be eligible for registration.[739]

e. Product Shape and Packaging as Marks

262. The Supreme Court has ruled that product shapes are deemed to lack inherent distinctiveness but may be shown to have acquired a secondary meaning through use; however, product shapes that are essentially functional or play an essentially aesthetic role cannot be registered even if they acquire a secondary meaning.[740] The

737. ACH 10639/06 *Tea Board India v. Delta Lingerie S.A.* (unpublished) [2008].

738. The Trade Marks Ordinance, s. 11(11): 'a mark whose ordinary signification is (…) a surname, unless represented in a special manner or unless having a distinctive character within the meaning of section 8(b) or 9'.

739. See the *Phoenicia* matter at 235; CC (TA Distr.) 225/96 *Eastman Kodak Co. v. Konco Ltd* (unpublished) [2003]. Accordingly, a shade of yellow was registered in the name of Eastman Kodak Co. Combination of colours [by way of a three-dimensional mark] has been refused when not sufficiently described, e.g., when the proportion between the two colours constituting a three-dimensional cube mark was not indicated (Application to register three-dimensional marks 182676, 182677, 182679, 182680 by Mann Hubbel GmbH [2008]).

740. CA 11487/03 *August Storck KG v. Alpha Intuit Foods Ltd* (unpublished) [2008] (*Storck*), Toffifee candy shape registration upheld in an infringement action; CA 3776/06 *Ein Gedi Cosmetics v. Registrar of Trademarks* (unpublished) [2008] (*Ein Gedi*), refusal to register gift set shape and candle shape as three-dimensional marks upheld. Following the *Storck* ruling, Circular Letter MN 28 of 2004, according to which product shape marks were allowed only in exceptional cases upon showing of secondary meaning, was replaced by Circular Letter MN 61 of April 2008 (which nevertheless viewed cases where product shapes would be eligible as 'special cases'). Said Circular Letter was in its turn subsequently replaced in 2015 by Circular Letter 032/2015. The current Circular Letter (032/2015) no longer limits registration of a product shape or packaging meeting the product-shape mark eligibility criteria to 'special cases' and provides for the possibility that a mark be registrable when it contains additional identification elements such as the applicant's house mark, even if it does not meet the product-shape eligibility criteria (namely the shape's role as a trademark, no essentially aesthetic or functional role; and a secondary meaning).

Subsequently, on the basis of the *Storck* criteria, certain product shapes were allowed for registration. Thus, in the wake of the *Storck* ruling, the Registrar allowed, upon a showing of secondary meaning, the registration of the shape of Ferrero 'Rocher' chocolate candy (Application by *Ferrero S.p.A.* to register marks No. 198944, 199650–3 [2011] (the 'Rocher' matter)).

By way of another example, Rubik's cube shape was allowed for registration for puzzles in class 28 and for advertising services in class 35 (Application to register marks 228232 and 228233 in the name of *Seven Towns SA* [2012], secondary meaning not shown but telle quelle registration

question as to whether product packaging (get-up) may rely on inherent distinctiveness for registration has been left open,[741] as the registration of packaging is seen as less detrimental to free competition. Yet, there is some uncertainty surrounding the susceptibility of product shapes to registration as the distinction between product shape and get-up may be blurred.[742]

3. Disclaiming of Non-distinctive Elements

263. Where a mark comprises elements that are deemed non-distinctive, it may be registered, provided that a disclaimer is placed with respect to such elements.[743] By way of illustration, composite marks containing the Hebrew word for 'grape juice' (*tirosh*), were held to be descriptive despite extensive sales and advertising by the proprietor. Consequently, the Supreme Court ordered that the marks be struck off the register, unless a disclaimer of exclusive use of the word is recorded.[744] As

---

allowed; held not to have an essentially aesthetic or functional role which would negate telle quelle registration), Crocs footwear model was allowed for registration in class 25 for footwear (Applications 212302 and 212303 in the name of *Crocs Inc* [2013], product shape held to have acquired a secondary meaning and not to have an essentially aesthetic function). Registration of certain other product shapes was disallowed – for example, the Tripp Trapp highchair was not allowed for registration in class 20 for furniture (in *Stokke AS v. Registrar of Patents, Designs and Trademarks* (MCA (TA Distr) 59175-12-12 [2013], the Tel Aviv District Court upheld the Registrar's refusal; product shape was not shown to have acquired a secondary meaning and was held to have a functional or aesthetic role; it suffices for such role to be non-negligible, rather than dominant, to negate registration) and the front view of Apple's iPhone 4 was not allowed for electronic devices (Application to register device mark 236294 in the name of *Apple Inc.* [2015], the product shape held not to serve a trademark function and held to serve substantial functional and aesthetic roles; the 2015 Circular Letter did not avail as the mark had no additional distinguishing elements).

741. See dictum in *Storck* and *Ein Gedi* that product packaging may be subject to less stringent standards of distinctiveness than product shape. Subsequently, the Registrar allowed, upon a showing of secondary meaning, the registration of the shape and design of Ferrero 'Rocher' transparent candy boxes (the *Rocher* matter) and the shape and design of certain liquor bottles (see *infra*).

742. *Ein Gedi* at para. 12. In practice, such shapes as bottles in which liquids are sold have been held to constitute products rather than packaging (Application to register mark No. 169606 [2009] in the name of *Spirits International Intellectual Property B.V.*, a vodka bottle shape refused registration in class 33 as product shape); registration was also refused to the Head & Shoulders shampoo bottle (Application to register mark No. 210043 [2011] in the name of *The Procter & Gamble Company*) and to the vitaminwater bottle (Application for the registration of mark 217460 [2014] in the name of *Energy Brands Inc.*); in several IPTO decisions, a bottle configuration was held eligible for trademark registration if perceived by the public as an indication of source due to long-established goodwill acquired through use or due to referencing a long-used trademark (Application by *Diageo North America, Inc.* to register mark No. 174402 [2011] (the configuration of the Crown Royal whisky bottle); Application by *Martell & Co.* to register mark No. 195184 [2011] (the configuration of the Martell cognac bottle)); a Fanta bottle was allowed for registration in Application for the registration of mark 184325 [2012] in the name of *The Coca-Cola Company*.

743. The Trade Marks Ordinance, s. 21(a). Disclaimers of exclusive use are further discussed in s. §7 'Limitations of the Scope of Trademark Protection', *infra*.

744. The *Tirosh* matter.

a matter of practice, the policy of the Trade Marks Office is not to require disclaimers as a general rule other than in cases where the Registrar deems appropriate to exercise this power.[745]

D. Absolute Grounds of Refusal Other Than Non-distinctiveness

264. Absolute grounds for refusing registration, other than for the absence of distinctiveness, are based on policy considerations. Such grounds are intended to protect the *ordre public* and to prevent deception or confusion of the public arising from the potentially misleading nature of the mark. A mark cannot be registered if it is likely to disturb the ordre public, to be injurious to morality or to mislead the public or if it encourages unfair competition.

1. Marks Involving Indications of Patronage: State and Religious Symbols – Official Signs

265. Registration cannot be used to appropriate for the use of a trademark proprietor 'flags and emblems of the State, State institutions, foreign States or international organizations', nor can a mark be registered if it resembles any of these.[746] Registration is denied to a mark identical with or similar to emblems of exclusively religious significance.[747]

Also ineligible are marks indicating a connection to the President, regardless of actual patronage.[748] The connection to the President has been narrowly interpreted.[749]

Certain other special emblems – namely, 'public armorial bearings, official signs or seals used by any state to indicate control or warranty, and any sign resembling any of these and any sign from which it might be inferred that its proprietor enjoys the patronage of or supplies goods or renders services to a head of state or a government' – are registrable only if the proprietor of the mark proves to the Registrar his right to use such mark.[750]

A further restriction on the use of emblems in trade and advertising is found in the Protection of Emblems Law, 5735 – 1974, which provides that a person may not use any name, emblem or flag, whether or not protected by an order of the Minister of Interior, for trade or advertising, in a manner leading to believe that such person is acting on behalf of the State, a governmental or local authority or in a

745. Circular Letter MN 84, 6 Sep. 2010.
746. The Trade Marks Ordinance, s. 11(2).
747. The Trade Marks Ordinance, s. 11(7).
748. The Trade Marks Ordinance, s. 11(1): 'a mark referring to some connection with the President of the State or his household or to presidential patronage or a mark from which any such connection or patronage might be inferred'.
749. For example, language clarifying absence of patronage sufficed to leave intact the registration of 'President's Wine' (*Yain Ha-Nasi*) (*Winemakers Cooperative Association of Rishon Lezion and Zichron Yaakov Ltd v. Hevrat Hakerem*, Application to cancel mark 82166 [2003]).
750. The Trade Marks Ordinance, s. 11(3).

manner injurious to public policy or public feelings.[751] A committee appointed by the Minister of Interior may certify at the request of a person that his use of a name, emblem or flag is not so misleading or injurious.[752] The State Flag, Emblem and Anthem Law, 5709 – 1949, specifically restricts the use of the national flag for trade or business purposes,[753] or any use of the State emblem,[754] unless authorized by the Minister of Interior. Certain additional statutes contain restrictions on the use of emblems misleadingly similar to those of a specific entity.

2. Marks Involving Indications of Registered Rights, Standardization or Supervision

266. A mark comprising words such as 'Patent', 'Patented', 'By Royal Letters Patent', 'Registered', 'Registered design', 'Copyrights', 'To counterfeit this is forgery', or words to a similar effect,[755] is not eligible for registration. Similarly, a mark cannot be registered if it contains words 'standard' or 'norm', or similar words, other than upon approval by the Minister of Industry and Trade.[756]

3. Marks Tainted with Immorality or Injurious to *Ordre Public*

267. Marks actually or potentially injurious to the *ordre public* or morality are not eligible for registration.[757] This ground has at times been invoked alongside relative refusal grounds such as confusing similarity to another's mark, and has at times been held to be inapplicable other than in cases of flagrant violation of general societal principles.[758]

4. Misleading Marks

268. Marks that are potentially deceptive or encouraging unfair competition. A mark is not eligible for registration if it is likely to deceive the public[759] or if it encourages unfair trade competition[760] (both grounds often invoked alongside the

751. The Protection of Emblems Law, 5735-1974, s. 5.
752. The Protection of Emblems Law, 5735-1974, s. 6(a).
753. The State Flag, Emblem and Anthem Law, 5709-1949, s. 2.
754. The State Flag, Emblem and Anthem Law, 5709-1949, s. 3(b).
755. The Trade Marks Ordinance, s. 11(4).
756. The Standards Law, 5713-1953, ss 13(a)(1) and 14.
757. The Trade Marks Ordinance, s. 11(5).
758. *Chaos Designers Ltd v. Fuzailov*, Opposition to the registration of mark 164130 'Fuz' [2007]; *BSN Medical Gmbh & Co. KG v. Farmaban S.A.*, Opposition to the registration of mark 146483 'Lenoplast' [2005].
759. The Trade Marks Ordinance, s. 11(6).
760. The Trade Marks Ordinance, s. 11(6).

relative grounds of a conflict with another's mark). A mark cannot be registered if it contains a 'false indication of origin'.[761]

Marks containing misleading geographical indications. In line with Article 22 of TRIPS, a mark containing a geographical indication that may be misleading as to the real geographical area in which the goods originated is barred from registration.[762] Also, a mark containing a geographical indication that is literally correct, but contains a false representation to the effect that the goods originated in a different geographical area, is unregistrable.[763] There exist specific provisions with respect to trademarks of wines or spirits that contain geographical indications. Such marks are barred from registration if such wine or spirit did not originate in that geographical area.[764]

Yet another specific restriction is imposed on the use of the name 'Jerusalem', which would be deemed a false trade description under the Merchandise Marks Ordinance, unless such use is proved lawful.[765]

E. *Relative Grounds for Refusing Registration*

269. Relative grounds for refusing registration are designed to bar the registration of such marks that are found to injure the proprietary rights of third parties, which may be the rights of the owner of an earlier registration, the rights of the owners of registered and unregistered well-known marks, and the rights of a person in his likeness.

1. Conflict with an Earlier Registered Mark Relating to the Same Goods

270. Section 11(9) of the Trade Marks Ordinance precludes the registration of a mark that is:

> identical with one belonging to a different proprietor which is already on the register in respect of the same goods or description of goods, or so nearly resembling such a mark as to be calculated to deceive.

The purpose of the provision is twofold: to prevent commercial harm to the proprietor of the mark in consequence of consumer confusion and to prevent injury to the consumer public in consequence of such confusion.[766]

---

761. The Trade Marks Ordinance, s. 11(6).
762. The Trade Marks Ordinance, s. 11(6a) 'a mark containing a geographical indication in respect of goods originating in the geographical area indicated, if the geographical indication may be misleading as to the real geographical area in which the goods originated'.
763. The Trade Marks Ordinance, s. 11(6b) 'a mark containing a geographical indication that is literally correct, however that contains a false representation to the effect that the goods originated in a different geographical area'.
764. The Trade Marks Ordinance, s. 11(12) 'a mark identifying wine or spirit beverages that contains a geographical indication, if such wine or spirit beverage did not originate in that geographical area'.
765. The Merchandise Marks Ordinance, s. 6B.
766. HCJ 178/57 *Aktiebolaget Astra v. the Registrar*, 12 (1) P.D. 708 [1958] at 712.

Assessing confusing similarity. In accordance with statutory language, where the propounded mark is not identical with the earlier registration, it will be barred from registration if it is found to be similar to a point of confusing the public.[767] Whether a mark is confusingly similar to the registered mark is subject to judicial determination. The criterion for determining confusing similarity is whether members of the public of ordinary intelligence acting with usual circumspection are likely to be confused as to the source of goods of the parties.[768] Confusion as to the source of goods is interpreted in an expansive manner so as to cover also confusion regarding their connection to, or sponsorship by, the trademark owner.[769] It has been held that consumers' doubt as to whether the goods of the two parties are related suffices to show confusing similarity.[770] The degree of similarity must be higher than a mere 'connection', and such determination is to be made with respect to 'people having common sense and applying reasonable diligence'.[771]

The *three-prong test for determining confusing similarity* was first enunciated by the courts in actions for passing off[772] and subsequently held to apply to the determination of confusing similarity between trademarks for registration and infringement purposes.[773] The three-prong test examines the visual and aural similarity between the two marks: the similarity of the goods, the relevant circles of customers and channels of distribution, and other surrounding circumstances.[774] The application of the three-prong test in each case is not uniform but rather is affected by the degree of the mark's distinctiveness and the degree of protection to which it is entitled.[775]

Among these factors, *the visual and aural similarity* has been held to be the central test in the assessment of confusing similarity.[776] The visual similarity consideration is more significant where products are sold off the shelf, and the relative weight attributed to aural similarity increases where the products are sold over the counter or marketed through radio and television; if the sale or advertising of the products appeals both to the eye and the ear, both visual and auditory prongs of the test are important.[777] For thepurpose of assessing confusing similarity, the marks should be examined and compared in their entirety, including any descriptive or otherwise non-distinctive elements (even if disclaimed) for overall impression.[778]

---

767. LCA 1400/97 *Pikanti Food Industries (Israel) Ltd v. Osem Food Industries Ltd*, 51(1) P.D. 310 [1997] at 313.
768. HCJ 476/82 *Orlogad Ltd v. Registrar of Trade Marks*, 39(2) P. D. 148 [1985] (*Orlogad*) at 158.
769. The *Toto* matter.
770. HCJ 197/51 *Coca-Cola Company v. Vita Plotkin Partnership*, 8 P.D. 772 [1954] at 783.
771. *Adidas 2012* at para.12; cited and applied by a district court in MCA 31303-09 *Wrangler Apparel Corp v. Weiss Brothers JSJ Manufacturing and Marketing Ltd* [2013] ('Wrangler') (appeal from the IPTO dismissal of an opposition to the registration of a cowboy mark, dismissed) at 5–6.
772. CA 261/64 *Frou-Frou Biscuit (Kfar Sava) Ltd v. Froumine & Sons Ltd*, 18 (3) P.D. 275 [1964] (*Frou-Frou*).
773. LCA 1400/97 *Pikanti Food Industries (Israel) Ltd v. Osem Food Industries Ltd*, 51(1) P.D. 310 [1997] at 313; LCA 5454/02 *Taam Teva (1988) Tivoli Ltd v. Ambrosia Supherb Ltd*, 57(2) P.D. 438 [2003] (*Taam Teva*) at 450.
774. For example, *Taam Teva* at 451 et seq.
775. *Adidas* 2012 at para. 12, *Wrangler* at 6–7.
776. *Taam Teva* at 451.
777. *Taam Teva* at 454.
778. *Taam Teva*; CA 1123/04 *Canali S.P.A. v. Canal Jean Co.* (unpublished) [2005].

Comparison of the marks to ascertain similarity does not consist of meticulous comparison of each individual element but rather makes allowance for a person's first impression and imperfect recollection (unless consumers are liable to encounter the marks side by side).[779] The examination of similarity between composite marks focuses on the dominant element of each mark.[780] Where the compared marks have common descriptive or generic components, such components are held to be transparent and ought not be taken into consideration when assessing confusion.[781] Furthermore, because protection of a mark is affected by its position on the spectrum of distinctiveness, where the mark or its component is descriptive or generic, rather than arbitrary or fanciful, slight variation may suffice to counteract confusing similarity.[782]

In the *Adidas* matter[783] in 2012, the Supreme Court noted, *inter alia*, that while it was held in the past that comparison of the marks ought to be made with reference to the registered mark as it appears on the register, rather than as the marks appear on the products themselves, this authority is good mostly with respect to word marks, while device marks, such as stripes sewn on a shoe, are to be considered together with the products which they designate.

The '*circle of customers*' prong examines, first, whether the goods are intended for the same target clientele and, second, whether the targeted customers are prone to be confused, e.g., because of their level of sophistication and their capacity for discrimination (e.g., clients requiring financial services, professionals or the general public including children).[784] Where each party targets a different clientele, the likelihood of confusion is diminished;[785] difference in goods and channels of distribution may also counteract a likelihood of confusion.[786]

Examining the goods. The confusing similarity test initially evolved in connection with the tort of passing off. Because the statutory definition of passing off, unlike the language of the refusal ground under the Ordinance, does not involve a

779. *Taam Teva* at 452.
780. The *Toto* matter (addition of non-dominant elements did not suffice to distinguish).
781. CA 1677/05 *Deutsche Telekom AG v. E! Entertainment Television Inc.* (unpublished) [2005] – word 'online'.
782. See, e.g., LCA 4322/09 *SA Ferromat Trade & Services (1994) Ltd v. AS Snir Ltd* (Gold) (unpublished) [2009] where the Supreme Court held that use of the trademark GOLD 55 for a fuel system cleaner did not infringe the registered trademark GOLD LABEL for identical goods. See also CA 8981/04 *Malka – 'Avazei Zahav Restaurant' v. Avazi Shchunat Hatikva 1997 Restaurant Management Ltd* (unpublished)[2006].
783. *Adidas 2012*. The Supreme Court held there that four-stripe sports shoes, which also prominently bore an unrelated word mark and were intended for sale at low price points at open-air markets, did not amount to the infringement of Adidas' registered and well-known mark, as there was no likelihood of confusion or association with Adidas' well-known three-stripe mark. The Supreme Court subsequently refused an additional hearing, holding that the examination of the mark as the mark appears on the goods was dictated by the circumstances of the case and did not diminish the distinction between the examination of confusing similarity in the context of trademark law and that in the context of passing off (*Adidas 2014*).
784. CA 210/65 *Bank Igud for Israel Ltd v. Bank 'Agudath Israel'*, P.D. 19(2) 673 [1965] (*Bank Igud*); CA 715/68 *Frou-Frou Biscuit Kfar-Sava Ltd et al. v. L. Froumine & Sons Ltd*, P.D. 23 (2) 43 [1969] (*Frou-Frou 1969*); *Taam Teva* at 453.
785. LCA 4196/93 *Shefa Bar Management and Services (1991) Ltd v. Shefa Restaurants Ready Meals Manufacturing and Marketing 1984 Ltd*, P.D. 47(5) 165 [1993].
786. CA 1123/04 *Canali S.P.A. v. Canal Jean Co.* (unpublished) [2005].

requirement that confusing use relate to 'goods of the same description', judicial examination of a likelihood of confusion for passing off purposes includes examining the goods involved. Therefore, the examination of confusing similarity as a bar to registration involves a comparison between each party's goods for both purposes – as a 'type of goods' consideration for determining the existence of confusing similarity and for deciding whether the later mark is requested for goods 'of the same description' as required by the Ordinance.

The *type of goods* aspect not only examines the similarity between the parties' goods but also whether the type of goods concerned affects the likelihood of confusion, e.g., higher-cost goods and important services typically induce consumers to make a more thorough examination, whereas basic, daily staples require less discrimination.[787]

The test as to whether the goods of the two parties are goods '*of the same description*' examines whether the goods are commonly dealt in by the same trader[788] and belong to the same 'commercial family', analysed on a case-by-case basis, in respect of which the consumer is likely to infer a connection to the registered mark owner or his sponsorship.[789] Services and goods may be found within the 'same description' if found to be within the same 'commercial family'.[790] Such approach succeeded a much narrower approach expressed in the past, according to which clothing and shoes were deemed goods not of the same description.[791]

The '*other circumstances of the case*' prong is a residual test relating to all other circumstances of the specific case, e.g., the advertising of the mark on which the opposition relies.[792]

An additional, independent test is the test of *conceptual similarity*, or *mental impression*, sometimes referred to as 'the *common sense* test',[793] which examines whether confusing similarity resides in the idea, or the concept, conveyed by the marks.[794]

2. Conflict with a Well-known Mark

271. The notion that famous trademarks enjoy protection from 'dilution' was adopted into Israeli jurisprudence by the Supreme Court in the *Bacardi* matter via the channel of section 11(6) of the Ordinance which is aimed at preventing the registration of marks which encourage unfair competition (see discussion below). In addition, there exist in the Ordinance specific statutory provisions that adopted the provisions of Article 16 of the TRIPS Agreement with respect to well-known trademarks.

---

787. *Taam Teva* at 453; *Bank Igud*; *Frou-Frou 1969*.
788. *Orlogad*.
789. *Toto* at 894.
790. *Toto* at 894–895.
791. CA 352/69 *Manhattan Co. v. Hamafger Ltd*, P.D. 23(1) 373 [1969].
792. HCJ 197/51 *Coca-Cola Company v. Vita Plotkin Partnership*, P.D. 8, 772; *Taam Teva* at 453.
793. CA 8441/04 *Unilever Plc v. Segev* (unpublished) [2006] (*Unilever*).
794. *Unilever Plc* (Dove's dove device); CA 6659/09 *Mul-T-Lock Ltd v. Rav Bariach (08) Industries Ltd* (unpublished) [2010] (muscleman device).

Non-registered Well-known Marks

Section 11(13) of the Trade Marks Ordinance, enacted in 1999 to ensure Israel's compliance with the TRIPS Agreement (Article 16(2)), bars from registration a mark that is:

> identical to, or misleadingly similar with, a well-known trade mark even if such mark is not registered in respect of goods for which the mark is well known or in respect of goods of the same description.

A well-known mark operates as a bar to registration in respect of the goods for which it is known or goods of the same description regardless of whether or not the well-known mark is registered.

Registered Well-known Marks

A registered well-known mark is afforded broader protection than that of a well-known mark that has not been registered or of a registered mark that is not well known.

Section 11(14) of the Trade Marks Ordinance, enacted in the wake of accession to the TRIPS Agreement (Article 16(3)), provides for the ineligibility for registration of a mark that is:

> identical to or similar to a well-known trade mark being a registered trade mark, even in respect of goods not of the same description, if the mark sought to be registered would indicate a connection between the goods in respect of which the mark is sought and the registered proprietor of the trade mark, and the registered proprietor of the trade mark is likely to be harmed as a result of the use of the mark sought.

The interpretation of the statutory requirements applicable to a well-known mark in respect of goods of the same description is evolving; formerly, the Supreme Court interpreted the statute as providing that, for a registered well-known mark, a likelihood of a harmful association suffices to bar registration of a conflicting mark both for goods of the same description and for goods of a different description;[795] recently, the Supreme Court (in an infringement context) interpreted the statutory language differently, observing that for a well-known mark (whether registered or unregistered) with respect to goods of the same description, likelihood of confusion must be shown and apparently only with regard to goods of a different description would a likelihood of association suffice.[796] (Also see the discussion in §10. I 'Infringement' *infra*).

Determination whether a mark is well known in Israel. A well-known mark is defined in the Ordinance as a mark, whether or not registered or actually used in Israel, that is well known in Israel as a mark owned by a person that is a citizen or

795. See the *Unilever* matter at 22–23.
796. CA 5066/10 *Shlomo A. Angel Ltd v. J & E Berman Ltd et al* [2013] at 32–34.

permanent resident of a Member State (a Paris Convention signatory or WTO member) or who has an active industrial or commercial business in such State.[797] Thus, a foreign mark may be considered well known even if not used in Israel but should be shown to have acquired a reputation in Israel.[798] It is statutorily provided under the Trade Marks Ordinance, that a determination whether a mark is well known in Israel shall take into account the extent to which the mark is known in public circles relating to it and the extent to which it is known as a result of marketing.[799]

Assessing likelihood of association. To bar registration in reliance on section 11(14) of the Ordinance (or to constitute infringement of a well-known registered mark, under section 46A(b) of the Ordinance), it suffices to show that the mark is likely to indicate, in the consumers' minds, a connection to the well-known mark owner and that such owner is liable to suffer harm from the applicant's use.[800]

However, the likelihood of association with a well-known mark varies depending on its degree of distinctiveness. For example, a well-known mark consisting of a dictionary laudatory word (ABSOLUT for vodka) was found not to bar the use of such word within another, composite mark for a dissimilar category of goods (Absolute Shoes);[801] a well-known mark consisting of a non-arbitrary word (CARMEL for wine) was not allowed to bar an arbitrary use of the same word for a dissimilar category of goods (electronics).[802]

Dilution of Famous Marks – The refusal ground of unfair competition set forth in section 11(6) of the Ordinance has been invoked to protect marks that have acquired international reputation and goodwill from free rides on such reputation, prior to the enactment of specific provisions protecting well-known marks.

In the *Bacardi* case, handed down before the TRIPS amendment,[803] the Supreme Court has imported the doctrine of dilution of famous marks into Israeli trademark law via the conduit of section 11(6), which provides, *inter alia*, that a mark that is likely to deceive the public or that encourages unfair trade competition[804] is incapable of being registered. In *Bacardi*, the Supreme Court afforded protection to a mark of international renown (Bacardi), registered in Israel for alcoholic beverages, from the registration of a similar mark for goods of a different description (clothing). Under the criteria of protection enunciated in *Bacardi*, an apprehension of dilution exists also absent likelihood of confusion, where the business is an internationally famous one, where the mark possesses strength transcending specific goods and where the accused use is designed to promote the business of another trader through free-riding on the famous mark's goodwill through blurring the uniqueness of its image amongst consumers.[805] The doctrine of dilution under

797. The Trade Marks Ordinance, s. 1.
798. The *Absolut* matter.
799. The Trade Marks Ordinance, s. 1.
800. The *Absolut* matter.
801. The *Absolut* matter.
802. *Winemakers Cooperative Association of Rishon Lezion and Zichron Yaakov Ltd v. Infineon Technologies AG*, Opposition to the registration of marks 120949, 129050 'Carmel' [2003].
803. CA 6181/96 *Kardi v. Bacardi & Co. Ltd*, 52 (3) P.D. 276 [1998] (*Bacardi*) at 282.
804. The Trade Marks Ordinance, s. 11(6).
805. *Bacardi* at 282; CA 10959/05 *Delta Lingerie S.A. v. Tea Board of India* (unpublished) [2006]; *Adidas 2012*.

the *Bacardi* authority is broader in scope since it confers upon unregistered well-known marks protection also in respect of those goods for which they are not known, even if not of the same description.

Notwithstanding the enactment of the statutory protection of well-known marks under section 11(3) and 11(4) of the Ordinance, the *Bacardi* dilution doctrine is still good law and may continue to be invoked with respect to well-known marks.[806]

In the *Adidas* matter, the Supreme Court noted that – while dilution does not require a likelihood of confusion – in the absence of a likelihood of confusion, dilution should not be adopted as a default position and should possibly be reserved for exceptional cases, such as where confusion is unlikely due to goods being of a different description.[807]

3. Unauthorized Use of a Third-Party's Image as a Bar to Registration

272. The registration of a mark containing the image of a person is subject to having obtained the consent of such person; in the case of the representation of a deceased person, the Registrar shall request the consent of his survivors unless, in his opinion, reasonable grounds exist for not doing so.[808]

4. Conflict with an Existing Business Name

273. Registration may be refused to a mark identical or similar to another person's name or business name (or containing an identical or similar name) if the mark is likely to mislead the public or cause unfair competition.[809]

III. Eligibility for *Telle Quelle* Registration of Foreign Marks

274. Telle quelle registration. A trademark applicant who is a national or domiciliary of a Paris Convention or WTO Member State or who maintains an industrial

806. ACH 10639/06 *Tea Board India v. Delta Lingerie S.A.* (unpublished) [2006]. The image of a leaping cat was disallowed for registration, inter alia, on the basis of diluting Puma's famous mark, even assuming an absence of confusion (*Puma AG v. City Wash Ltd*, Opposition to the registration of device mark 913791 TIGRIS [2011]); the determination of dilution was adopted in the infringement proceedings between the parties in CC (TA Distr.) 1245-08 *Puma SE v. City Wash Ltd* [2013].

807. *Adidas 2012* (due to an absence of a likelihood of confusion that the defendant's goods were manufactured by Adidas, consumers unlikely to associate their quality with Adidas and hence no dilution); additional hearing refused in *Adidas 2014*. In the wake of the *Adidas* ruling, a district court in a different *Adidas* matter, while finding infringement due to the use of a three-stripe mark virtually identical to that of Adidas, held that, in the absence of a likelihood of confusion there was no dilution of the Adidas triple mark stripe, because consumers would be unlikely to associate the quality of the defendant's goods with Adidas (CA (TA Distr.) 2028-08 *Adidas AG et al v. Batash et al* [2014]).

808. The Trade Marks Ordinance, s. 11(8).

809. The Trade Marks Ordinance, s. 12.

or commercial establishment in such state, may base his application on a home registration; in such case, the Trade Marks Office will apply more temperate criteria of examination than the grounds of refusal applicable to national marks.[810] The grounds for refusal of a *telle quelle* registration[811] are as follows:

(1) registration of the mark in Israel will infringe rights acquired in Israel by another person; or
(2) the mark is devoid of any distinctive character (a trademark shall not be disqualified from registration if it is different from the trademark registered in its country of origin in a manner that does not alter its distinctiveness, and does not adversely affect its identity in the form in which it has been registered in the said country of origin);
(3) the mark consists exclusively of signs or indications which may serve in trade to designate the kind, quality, quantity, place of origin, intended purpose, time of production or value of the goods; or
(4) the mark is customary in current language or in the bona fide and established trade practices in Israel; or
(5) the mark is contrary to public order or morality; or
(6) the mark is likely to deceive the public.

Where a mark is accepted as a *telle quelle* registration but would not have been registrable otherwise, such fact shall be indicated in the publication of the application and in the register.[812]

§4. Formalities (Procedure for Obtaining Protection, Establishing and Maintaining Trademarks)

I. Procedure for Obtaining Registration

A. *Applying for Registration*

275. Who may apply. An application for registration may be made by any person claiming to be the proprietor of the mark used or intended to be used by him either as a manufacturer or as a trader.[813] Applications for an identical mark, or similar marks, may be filed by rival applicants.[814]

Registration in respect of goods/classes; classification. A trademark must be registered in respect of particular goods or classes of goods.[815] Registration follows classes of goods and services set forth in the Nice Classification of Goods and

810. Set forth in ss 8–11 of the Ordinance.
811. The Trade Marks Ordinance, s. 16.
812. The Trade Marks Ordinance, s. 16(c).
813. The Trade Marks Ordinance, ss 17 and 1.
814. Discussed in s. §5 'Ownership'.
815. The Trade Marks Ordinance, s. 10(a).

Services; the ninth edition is currently adopted.[816] The final determination of the class into which the goods fall is made by the Registrar.[817] Following Israel's accession to the Madrid Protocol (effective 1 September 2010), a single application may relate to multiple classes of goods. Separate single-class applications simultaneously submitted for the same mark may, at the applicant's request, be consolidated into one multiple-class application;[818] such registrations may also be consolidated after the registration.[819] Multi-class applications may be divided at the request of the applicant;[820] division may also be ordered by the Registrar.[821]

Priority. Priority of an application filed in any Paris Convention or WTO Member State may be claimed.[822] Priority must be claimed within six months of filing an application in Israel.[823]

Application designating Israel under the Madrid System. International applications filed in accordance with the Madrid Protocol may designate Israel. Processing of international applications is governed by the amended Ordinance (and regulations thereunder) and, to the extent not provided for therein, by the Common Regulations under the Madrid Agreement Concerning the International Registration of Marks and the Protocol Relating to that Agreement.[824]

B. Examination, Acceptance, Publication

276. Examination and office actions. Applicants must respond to office actions within a three-month period, which may be extended; absent timely response, an application will be deemed abandoned.[825] The Trade Marks Office conducts both a formal examination of the applications (for such issues as classification of goods and services, completeness, priority claims) and a substantive examination of the registrability of the mark and absence of applicable grounds of refusal.

Acceptance; appeal of refusal. The Registrar may refuse an application or accept it absolutely or subject to conditions, amendments or modifications, or subject to such limitations as to mode or place of use or otherwise as it may think right to impose.[826] A refusal to accept is subject to appeal to the district court.[827] District court decisions are appealable by leave to the Supreme Court.[828]

---

816. The Trade Marks Regulations, s. 5.
817. The Trade Marks Ordinance, s. 10(b).
818. The Trade Marks Ordinance, s. 17B.
819. The Trade Marks Ordinance, s. 36A.
820. The Trade Marks Ordinance, s. 17A.
821. The Trade Marks Ordinance, s. 18(b).
822. The Trade Marks Ordinance, s. 55(a).
823. The Trade Marks Ordinance, s. 55(c).
824. The Trade Marks Ordinance, s. 56B(b).
825. The Trade Marks Ordinance, s. 22.
826. The Trade Marks Ordinance, s. 18(a).
827. The Trade Marks Ordinance, s. 18(b).
828. The Trade Marks Ordinance, s. 63B(a).

Publication. Upon acceptance, the application as accepted is published for oppositions in the *Trademark Journal* that is part of the *Official Gazette* (*Reshumot*), specifying every condition and limitation subject to which it has been accepted.[829]

C. *Opposition*

277. Timeframe for opposition and response. Opposition may be made, by any person, by way of filing a notice of opposition with the Registrar, within three months of the publication of the accepted application.[830] The applicant's failure to respond to an opposition by way of a counter-statement within two months of receipt of the notice of opposition leads to the application being considered abandoned.[831]

Grounds for opposition. The registration of a mark may be opposed either on the ground that a reason exists for which the application may be refused, under the provisions of the Trade Marks Ordinance[832] (grounds for refusal are discussed in section §3 'Conditions of Protection' *supra*), or on the ground that the opponent, and not the applicant, is the owner of the mark[833] (rival claims to the ownership of a mark are discussed *infra* at section §5 'Ownership').

Decision in an opposition; appeal. The Registrar's decision in an opposition proceeding is subject to appeal to the district court,[834] to be made within thirty days from the date of the decision of the Registrar.[835] District court decisions are appealable by leave to the Supreme Court.[836]

D. *Grant*

278. If no opposition was filed to the accepted application, or if the opposition is not successful, the mark is registered unless the court otherwise directs[837] and the applicant is issued a certificate of registration.[838]

E. *International Applications*

279. The Registrar must, within eighteen months from receipt of an application designating Israel, advise the International Bureau that the mark is unsuitable for registration or is eligible for registration subject to conditions, restrictions or

829. The Trade Marks Ordinance, s. 23.
830. The Trade Marks Ordinance, s. 24(a).
831. The Trade Marks Ordinance, s. 24(d) and (e); the Trade Marks Regulations, s. 37.
832. The Trade Marks Ordinance, s. 24(a1)(1).
833. The Trade Marks Ordinance, s. 24(a1)(2).
834. The Trade Marks Ordinance, s. 25(a).
835. The Trade Marks Ordinance, s. 25(b).
836. The Trade Marks Ordinance, s. 63B(a).
837. The Trade Marks Ordinance, s. 26.
838. The Trade Marks Ordinance, s. 28.

changes, or that oppositions have been filed or may be filed;[839] any oppositions must be notified to the International Bureau within a month after the end of the period for their filing.[840] Absent such notice, the Registrar shall register the mark.[841] Decisions on unappealed oppositions or appellate judgments must be notified to the International Bureau.[842]

Registration as an international mark will replace domestic registration if the domestic mark was on the register at the time of filing of the international application in the name of the international applicant and the international application covers all the goods for which the domestic mark was registered.[843] International registration will not prejudice rights acquired under the domestic registration.[844]

II. Maintaining a Trademark

280. For a trademark to continue on the register, the trademark owner must pay the prescribed maintenance fees at prescribed times. A trademark for which such fees were not paid is removed from the register after a grace period and is subject to reinstatement for a limited additional period, as discussed below in section §9 'Duration'.

§5. Ownership and Transfer (Assignment: Licenses)

I. Ownership of a Registered Mark: Joint Ownership

281. A mark may be registered in the name of one person and as a matter of practice also in the name of several persons who may own the mark jointly, under conditions set out by the Registrar.

Determining ownership for the purpose of registration. An application to register a mark may be brought by any person claiming to be the proprietor of such mark.[845] The question of ownership at registration may arise before acceptance of the application, if another person applies to register an identical mark,[846] or following acceptance, as a ground of opposition.[847] Ownership of a mark is determined based on the rights acquired to the mark; an earlier filing date of an application would not, by itself, determine the rights to the mark.

839. The Trade Marks Ordinance, s. 56F(a).
840. The Trade Marks Ordinance, s. 56F(b).
841. The Trade Marks Ordinance, s. 56G.
842. The Trade Marks Ordinance, s. 56H.
843. The Trade Marks Ordinance, s. 56I(a).
844. The Trade Marks Ordinance, s. 56I(b).
845. The Trade Marks Ordinance, s. 17(a).
846. The Trade Marks Ordinance, s. 29.
847. The Trade Marks Ordinance, s. 24(a)(2).

A. Rival Claims and Concurrent Registration

282. Rival claims to an identical mark or to similar marks. Where there is a conflict between different applicants who claim ownership of identical or similar marks in respect of the same goods or description of goods, and provided that the examination of such applications has not ended, the Registrar may initiate contentious proceedings for deciding which of the rival applicants has better rights in the mark.[848] Such decision is appealable to the district court within thirty days from the date of the Registrar's decision.[849]

Contentious proceedings between rival applicants under section 29 of the Ordinance are determined primarily on a 'first to use' basis while the manner and extent of use by each applicant in Israel, both before and after the date of filing, are also taken into account. Other considerations that may impact such decision are good faith in choosing the mark (e.g., the choice of a mark similar to an internationally renowned mark) and the filing date (the filing date being secondary to good faith and extent of use).[850] In deciding the relative rights of the parties, the Registrar would also take into consideration respective use of the rival marks after the filing date until the case is heard. Nonetheless, it was noted that the taking into consideration of post-filing use must be made with caution, lest one party *mala fide* attempt to massively use a mark after filing in order to usurp another's goodwill.[851] In order for one trader to prove rights to a mark in preference over another trader, long-term or extensive use per se would not suffice; the use must be such as to create an association between the mark and the trader.[852]

Where several traders show that they have extensively used the mark, the mark may be deemed to have lost its distinctive character and thus not eligible for registration.[853]

Parallel registration in case of honest concurrent use. Where the Registrar is satisfied that there has been honest concurrent use of identical or similar marks by the rival parties, or that 'other special circumstances' justify the registration of identical or similar marks by different applicants in respect of the same goods (or description of goods), the Registrar may order the separate registration of the rival applications subject to such conditions and limitations as the Registrar may prescribe.[854] Such decision is appealable to the district court.[855] In deciding whether concurrent registration of rival marks is applicable, great importance is attributed to the good faith,

848. The Trade Marks Ordinance, s. 29(a).
849. The Trade Marks Ordinance, s. 29(b).
850. CA 8778/04 *Yotveta Dairies Ltd v. Tnuva Cooperative Center*(unpublished) [2007]; CA 11188/03 *Kontakt Linsen Israel Ltd v. Registrar et al.* (unpublished) [2005]; CA 8987/05 *Malchi v. Soap Like the Old Times (2000) Ltd* (unpublished) [2007] (*Malchi*).
851. CA 8778/04 *Yotveta Dairies Ltd v. Tnuva Cooperative Center* (unpublished) [2007].
852. *Malchi*.
853. HCJ 450/80 *Al Addin v. Registrar*, 35(2) P.D 187; CA 2673/04 *Coffee To Go Marketing (1997) Ltd v. Shaked* (unpublished) [2007].
854. The Trade Marks Ordinance, s. 30.
855. The Trade Marks Ordinance, s. 30(b).

or lack thereof, in the choice and use of the mark; bad faith such as an intention to benefit from a foreign mark's goodwill results in a refusal of registration.[856]

Each of the registered owners of an identical mark in respect of the same goods has rights as if he were the sole registered proprietor of the mark, but none has the right of exclusive use as against the other owners, unless the owners' respective rights have been determined by the Registrar or the district court.[857]

II. Transfers

283. A registered trademark may be transferred by assignment or pass by operation of law.

A. *Transfer of Trademarks*

284. Trademark registrations and trademark applications may be assigned together with the goodwill of the business, or separately.[858] An assignee is to apply to the Registrar to record the assignment[859] and shall be registered as owner upon proof of its rights.[860] Recordal of an assignment is essential in order for the use by the assignee to be deemed use by the owner.[861] The same applies to a transfer by operation of law.[862] However, the Registrar may refuse to register an assignment or transfer of a mark if, in its opinion, the use of the mark by the transferee is likely to deceive the public or if the transfer is contrary to public order.[863]

Absent recordal in the register, documents evidencing a transfer shall not be admissible in any court proceedings as evidence of title, unless specifically permitted by the court.[864]

B. *Transfer of Collective Marks and Certification Marks*

285. Transfer of a collective mark or of a certification mark requires the Registrar's approval.[865]

856. HCJ 53/54 *Alpha Ltd v. Societé Technique de Parfumerie F. Millot SA*, 9 P.D. 121[1955]; HCJ 95/68 *Mittperet Hadarom Ltd v. H.D. Lee Co.*, 22(2) P.D. 189 [1968].
857. The Trade Marks Ordinance, s. 46(b).
858. The Trade Marks Ordinance, s. 48.
859. The Trade Marks Ordinance, s. 49(a).
860. The Trade Marks Ordinance, s. 49(a).
861. CA 2209/08 *Gigiesse Confezioni S.p.A. v. Wampum Ltd* (unpublished) [2010] (*Gigiesse*); CA 7038/04 *Miss L Women's Fashion 1992 Ltd v. Lagotte Bekleidungsfabrik Paula Gottesdiener GmbH* (unpublished) [2007].
862. The Trade Marks Ordinance, s. 49(a).
863. The Trade Marks Ordinance, s. 48(a).
864. The Trade Marks Ordinance, s. 49(c).
865. The Trade Marks Ordinance, ss 15 and 14, respectively.

III. Authorization of User

286. The owner of a registered mark has the right to authorize another to use the mark in respect of all the goods for which the mark is registered or in respect of some of them.[866] The authorization to use must be recorded in order for it to have effect.[867] It has been held that the parties' intention to permit use without duly recording the authorization makes such authorization not only invalid but also illegal.[868]

The use of the mark by a recorded authorized user in accordance with the terms of the authorization accrues to the registered owner; the use by an unrecorded licensee does not accrue to the registered owner.[869] It has been left open whether recordal of a license is required between affiliated companies.[870]

An application to record an authorization shall be submitted by the proprietor of the mark and the proposed authorized user[871] and needs *inter alia* to indicate the extent of the proprietor's control over the use of the mark by the authorized user.[872] The Registrar may prescribe conditions and restrictions at the time of recording the authorization[873] and may register the authorization if satisfied that the use of the trademark in relation to the goods in respect of which registration of the authorization is sought is not contrary to public order and is not likely to deceive.

§6. Scope of Exclusive Rights

I. Exclusive Use of the Owner of a Registered Mark

287. A valid registered mark grants its owner the right to the exclusive use of such trademark upon, and in every matter relating to, the goods or services in respect of which it has been registered.[874]

A. Exclusive Use of a Well-known Trademark

288. Under the TRIPS-related amendment of the Ordinance, the owner of a well-known mark enjoys exclusive right to use his mark, regardless of registration. Section 46A(a) of the Trade Marks Ordinance provides:

866. The Trade Marks Ordinance, s. 50(a).
867. The Trade Marks Ordinance, s. 50(b).
868. CA 364/74 *Davidovich v. Miromit Metal Works Ashkelon Ltd*, 29(1) P.D. 703 [1975].
869. The Trade Marks Ordinance, s. 50(c).
870. CA 7038/04 *Miss L Women's Fashion 1992 Ltd v. Lagotte Bekleidungsfabrik Paula Gottesdiener GmbH* (unpublished) [2007].
871. The Trade Marks Ordinance, s. 51(a).
872. The Trade Marks Ordinance, s. 51(a)(1).
873. The Trade Marks Ordinance, s. 50(b).
874. The Trade Marks Ordinance, s. 46(a).

> The proprietor of a well-known trade mark, even if it is not a registered trade mark, shall be entitled to exclusive use of the mark in respect of the goods for which it is well-known in Israel or in respect of goods of the same description.

B. Exclusive Use of a Well-known Registered Trademark

289. Where a well-known mark has also been registered, the scope of exclusive use to which its owner is entitled, is broadened beyond the goods for which the mark is known or goods of the same description. Section 46A(b) of the Ordinance provides:

> The proprietor of a well known trade mark that is a registered trade mark shall also be entitled to the exclusive use of that mark in respect of goods which are not of the same description if use of that mark by a person other than the proprietor would be likely to indicate a connection between the said goods and the registered proprietor of the mark, and the registered proprietor of the mark is likely to be damaged by such use.

II. Temporary Protection during Exhibitions

290. If a mark that is not registered in Israel is used during official or officially recognized international exhibitions where the goods on which such mark is used are exhibited, it enjoys temporary protection as a registered mark, for the duration of such exhibition.[875]

§7. Limitations of the Scope of Trademark Protection

291. Trademark protection is territorial in its nature. The scope of rights conferred by the registration of a mark may also be subject to any limitations and disclaimers recorded in the register, which limit the exclusive use of the mark owner. The rights to exclusive use may be subject to statutory exceptions of legitimate third-party use.

I. Territorial Protection

292. Due to the territoriality of trademark rights, the rights conferred on the owner of a protectable trademark, whether by virtue of registration or the international goodwill of his well-known mark, are national in their scope – that is, limited to acts done in the territory of the State of Israel. Importation of goods for sale,

875. The Trade Marks Ordinance, s. 46B.

marketing or other trade purpose into territories under the administration of the Palestinian Authority is equivalent to importation into Israel.[876]

II. Limitations and Disclaimers

293. Use of disclaimed elements. Under the Trade Marks Ordinance, the Registrar may require an applicant for registration of a mark to disclaim the right to the exclusive use of an element of the mark that is common to the trade or otherwise non-distinctive, and has power to make registration conditional upon disclaimer.[877]

A registered owner may also subsequently request that a disclaimer in respect of the mark be recorded[878] or request that the list of goods or services for which the mark is registered be limited.[879]

Any disclaimers are included in the trademark's registration on the register.[880] A disclaimer under the Ordinance shall not affect any rights of the proprietor of the trademark except those which arise out of the registration of the mark.[881]

Conditions and limitations. The Registrar may accept a mark for registration subject to conditions or restrictions[882] or prescribe conditions in his decision in an opposition.[883] Any conditions and restrictions imposed by the Registrar are included in the trademark's registration on the register.[884]

III. Legitimate Third-Party Use

A. General

294. The proprietor's right to make exclusive use of his registered mark conferred under the Ordinance is not absolute and cannot prevent legitimate use by others, whether by virtue of the statutorily excused 'genuine use' or by falling outside the scope of infringing use; for a discussion of what use is considered infringing, see section §10 'Infringement and Remedies' *infra*. As noted, where the registration of a mark contains elements in respect of which a disclaimer of exclusive use has been registered, such elements do not by themselves form a bar to the registration

876. LCA 2736/98 *Habboub Bros. Co. v. Nike International Ltd*, 54(1) P.D. 614 [2000].
877. The Trade Marks Ordinance, s. 21(a). As a matter of practice, the policy of the Trade Marks Office is not to require disclaimers as a general rule other than in cases where the Registrar deems appropriate to exercise this power, except in specified cases (Circular Letter MN 84, 6 Sep. 2010); for a more detailed discussion of disclaimers of non-distinctive elements see s. §3 'Conditions of Protection', Part II -C. 3 (overcoming non-distinctiveness through disclaimer).
878. The Trade Marks Ordinance, s. 36(a)(4).
879. The Trade Marks Ordinance, s. 36(a)(3).
880. The Trade Marks Ordinance, s. 4(3).
881. The Trade Marks Ordinance, s. 21(b).
882. The Trade Marks Ordinance, s. 18(a).
883. The Trade Marks Ordinance, s. 24(f).
884. The Trade Marks Ordinance, s. 4(4).

of other marks. Nonetheless, when assessing similarity between marks as a whole, including for infringement purposes, disclaimed elements may be included.[885]

B. Permitted Genuine Use

295. The rights conferred on the owner of a registered trademark by virtue of registration do not prevent legitimate use by others, which fall within the ambit of the statutory exception of permitted genuine use. The 'genuine use' exception is set forth in section 47 of the Ordinance in the following language:

> Registration under this Ordinance shall not prevent any genuine use by a person of his own name or of the name of his business or the geographical name of his place of business or the name of the business of any of his predecessors in business, or the use by any person of any genuine description of the character or quality of his goods.

1. The Use of a Person's Name or Business Name

296. The primary assumption is that use of a person's name for business is a natural right, which may be exercised as long as the name being used is the actual name and there is no apprehension of consumer confusion; the trademark proprietor objecting to such use must show an imminent risk of confusion. However, no absolute protection is afforded to the right to use a name where there exists an apprehension of confusion; the use of a nickname increases the apprehension of confusion.[886]

To be protected, the use of a personal name, business name or geographical location of a business must be made in good faith without free-riding on the goodwill of the trademark owner, and only to the extent necessary for identifying the user.[887]

2. Genuine Description of Character or Quality of the Goods

297. Section 47 of the Ordinance provides for a third party's right to use the mark to indicate 'genuine description of the character or quality of his goods'. The Supreme Court in the *Toto* matter[888] enunciated the criteria of permissible truthful use as follows: (1) that the goods are difficult to identify without using the mark and the use is necessary for identifying the goods, (2) that the use of the mark is made to such extent as does not exceed what is reasonably and fairly necessary for

885. LCA 5454/02 *Taam Teva (1988) Tivoli Ltd v. Ambrosia Supherb Ltd*, 57(2) P.D. 438 [2003] (*Taam Teva*) at 450.

886. CA 7980/98 *Freundlich v. Chaliva*, 58(2) P.D. 856, 876 [2000].

887. CA 3559/02 *Toto Gold Subscribers Club Ltd v. Sports Lottery Council*, P.D. 59(1) 873 at 898; The *McDonald* matter.

888. *Toto* at 898–899.

identifying the goods; and (3) that such use does not imply sponsorship by the trademark owner. Accordingly, a trademark may be used by another trader to describe truthfully the character or quality of his goods – for example, to identify the genuine merchandise of the trademark owner dealt in by such trader, whether or not authorized to deal in such merchandise (e.g., in situations of parallel importation),[889] to indicate the intended purpose or compatibility of the user's goods or services with those of the trademark owner – e.g., repair services or spare parts for the trademark owner's products.[890] Such use of a mark will be deemed permitted 'genuine use', provided there is no likelihood of confusion and the mark is used as reasonably necessary and in proportionate manner (e.g., not in overly prominent display or overly large font size).[891] In the context of parallel importation, it has been held that the most important factor is the likelihood of confusion as to sponsorship.[892] The Supreme Court also held that, in the context of parallel importation, distribution of genuine merchandise in less exclusive settings at lower prices did not by itself constitute dilution.[893]

C. Continued Use of a Mark Not Prejudiced by Well-known Mark

298. Under section 52A of the Ordinance, enacted as part of the implementation of the undertakings under the TRIPS Agreement, a well-known trademark protected under the Ordinance shall not prejudice the registrability, or validity of registration,

---

889. CA 471/70 *J.R. Geigy S.A. v. Pazchem Ltd*, 24(2) P.D. 705 [1970](parallel importation of genuine goods bearing the owner's trademarks, which had been manufactured abroad with the authorization of the trademark owner, is not infringement); CA 8848/12 *Tommy Hilfiger Licensing LLC et al v. Swissa* [2014], additional hearing refused (ACH 8619/14 *Tommy Hilfiger Licensing LLC et al v. Swissa* [2015]). LCA 8977/11 *American Eagle Outfitters Inc. v. Hamashbir Department Stores Ltd* [2011] (the law is not settled on whether a territorial restriction in the contractual relations between the trademark owner and the foreign trader (from whom the parallel importer acquires) would affect the determination regarding infringement).

890. OM (TA) 5115/97 *Gillette Co. v. Amir Marketing* (unpublished) [1997] (indicating compatibility of razor blades to Gillette sensor razors not infringement).

891. OM (TA) 5115/97 *Gillette v. Amir Marketing* (unpublished) [1997] (necessary use was not deemed infringement); CC (TA) 652/92 *Gillette Co. v. Adi Marketing & Distribution Ltd* (unpublished) [1996] (prominently displayed mark was deemed to constitute infringement); CC (TA) 3674/68 *Rechev Nir v. Peugeot* (prominently displayed mark Peugeot on garage board was deemed not to be a good faith description of garage services). The very stringent restrictions on the scope and quantity of the parallel importer's use of the owner's marks, imposed in CC (TA Distr.) 11296-09-10 *Tommy Hilfiger Licensing LLC et al. v. Swisa et al.* [2012] (overly broad and overly prominent use of the Tommy Hilfiger marks (on storefront, outdoor signage, website and in advertising) by parallel importers of genuine products exceeded what was reasonably and fairly necessary for genuinely describing the goods and was likely to imply sponsorship by the trademark owner, thus falling outside the statutory defence of genuine description; all but limited use of the marks was enjoined) were relaxed on appeal by the Supreme Court (CA 7629/12 *Swissa et al. v. Tommy Hilfiger Licensing LLC et al.* [2014]), additional hearing refused (ACH 8619/14 *Tommy Hilfiger Licensing LLC et al v. Swissa* [2015]).

892. *Tommy Hilfiger 2014.*

893. *Tommy Hilfiger 2014.*

of an identical or similar mark if such mark had been applied for, or registered, in good faith prior to the day when the well-known mark became well known.[894]

A well-known trademark shall also not prejudice another's right to use an identical or similar mark if such right had been acquired through good faith use of it prior to the day when the well-known mark became well known.[895]

§8. Use Requirements

I. Use Requirement Following Registration

299. Loss of rights due to non-use. The Trade Marks Ordinance does not require an owner of a registered mark to use it in order to maintain the registration. However, in light of the concept of the integrity of the register, which should reflect actual trade practice, 'defensive' registrations are liable to be struck off the register for non-use pursuant to section 41 of the Trade Marks Ordinance.[896]

II. Removal Due to Non-use

A. General

300. Lack of *bona fide* use of the mark exposes a mark to removal for non-use. The Trade Marks Ordinance provides that removal of a registration may be applied for, in respect of all goods or classes of goods for which the mark is registered or in respect of part thereof:

> on the ground that there was no bona fide intention to use the trade mark in connection with the goods in respect of which cancellation of registration is requested and that there has been in fact no bona fide use of the trade mark in connection with the goods in respect of which cancellation of registration is requested or that there had not been any such use during the three years preceding the application for cancellation.[897]

---

894. The Trade Marks Ordinance, s. 52A:

> Notwithstanding the provisions of this Ordinance, where an application for registration of a trade mark is filed, or where a trade mark has been registered in good faith, or where rights to a trade mark have been acquired through use of it in good faith, neither the eligibility of the mark for registration, the validity of registration, nor the right to use such trade mark, shall be prejudiced for the sole reason that the trade mark is identical or similar […] to a well-known trade mark, provided that the application for registration of the trade mark, the registration or the acquisition as aforesaid were effected prior to—(1) in the case of a well-known trade mark—the day on which the trade mark became a well-known trade mark; […].

895. The Trade Marks Ordinance, s. 52A.

896. The *Gigiesse* matter.

897. The Trade Marks Ordinance, s. 41(a).

A trademark is not subject to cancellation where 'it is proved that the non-use is due to special circumstances in the trade and not to any intention not to use, or to abandon, the mark in respect of the said goods'.[898]

B. Who May Apply for Removal Due to Non-use?

301. Application to remove a mark for non-use may be submitted by 'any person interested'.[899] Because the removal is intended to protect the integrity of the register, an 'interested person' has been given a liberal interpretation.[900]

C. What Constitutes 'Use'?

302. In order to sustain an attack on the grounds of non-use, the owner of the mark must show that he has used the mark in good faith during a period of three years that preceded the application for cancellation, and if the allegation of non-use is based on lack of *bona fide* intention to use the mark (before the elapse of a three-year period), he must show otherwise. Use of a mark in a manner that differs from the mark as appears on the register in such a way as not to change the distinctive character of the mark, also counts as use in good faith of a registered mark.[901] There exist certain statutory guidelines for types of use that are not to be considered as use in good faith. Thus, mere use in advertisements does not amount to *bona fide* use of the mark in Israel. Nonetheless, where there are special circumstances that, in the opinion of the Court or the Registrar, justify the non-use in Israel, the mark may not necessarily be cancelled.[902]

Similarly, rescinding a use authorization granted to an Israeli manufacturer may be deemed bad faith use in Israel, unless it is shown that such authorized user has breached the terms of the authorization or that the grantor of the authorization intends to manufacture the goods by himself or to grant authorization to another manufacturer in Israel.[903]

Use by an 'authorized user' would satisfy the requirements of 'use' under section 41 of the Trade Marks Ordinance only if such authorized user has been recorded and on condition that such use is subject to the control of the proprietor of the mark.[904]

Otherwise, the quantum and nature of use that would meet the requirement of 'use of a trademark in good faith' is not anchored in legislation and was addressed in case law. Thus, it was held, for example, that intent to use does not alone suffice

898. The Trade Marks Ordinance, s. 41(b).
899. The Trade Marks Ordinance, s. 41(a).
900. HCJ 67/71 *Premo Ltd v. Schmidgall*, P.D. 25(1) 802, 810 [1971].
901. The Trade Marks Ordinance, s. 41(f)(1).
902. The Trade Marks Ordinance, s. 41(c)(1).
903. The Trade Marks Ordinance, s. 41(c)(2).
904. The Trade Marks Ordinance, s. 41(f)(2).

to negate cancellation.[905] Similarly, enforcement actions such as detention of merchandise by Customs did not negate a finding of non-use.[906]

Where a word is used to indicate the nature or quality of goods, this is not considered as trademark use. Thus, the use of the registered mark 'lights' in relation to cigarettes, as in 'Marlboro Lights', did not constitute good faith use of the mark, because it was not intended to indicate the origin of the goods but rather their nature or quality.[907]

D. Excusing Non-use

303. Statutory exception of 'special circumstances in the trade'. Under the statutory exception, the registration would not be removed on the grounds of non-use if the Registrar is satisfied that non-use resulted from 'special circumstances in the trade' that prevented the use and not from the owner's intention not to use or to abandon the mark in respect of the goods in question.[908] The statutory exemption is analysed under a two-pronged test of 'special circumstances in the trade' and the proprietor's intention.[909] Such circumstances would typically be circumstances beyond control of the owner, for example, such as governmental policy not to grant import licenses,[910] but not the owner's failure to obtain an import license[911] or the owner's difficulty in finding another licensee.[912] It has been held that extensive infringing use may constitute a 'special circumstance in the trade' excusing non-use by the proprietor.[913]

Discretion to excuse non-use due to exceptional circumstances. Even where non-use has been demonstrated and the statutory exemption of 'special circumstances in the trade' does not apply, under the case law the Registrar may, in his discretion, refuse cancellation if exceptional circumstances exist, due to considerations of justice.[914] Such exceptional circumstances may be individual to the owner and not pervasive throughout the trade.

E. Partial Revocation on the Ground of Non-use

304. Following the Madrid amendments, revocation may be requested in respect of specific goods or specific classes of goods in a multiple-class registration. If

905. The *Gigiesse* matter.
906. The *Gigiesse* matter.
907. HCJ 296/86 *Philip Morris Inc. v. Moorgate Tobacco Co. Ltd*, P.D. 41(1) 485 [1987] (the mark 'lights' cancelled for non-use because the use made was not trademark use).
908. The Trade Marks Ordinance, s. 41(b).
909. The *Gigiesse* matter.
910. HCJ 95/54 *Schnell v. General Registrar*, 9 P.D. 127 [1955] (*Schnell*); HCJ 302/74 *Nicholas Overseas Ltd v. Nisan Preminger Ltd*, 29(1) P.D. 676 [1975] (*Preminger*).
911. *Schnell*; *Preminger*.
912. The *Gigiesse* matter.
913. The *Gigiesse* matter.
914. The *Gigiesse* matter.

grounds of revocation – in this context, use – exist only in respect of some of the goods or services for which the mark is registered, revocation shall be limited to such goods.

§9. Duration Of Protection: Renewal – Termination

I. Duration of Protection and Renewal

A. *Duration of Registration*

305. The date of registration is the date when the application for registration was filed.[915] Trademarks are due for renewal ten years from the application date.[916] Subsequent renewal terms are for ten years;[917] registrations renewed prior to 1 September 2010 are due for renewal after fourteen years (the renewal term prior to Israel's accession to the Madrid Protocol). If duly renewed and not removed, a trademark may enjoy perpetual protection.

At the timely request of the registered owner of a mark, the Registrar shall renew the registration of such trademark, in respect of all or part of the goods or classes of goods, for a period of ten years from the date of expiration of the original or renewed registration.[918] The expiry date is notified to the registered owner.[919]

B. *Lapse Due to Non-renewal: Restoration*

306. A trademark lapsed through failure to pay renewal fees is removed from the register after a grace period of six months from the original expiry date if the owner does not pay the prescribed fees within such six-month grace period.[920]

During the additional six-month period following the expiry of the grace period, the mark may be restored at the request of the registered owner if the Registrar is satisfied that such restoration is just, subject to such conditions as the Registrar may deem fit.[921] The owner's application must set forth the reasons for failure to pay maintenance fees and contain a declaration that the use of the mark has not ceased; in his decision on restoration, the Registrar will, *inter alia,* consider any injury to third parties.[922]

Lapsed registration temporary bar to registration. A lapsed trademark registration acts as a bar against registration of conflicting marks for one year following its removal from the register[923] unless the Registrar is satisfied that there was no *bona*

915. The Trade Marks Ordinance, s. 27.
916. The Trade Marks Ordinance, s. 31.
917. The Trade Marks Ordinance, s. 32.
918. The Trade Marks Ordinance, s. 32.
919. The Trade Marks Ordinance, s. 33(a).
920. The Trade Marks Ordinance, s. 33(b); the Trade Marks Regulations, ss 52–53.
921. The Trade Marks Ordinance, s. 33(b)(2).
922. The Trade Marks Ordinance, s. 33(b)(2).
923. The Trade Marks Ordinance, s. 34.

fide use in trade of the lapsed registration, or that the requested new registration is not likely to cause deception or confusion in consequence of the use previously made of the trademark subject of the lapsed registration.[924]

Termination due to grounds other than its expiry for non-renewal is addressed in Part II 'Termination', *infra*.

II. Termination

307. Trademark registration may lapse if not renewed, on the terms discussed above, or be cancelled at the initiative of the proprietor if approved by the Registrar or at the request of a third party. A third party may request cancellation if the mark does not meet the requirements for registration, on the grounds discussed below, or on the ground of non-use, addressed in section §8 'Use Requirement', *supra*.

A. *Cancellation at the Request of the Proprietor*

308. The Registrar may, at the request of the registered proprietor, cancel the entry of the trademark in the Register[925] or strike out any goods or classes of goods from those for which the trademark is registered.[926] Any decision of the Registrar shall be subject to appeal to the district court.[927]

B. *Cancellation Due to Ineligibility for Registration or for Continuation on the Register*

1. Grounds of Cancellation of a Regular National Mark

309. Rectification of the register, including cancellation of a registration, may be requested by any person aggrieved by 'the non-insertion or omission from the Register of any entry, or by any entry made in the Register without sufficient cause, or by any entry wrongly remaining on the Register, or by any error or defect in any entry in the Register'.[928] Cancellation may be requested in respect of specific goods or classes of goods.[929] If grounds of cancellation exist only in respect of some of the goods or services for which the mark is registered, cancellation shall be limited to such goods.

Specific grounds include ineligibility for registration under the various refusal grounds listed in sections 7 through 11 of the Ordinance,[930] the fact that the mark

924. The Trade Marks Ordinance, s. 35.
925. The Trade Marks Ordinance, s. 36(a)(5).
926. The Trade Marks Ordinance, s. 36(a)(3).
927. The Trade Marks Ordinance, s. 36(b).
928. The Trade Marks Ordinance, s. 38(a).
929. The Trade Marks Ordinance, s. 39(a).
930. The Trade Marks Ordinance, s. 39(a).

creates an unfair competition in respect of the applicant's rights in Israel[931] and bad faith at the time of filing of the mark. Bad faith at the time of filing may be inferred from the applicant's conduct after filing, e.g., if he attempts to free-ride on another mark's goodwill.[932] Another example of bad faith at the time of filing of the application may consist of an attempt to obtain trademark protection for purely functional or purely aesthetic embodiments that are protectable by a patent or a design, and thus to create unwarranted perpetual monopoly.[933]

Statute of limitations. There is a five-year limit for filing an application to cancel on the ground that the mark is not eligible for registration on the grounds of ineligibility under sections 7–11 of the Ordinance or on the ground that the mark 'creates an unfair competition in respect of the applicant's rights in Israel';[934] the five-year period commences upon the issuance of the certificate of registration.[935]

Although it was held that a mark may become incapable of being registered due to loss of its distinctive character through extensive use by others (e.g., it became a generic term),[936] the Ordinance does not specifically provide for such ground for cancellation of a registered mark.

There is no time limit for an application for removal of a trademark on the grounds that the application for registration of the mark was filed in bad faith;[937] a trademark registered in bad faith, under section 39(a1) of the Ordinance, remains open to attack at any time.

2. Grounds of Cancellation of *Telle Quelle* Registrations

310. The registration of a foreign trademark, which continues to be registered in the country of origin, may be removed from the register only on the grounds which under section 16 preclude registration[938] (discussed in section §3 'Conditions of Protection', *supra*). A trademark of a non-resident which is not eligible for registration under the domestic criteria of eligibility and has been registered *telle quelle* may be removed from the register at any time on the grounds precluding its registration under the domestic criteria of eligibility (namely, sections 8–11 of the Ordinance) when it is no longer registered in the country of origin; the foreign proprietor of the mark may, however, prove that at the time of application for removal, the mark would have been eligible for registration upon application by an Israeli applicant.[939]

931. The Trade Marks Ordinance, s. 39(a).
932. CC (TA Distr.) 2960/00 *Gianni Versace S.p.A. v. Versace 83 Ltd et al.* (unpublished) [2010] (*Versace*).
933. MCM 16540/06 *Koninklijke Philips Electronics N.V. v. Sarig Electronic Ltd* (unpublished) [2006].
934. The Trade Marks Ordinance, s. 39(a).
935. The Trade Marks Ordinance, s. 39(a).
936. CA 2673/04 *Coffee To Go Marketing (1997) Ltd v. Shaked* (unpublished) [2007].
937. The Trade Marks Ordinance, s. 39(b).
938. The Trade Marks Ordinance, s. 39(b)(1), discussed in s. §3 'Conditions for Registration', *supra*.
939. The Trade Marks Ordinance, s. 39(b)(2).

3. Who May Apply for Cancellation?

311. 'Person aggrieved'. Application may be made by 'any person aggrieved' by the improperly entered or remaining registration.[940] 'Person aggrieved' has been liberally construed to include any competitor deprived of an advantage due to the benefit accruing to the registrant pursuant to the improper registration,[941] or potentially deprived of an advantage in the future.[942]

Registrar's power to cancel at his initiative. There is no express statutory provision in the Ordinance that provides for the Registrar's power to initiate cancellation of a mark. Prior to September 2010, an express provision of the Ordinance allowed the Registrar to apply to the High Court of Justice for cancellation of a registered mark in the case of fraud in its registration or transfer,[943] repealed in 2010. It appears from the explanatory notes of the governmental bill for the 2010 amendment of the Trade Marks Ordinance that repealed such provision, that the legislator assumes that the authority to invalidate such registrations *ex officio* vests in the Registrar by virtue of its inherent power to protect the integrity of the register.[944]

§10. Infringement and Remedies

I. Infringement

312. An infringement action may be brought for the infringement of a registered mark or, following the 1999 amendment of the Trade Marks Ordinance, for the infringement of a well-known unregistered mark.[945] Unregistered marks that are not well known do not give rise to an action for infringement, so that other causes of action would need to be invoked for obtaining protection.[946] Infringement is defined in the Ordinance as:

> the use by a person not entitled thereto –
>
> (1) of a registered trade mark, or of a mark resembling such a trade mark, in relation to goods in respect of which the trade mark is registered, or to goods of the same description;
> (2) of a registered trade mark in advertising goods of the class in respect of which the mark is registered or goods of the same description;
> (3) of a well-known trade mark even if it is not a registered trade mark, or of a mark so similar to it as to be misleading, in respect of goods for which the mark is well known or in respect of goods of the same description;

940. The Trade Marks Ordinance, s. 38(a).
941. *Tirosh.*
942. *Klil* at 316–317.
943. The Trade Marks Ordinance, s. 38(d).
944. Government bill 477 of 25 Jan. 2010; protocol 204 of the Constitution, Law and Justice Committee of the *Knesset* of 2 Jun. 2010.
945. The Trade Marks Ordinance, s. 57.
946. See s. §11 *infra* for other causes of action.

(4) of a well-known trade mark which is registered, or a mark similar thereto, in respect of goods not of the same description, provided that such use could indicate a connection between such goods and the proprietor of the registered trade mark and the proprietor of the registered trade mark might be harmed as a result of such use.

We shall address below each alternative in the statutory definition.

A. *Infringement of a Registered Mark by Use in Relation to Goods or Services in Respect of Which the Trademark Is Registered, or to Goods of the Same Description*

1. Assessment of Similarity between the Marks

313. Where allegedly infringing use is made of a mark that is not identical with a registered mark, the issue is whether the marks are deemed similar for the purpose of 'infringement' as defined in the Trade Marks Ordinance. The statutory definition of infringement of a registered mark does not require that similarity be confusing; however, it has been held that, in light of the twofold role of trademark protection – to protect the public from confusion and to protect the goodwill acquired by a trader – a plaintiff in an infringement action should usually demonstrate that the infringing mark is similar to the point of causing confusion among the public;[947] the examination of confusing similarity is guided by the same tests that are used for examining eligibility of a mark for registration.[948] For a detailed discussion of assessing confusing similarity between the marks, see section §3 'Conditions of Protection' (Assessing Confusing Similarity) *supra*.

In the context of infringing use, the question arises as to whether a trademark can be infringed by use for services and *vice versa*. It has been held that when a mark is registered in respect of goods, the owner of a registered trademark cannot prevent the use of the mark in respect of services rendered in respect of his goods, e.g., repair services.[949] In certain circumstances, however, use in relation to services was deemed to infringe a mark registered in respect of goods, or *vice versa*, if they belong to the same 'commercial family', to be defined on a case-by-case basis, and likely to confuse vis-à-vis*as to* sponsorship.[950]

947. *Taam Teva* at 450.
948. *Taam Teva* at 450.
949. CA 788/70 *Volkswagenwerk AG v. Tenus et Nadjar Garage*, P.D. 25(2)315 [1971] (*Volkswagen*) – the claim of the owner of a trademark registered in respect of cars against a defendant who provided services for such cars dismissed because the owner did not hold a registration in respect of services; in CC (TA) 1769/83 *The Boeing Company v. Boeing Tours Ltd*, 5749/1989 (3) P.M. 108 [1989], tour services did not infringe the trademark registered in respect of goods (land vehicles, aircraft and parts thereof), as these cannot be of the same description; in reliance on the *Volkswagen* case, held: in order to gain protection, a service mark should be registered, regardless of any connection that may exist between the type of services in question and the type of goods for which the trademark is registered.
950. The *Toto* matter (lottery goods and services held to belong to the same 'commercial family').

2. Use 'By a Person Not Entitled Thereto'

314. Only use made by a person 'not entitled thereto' may constitute infringement, that is, a person other than the lawful proprietor of the mark in question or acting under the proprietor's authorization under section 50(a) of the Ordinance, and whose use falls outside the exception of 'genuine use' under section 47 of the Ordinance.

3. Nature of Infringing Use

315. What constitutes 'use of a mark' for infringement purposes is not defined in the Ordinance. There is also no statutory requirement for use 'in trade' or 'for commerce'. One commentator notes that infringing use should be 'use by way of trade', despite the silence of the definition of infringement, because the purpose of the Ordinance is to afford a trademark proprietor protection in trade and not to grant him an absolute right for any other purpose.[951]

It is submitted that when a mark is not used as a 'trademark', infringement cannot be established.[952] Registration of a domain name identical or misleadingly similar to a mark entitled to protection was held to constitute infringement.[953] While the question of whether use of a competitor's mark as a targeted search keyword (meta tag) in a search engine (e.g., Google AdWord) would constitute trademark use has not been conclusively resolved, case law appears to indicate that such use would not be deemed infringing.[954]

4. Infringing Use: Is Likelihood of Confusion Required?

316. The statutory definition of trademark infringement in the Ordinance does not expressly require that use always be confusing or misleading. While judicial determination of what constitutes infringing 'use' has usually taken into account the primary goal of trademark protection to prevent confusion of consumers as to source, it has been acknowledged that in principle in some cases infringement may occur also in the absence of confusion as to source.[955] A pronouncement of the

---

951. Seligsohn at 76.
952. Cf. HCJ 296/86 *Philip Morris Inc. v. Moorgate Tobacco Co.*, 41(1) P.D. 485 [1987] (the registered mark 'lights' cancelled for non-use because it was used to designate a type of cigarette rather than the identity of its manufacturer, namely 'Marlboro Lights'.
953. MCM (TA District) 14377/01 *Israel Bar Association v. Ben David* (unpublished) [2001] (registration of domain name 'hapraklit' (Hebrew for 'the attorney') held to infringe the unregistered mark of the Israel Bar Association in long-term use as the name of a professional journal).
954. In one district court decision, it was held that use of a trademark as a meta tag would not amount to infringement (OM 506/06 *Mat'im Li Fashion Ltd v. Crazy Line Ltd*, 5764-2004 (2) P.M. 702). The Supreme Court in *Tommy Hilfiger 2014* noted in an *obiter dictum* that use of another's trademark as keyword or meta tag in a search engine would not be deemed infringement.
955. Cf. CA 471/70 *J.R. Geigy S.A. v. Pazchem Ltd*, 24(2) P.D. 705 [1970] at 707; CA 8483/02 *Aloniel Ltd v. McDonald*, 58(4) P.D. 314 [2004] (*McDonald*) at 331–332 and the *Toto* matter at 892.

Supreme Court in a recent case appears to indicate that a defendant's intention to mislead consumers does not suffice if there was no likelihood of confusion.[956]

B. Infringement of a Registered Mark by Use in Advertising

317. Infringement of a registered trademark also extends to use in advertising regardless of whether confusion may arise. A registered mark is infringed when a person not entitled thereto makes use of a registered mark in advertising goods of the class in respect of which the mark is registered or goods of the same description.[957]

Does 'use of a mark' exclude non-identical marks? A literal interpretation of the statutory language suggests that use in advertising is infringing only if made of a mark identical with the registered mark. However, the Supreme Court held that infringement through use in advertising is not limited to strictly identical marks (McDonald's and McDonald were deemed practically the same).[958]

Is any use in advertising infringing? Statutory definition of infringement through advertising is broad enough to suggest that no use of a mark in advertising is permitted; the Supreme Court has confirmed that such use need not be confusing for establishing infringement.[959] It noted, however, in a *dictum* that truthful comparative advertising, which serves the principle of free speech and increases the pool of knowledge by presenting accurate facts about products or services, may be exempted if done in a strictly informative manner.[960] The majority opinion was that denigrating mention of another's mark in advertising falls within the definition of infringement.[961]

C. Infringement of a Registered Mark That Is Well Known

318. The definition of infringement of a registered well-known mark is broader than that of infringement of a registered mark which is not well known, so that, in addition to the infringement discussed above, infringement of a registered well-known mark occurs also when use is made in respect of goods not of the same description, provided that such use could indicate a connection between such goods and the proprietor of the registered trademark and that the proprietor of the registered mark might be harmed as a result of such use.[962]

956. CA 5066/10 *Shlomo A. Angel Ltd v. J & E Berman Ltd et al* [2013] at 22–23.
957. The Trade Marks Ordinance, s. 1.
958. *McDonald* at 331, majority opinion.
959. *McDonald*; see also OM 506/06 *Mat'im Li Fashion Ltd v. Crazy Line Ltd*, P.M. 5764-2004 (2) 702.
960. *McDonald*, at 334.
961. *McDonald* at 334–335. The dissenting opinion was that use in advertising should not be given broad interpretation and should constitute infringement only if the user benefits from the proprietor's goodwill through deception, *McDonald* at 376.
962. The Trade Marks Ordinance, s. 1.

1. Determination Whether a Mark Is Well Known

319. There is no separate registration of well-known marks, so that the determination whether a registered mark is well known is a judicial determination. The criteria governing the determination whether a mark is well known are discussed in section §3 'Conditions of Protection', *supra.*

2. Assessing Similarity between Marks

320. Where the alleged infringement relates to a mark that is similar to but not identical with the well-known mark, statutory language does not require that such similarity be confusing (the applicable requirement is that a harmful association is liable to be created between the goods bearing the accused marks and the proprietor of the well-known mark).[963] However, in a recent judgment, the Supreme Court interpreted the statutory language differently, observing that to establish infringement of a well-known mark (whether registered or unregistered) with respect to goods of the same description, likelihood of confusion must be shown; only with regard to goods of a different description would a likelihood of association suffice.[964] The scope of protection depends on the strength of the mark on the spectrum of distinctiveness. Where the well-known mark is, or includes, a dictionary word which is descriptive or commonly used in the trade (e.g., 'family' (in Hebrew) for the same type of goods such as family magazines) or as a laudatory word ('absolute'), it will be afforded a narrower protection;[965] generally the more arbitrary the mark, the lesser degree of similarity required to establish infringement.[966]

3. Infringing Use of a Registered Well-known Mark: Likelihood of Association

321. Infringing use of a registered well-known mark requires a showing of likelihood of association with the proprietor of the well-known mark, in a manner that would be harmful to the proprietor.[967]

Infringing use of a registered well-known mark encompasses use in relation to goods that are not of the same description. Unlike an ordinary registered trademark, the protection of a registered well-known mark transcends 'goods of the same description'.[968] The courts have, however, noted that caution should be exercised when extending protection beyond the goods of the same description, even for

963. See the *Unilever* matter at 22–23.

964. CA 5066/10 *Shlomo A. Angel Ltd v. J & E Berman Ltd et al* [2013] at 32–34.

965. Cf. the *Bacardi* matter where it was held that the use of 'Bakardi' with respect to jeans wear unlawfully conflicted with the trademark 'Bacardi', which is well known in respect of rum, versus the *Absolut* matter where it was held that the use of 'Absolute Shoes' did not unlawfully conflict with the trademark 'Absolut', which is well known in respect of vodka. See also discussion in The *Good Family* matter.

966. *Taam Teva* analysed in the *Absolut* matter.

967. The Trade Marks Ordinance, s. 1; the *Absolut* matter.

968. The Trade Marks Ordinance, s. 1.

well-known marks.[969] The protection afforded to a mark depends on its inherent distinctiveness; arbitrary, inherently distinctive well-known marks such as 'Bacardi' would be entitled to protection for a category of goods dissimilar from the goods for which it is registered.[970] With respect to marks of lesser inherent distinctiveness, their protection would not extend as far beyond the description of goods for which they are registered.[971]

4. Use 'By a Person Not Entitled Thereto'

322. In addition to other exceptions permitting use of a trademark, a person may be entitled to make such use of a mark identical or similar to a well-known mark due to his prior rights, in accordance with section 52A of the Ordinance.[972]

D. Infringement of an Unregistered Well-known Mark

323. While as a general rule an unregistered mark does not give rise to an action for infringement, an exception exists for an unregistered well-known mark. An unregistered well-known mark is infringed by use by a person not entitled thereto:

> of the well-known mark or of a mark so similar to it as to be misleading in respect of goods for which the mark is well known or in respect of goods of the same description.[973]

An unregistered well-known mark, unlike an ordinary unregistered mark which cannot form a basis for an infringement action, affords its owner a right of action in infringement for unauthorized use of such mark or confusingly similar mark in respect of goods for which the mark is well known or in respect of goods of the same description.[974] The criteria governing the determination whether a mark is well known, and the determination of confusing similarity, are discussed in section §3 'Conditions of Protection', *supra*.

Another difference between infringement of non-registered well-known marks and that of registered marks resides in the ability to implement administrative measures at the borders, which is possible only for registered trademarks. Similarly, the infringement of a well-known trademark that is not registered does not amount to a criminal offence. See discussion below.

---

969. The *Absolut* matter.
970. The *Bacardi* case and others analysed in the *Absolut* matter at 885.
971. *Winemakers Cooperative Association of Rishon Lezion and Zichron Yaakov Ltd v. Infineon Technologies AG*, Opposition to the registration of marks 120949, 129050 'Carmel' [2003]. See also the *Absolut* matter.
972. Discussed in s. §7 'Limitations of the Scope of Trademark Protection', *supra*.
973. The Trade Marks Ordinance, s. 1.
974. The Trade Marks Ordinance, s. 1.

E. Who May Sue for Infringement?

324. An action for infringement may be brought only by the owner of a registered mark,[975] or the owner of a well-known unregistered mark.[976] A licensee (an authorized user), even if recorded in accordance with the provisions of the Ordinance, cannot bring an action for infringement; he can, however, act under a specific power of attorney from the trademark owner.[977]

It follows from the language of the Ordinance that, unless the action relies on a well-known mark, for which registration is not required to support a claim, an action for infringement may be brought only after the registration of a trademark has been completed.

II. Remedies

A. Civil Remedies for Trademark Infringement

325. The remedies for registered trademark infringement provided for by the Ordinance are as follows: injunction; damages; the destruction of goods produced during the performance of the infringement or which served in performing the infringement;[978] at the plaintiff's request, the transfer to the plaintiff of ownership of the goods produced during the performance of the infringement or which served in performing the infringement, in consideration for payment of their value but for the infringement;[979] any other disposition of the goods produced during the performance of the infringement or which served in performing the infringement.[980] The defendant shall not be allowed to possess the goods, even after he has removed the infringing marks, except in extraordinary cases.[981] The plaintiff is also entitled to 'any other relief which the court dealing with the case is competent to grant'.[982] Such other relief may include accounting for profits or declarative judgment.

Under the language of the Ordinance in the wake of the TRIPS amendment, the only remedy available for the infringement of an unregistered well-known trademark is injunction.[983] This ought not exclude remedies under other causes of action, e.g., passing off.

975. The Trade Marks Ordinance, s. 57(a).
976. The Trade Marks Ordinance, s. 57(a).
977. CA 650/80 *Empisal Israel Ltd v. Naimi*, 37(3) P.D. 780 [1983].
978. The Trade Marks Ordinance, s. 59(a) and 59A(a)(1).
979. The Trade Marks Ordinance, s. 59(a) and 59A(a)(2).
980. The Trade Marks Ordinance, s. 59(a) and 59A(a)(3).
981. The Trade Marks Ordinance, s. 59A(a)(3).
982. The Trade Marks Ordinance, s. 59(a).
983. The Trade Marks Ordinance, s. 59(b).

Damages. An award of damages may be based on a proof of damage suffered by the owner, or – because, as set forth in an early Supreme Court judgment, infringement entitles the plaintiff at least to nominal compensation even without proof of damage and because even actually suffered damage may be difficult to gauge accurately – may be granted by way of judicial assessment.[984]

Compensation without proof of damage. The Ordinance contains no express provision for awarding compensation for trademark infringement without proof of damage (in contradistinction to the tort of passing off under the Commercial Torts Law, for which a remedy of statutory damages is available). As noted, an early Supreme Court judgment handed down in 1969 permitted, based on English law, damages without proof of damage in trademark cases. In 2014, the Supreme Court held that compensation without proof of damage could not be awarded for trademark infringement, since the Ordinance did not vest the courts with the power to award it.[985] (It should be noted, however, that in other intellectual property contexts, the question of the courts' power to award compensation without proof of damage without express authorization in the statute is not yet conclusively resolved and raises some concern, after the Supreme Court opined in 2013, in a design infringement case, in an *obiter dictum*, that it was possible to award compensation for design infringement without proof of damage, even though the awarding of such damages is not anchored in statute,[986] and in the wake of this pronouncement, a 2013 District Court decisionawarded compensation without proof of damage for patent infringement (also not anchored in statute) but was reversed on appeal, as the Supreme Court held that compensation without proof of damage was inappropriate for patent infringement).[987]

Once a trademark is registered, damages could be awardable from the date of the registration, which is the date when the application for registration was filed.[988] Damages for infringement of marks registered pursuant to priority claims do not extend to infringement committed before the date of filing of the application for registration of the mark in Israel.[989]

Interim relief. Interim relief may, in appropriate cases, be granted *ex parte* and may include interim injunction, attachment, *Anton Piller*-type search and seizure order. For a detailed discussion of interim relief, see Chapter 2 Patents in section §9 'Infringement and Remedies'.

984. *Frou-Frou 1969* at 49–50. See, however, the recent judgment of the Supreme Court in the *Tommy Hilfiger* matter (CA 7629/12) discussed below. The majority opinion in CA 1203/13 *Tomashover v. Art Optic Ltd* [2015], while affirming an award of damaged by assessment due to evidentiary difficulties, noted that damages by way of judicial assessment should be reserved for exceptional cases, whereas the minority suggested that it should not be exceptional in IP cases.
985. CA 7629/12 *Swissa et al. v. Tommy Hilfiger Licensing LLC et al.* [2014] at 44 and 48, additional hearing refused (ACH 8619/14 *Tommy Hilfiger Licensing LLC et al v. Swissa* [2015].
986. CA 3853/11 *Ronit National Flags Ltd. et al. v. Shatan et al.* [2013].
987. CC (TA Distr.) 1133-09-10 *Twitoplast Ltd. v. Tavig - Israel Gruber Ltd. et al.* [2013]; this issue reversed on appeal in CA 7201/13 *Tavig - Israel Gruber Ltd. Et al. v. Twitoplast Ltd.* [2015].
988. The Trade Marks Ordinance, s. 27.
989. The Trade Marks Ordinance, s. 55(c).

B. Administrative Measures

326. In addition to civil liability for infringement, the proprietor of a registered mark whose right has been infringed or faces infringement may be able to resort to administrative measures of protection.

Detention at Customs. The owner of a registered mark whose rights have been infringed, or who faces 'reasonable suspicion' that his rights will be infringed, may give written notice to the Customs Director to detain the release of allegedly infringing goods.[990] The Customs Director may, either upon receiving such notice or at his own initiative, detain goods that *prima facie* infringe registered trademark rights.[991] Detention by Customs is subject to the deposit of an indemnification guarantee by the trademark owner[992] and will be cancelled if the owner fails to bring legal action within ten days of the notice of detention.[993]

Owners of unregistered marks do not have a procedure for enlisting the assistance of Customs and have to apply for an interim injunction to enjoin the release of infringing goods from Customs. Goods imported for personal use are not subject to Customs detention.[994]

It is to be noted that Customs has the power to detain goods also in accordance with the Merchandise Marks Ordinance[995] and with the Consumer Protection Law - 1981.[996]

C. Penal Measures

327. In addition to civil liability for infringement, a range of activities involving unauthorized use of registered trademarks and of their imitations incurs criminal liability under the Trade Marks Ordinance[997] or the Merchandise Marks Ordinance.[998]

Activity incurring criminal liability. Criminally punishable activities are unauthorized commercial marking of goods for which the mark is registered which is liable to confuse[999] and unauthorized commercial importation of goods marked with a mark registered for such goods or imitation of such mark which is liable to confuse (unless the marking abroad was done with the authorization of the mark owner there),[1000] as well as commercial sale, distribution, or rent of goods so marked or imported,[1001] and possession for trade purposes of goods so marked or

990. The Trade Marks Ordinance, s. 69A.
991. The Customs Ordinance, s. 200A.
992. The Trade Marks Ordinance, s. 69A(d); the Customs Ordinance, s. 200A(c).
993. The Customs Ordinance, s. 200A(a)(4).
994. The Trade Marks Ordinance, s. 69A(e).
995. The Merchandise Marks Ordinance, s. 14.
996. The Consumer Protection Law, s. 35.
997. The Trade Marks Ordinance, s. 60.
998. The Merchandise Marks Ordinance, s. 3(2).
999. The Trade Marks Ordinance, s. 60(a)(1).
1000. The Trade Marks Ordinance, s. 60(a)(2).
1001. The Trade Marks Ordinance, s. 60(a)(3).

imported.[1002] Corporate officers are under a duty to prevent offences under the Trade Marks Ordinance and may be criminally liable.[1003]

While liability under the Trade Marks Ordinance is limited to activities in respect of registered marks or their imitations, under the Merchandise Marks Ordinance, it is an offence to sell or possess for commercial or industrial purposes goods or items designated by forged trademark or false trade description or falsely designated by a trademark or a mark confusingly similar to it[1004] – that is, there is no requirement under the Merchandise Marks Ordinance that a trademark be registered to trigger an offence. Defences of reasonable precautions and otherwise good faith conduct are available under the Merchandise Marks Ordinance.[1005]

Additional offences. It is also an offence to provide false information to the Registrar in connection with an application.[1006] It is an offence to make an explicit or implied misrepresentation that a trademark is registered.[1007]

Procedure. To initiate a criminal proceeding, the mark owner may file a complaint with the police or file a private criminal complaint with the court.[1008]

Penalties. Penalties for criminal offences under the Trade Marks Ordinance range from the imposition of a fine to three years' imprisonment.[1009] Presenting false information to the Registrar at registration is subject to one year's imprisonment.[1010]

§11. Overlapping and Relation to Other Intellectual Property Laws

I. Trademarks and Other Intellectual Property Rights: General

328. The primary goal of trademark protection has been held to confer protection on marks insofar as these serve to indicate the source of goods and distinguish between the goods of different traders, so as to protect consumers from confusion and traders from misappropriation of their goodwill,[1011] at times removing for this purpose from the public domain names or other signs that are not uncommon. Such goal accounts for the unlimited duration of trademark protection as long as a mark meets the criteria. By contrast, patents, industrial designs and copyright enjoy protection of a limited duration, intended to encourage creativity and innovation in return for making the fruit of such creativity public and subsequently including it in the public domain. Because of the different goals dictating different terms of protection, the question arises at times as to whether trademark protection may

1002. The Trade Marks Ordinance, s. 60 (4).
1003. The Trade Marks Ordinance, s. 60(d).
1004. The Merchandise Marks Ordinance, s. 3(2).
1005. The Merchandise Marks Ordinance, s. 3(2).
1006. The Trade Marks Ordinance, s. 60(c).
1007. The Trade Marks Ordinance, s. 63.
1008. The Criminal Procedure Law [Consolidated Version], 5742-1982, s. 68.
1009. The Trade Marks Ordinance, s. 60(a).
1010. The Trade Marks Ordinance, s. 60(c).
1011. CA 11487/03 *August Storck KG v. Alpha Intuit Foodstuffs Ltd* (unpublished) [2008]; LCA 5454/02 *Taam Teva (1988) Tivoli Ltd v. Ambrosia Supherb Ltd*, P.D. 57(2) 438 [2003].

complement the intellectual property rights of limited duration or should not be available for the same subject matter.

The laws of unfair competition (such as the tort of passing off) are similar in their objective to the law of trademarks and therefore can apply alongside trademark protection.

II. Complementary Protection: Passing Off and Other Torts under the Commercial Torts Law

329. Protection of marks regardless of their registration under the Trade Marks Ordinance may be available under other doctrines, such as the tort of passing off under the Commercial Torts Law and other commercial torts thereunder, unjust enrichment under the Unjust Enrichment Law, and consumer deception under the Consumer Protection Law.

A. *Passing Off*

330. The tort of passing off. A mark, regardless of registration, may be entitled to protection under the tort of passing off under the Commercial Torts Law.

The tort of passing off is defined in the Commercial Torts Law, which prohibits a trader from causing an asset he sells or a service he provides, to be mistaken for the asset or service of another trader, or for an asset or service that is connected with another trader.[1012] The courts have viewed the objective of the tort in protecting the goodwill acquired by a trader.[1013] To establish passing off, the plaintiff must prove two elements: (1) his goodwill (reputation) in his goods; and (2) reasonable apprehension of public confusion as to the origin of the goods/services.[1014] Actual confusion is not required to establish passing off.[1015] It has been ruled that passing off is not available for the protection of functional features[1016] or aesthetic shapes.[1017]

Upon the enactment of the Commercial Torts Law, the definition of passing off expressly covers services; the earlier statutory definition did not refer to services, which were judicially read into the definition of the tort.[1018]

Demonstrating goodwill. Under Israeli case law, the plaintiff – in contrast to a trademark infringement action – needs to show that his goods have acquired recognition by the public, that is, that the public associates them with the plaintiff or with a certain source even if not identified by name.[1019] If the plaintiff succeeds in

1012. The Commercial Torts Law, 5759-1999, s. 1.
1013. CA 634/89 *Rein v. Fuji Electronics Mfg Co.,* P.D. 45(4) 837, 846 [1991]; *Good Family* at 943.
1014. CA 4030/02 *Amichai Trade Ltd v. Source Vagabond Systems Ltd,* 58(5) P.D. 632 [2004] (*Amichai Trade*); *the Good Family* at 944–955; *Storck.*
1015. CA 3471/98 *Salem v. Intar,* 54(2) P.D. 681 [2000].
1016. *Amichai Trade* at 636–637; *Storck.*
1017. *Phoenicia*; *Storck.*
1018. CC (TA) 1769/83 *The Boeing Company v. Boeing Tours Ltd,* 5749/1989 (3) P.M. 108 [1989].
1019. *Phoenicia Glass Factories Ltd v. Les Verreries de Saint Gobain,* 45(3) P.D. 224, 230–232 [1991].

showing goodwill, the action under passing off would depend on the likelihood of confusion.

Demonstrating likelihood of confusion. It is established law that likelihood of confusion for the purpose of passing off, as well as for the infringement of registered trademarks, is examined under the three-prong test, which considers the visual and aural similarity, the type of goods and the circle of customers, and other surrounding circumstances, as discussed in more detail in section §3 'Conditions of Protection' *supra.*[1020] It has been pointed out in subsequent case law that for the purposes of passing off, likelihood of confusion is examined having regard to the entirety of the defendant's actions, including overall get-up of the products. This is in contrast to trademark infringement actions where the focus is on the confusing similarity between the marks themselves, and the overall difference of the product get-up may be disregarded.[1021]

Under the tort of passing off, as in the law of trademarks, maximum protection is afforded to arbitrary or fanciful names where likelihood of confusion is easily inferred; descriptive names would be entitled to protection only where it has acquired distinctiveness through use, and would be limited in scope;generic names are not usually entitled to protection so as not to be monopolized.[1022]

Remedies for passing off; statutory damages. The provisions of the Civil Wrongs Ordinance apply to the tort of passing off.[1023] A plaintiff successful in a passing off action may be entitled to statutory damages (i.e., without proof of damages) in an amount of up to ISL 100,000 for each tort.[1024] The Supreme Court in the *Toto* matter[1025] held that the rationale for the remedy lies in addressing the difficulty in proving damage and in the need for determent. In determining the amount of statutory damages, the court must have regard, *inter alia*, to the gravity, number and duration of the torts, the fault attached to the tortfeasor's conduct, and the nature and size of his business. In the *Anderson* matter,[1026] the Supreme Court held that absent a showing of significant injury to the plaintiff and absent other justification for doing so, the court will not award statutory damages under this section.

The defendant may be ordered to give an account.[1027] A receiver may be appointed by the court to search the defendant's or third party's premises and seize infringing goods (or goods used for wrongdoing) or evidence,[1028] including such order *ex parte.*[1029] The court may order the destruction of infringing goods (or goods used for wrongdoing) or their transfer to the plaintiff for consideration or any other act in respect of the goods.[1030]

1020. *Frou-Frou* at 278.
1021. CA 1400/97 *Pikanti Food Industries (Israel) Ltd v. Osem Food Industries Ltd*, 51(1) 310 [1997]; *Taam Teva* at 450–451.
1022. *Good Family* at 944–955.
1023. The Commercial Torts Law, s. 11.
1024. The Commercial Torts Law, s. 13(a).
1025. *Toto* at 903–904.
1026. CA 5671/11 *Anderson Medical Ltd v. Unipharm Ltd* [2012].
1027. The Commercial Torts Law, s. 15.
1028. The Commercial Torts Law, s. 16.
1029. The Commercial Torts Law, s. 17.
1030. The Commercial Torts Law, s. 21.

Comparison with trademark protection. The courts have noted that the difference between passing off and infringement of a registered mark is in the burden placed on the plaintiff; the claim under trademark infringement (other than the infringement of a well-known mark) relies on the registration of a mark, whereas a plaintiff invoking passing off has to prove that he has acquired goodwill (reputation) worthy of protection.[1031] In addition, passing off requires a showing of a likelihood of confusion, which is not always the case for trademark infringement.

It has been held that the tort of passing off and trademark infringement are not co-extensive, since passing off addresses the overall conduct of the defendant while trademark infringement is limited to the use of the mark. Thus, it may well be that a certain conduct of a defendant would not amount to passing off but would nonetheless constitute trademark infringement, and *vice versa.*[1032] Also, similarity between the marks may be outweighed by the overall presentation of the goods.

In addition, the tort of passing off allows for statutory damages whereas trademark infringement does not.

B. False Trade Description under the Commercial Torts Law

331. The tort of false trade description. The definition of the tort of false trade description under the Commercial Torts Law provides that:

> A business shall not advertise, nor cause to be advertised, something that he knows or that he ought to know is untrue with respect to his own business, profession, goods or services or those of another business.[1033]

Advertisers or people disseminating third-party advertisements containing a false description will only be liable if they knew that the description was a false description or if the description was, on its face, a false description.[1034]

Formerly, such conduct was covered only by the tort of 'injurious falsehood' in the Civil Wrongs Ordinance, which requires 'malicious intent' and only applies to false advertising in respect of another; under the Commercial Torts Law, constructive knowledge suffices and the advertising may relate to one's own business.

The tort of false trade description under section 2 of the Commercial Torts Law has been successfully invoked where the source of goods is misrepresented[1035] and where the trademarks were used in a manner that did not accurately reflect the reality.[1036]

1031. *Phoenicia* at 231–232; *Toto* at 901.
1032. See for example the *Adidas* matter.
1033. The Commercial Torts Law, s. 2(a).
1034. The Commercial Torts Law, s. 2(b).
1035. CC (Mag. Haifa) 8843/05 *Amisragas v. Abadu Gas Tamra Ltd et al.* (unpublished) [2008].
1036. OM (TA) 1503/04 *Champion Motors (Israel) Ltd v. Haggai* (unpublished) [2008] (trademarks of car manufacturers prominently displayed by garage after termination of its license from exclusive importer as authorized service garage; the plaintiff did not succeed in showing its authority to sue in reliance on trademark registrations). CC (TA Distr.) 11296-09-10 *Tommy Hilfiger Licensing LLC et al. v. Swissa et al.* [2012] (a genuine parallel importer's use of the owner's trademark in

Remedies. The tort of false trade description does not entail the remedy of statutory damages;[1037] actual damage needs to be shown in order to obtain compensation.

C. *Tort of Unfair Interference with Access to Another's Business under the Commercial Torts Law*

332. The tort of unfair interference with access to another's business. The definition of the tort of unfair interference with access to another's business under section 3 of the Commercial Torts Law provides that an enterprise 'shall not unfairly prevent or burden the access of customers, employees or agents to the business, goods or services' of another enterprise. For example, in one instance[1038] the Tel Aviv District Court held that a defendant that had placed information booths and distributed advertising booklets on an access path leading to a career fair organized by the plaintiff had committed the tort of unfair interference with access to the plaintiff's business and had unjustly enriched itself at the plaintiff's expense; however, the claim of passing off was rejected, as the court found that the plaintiff did not have independent goodwill in the fair.

The tort of unfair interference with access has been at times invoked to supplement bad faith registration of domain names identical or similar to trademarks used by another trader, without good faith use of such domain name (users were rerouted to another domain), has been held to constitute unfair interference with access to such other trader's business, under section 3 of the Commercial Torts Law, as it hinders access to the trader's website,[1039] but were not held, for example, to constitute unfair interference when used as part of the domain name of a genuine parallel importer.[1040] Use of a competitor's mark as a targeted search keyword (meta tag) in search engines that resulted in sponsored ad links (Google AdWord) has been held

---

its store name and domain name created a false representation that its goods were sourced directly from the trademark owner and that its business was sponsored by the trademark owner, and thus fell within the scope of the tort); the Supreme Court in CA 7629/12 *Swissa et al. v. Tommy Hilfiger Licensing LLC et al.* [2014] lifted some of the restrictions on the parallel importer and in particular on its use of the domain name; additional hearing refused (ACH 8619/14 *Tommy Hilfiger Licensing LLC et al v. Swissa* [2015].

1037. The Commercial Torts Law, s. 12.

1038. *The Israeli Trade Fairs and Convention Centre Ltd v. Bashan Bar Ilan Management Services Ltd* (CC 27080-06-11 (TA Distr), 22 May 2012).

1039. CC (TA) 1627/01 *M.S. Magnetics v. Discopy (Israel) Ltd* [2001](unpublished); MCM (TA District) 14377/01 *Israel Bar Association v. Ben David* (unpublished) [2001] (registration of domain name 'hapraklit' (Hebrew for 'the attorney') held to infringe the unregistered mark of the Israel Bar Association in long-term use as name of a professional journal, and constitute unfair interference with access).

1040. CC (TA Distr.) 11296-09-10 *Tommy Hilfiger Licensing LLC et al. v. Swisa et al.* [2012] (the use of the mark TOMMY in the domain name of a parallel importer's website was held not to prevent or encumber access to the plaintiff's businesses and thus not to constitute the tort of interference with access to the business of the trademark owner), on appeal the Supreme Court found the importer's use of the domain name legitimate in light of the additional elements preventing confusion (CA 7629/12 *Swissa et al. v. Tommy Hilfiger Licensing LLC et al.* [2014], additional hearing refused (ACH 8619/14 *Tommy Hilfiger Licensing LLC et al v. Swissa* [2015]).

not to constitute unfair interference with access to a business.[1041] No unfair interference with access to another's business has been found in a case of trademark infringement and misrepresentations where neither physical nor telephonic nor online access was interfered with.[1042]

Remedies for unfair interference with access to a business. The tort of unfair interference with access to a business does not entail the remedy of statutory damages.[1043]

D. Torts under the Consumer Protection Law

333. The Consumer Protection Law, 5741 – 1981, makes certain deceptive practices, including misrepresentation as to the name, commercial appellation or sponsorship of a product or service, as well as misrepresentation as to the manufacturer of a product or the provider of a service,[1044] a civil wrong actionable under the Civil Wrongs Ordinance;[1045] criminal liability is also imposed.[1046] The civil action under the Consumer Protection Law is available not only to an aggrieved consumer[1047] but also to an aggrieved trader.[1048]

The tort of misleading acts under section 2 of the Consumer Protection Law may occur through a trader's action such as misrepresentation, or failure to act, through non-disclosure of particulars that needed to be disclosed.[1049] For the purpose of the misleading acts tort, likelihood of confusion suffices, even if no actual confusion occurred.[1050]

III. Trademarks and Plant Variety Names

334. Existing trademarks may prevent the registration of a plant variety under a certain name; the registration of a plant variety name is subject to the absence of a registration of an identical or similar name or description under the Trade Marks

1041. OM 506/06 *Mat'im Li Fashion Ltd v. Crazy Line Ltd*, 5764-2004 (2) P.M. 702.
1042. CC (Mag. Haifa) 8843/05 *Amisragas v. Abadu Gas Tamra Ltd et al.* (unpublished) [2008].
1043. The Commercial Torts Law, s. 12.
1044. Consumer Protection Law, s. 2(a).
1045. Consumer Protection Law, s. 31(a).
1046. Consumer Protection Law, s. 23(1).
1047. Consumer Protection Law, s. 31(a1).
1048. Consumer Protection Law, s. 31(a1), e.g., in CC (Centre) 07-08-1967 *Ferrero SPA v. N. A. Kastro Import & Export Ltd* (unpublished) [2009] (marketing chocolates misleadingly similar to plaintiff's Ferrero Rocher chocolates held to be consumer deception and therefore tort actionable by trader); OM (TA) 1503/04 *Champion Motors (Israel) Ltd v. Haggai* (unpublished)[2008] (trademarks of car manufacturers prominently displayed by garage after termination of its license from exclusive importer as authorized service garage).
1049. LCA 2837/98 *Arad v. Bezeq Israeli Communications Company Ltd*, P.D. 54(1) 600; OM (TA) 1503/04 *Champion Motors (Israel) Ltd v. Haggai* (unpublished) [2008].
1050. ACH 5712/01 *Berezny v. Bezeq Israeli Communications Company Ltd*, 57(6) P.D. 385 [2003]; OM (TA) 1503/04 *Champion Motors (Israel) Ltd v. Haggai* (unpublished) [2008].

Ordinance in respect of agricultural crops of the same species.[1051] For eligibility of a plant variety for registration, see Chapter 5 'Plant Breeders Rights'.

IV. Trademarks, Trade Names and Company Names

A. *Trademark Protection of Trade Names*

335. A trade name used by a business or a company name may function as its trademark and to be entitled to trademark protection, the conditions and scope of which is discussed elsewhere in this Chapter. Protection of trade names under other doctrines, such as the tort of passing off, is discussed *supra* in this section.

1. Conflict between Trademark (Registered or Propounded) and Trade Name

336. A trade name used by a business or a company name may come into conflict with another's trademark.

Trade name a bar to trademark registration. To resolve such conflicts in accordance with the principles of rights acquired through use and preventing consumer confusion, under the Trade Marks Ordinance, the Registrar may refuse registration of a trademark which is identical with another's name or business name, or resembles it, or containing such identical or resembling name, if the propounded mark is liable to confuse the public or constitute unfair competition.[1052] The examination of confusing similarity to a trade/business name makes use of the three-fold test of visual and auditory similarity, type of goods and kind of customers, and other circumstances, which is applied to the tort of passing off and conflicts between trademarks[1053] (discussed in section I, *supra*).

Genuine use of a trade name. Where a conflicting trademark is registered, such registration does not prejudice continued genuine use of a person's name or of the name of a business (or a predecessor's business), which is allowed under the genuine use exception.[1054]

2. Conflict between a Trademark and a Corporate Name

337. Trademark a bar to registration of a company name. Trademark rights may bar the registration of a conflicting corporate name. The Companies Law 5759 – 1999, which as a general principle permits a company to be registered under any

1051. Plant Breeders Rights Law, 5733-1973, s. 31(a).
1052. The Trade Marks Ordinance, s. 12.
1053. HCJ 226/63 *Sigma Chemical Co. v. Registrar of Trademarks*, 17 P.D. 2594 [1963] ('Sigma' allowed for registration for chemical preparations as no likelihood of confusion between it and Sigma Ltd).
1054. The Trade Marks Ordinance, s. 47.

name, subject to the provisions of the Companies Law and any other law,[1055] bars from registration, *inter alia*, deceptive or misleading corporate names.[1056] A company may not be registered under a name identical or confusingly similar to a trademark registered in Israel in respect of goods or services dealt in for purposes similar to the purposes of the company that applied for registration, unless it was proven to the Companies Registrar that the registered trademark owner agreed to it in writing.[1057]

The Companies Registrar may require a company to change the name that should have been barred from registration.[1058] A party aggrieved by the registration of a company name identical or misleadingly similar to a registered trademark, or by the registration of a deceptive or misleading company name, may apply to the court to enjoin such use; the court may grant such injunction unless persuaded that the respondent's right to use the name precedes that of the applicant.[1059]

Whether a company name is misleadingly similar is examined in accordance with the same three-fold test of visual and auditory similarity, type of goods and kind of customers, and other circumstances, which is applied to the tort of passing off and conflict between trademarks (discussed in section I, *supra*).[1060]

Use of a mark as part of a corporate name. Incorporation under a corporate name does not by itself confer any rights in such name as a mark or as a trade name.[1061] However, the use, within a company name, of an element (letter combination, word or phrase) claimed to be a mark may be deemed trademark use if such element appearing within a company name is intended to indicate the origin of goods or services and is perceived by the target customers as indicating their origin.[1062]

B. Trademarks and Unjust Enrichment

338. Under the *A.S.I.R.* ruling[1063] of the Supreme Court, protection under the unjust enrichment laws – discussed in more detail in Chapter 6 'Unjust Enrichment' – may be available in certain circumstances where specific intellectual property laws do not provide for a remedy and contain no contrary provision. In the *Adidas* matter[1064] in 2012, the Supreme Court held, by a majority opinion, that in the

1055. The Companies Law, s. 25.
1056. The Companies Law, 5759-1999, s. 27(b).
1057. The Companies Law, 5759-1999, s. 27(a)(2).
1058. The Companies Law, s. 29(a).
1059. The Companies Law, s. 30.
1060. *Bank Igud.*
1061. *Frou-Frou* at 279.
1062. *NBA Ltd v. NBA Properties Inc.*, Opposition to the registration of trademark 'NBA' 79593 [22 Mar. 2006] (whether use conferred goodwill to support an opposition); *Off Oz Industries (1991) Ltd v. Off Tenne Meat Enterprises Ltd*, Application to strike mark No. 169322 [20 Feb. 2011](cancellation for non-use).
1063. LCA 5798/94 et al. *A.S.I.R. Import Manufacture and Distribution Ltd v. Forum Accessories and Consumer Goods Ltd*, 52(4) P.D. 289 [1998].
1064. The dissenting opinion was that notwithstanding the absence of a likelihood of confusion or association among consumers that would have amounted to traditional trademark infringement, the defendant committed unjust enrichment as it free-rode the plaintiff's goodwill.

absence of a likelihood of confusion or of association with Adidas' well-known three-stripe mark, which would have afforded protection on the grounds of trademark infringement, Adidas has no cause of action under the laws of unjust enrichment against an importer of four-stripe sports shoes. In 2014, in a decision refusing an additional hearing of the *Adidas* matter, the Supreme Court clarified that the *Adidas* ruling in 2012 did not foreclose reliance on the unjust enrichment laws where the intellectual property laws do not afford protection due to issues of substance (such as the absence of a likelihood of confusion) rather than of form (such as absence of registration) but left it open for future consideration.[1065]

1065. ACH 6658/12 *Adidas Salomon AG v. Yassin* [2014].

Chapter 4. Industrial Designs

§1. Sources: Legislation

339. Industrial Designs may be protected under Israeli law by an Act specifically dealing with Industrial Designs – Patents and Designs Ordinance (1924)[1066] (hereinafter 'the Design Act') – which was applied to Palestine during the British Mandate, and was subsequently incorporated into Israeli law following independence in 1948.[1067] The Design Act has been amended twelve times in order to adapt it to international obligations as well as to contemporary needs[1068] (including nullification of the section dealing with patents on 1967 due to the legislation of a new modern patent act); nevertheless, it is still an obsolete piece of legislation. It should be noted that a new and comprehensive governmental Design Law bill has been drafted,[1069] and it proposes to introduce significant changes to the current law. In particular, there are two major proposed changes: establishment of a non-registered design right for a shorter term of protection, and adoption of sections that would allow Israel to sign the Hague Agreement Concerning the International Deposit of Industrial Designs, Geneva Act of 2 July 1999. The *Knesset* has approved the transfer of the bill to discussions at the *Knesset's* Economic Committee.[1070]

Industrial designs may be protected also, to a limited extent, by copyright law.[1071] A third legal path for protecting industrial designs is the unjust enrichment doctrine, developed by courts in order to fill the gaps in those cases where industrial designs fail to enjoy the protection of institutional intellectual property law.[1072] Copyright law and unjust enrichment are discussed below in section 10, which deals with overlapping protection.

Article 56 of the Design Act empowers the Registrar, with the approval of the Minister of Justice, to make rules regulating different issues, which are technical by nature, such as the practice of registration.[1073] Accordingly, a design regulation

1066. Officially published in Chukey Eretz-Israel vol. 2 (English) 1076 (1933).
1067. The authority of the British High Commissioner was transferred to the first Israeli Minister of Justice on 16 Jun. 1948, 5, 22.
1068. Three amendments were introduced by the British High Commissioner in the years 1937, 1938 and 1948, and nine amendments were introduced by the *Knesset* in the years 1951, 1952, 1961, 1967, 1999, 2000, 2002, 2007 and 2008.
1069. Government Bills 928 – Design Law Bill, 6 Jul. 2015.
1070. Design Law Bill, approved in *Knesset* first vote, 13 Jul. 2015.
1071. Copyright Act, 2007.
1072. Unjust Enrichment Act, 1979; CA 5768/94 A.S.I.R. *Import Export and Distribution et al. v. Forum Products Ltd*, P.D. 52 (4) 289 (1998).
1073. According to the Design Act, Art. 56:The Registrar, with the sanction of the Minister of Justice, may make such general rules and do such things as he thinks expedient, subject to the provisions of this Act, (1) for regulating the practice of registration under the Act; (2) for classifying goods for the purposes of designs; (3) for making or requiring duplicates of specifications, drawings and other documents; (4) for securing and regulating the publishing and selling of copies at such prices and in such manner as he thinks fit, of specifications, drawings and other documents; (5) for securing and regulating the making, printing, publishing and selling of indices to, and abridgements of, specifications and other documents in the registry of patents, and providing for the inspection of indices and abridgements and other documents; (6) for regulating the keeping of the register of patent agents under this Act; (7) prescribing the fees to be paid in respect of the grant of a patent

(hereinafter 'the Design Regulation') has been in effect since 1925.[1074] The Design Regulation has been amended several times; the last amendment is of 30 June 2014. The Design Regulation was amended in 2013 in order to update the classification of goods, required for registration. A common practice, which has developed in recent years, is for the Registrar to publish 'notices', clarifying different issues such as the practice of registration. These notices are internal guidelines of the Patent Office, and serve as a complimentary source to the Design Regulation.

Israel is a party to the Paris Convention of 1883, as revised in 1900, 1911, 1925, 1934, 1958, 1967 and as amended in 1979;[1075] the Hague Agreement;[1076] and the TRIPS Agreement.[1077] Under Israeli law, international conventions are not self-executed, and therefore there is a need to internalize the conventions through legislation.

§2. Subject Matter of Protection

340. Article 1 of the Design Act defines the subject matter of protection – 'design' – as 'features of shape, configuration, pattern or ornament applied to any article by any industrial process or means, whether manual, mechanical or chemical, separate or combined, which in the finished article appeal to, and are judged solely by, the eye, but does not include any mode or principle of construction or anything which is in substance a mere mechanical device'. The Article further defines an 'article' as 'any article of manufacture and any substance, artificial or natural, or partly artificial and partly natural'.

This definition of the subject matter contains four fundamental components:

(i) The subject matter should refer only to 'features of shape, configuration, pattern or ornament'. 'Features of shape and configuration' refers to the shape or form of a three-dimensional article. Examples of such designs reflected in shape or configuration of an article are chairs, bottles and cars. Pattern or ornament refers to decorations attached to a useful article, whether two- or three-dimensional. Examples of such two-dimensional decorative designs are drawings printed on wallpaper, textile or teapots, or decorative patterns appearing on tapestry and carpets. However, mere letters, words or numbers and text arrangements are not eligible for registration since they do not involve any shape or ornament

---

and the registration of designs and applications therefore and in respect of other matters in relation to patents and designs under this Act.

1074. Design Regulation, 1925, officially published in Chukey Eretz-Israel vol. 3 (English), 1910.

1075. Paris Convention for the Protection of Industrial Property of 1883, 14 Jul. 1967, 21 U.S.T. 1583 [hereinafter 'Paris Convention'].

1076. Geneva Act of the Hague Agreement [of 6 Nov. 1925] Concerning the International Registration of Industrial Designs Art. 14(1), 2 Jul. 1999 (extending the Hague Agreement Concerning the Deposit of Industrial Designs of 1934, amended in 1960) [hereinafter 'Hague Agreement'].

1077. Agreement on Trade-Related Aspects of Intellectual Property Rights, 15 Apr. 1994, Marrakesh Agreement Establishing the World Trade Organization, Annex 1C, The Legal Texts: The Results of the Uruguay Round of Multilateral Trade Negotiations 320 (1999), 1869 U.N.T.S. 299, 33 I.L.M. 1197 (1994) [hereinafter 'TRIPS Agreement'].

aimed at pleasing the eye.[1078] Examples of three-dimensional decorative designs are small sculptures attached to dishes.

(ii) The subject matter should be applied to an 'article'. The design is not the article itself but is should be applied to one. The term 'article' is defined as: 'any article of manufacture and any substance, artificial or natural, or partly artificial and partly natural'.[1079] A leading commentator has interpreted the term 'article' as referring to chattels (i.e., movable tangible goods).[1080] This interpretation was supported by a recent court decision holding that typefaces are not eligible for design protection, since they are not attached to an 'article'.[1081] Typefaces are the graphical design of language symbols, such as letters and numbers. However, as in the digital age they are not attached to physical plates and are used only as digital fonts, the court concluded that acknowledging typefaces as eligible for design protection might lead to an absurd situation in which the letters of the language itself are the 'article' to which the typefaces are attached. Since the subject matter should be attached to a tangible article, the Court held, it would be better to view typefaces as works subject to copyright protection rather than industrial design's subject matter.[1082]

(iii) The subject matter should be produced by an 'industrial process or means'. In order for a design to be eligible for protection, it has to be accompanied by manufacture (or an intention to manufacture) on an industrial scale. The Design Regulation clarifies that when a design is reproduced, or intended to be reproduced, in more than fifty single articles, then the design is deemed to be used in an industrial process, unless all the articles together form a single set.[1083] The Design Regulation further clarifies that a design is regarded as fulfilling the industrial process requirement when it is intended to be applied to: printed paper curtains (upper hangings); carpets, rugs (floor cloth) or table covers (oil cloth) manufactured or sold in lengths or pieces; textile piece goods or textile goods manufactured or sold in lengths or pieces; and lace not made by hand.[1084] It should be noted that the line separating copyright protection for an artistic work such as a sculpture and industrial design protection for the same sculpture if attached to an article reproduced in more than fifty single articles is not clear. The issue is complicated by

1078. CC 2377/98 *The Israeli Center for Discs Ltd Yail D.S.S. Ltd* (TA District Court, Judge A. Azar) (unpublished, 2000).
1079. Design Act, Art. 1.
1080. A.H. Seligsohn, Fundamentals in Copyright, Trademark, Patent and Design Laws, 195 (1963).
1081. CC 5311/04/08 *Zvi Narkis Estate and Others v. Microsoft Israel Ltd and Others* (Central District Court, Judge Ofer Groskopf, not published yet), 22–23.
1082. See *Zvi Narkis Estate and Others v. Microsoft Israel Ltd and Others*, *ibid.*, at 22–23.
1083. Design Regulation, Art. 72(a). The District Court held that if a contract that commissions the production of a design, specifies an order of more than fifty pieces of the design, then the design qualifies for the industrial scale manufacture requirement regardless of whether eventually fifty pieces are indeed manufactured, see: CC 10-03-22913 *Tamari v. Comfy War Ltd* (20 Mar. 2014).
1084. Design Regulation, Art. 72(b).

the 'either-or' principle of copyright law, according to which there can be no cumulative protection.[1085]

(iv) The subject matter should be one that it is appealing to the eye. This fundamental requirement will be discussed at length below.

§3. Conditions of Protection

341. The conditions for protecting Industrial Designs are set forth in Article 1 of the Design Act, defining the subject matter and Article 30 of the Design Act setting the eligibility for registration. A number of requirements must be met as a prerequisite for protection:

I. New or Original

342. Article 30 of the Design Act expressly defines the eligibility threshold for protection of a registered design as 'new or original'. It is worth mentioning that the Paris Convention merely provides an obligation to protect designs, but does not set any standard with respect to eligibility for, or scope of, such protection.[1086] The TRIPS Agreement does not set clear conditions for protection either, stating that Member States 'shall provide for the protection of independently created industrial designs that are *new or original*'.[1087] Originality is a requirement for protection used in copyright law, while novelty is a requirement found in the patent realm. These two requirements for eligibility reflect the complexity of locating industrial design in the intellectual property field: is it more akin to copyright or to patent law?[1088] The Israeli Patent, Trademark and Designs Registrar typically require novelty, rather than originality, as the threshold requirement for protection, as do the courts. However, in some decisions there is an attempt to combine the two requirements. For example, an explanation given to the two requirements is that the novelty standard is as in patents, namely something not known before, and the originality standard as used in design law means a new use of a known design.[1089] This interpretation is based on patent law doctrines, allowing registration of a known invention having a new aim for function.[1090] Interpreting 'original' as a new use of a known design

1085. For the no-commutation rule in Copyright Law, see Copyright Act 2007, Art. 7. For the overlap between industrial designs and copyright see *infra* Ch. 10. See also Orit Fischman Afori, *Reconceptualizing Property in Designs*, 25 Cardozo Arts & Ent. L. J. 1105 (2008).

1086. Paris Convention, Art. 5(5).

1087. TRIPS Agreement, Art. 25(1).

1088. For a review of this complexity in design law see: Orit Fischman Afori, *Reconceptualizing Property in Designs*, 25 Cardozo Arts & Ent. L. J. 1105 (2008).

1089. See CA 3406/96 *Sela – A Company for Concrete Products LTD v. Akerstein Industries Ltd* (unpublished 1999); Registrar Decision as of 1 Jun. 1989 Re Design No. 9946, *Pal-Mat Ltd v. Isaac Peled.*

1090. See for example CA 244/72 *Plantex Ltd v. The Welcome Foundation Ltd*, P.D. 27 (2) 29 (1973).

emphasizes that the two requirements of 'new or original' are not cumulative but rather constitute two alternative thresholds.[1091]

The novelty requirement is understood as 'substantially different from what was previously known'.[1092] Slight variations from prior design will satisfy the novelty requirement. In some areas, the requisite degree of novelty is more modest than in others. For example, in areas in which the form of a design is more limited due to the nature, function or way of use of the designed product or in areas in which the development of new designs is rapid, a small difference will satisfy the newness requirement.[1093] Ultimately, the question is whether the form is sufficiently modified, and the emphasis is not on the number of modification but on the overall impression it creates.[1094]

II. No Prior Publication

343. As in patent law, in industrial design law, too, the novelty threshold is examined through, *inter alia*, the prior publication test. Prior publication of the design prevents its registration.[1095] However, the prior publication test is examined on a territorial basis, namely only prior publication *in Israel* prevents registration of the design. This is, of course, a major difference from the novelty requirement as examined in patent law. However, since 2008 publication online, even if on a foreign website, may be regarded as prior publication in Israel. Therefore, publications of designs in online databases such as those of the US Patent and Trademark Office or WIPO may be regarded as prior publication in Israel.

With regard to the criteria for establishing prior publication, the most fundamental one is prior application for registration of the same design or of a similar design.[1096] Thus, as in patent law, there is a rush to apply for registration, since the first application bars all subsequent registration of the same or similar design by other persons. However, where a design has been registered in one or more classes of goods, the proprietor of the design may register it in other classes, registration not being refused on grounds that the design is not new or original or that the design has been previously published in Israel.[1097] Moreover, application for having priority in registration according to international agreements, which refers to a design

1091. CC 1187/94 and 1772/94 *Sela – A Company for Concrete Products Ltd v. Akerstein Industries Ltd* (TA District Court, Judge Uri Goren) P.M. 1996 (2) 281, 293.

1092. See *Sela – A Company for Concrete Products Ltd v. Akerstein Industries Ltd, supra.*

1093. *Sela – A Company for Concrete Products Ltd v. Akerstein Industries Ltd, supra.*

1094. *Sela – A Company for Concrete Products Ltd v. Akerstein Industries Ltd, supra* (Quoting from Lord Herschell, in Re: Rollanson's Registered Design ([1898] 15 R.P.C. 441, 447).

1095. Design Act, Art. 30.

1096. CC (TA Distr.) 1751/81 *Erling Vangedal Nielsen v. Polydan Ltd*, P.M. 1983 (1), 145 [1982]. (Submission of a document to the Patent, Industrial Design and Trademark Registrar's library consists of prior publication.)

1097. Design Act, Art. 31. See also Registrar Decision as of 2 Aug. 1999 Re Design No. 28206-7, Daphna Arieli.

that was registered abroad, does not constitute prior publication, which prevents registration in Israel.[1098]

As to the typical situation of prior publication through registration, some complexity stems from the rule according to which the design is not open to the public for two years from the registration's commencement, and thus is not 'published' by the mere act of application or registration.[1099] For example, in one case a design was registered but was not available to the public under the two-year non-disclosure rule, and the design was not published in any other way, and therefore a later registration of the same design by another person could not be cancelled by the Registrar due to existence of 'prior publication' of the design.[1100] The way to solve this problem is to petition the district court to cancel the registration of the later design under the courts' general authority to add, cancel or change any registration in the industrial design registry.[1101]

Other acts, which constitute prior publication, are deposit of the design or its description in public place, such as a library the public has access to;[1102] sale of products incorporating the design;[1103] and the publication of the designed product in catalogues.[1104] If registration is planned, then an application should be filed before any commercial steps are taken, such as import, sale and marketing. However, in one case, a court concluded that trademark registration, which included the appearance of the design, should not be regarded as prior publication preventing the registration of a design, since there is no logic in forcing the proprietor to register a design before registering a trademark.[1105]

The 'prior publication' condition prevents subsequent registration if the *same* lines of features or shapes appear in the prior publication at stake.[1106] Such 'prior publication' should also include clear instructions on how to prepare the designed article, so as to be the same as the pending design.[1107] The test that is used to determine the substance of the prior publication is the 'eye test', which is not necessarily the same test as the one used in order to conclude the existence of infringement. The publication needs to include clear lines of the form or shape such that an observer

1098. Registrar Decision as of 27 May 2004 Re Design No. 38326, *Pepsico Inc. v. Promociones Premier International, S.A.* For priority in applications, see Design Act, Art. 52.

1099. Design Act, Art. 35.

1100. Registrar Decision as of 3 Mar. 2009 Re Design No. 41596 *Carmel Ma'arachot Meichalim Ltd v. Mr Menashe Rogotner*. This determination stemmed also from the somewhat limited authority of the Registrar to cancel registered design only due to prior publication in Israel. All other reasons for such cancellation should be discussed in the district court, see Design Act, Arts 36, 44.

1101. Design Act, Art. 44. For a leading decision discussing the separation of authorities between the Registrar and the district court as to the registry, see: CA 733/95 *Arpal Aluminium Ltd v. Kalil Industries Ltd*, P.D. 51(3) 577 (1997).

1102. CA 430/67 *Sarnoa Ltd v. Tnuva Ltd*, P.D. 22(1) 113, 119 (1968).

1103. CA 430/67 *Sarnoa Ltd v. Tnuva Ltd,* P.D. 22(1) 113, 119 (1968); CA 7125/98 *Mifromal Industries Ltd v. Kalil Industries Ltd,* P.D. 57(3) 702, 720 (2002).

1104. CC 1756/77 *Kibutz Dan v. Ambin Plastic Industries for Building Ltd*, P.M. 1979 (2) 156 (1979) (Publication in a catalogue hindered novelty).

1105. CC (Tel Aviv) 1509/93 *Hamratza* (Tel Aviv) 12261/93 *Rav Bariach Ltd v. Beit Mishar for Avizarei Rechev Havshush (1987) Ltd* (Judge Shtruzman, not published).

1106. CC (Tel Aviv) 758/85 *Hamaslul Industries Ltd v. Ackestein Co*., P.M. 1985 (2) 213 (1985).

1107. See *Hamaslul Industries Ltd v. Ackestein Co., ibid.*

could copy the design from the publication itself.[1108] This requirement is also based on patent law doctrine, according to which a prior publication depriving registration is regarded as such only if an average skilled person could have created the invention based on the description included in that publication.[1109] The Registrar's Office permits the applicant to add a 'Statement of Novelty' identifying the special features with respect to which the threshold of novelty and no prior publication should be inspected. The 'Statement of Novelty' is not obligatory. Its inclusion, however, works to prevent the application of a general inspection by means of the 'eye test', and its effect is that registration of the design is denied only if there is prior publication of the feature that was identified in the statement.[1110] This practice solves a common design registration problem, where minor differences between two or more designs nevertheless represent significant variation. The Supreme Court has held that the eye test should be applied from the perspective of a consumer,[1111] due to the fact that the appearance of the design is aimed at attracting consumers, at meeting their needs and their visual preferences. A discussion of the eye test in the context of determining whether there is an infringing act can be found below at Chapter 6.

For a 'prior publication' to result in the denial of registration, it must have been presented to at least one member of the public, in other words to a person who has no confidentiality obligations to the design publisher. If such person is free to use the information containing the design then revealing such information to a single such person constitutes prior publication.[1112]

III. Non-functional Elements

344. A basic principle of the protection granted to industrial designs is that it covers non-functional elements only, and does not extend to functional elements. This principle is expressed in the Design Act by the exclusion from protection of 'technical devices',[1113] which are devices whose form are dictated entirely by their technological function, and whose protection (if at all) is therefore covered under patent law.[1114] The application of principle has resulted in much of the complexity of industrial design law, since in many, if not most, cases, functional and non-functional elements are merged in one form.[1115] Given contemporary stylistic sensibilities, as expressed in the well-known design principle that 'form follows

1108. See *Hamaslul Industries Ltd v. Ackestein Co., ibid.*
1109. Patents Law, 1967, Art. 4.
1110. CC (Tel Aviv) 1239/80 *Big Plastic Industries Ltd v. Betzalel*, P.M. 1981 (1) 481 (1980).
1111. CA 3406/96 *Sela – A Company for Concrete Products Ltd v. Akerstein Industries Ltd* (unpublished 1999).
1112. Registrar Decision as of 20 Dec. 2005 Re Design No. 26649 *Super Plast Ltd v. Star Plast Industries (1967) Ltd.*
1113. Design Act, Art. 1.
1114. See CA 430/67 *Sarnoa Ltd v. Tnuva Ltd*, P.D. 22(1) 113 (1968).
1115. See Orit Fischman Afori, *The Role of the Non-functionality Requirement in Design Law*, 20 Fordham Intell. Prop. Media & Ent. L.J. 841 (2010).

function', it is often difficult to separate functional elements from non-functional ones. In such case, under Israeli law the entire form is entitled to protection.[1116]

There are many court decisions providing guidance on how to protect only non-functional elements.[1117] In an early, seminal decision, it was held that if the form is entirely dictated by its function and at the time of registration there was no other equally effective known way to achieve the same function, then the design could not be registered.[1118] In some later decisions, the same test was articulated in the opposite way: if the functional aim can be achieved, equally effectively, by another design, then the design is eligible for registration.[1119] However, the mere fact that the design incorporates functional features does not, by itself, deprive eligibility.[1120]

In a much later seminal decision, a court held that the non-functionality requirement is anchored in another explicit condition for protection under the Design Act, namely the 'appealing to the eye' test.[1121] The Supreme Court held that the non-functionality requirement is composed of both positive and negative aspects: the positive one is that the design is focused on parts which are visually appealing and which attract consumers. The form by itself should be the element, which achieves such attraction. The negative aspect of this requirement is that when the form is entirely dictated by function, there is no attraction of consumers based on visual appeal, and therefore the design is ineligible for protection.[1122]

One example of a case which has fulfilled Supreme Court guidelines on the matter relates to the design of a greenhouse. The District Court held that the design was not eligible for registration because, *inter alia*, it was functional. The elements claimed as new did not relate to the shape of the article in question, which was not only aimed at attracting consumers, but rather to the design's functional advantages, such as more air or space. On this basis, the design was held to be functional.[1123]

IV. Usefulness

345. To be protected under industrial design law, it is not enough that the design contain non-function elements (which are the only ones afforded such protection). The article afforded protection must be of actual use. Therefore, an object, which

1116. See CC 1756/77 *Kibutz Dan v. Ambin Plastic Industries for Building Ltd*, P.M. 1979 (2) 156 (1979) (The form of the mechanical device is dictated entirely by its function and therefore is not eligible for registration).
1117. See, for example, *Sarnoa Ltd v. Tnuva Ltd, supra*; *Kibutz Dan v. Ambin Plastic Industries for Building Ltd, supra*; CC (Haifa) 373/89 *Center of Boxes Ltd (Con.) v. Atzmon Plast Ltd*, P.M. 1990 (1) 89 (1989).
1118. *Sarnoa Ltd v. Tnuva Ltd, supra.*
1119. CC (Tel Aviv) 1516/88 *Oz On – Cooperative for Electric Devices in Tel Aviv, Ltd v. Electron Ltd*, P.M. 1990 (1) 149 (1990).
1120. *Sarnoa Ltd v. Tnuva Ltd, supra.*
1121. Design Act, Art. 1. The 'appealing to the eye' test is discussed *infra*.
1122. CA 3406/96 *Sela – A Company for Concrete Products Ltd v. Akerstein Industries Ltd* (unpublished 1999).
1123. CC 2138.96 *Razkalla Brothers – A Company for Manufacture and Construction of Green Houses Ltd v. Az-Rom Metal Industries Ltd*, P.M. 2002 (1), 271, 284–286 (2002).

has no useful purpose and no function beyond its external appearance, cannot be classified as an industrial design, but rather as an artistic work, and as such may be protected under copyright law.[1124] In one case, a court held that raw materials, which were devoid of use when detached from the design, could not be protected. Consequently, forms printed on paper could not be registered as a design, since the paper itself had no practical purpose without the printed form on it.[1125] By contrast, cover pages of notebooks have been held to be eligible for registration, as they constitute an ornamental print, which is attached to a useful article.[1126] In yet another case, a court held that the arrangement of words on a paper were not eligible for protection as a design, since there was no form or pattern, and the 'design' did not meet the 'appealing to the eye' requirement, which is discussed below.[1127]

V. Appealing to the Eye

346. Another fundamental requirement for protection is that the essence of the design is such that 'the finished article appeal to, and be judged solely by, the eye'.[1128] This 'appealing to the eye' requirement clarifies that the subject matter of industrial designs is the aesthetics of industrial articles. As explained above, this requirement complements the denial of protection for functional elements; both elements are aspects of the same fundamental principle with respect to designs subject matter: the focus is not on technology but on its aesthetical manifestation.[1129] A design is not regarded as being 'appealing to the eye' if the attraction of the eye is channelled to the function of the article in contrast to attraction made only by the shape of the product.[1130] And an industrial product which has only functional features is not eligible for design registration.[1131] One court has held that when the registration application does not refer to the external features of the design then it might

1124. CC (Tel Aviv) 1454/79 *Strusky Ltd v. Vitman Icecream Com. Ltd*, P.M. 1983 (2) 460 (1983) (Commercial sign cannot be regarded as an industrial design since it has no use by itself and it has nothing but its external appearance. Therefore, a sign should be classified as an artistic work. In order for a design to be regarded as an industrial design, it has to be attached to an object, which has a purpose other than itself). On appeal, the protection through industrial design was denied due to lack of industrial manufacture scale, CA 360/83 *Strusky Ltd v. Vitman Icecream Com. Ltd*, P.D. 40(3) 340 (1985). For the need that a design will be attached to a useful object see also CC (Tel Aviv) 557/79 *Kotlitzky v. Alkelei*, P.M. 1982 (1) 387 (1981).

1125. CC (Tel Aviv) 1127/87 *Hamratza* 87/4648, *K.S. Ltd v. Ofek Jerusalem Paper Products*, P.M. 1988 (1) 455 (1987).

1126. CC 1334/91 *Lafayet Agencies Ltd v. Dafron Petach Tikva Ltd* (unpublished).

1127. See CC 2377/98 *The Israeli Center for Discs Ltd Yail D.S.S. Ltd* (Tel Aviv District Court, Judge A. Azar) (unpublished, 2000).

1128. Design Act, Art. 1.

1129. CA 3406/96 *Sela – A Company for Concrete Products Ltd v. Akerstein Industries Ltd* (unpublished 1999).

1130. See Sela – *A Company for Concrete Products Ltd v. Akerstein Industries Ltd, ibid.*

1131. See CC (Haifa) 373/89 *Center of Boxes Ltd (Con.) v. Atzmon Plast Ltd*, P.M. 1990 (1) 89 (1989) (in this case a simple rectangle shape for a box was found as non-eligible for registration).

lead to the conclusion that the design is not 'new or original'.[1132] However, the'appealing to the eye' requirement does not constitute an artistic threshold. Rather, it focuses on the external, non-functional appearance of the object, and the threshold of such external appearance is 'new or original'. The 'appealing to the eye' requirement, nevertheless, can be fulfilled by external shape or configuration, which has a functional purpose also.[1133] Thus, designs that combine functionality and aesthetics in the same shape or configuration are not automatically denied from registration.

The 'appealing to the eye' requirement implies that only external parts of an article can be registered as a design. Internal parts, such as filters and other mechanical devices which the consumer cannot see, have by definition a purely functional purpose, and therefore cannot be registered.[1134]

VI. Exclusions

347. The Design Act specifies three exclusions for registration within the definition of the protected subject matter, which includes mode (or method), principle of construction and anything which is in substance a mere mechanical device.[1135] As to 'modes' or 'methods', these are not covered by industrial design laws since they are abstract concepts with no configuration. As 'ideas', they are potentially candidates for patent protection. Mere mechanical devices, as already explained, are also excluded from industrial design law, since protection is granted only to the aesthetical appearance of industrial products.[1136] And, 'principle of construction' should be interpreted as building methods and not as the buildings themselves. Though architectural work is usually protected as a copyrighted work, in certain cases it may fall within the subject matter of industrial design.[1137] Furthermore, the Registrar may, if it thinks fit, refuse to register any design the use of which, in his opinion, will be contrary to law, morality or public policy.[1138]

1132. See CC 2138/96 *Razkalla Brothers – A Company for Manufacture and Construction of Green Houses Ltd v. Az-Rom Metal Industries Ltd*, P.M. 2002 (1), 271 (2002).

1133. A.H. Seligsohn, *Fundamentals in Copyright, Trademark, Patent and Design Laws*, 195 (1963).

1134. *Ibid.*

1135. Design Act, Art. 1.

1136. For example, in one case the court decided that folding plastic boxes were unsuitable for design registration since they were merely a mechanical device, see: CC (Haifa) 373/89 *Center of Boxes Ltd (Con.) v. Atzmon Plast Ltd*, P.M. 1990 (1)89 (1989). However, in later cases, folding boxes were registered.

1137. Class 25 of designs' registration includes buildings units and houses, garages and other buildings. Thus, it seems that there is no prevention from registering buildings, in contrast to building methods. For the view that industrial manufacture of buildings, such as bus-stops, booths and even houses, should be protected through industrial design right, and that such buildings could be classified as chattels thus eligible for registration see: Meir Noam, *Protection of Architectural Works as Designs in Israel*, 15 Eyuney Mishpat (Tel Aviv University Law Review) 343 (1990).

1138. Design Act, Art. 30(3). No decision executing such authority was located.

§4. FORMALITIES: PROCEDURE FOR OBTAINING PROTECTION

I. Registration

348. In order to register a design, a prescribed application form must be submitted.[1139] If the application is accepted, the design is deemed registered as of the date of the application.[1140] An application which, because of the applicant's fault or negligence, has not been completed in a way that enables registration to be effected within the prescribed time, is deemed to have been abandoned.[1141] Registration with private registries, such as registries offered by different commercial companies, has no legal status.[1142]

The Design Regulation specifies in detail what should be included in the application and how. In 2014, the Design Regulation was updated by a comprehensive amendment. Of all the technical specifications, it is worthwhile mentioning the rules regarding drawings that should be attached to the application. When words, letters or numbers are not of the essence of the design itself, then they should be removed from the drawing, and in cases where such elements are of the essence of the design, the Registrar may require the insertion of a disclaimer of any right to their exclusive use.[1143] Where the names or representations of living persons appear on a design, the Registrar may require such persons' consent before proceeding to register the design, and in case of use of names or representations of recently dead persons, the Registrar may require the consent of their legal representatives before registration.[1144]

The same design may be registered in more than one class of goods, and, in case of doubt as to the class in which a design ought to be registered, the Registrar may decide on the question.[1145] The Design Act further provides that where a design has been registered in one or more classes of goods, the application of the proprietor of the design to register it in some more other classes shall not be refused on the ground that the design is not being new or original because it has been previously registered or has been previously published in Israel.[1146] The Design Act was amended in 2007 in order to clarify that such subsequent registration shall not extend the period of the registered design beyond that arising from the initial registration.[1147]

1139. Design Act, Art. 30(1); Design Regulation, Art. 4.
1140. Design Act, Art. 30(5).
1141. Design Act, Art. 30(4).
1142. CC 7361/05 *Meizlik Ze'ev v. Karshi International Ltd* (Jerusalem District Court, Judge Shapira, unpublished).
1143. Design Regulation, Art. 24. In the case of CC 2377/98 *The Israeli Center for Discs Ltd Yail D.S.S. Ltd* (Tel Aviv District Court, Judge A. Azar) (unpublished, 2000), court clarified that this rule must not lead to the wrong conclusion that words, letters or numbers are potentially eligible for registration.
1144. Design Regulation, Art. 27.
1145. Design Act, Art. 30(2).
1146. Design Act, Art. 31.
1147. Design Act, Art. 31 (Design Act 8th Amendment, 2007).

The Registrar shall grant a certificate of registration to the proprietor of the design when registered.[1148] In case of loss of the original certificate, or in any other case in which the Registrar deems it expedient, the Registrar may furnish one or more copies of the certificate.[1149] The Registrar's decision to refuse to register a design may be appealed to the district court within one month from the date of the decision.[1150]

II. Prior Application in Member Countries

349. Pursuant to Article 52 of the Design Act, a person who has applied for a design in any of the member countries, defined as countries party to the Paris Convention or to the WTO,[1151] may apply for registration of the same design in Israel within six months from the first application for registration of that design abroad, and the application shall have priority over any other application subsequent to this application abroad. The date of the application in Israel is not determined based on the date of the application abroad.[1152] However, the novelty of the design is assessed in relation to the date of the foreign application. The result is that publication in Israel following application abroad will not affect the novelty with respect to the Israeli application if such request for priority was appealed on time.

III. Inspection of Registered Design

350. A basic principle underlying intellectual property systems is that the registration is open to the public for inspection. However, under the Design Act, during the existence of a design right in a design or for a shorter period, which is not less than two years from the registration of the design, the design is not open to inspection except by the proprietor, by a person authorized in writing by him, or by a person authorized by the Registrar or a court of law.[1153] Under the Design Regulation, the period during which a design is not open to inspection is two years from the date of registration.[1154] The reason for this rule is to prevent the act of registration from being used as a source of information for competitors and to protect registered designs at an early stage of commercialization. An exception to this rule is if the Registrar denies registration on the grounds of similarity to an already registered design. In such case, the applicant may inspect the registered design even within the two-year period.[1155] After the expiration of the two-year period, designs

1148. Design Act, Art. 32(1).
1149. Design Act, Art. 32(2).
1150. Design Act, Art. 51.
1151. Design Act, Art. 1.
1152. Registrar Decision as of 27 May 2004 Re Design No. 38326, *Pepsico Inc. v. Promociones Premier International, S.A.*
1153. Design Act, Art. 35(1).
1154. Design Regulation, Art. 58.
1155. Design Act, Art. 35(1).

are open to inspection, and copies may be made by any person on payment of the prescribed fee.[1156]

IV. Cancellation of a Registered Design

351. Under Article 36 of the Design Act, the Registrar has the authority to cancel an already registered design only on the grounds of prior publication in Israel. The consequence of this restricted authority is that any other grounds for cancelling the registration of a design must be brought before a district court, which, in addition to its general jurisdiction, has specific authority to make changes to the design registry.[1157] The Supreme Court has held that the district court's broad jurisdiction in matters of design registration also includes the authority to cancel registration on the grounds of prior publication. In other words, cancellation of a registration on these grounds is not exclusive to the Registrar.[1158] The validity of a registered design can be challenged in the context of an infringement lawsuit, and even during the initial stages of a petition for an interlocutory injunction.[1159] The burden of proof concerning the non-eligibility of a registered design for registration, challenged in the context of an infringement lawsuit, is on the defendant. However, the Supreme Court has acknowledged that the lack of any prosecution in the process of the design registration may be taken into account within the evaluation of the evidential weight of the fact that the design has been registered.[1160] However, the Supreme Court has held that a potential defendant in a lawsuit may petition the district court for cancellation of a registered design, and should not be forced to risk being sued and then challenge the validity of the registered design indirectly.[1161]

The Registrar is also authorized to correct clerical errors, which may relate to the whole registration of a design or to part of it,[1162] but such authority should not be confused with the rather limited substantive authority to cancel the registration of a design only in cases of prior publication.

Prior to deciding whether to cancel a registered design, as with any decision that affects a person's rights, the Registrar will hear the parties' claims, if a request for a hearing has been made.[1163] The Design Regulation specifies the procedure for such hearing, including the timetable for submitting claims and providing evidence.[1164] The hearing is conducted similar to a court trial, but the Registrar is

1156. Design Act, Art. 35(2).

1157. Design Act, Art. 44. See also CA 733/95 *Arpal Aluminium Ltd v. Kalil Industries Ltd*, P.D. 51 (3) 577 (1997). Registrar Decision as of 3 Mar. 2009 Re Design No. 41596 *Carmel Ma'arachot Meichalim Ltd v. Mr Menashe Rogotner*.

1158. See *Arpal Aluminium Ltd v. Kalil Industries Ltd, supra*.

1159. CA 430/67 *Sarnoa Ltd v. Tnuva Ltd*, P.D. 22 (1) 113 (1968); CA 8951/10 *Oren Yoram Packages Ltd v. Skolnik H.Y. Ltd* (2 Nov. 2014).

1160. CA 8951/10 *Oren Yoram Packages Ltd v. Skolnik H.Y. Ltd* (2 Nov. 2014).

1161. See *Arpal Aluminium Ltd v. Kalil Industries Ltd, supra*.

1162. Design Act, Art. 42(2).

1163. Design Regulation, Art. 48 (Before exercising any discretionary power given to the Registrar by the Ordinance, or these rules adversely to any person, the Registrar shall, if so required, hear the person who is affected by the exercise of such power).

1164. Design Regulation, Arts 48, 57–68.

authorized to decide what type of evidence is required, and not to insist on evidence that was required by the Design Regulation.[1165] This rule is in accordance with the general rule that proceedings in the Patent Office are not subject to the general evidence and procedure laws, but the Registrar may apply such rules *mutatis mutandis*. A notice on a request that has been submitted to the district court to add, cancel or change the registry should be delivered to the Registrar,[1166] and the successful party to litigation is obliged to inform the Registrar of the court's decision with respect to any change in the Registry.[1167]

§5. Ownership and Transfer: Assignment – Licenses

352. The general rule is that the author (i.e., designer) of a design is its first owner.[1168] From this general rule stems also the subsequent rule that when ownership of rights in the design has been transferred from the original proprietor to any other person, then that other person is the legal proprietor of the design, namely ownership is transferable.[1169] However, there is a major exception to this general rule, 'where the author of the design for good consideration executes the work of some other person', in which case the person for whom the design has been executed is the original owner of the design.[1170] It is clear that this exception applies not only in situations in which the design was created in the course of employment, but also when a design is commissioned. However, there are no court decisions on this matter.

When a person becomes entitled by assignment, transmission, license or any other legal way to a design right (or any interest) in a registered design, he needs to apply to the Registrar to register his title, and the Registrar is required to register such person as the owner of the design once proof of title has been shown to the Registrar's satisfaction.[1171] Under the Design Act, the person who is registered as the proprietor of a design has, subject to the provisions of the Act and to any rights appearing on the register to be vested in any other person, power to assign, grant licenses as to, or otherwise deal with, the design.[1172] Therefore, it seems that the entry of any assignment or transmission of title in registers has substantive force and is not only of declaratory value.[1173] The registration of an assignment creates a presumption of a good title. However, this presumption may be rebutted by sufficient evidence.[1174]

1165. Design Regulation, Art. 52, Design Act, Art. 47.
1166. Design Regulation, Art. 69.
1167. Design Regulation, Art. 70.
1168. Design Act, Art. 2, definition of the term 'proprietor of a new or original design'.
1169. Design Act, Art. 2, definition of the term 'proprietor of a new or original design'.
1170. Design Act, Art. 2, definition of the term 'proprietor of a new or original design'.
1171. Design Act, Art. 43(1).
1172. Design Act, Art. 43(2).
1173. CC 1562/04 *Ronit Nationals Flags Ltd v. Parketmatia Marketing Ltd* (Tel Aviv District Court, Judge Binyamini, 2009, unpublished).
1174. CC 3155/99 *Isi Yogev Industries Ltd v. Abu Brothers Workshop Ltd* (Tel Aviv District Court, Judge Pilpel, 2002, unpublished).

§6. Scope of Exclusive Rights

I. General Overview

353. The scope of the exclusive right is specified in Article 37 of the Design Act, and provides that during the existence of the registered design:

> it shall not be lawful for any person, for the purposes of sale, to apply to any article in any class of goods in which the design is registered the design of any fraudulent or obvious imitation thereof, except with the license or written consent of the registered proprietor, or to do anything with a view to enable the design to be so applied.[1175]

The Supreme Court has clarified that the scope of exclusivity applies only with respect to the class of goods that the design was registered in, and there is no infringement in case of use of the design with respect to another non-registered class of goods.[1176] Acts that may infringe a registered design includes unlawful manufacture, sale, marketing and importing. In this respect, there is no requirement that both the manufacture and the commercial activity are conducted in Israel. The sale of imported infringing articles in Israel also infringes the exclusive right.[1177] However, since the Design Act is territorial by nature, at least one of the infringing acts must occur in Israel. If both the manufacture and sale of unauthorized designs took place abroad, then there is no infringement of the design right in Israel, even if the financing of these acts originated in Israel.[1178]

Article 37 of the Design Act further defines the scope of the exclusive right as including secondary liability, by providing that 'it shall not be lawful for any person […] knowing that the design or any fraudulent or obvious imitation of it has been applied to any article without the consent of the registered proprietor, to publish or to expose for sale that article'.[1179] This Article, similar to other articles defining secondary liability in intellectual property law, requires that the infringer have knowledge of the infringing acts. Such knowledge includes situations in which the infringer was aware of the existence of rights with respect to the article at stake but chose to ignore the possible legal implications of his acts.[1180] Article 37 of the Design Act has also been interpreted as territorial in scope, and therefore publishing or offering for sale an unauthorized design abroad does not infringe the design right in Israel, even if the conflict is between two Israeli companies.[1181]

It should be noted that until 2007 the exclusive right of a registered design was specified by the Design Act as a 'copyright'. In 2007 a new copyright law came into

1175. Design Act, Art. 37(1)(a).
1176. CA 723/71 *Tagenski v. Damet Industries Ltd*, P.D. 26(2) 255 (1972).
1177. CC 10340/97 *Eruit Marketing Importing & Exporting 1993 Ltd v. Roni Yair* (District Court of Haifa, judge Bein, 1999, Unpublished).
1178. CC 681/00 *Super Plast Ltd v. Starplast Industries 1967 Ltd*, P.M. 2003 (2) 79, 87, 90–91 (2005).
1179. Design Act, Art. 37(1)(b).
1180. See CC *1562/04 Ronit Nationals Flags Ltd v. Parketmatia Marketing Ltd* (Tel Aviv District Court, Judge Binyamini, 2009, unpublished).
1181. See *Super Plast Ltd v. Starplast Industries 1967 Ltd*, *supra* at 92.

effect, which included an amendment of the Design Act referring to the term 'copyright', replacing it with a new term 'design right'.[1182] This amendment, however, did not refer in any way to the scope of the exclusive right, and was aimed only at clarifying the difference between 'copyright' as defined by the Copyright Act and 'design right' as defined by the Design Act.

II. The 'Eye Test'

354. An unlawful application of the registered design to an article occurs either when the *same* or *similar* design is used without the permission of the owner of the design. Some differences between the registered design and the used design which is claimed as infringing, therefore, does not prevent court's determination that there has been an infringement.[1183] The test which is used by courts to decide whether there has been an infringement is the 'eye test'.[1184] The 'eye test' usually consists of inspecting the general appearance of the two designs under discussion in order to assess the degree of similarity, and does not entail comparing each detail separately.[1185] In applying this test, a court should ignore the question of whether the operation of the articles is identical, as it pertains only to the external appearance of the designs at issue.[1186] If a substantial part of the registered design has not been copied, then usually an infringement claim should be dismissed.[1187] In industrial areas in which there are limited possibilities for differentiating one design from another, and the Registrar has nevertheless accepted for registration different variations of a design, then the court interprets the scope of the exclusive right narrowly, with the result that use of a design that varies only slightly from the one that is registered may still be found to be not infringing.[1188] The Supreme Court has generalized this rule into a more fundamental principle, according to which the scope of the exclusive design right is derived from the extent of novelty or originality reflected in the design.[1189]

Courts have held that the 'eye test' must be applied from the perspective of a consumer and not that of the court;[1190] if a typical consumer would not be confused by the two designs in the course of ordinary use of the products, then there is no infringement.[1191] By the same token, courts have concluded that if there is a substantial differentiating element between the registered design and the alleged

1182. Copyright Act, 2007, Art. 70.
1183. CC (Tel Aviv) 1751/81 *Erling Vangedal Nielsen v. Polydan Ltd*, P.M. 1983 (1), 145 (1982).
1184. See *Erling Vangedal Nielsen v. Polydan Ltd*, *ibid.*
1185. CA 7125/98 *Mifromal Industries Ltd v. Kalil Industries Ltd*, P.D. 57(3) 702, 712 (2002).
1186. See *Erling Vangedal Nielsen v. Polydan Ltd*, *supra.*
1187. *Ibid.*
1188. CA 733/95 *Arpal Aluminium Ltd v. Kalil Industries Ltd*, P.D. 51(3) 577 (1997); *Mifromal Industries Ltd v. Kalil Industries Ltd*, *supra* at 717; CC 10340/97 *Eruit Marketing Importing & Exporting 1993 Ltd v. Roni Yair* (District Court of Haifa, judge Bein, 1999, unpublished).
1189. CA 3406/96 *Sela – A Company for Concrete Products Ltd v. Akerstein Industries Ltd* (unpublished 1999); *Mifromal Industries Ltd v. Kalil Industries Ltd*, *supra* at 716.
1190. See *Mifromal Industries Ltd v. Kalil Industries Ltd*, *supra* at 709. See also *Erling Vangedal Nielsen v. Polydan Ltd*, *supra.*
1191. See *Erling Vangedal Nielsen v. Polydan Ltd*, *supra.*

infringing design, then there is no infringement, since the consumer would not confuse between the designs.[1192] The comparison between the two designs should be made by the general appearance of the products as seen by the relevant consumer. The general rule is that the consumer is not inspecting the product in the manner an expert would. However, he pays more attention to the product than an accidental viewer would.[1193] The comparison between the two designs should not be made by placing them side-by-side, since consumers' recollection is imperfect and there is no need for the two designs to be identical.[1194] In each case, the court should determine who the relevant consumer is in order to apply the test.[1195] In general, the relevant consumer in question is the 'average consumer' or the 'reasonable consumer' who purchases the product without paying much attention to it and without comparing in detail similar products in the market.[1196] In special cases, however, the product's nature may require closer inspection of the differences between the two designs by an expert, if the relevant consumer is an expert.[1197] Moreover, after identifying the relevant consumer, the court should determine how the product incorporating the design is sold in order to apply the test in the proper location and context. For example, the product might be inspected by the relevant consumer when it is still on the store shelf, or else it might be inspected after it is installed in the location where it will be used.[1198] In a case involving window profiles, the Supreme Court held that the relevant consumer is the professional who installs the window profiles, and therefore the differences between two similar designs should be viewed from the perspective of the expert comparing the two products on the store shelf, rather than after they have been installed in the end-user's house. In such a case, small differences may be significant, thus leading to a conclusion that there is no infringement of the registered design.[1199]

It is clear that this version of the eye test, focusing on the 'consumer eye', is taken from the realm of trademark law, focusing on the effect of the defendant's acts on consumers, asking whether confusion may occur.[1200] But such legal borrowing may create confusion when it is used not simply as a tool to aid in determining the existence of infringement, but rather as the concluding test. For example, one court concluded that if the similarity between the designs could end with a court determination of a passing off claim, then a design infringement could be concluded as well.[1201] This interpretation of the 'eye test' could be criticized as undermining the justifications for design law, which are to promote both the private interests of designers and the public's interest in the development of new and

1192. See CC 10340/97 *Eruit Marketing Importing & Exporting 1993 Ltd v. Roni Yair* (District Court of Haifa, judge Bein, 1999, unpublished).
1193. See *Mifromal Industries Ltd v. Kalil Industries Ltd, supra* at 712.
1194. See *Mifromal Industries Ltd v. Kalil Industries Ltd, supra* at 715.
1195. See *Mifromal Industries Ltd v. Kalil Industries Ltd, supra* at 710.
1196. *Ibid.*
1197. See *ibid.*, 711.
1198. *Ibid.*
1199. See *ibid.*, at 717–719.
1200. See *ibid.*, at 714.
1201. CA 480/93 *Joshua Kerolfeld v. Sharfman Metal Indust. Ltd* (Judge Shtruzman, unpublished).

original aesthetic designs.[1202] Therefore, the focus of the infringement test should be on whether the similarity between the designs exceeds an objective degree that reflects an appropriation of the essence of the registered design. The consumer test, in contrast, examines only the consequences of the appropriation from a rather limited point of view. For example, the consumer test may lead to a conclusion that there is no infringement in a case in which there is an unauthorized use of exactly the same design as the registered one and a clear notice clarifies that the used design is not originated from the registered owner. The consumer is therefore not confused, but the incentive to the original designer to invest in developing new designs may be significantly harmed.

§7. Limitations of the Scope of Protection

355. A major limitation on the scope of protection granted to registered designs is when they are needed for governmental use. Under the Design Act, the minister (which will be appointed by the government) may permit the use of a design, whether registered or in the process of application, by government departments, State-owned factories or State institutions, if such use is required in order to protect the State or to enable the supply of essential goods or services.[1203] Furthermore, the minister may permit any person who is acting under a contract with the State to use the design for such purposes, in order to enable the prosecution of such contract as long as it serves the State needs.[1204] The Patent Act rules, referring to use of patents by the State, including the procedure for setting compensation because of such use to the owner of the design rights, applies here *mutatis mutandis*.[1205] This limitation has never been applied to date.

§8. Duration of Protection

356. A design is registered for a period of five years, which may be extended twice, each for another period of five years, and in total the protection of designs can last for fifteen years.[1206] Each application for an extension must be submitted before the expiration of the current five-year period, in the prescribed time and manner, and is subject to payment of a fee.[1207] There is a sixmonth grace period for applying for an extension after the end of each five-year period, subject to payment of a fee.[1208]

As explained above, where a design has been registered in one or more class of goods, the application to register the same design in one or more other classes does

1202. See *Mifromal Industries Ltd v. Kalil Industries Ltd*, *supra* at 709.
1203. Design Act, Art. 39A(1) (2008 amendment).
1204. Design Act, Art. 39A(2) (2008 amendment).
1205. Design Act, Art. 39A(3) (2008 amendment).
1206. Design Act, Art. 33.
1207. Design Act, Art. 33(2)(3).
1208. Design Act, Art. 33(4) (Design Act 8th Amendment, 2007).

not extend the period of protection in the design beyond the initial registration period.[1209]

§9. Infringement and Remedies

357. The Design Act allows the owner of a design whose exclusive rights were infringed to elect one of two paths for remedies: the first is to bring an action for the recovery of damages and for an injunction against the repetition of infringing acts; the second is to seek statutory damages in 'a sum not exceeding 50 Israeli Lira as liquidated damages' per each infringement, provided that the total sum recoverable as liquidated damages in respect of any one design does not exceed 100 Israeli Lira.[1210] However, the statutory damages path, which originally appeared in the 1924 Act, has never been updated, and has become in effect a dead letter, as the value of the limited sum for available damages (100 Israeli Lira) has diminished to the point where it has no real value, and the local currency was replaced in the 1980s. Therefore, currently, the only course of action available to a proprietor of a registered design is to seek the basic remedies in a civil action, including damages and an injunction. It should be noted that under Israeli law, in any civil action the plaintiff may seek, in addition to proved damages, a restitutionary remedy pursuant to the unjust enrichment law.[1211] In a Supreme Court decision, handed down in 2013, the issue of remedies was thoroughly discussed.[1212] The Court ruled that under the Design Act framework, the plaintiff may ask for compensation for his lost profits and for the profits of the defendant, stemming from the act of infringement – namely a remedy against unjust enrichment. The Court perceived the defendant's actual profits, stemming from the infringement, as a legitimate basis for calculating the damages aimed at compensating for the lost profits. Such method for evaluating damages was preferred by the Court since it compensates actual and real loss of profits and not potential and speculative ones. Yet the Court stressed the need to establish a causal connection between the infringement and the plaintiff's lost profits, according to common Tort Law doctrines (such as market demand for the relevant items and the plaintiff's supply capacity, existence of market substitutes, etc.). In this case, after a thorough analysis of the circumstances at stake, the Court was willing to accept a calculation of the lost profits on the basis of the defendant's sales, assuming that each infringing item sold by the defendant reflected a lost sale for the plaintiff. Moreover, the Supreme Court held that the question of whether the plaintiff may seek statutory damages according to the Commercial Torts Act, despite the fact that there is no obstacle for proving actual damages, should be left open. It should be explained that the Commercial Torts Act governs various topics, such as passing off and trade secrets; however, industrial designs are not regulated under

1209. Design Act, Art. 31.
1210. Design Act, Art. 37(2).
1211. CA (Additional Hearing) 20/82 *Adras – Building Materials Ltd v. Harlo & Jones GMBH*, P.D. 42(1) 221 (1988).
1212. CA 3853/11 *Ronit Nationals Flags Ltd v. Satan* (13 May 2013).

this piece of legislation. Therefore, it is not clear how an infringement regulated by the Design Act may yield remedies set by a different statute.

§10. Criminal Offences

358. The Design Act sets a very limited range of criminal offences, in comparison to copyright law, and such reference that exists is made through obsolete language. The infringement of a design right in itself does not constitute a criminal offence, and the criminal offences relates only to false presentation. Under the Design Act:

> Whoever, after the design right in a design has expired, puts or causes to be put on any article to which the design has been applied the word 'registered' or any infringe word or words implying that there is a subsisting design right in the design, is guilty of an offence and is liable to a fine of twenty five pounds.[1213]

The penalty for this offence has never been updated, and it appears to have become a dead letter. The Design Act further sets a general offence relating to false entry in the register kept under the Design Act.[1214]

§11. Relation to Other Industrial Property Laws

359. The relation between design rights and other intellectual property laws is complex, and not all legal questions have been resolved in this regard. The most problematic overlap is between design right and copyright, and the possibility of protecting designs through trademarks. Moreover, the unjust enrichment law has been interpreted by the Supreme Court in a very broad manner, thus providing the possibility of protecting designs by applying other legal principles and theories that are outside the realm of intellectual property. Each one of these areas of overlap has received considerable attention from the courts. The interrelation between design rights and the unjust enrichment law is discussed below in section VII.

1213. Design Act, Art. 55(4).

1214. Design Act, Art. 55(1). (Whoever makes or causes to be made a false entry in any register kept under this Ordinance or a writing falsely purporting to be a copy of an entry in any such register, or produces in evidence any such writing, knowing the entry or writing to be false, is guilty of an offence and is liable to imprisonment for one year or a fine of one hundred pounds.)

Chapter 5. Plant Variety Protection

Definitions

'*The Convention*' or '*The UPOV Convention*': Unless defined otherwise – the Act of 1991 of the International Convention for the Protection of New Varieties of Plants.
'*Union Countries*': defined in the Plant Breeders Rights (PBR) Law as '*a foreign state, in respect of which the Registrar announced in the Official Gazette that, by virtue of the Convention, it is a member of the Union for the Protection of New Varieties of Plants.*'
'*Contracting Party*': as defined in the International Union for the Protection of New Varieties of Plants (UPOV) Convention.

§1. Sources: Legislation

360. PBRs are granted and enforced in Israel through the Plants Breeders' Rights Law, 5733-1973 ('*the PBR Law*' or '*the Law*').

The PBR Law was enacted in 1973[1215] to give effect[1216] to Israel's undertakings pursuant to the 1961 Act of the UPOV Convention.[1217]

In 1996, the PBR Law was amended in order to incorporate into Israeli law the provisions of the 1991 Act (*the 1996 Amendment*).[1218] Certain provisions of the PBR Law, as they were before the enactment of the 1996 amendment, continue to apply to certain categories of varieties. Thus, where necessary, reference will be made to the different provisions of the two versions of the Law.

The PBR Law is implemented through the PBR Regulations, 5734 – 1974.

§2. Subject Matter of Protection

361. Section 1 to the PBR Law defines a 'Variety' as follows:

> A group of plants within a botanical taxon unit of the lowest known rank which, irrespective of the extent to which conditions for the grant of a breeder's right have been met, can be –
>
> (1) defined by the expression of the characteristics that result from a given genotype or combination of genotypes;

1215. The Plants Breeders' Rights Law, 1973 *Seffer Hukim* 713.
1216. Unlike the laws of various European countries, under Israeli law, similar to English law, the provisions of international conventions do not automatically become part of the laws of the State of Israel (except for provisions reflecting customary international law). They become part of Israeli law only when imported by means of enactment of the *Knesset.*
1217. Israel joined the UPOV on 12 Dec. 1979 by ratifying the 1961 Act of the UPOV Convention.
1218. Prior to 1996, the PBR Law was amended only once in 1983 published in *Seffer Hukim* 1098, 23.

(2) distinguished from any other group of plants by the expression of at least one of the characteristics stated in paragraph (1);
(3) deemed as an independent unit in all respects of its suitability for being propagated without change.

This definition was incorporated into the PBR Law as part of the 1996 Amendment. It is substantially similar to the definition of a 'Variety' in the UPOV Convention. Pursuant to section 2 of the PBR Law, the Law applies to all plant genera and species.[1219]

§3. Conditions of Protection

I. General

362. A breeder's right is granted in Israel, in accordance with the UPOV Convention,[1220] where the variety is new, Distinct, Uniform and Stable (the latter three requirements often referred to as the DUS Requirements).

These requirements for eligibility are set in section 6 of the PBR Law:

> 6. A variety is eligible for registration of a breeder's right in the PBR Register if all the following hold true for it:
>
> (1) it is new;
> (2) it is sufficiently uniform in its basic characteristics, as stated in the application and taking the propagating method of the variety into consideration;
> (3) its basic characteristics are stable, its description and characteristics are maintained even after repeated propagation, and – if the breeding constitutes a complete cycle –its characteristics are maintained at the end of each cycle.

As can be seen from the language of section 6, the Law requires that the variety be new (section 6(1)), uniform (section 6(2)) and stable (section 6(3)) while the distinctness requirement is not expressly stated in section 6 to the PBR Law. As will be further explained below, the distinctness requirement is included in the novelty requirement. Naturally, this may create some confusion regarding the scope of the novelty requirement.

II. Novelty and Distinctness

363. The scope of the novelty requirement[1221] is addressed in section 7(c) to the PBR Law. Section 7(c) provides as follows:

1219. This is in compliance with Art. 3 of the UPOV Convention. Prior to the 1996 Amendment, the PBR Law applied only to a limited list of plants that appeared in a schedule of the PBR Law.
1220. See Art. 5 of the Convention.
1221. Cf. Art. 6 of the Convention.

> A variety shall be deemed new even if – prior to the filing of the application for the registration of breeders' rights – the propagating material[1222] or the harvested material of the variety was sold or otherwise transferred by or with the consent of the breeder of the variety, during a period no longer than–
>
> (1) In Israel – one year from the determining day;
> (2) Outside of Israel – in respect of grape vines, forest trees, fruit trees and ornamental trees – six years from the determining day, and in respect of other plants – four years from the determining day.

The novelty is examined as at the *'determining day'* which, in turn, is defined as the date of filing of the PBR Application.[1223] If priority from a foreign application is validly claimed, the priority date shall be the determining day.[1224]

Comparison of section 6 of the Israeli PBR Law with its counterpart in the UPOV Convention (Article 6) shows that while the latter defines the novelty-destroying act as '*sale*' or '*disposal*' of the propagation or harvested material *'for the purpose of exploitation of the variety*', the PBR Law defines it as *'sale'* or '*transfer*'. As it seems, the distinction between the word *'disposal*' and '*transfer*' is insignificant and can be interpreted in the same manner.

The legislative history of the amendment does not explain why the phrase *'for the purpose of exploitation of the variety'* is missing from section 6; thus, its omission is not entirely clear. Legislation that is enacted in order to implement Israel's international undertaking is to be interpreted in a manner that is consistent with the international undertakings (the treaty or convention);[1225] therefore, it stands to reason that said omission was made because it was deemed insignificant. In any event, the law is interpreted purposively. Thus, for example, delivery of a propagation material to a quarantine station for the purpose of obtaining an importation permit, even if literally constituting '*transfer*', cannot be deemed a novelty-destroying act. Likewise, it would seem that experimental use should not destroy novelty as stated in Article 15 to the Convention.

The Supreme Court of the State of Israel addressed the novelty requirement in the case of *Hazera.*[1226] The novelty of the variety in question was determined on the basis of the language of section 7 of the Law, as it was before the 1996 Amendment[1227] and the varieties in question were varieties of barley. As was agreed by all parties, the process of breeding of barley extends over five generations of barley

1222. The 1996 Amendment added, for the first time, a definition of the term 'propagating material'. This is defined as 'a plant and any part of it, which is intended for cultivation or propagation, including seeds and tissue cultures' (s. 1 of the Law, as amended).
1223. In s. 7(a) to the PBR Law.
1224. Section 72 of the PBR Law.
1225. See, for example, ACH 376/90 *Anheuser – Busch Inc. et al. v. Budejovicky Budvar, Narodni Podnik Ceske Budejovice et al.* 46(4) P.D. 843; HCJ 279/51 *Amsterdam v. The Finance Minister*, 6 P.D. 966 (Sup. Ct., 1952), at 945; Cr.A. 336/61 *Eichmann v. AG*, 16 P.D. 2033 (Sup. Ct., 1962), at 2041; HCJ 302/72 *Hilu et al. v. The State of Israel* 27(2) P.D. 169 (Sup. Ct., 1973).
1226. CA 2909/98 *Taarovot Hatzafon Ltd v. Hazerah (1939) Ltd*, P.D. 54(3) 652 (Sup. Ct., 2000).
1227. Prior to the 1996 Amendment, a variety was deemed known, if the 'propagating material' of the variety was exploited for certain defined periods prior to the filing date of the PBR application.

seed,[1228] commencing with the 'breeder's seeds' and ending with 'regular seeds'. The PBR proprietor argued that the definition of 'propagating material' is confined to the marketing and sale of 'breeder's seeds' and, thus, the marketing of the later seed generations does not destroy novelty.[1229] The Court held that the term 'propagating material', with respect to the novelty requirement, requires broad definition, and that it applies to all generations of the seeds (not just the first generation of 'breeder's seeds'); that is, the sale or marketing of any of the seed generations will destroy novelty.

The second feature of the Israeli PBR Law *'novelty'* requirement is the distinctness requirement.[1230] Section 7(a) and 7(b) of the PBR Law were introduced by the 1996 Amendment and provides that:

> 7.(a) A new variety is a variety that is clearly different from any other known variety when the application for the registration of breeders' rights is filed (hereafter: determining day).
>
> (b) Without derogating from the generality of the provisions of subsection (a), a variety shall be deemed to be known if an application for the registration of breeders' rights to the variety was filed with the official registers of any state, on conditions that the application resulted in the grant of the right or in its registration in the Register, as the case may be.

It is submitted that when read in context, section 7(b) should be interpreted as relating to the *'other variety'* of section 7(a), thereby rendering section 7(a)–(b) substantially in conformity with Article 7 of the UPOV Convention.

Notably, a district court decision, in an appeal on the PBR Council's decision to register a PBR in the name of the appellee, approved the Council's decision not to take into consideration evidence of genetic examinations (DNA analysis) which the opponent offered in order to show that the variety in question is not novel (distinct) from the opponent's variety. This was because morphological differences were found and, under these circumstances, the Council and the Court held that the DNA evidence is not relevant to the novelty determination. In the future, this might mean that the comparison of the new variety with the known varieties shall be based solely on morphological examinations and the DNA analysis may be, at the most, a tool to monitor the adequacy of morphological examinations.[1231]

The term 'propagating material' was not defined in the PBR Law prior to the 1996 Amendment. The corresponding provision of the 1978 Act of UPOV referred to offering for sale or marketing of 'the variety'.

1228. The five generations of seeds are: breeder's seeds, basic seeds, propagating seeds, sorted seeds regular seeds.

1229. The PBR proprietor argued that only the 'breeder's seeds' retain the exact characteristics of the variety in question.

1230. Required by Art. 5(ii) of the Convention and defined in Art. 7 thereof.

1231. CC 2056/03 (Jerusalem) *Danzinger Flower Farm v. Shmuel Mor et al.*, Dinim-District 2008 (9) 1978, ss 85–86.

III. Uniformity

364. The third condition for PBR eligibility is uniformity. A variety is deemed uniform if '*it is sufficiently uniform in its basic characteristics, as stated in the application, having regard to the method of propagating of the variety*'.[1232] The language in the UPOV Convention refers to '*relevant characteristics*'.[1233]

The phrase '*basic characteristics*' referred to in section 6(2) of the PBR Law is defined in section 1 to the PBR Law[1234] as '*one characteristic or a combination of characteristics, which are recognizable and capable of description and which differentiate the variety from all varieties of its kind*'. This may be reminiscent of the 1968 Act of UPOV that referred to the variety's '*important characteristics*'.[1235] Indeed, reference to the '*basic characteristics*' was included in section 6(2) of the PBR Law as it stood prior to the 1996 Amendment.

IV. Stability

365. The fourth and last condition for PBR eligibility is stability. A variety is deemed stable if '*its basic characteristics are stable and its description and characteristics are maintained even after repeated propagation, and – if the breeding constitutes a complete cycle – its characteristics are maintained at the end of each cycle*'.[1236] The language in the UPOV Convention refers to '*relevant characteristics*'.[1237]

§4. Formalities: Procedures for Obtaining Protection

I. The PBR Registrar, the PBR Council

366. A PBR application is handled by the PBR Registrar and the PBR Council. The PBR Registrar is appointed by the Minister. The sole requirement set out in the PBR Law in connection with the appointment of the PBR Registrar is that he would be selected from the employees of the Ministry of Agriculture.[1238]

As will be seen below, the functions of the PBR Registrar are administrative.[1239] The substantive functions of examining a PBR application and granting a PBR are assigned to the PBR Council. The Council is a body constituted of nine members,[1240] all appointed for a three-year term by the Minister who also appoints the

1232. Section 6(2) of the PBR Law (cf. Art. 8 of the Convention).
1233. Article 8 to the UPOV Convention.
1234. In s. 1 of the PBR Law.
1235. Article 6(1)(a) to the 1968 UPOV Convention.
1236. Section 6(3) of the PBR Law (cf. Art. 8 of the Convention).
1237. Article 9 to the UPOV Convention.
1238. Section 14(a) of the PBR Law.
1239. Section 14(b) of the PBR Law.
1240. The Minister may, with the approval of the Economics Committee of the *Knesset*, enlarge the number of the members of the Council to not more than thirteen.

Council's Chairman. Three of the Council members are representatives of the government and six are appointed from among scientists, researchers, seed growers and plant breeders.[1241] The Council is entitled to establish sub-committees, comprised of either Council Members or non-members that may submit recommendations in any manner prescribed by the Council. In practice, the Council often establishes sub-committees in order to obtain an expert opinion regarding different aspects in the process of the variety's examination.[1242] In this regard, a court ruling held that the recommendations of such a sub-committee, including the evidence it relied upon, must be forwarded to the applicant in order to allow the applicant to realize his right to testify before the Council prior to issuing its decision and enable the applicant to realize his right to appropriately appeal the Council's decision.[1243]

II. Submission of the PBR Application

367. A PBR application is filed with the PBR Registrar.[1244] The PBR application will include certain details prescribed by the PBR Law.[1245]

These include: (1) the applicant's name; (2) address in Israel for delivery of documents, and if the applicant is not an Israeli resident, a name of an Israeli resident who shall serve as the applicant's representative in all matters pertaining to the application; (3) a description and details of the variety including specification of its characteristics; (4) a proposed denomination; (5) a claim or claims that specify the uniqueness of the variety, each claim reasonably arising from the particulars described under (3) above;[1246] and (6) any other particular related to the implementation of this Law, as may be prescribed.

In addition, if the breeder applicant is not the actual breeder of the variety, he will explain in his application his entitlement to the PBR (e.g., by way of assignment or by way of operation of Law).[1247]

The PBR Law distinguishes between varieties cultivated in Israel and varieties cultivated outside of Israel. The right to apply for a PBR in respect of a variety cultivated in Israel is granted to any breeder and his successors, whether Israeli or not. The right to apply for a PBR in respect of a variety cultivated outside of Israel is granted only to citizens or residents (including corporations) of Israel and of the Paris Union Countries.[1248] However, the Minister of Agriculture is empowered to order registration of PBR applications applied for by non-qualifying applicants, if such registration is necessary to meet the obligations of the State of Israel pursuant

1241. Section 10(a) of the PBR Law.
1242. Section 10(d) of the PBR Law.
1243. CC 2056/03 (Jerusalem) *Danzinger Flower Farm v. Shmuel Mor et al.*, Dinim-District 2008 (9) 1978, ss 42–44.
1244. Section 15(b) of the PBR Law.
1245. Section 20(a) of the PBR Law.
1246. As will be explained, there is a considerable ambiguity as regards the significance of the 'claims' of a PBR.
1247. Section 20(b) of the PBR Law.
1248. Prior to the 1996 Amendment, the right to apply for a PBR in respect of a variety cultivated outside of Israel was granted to only Israeli citizens or residents. See, however, s. 71 of the PBR Law that is referred to in the ensuing sentence.

to international agreements, on the basis of reciprocity.[1249] The Minister may also order such registration if he deems such registration a matter of public interest.[1250]

Notably, in 2011 the Minister made use of the authority granted to him pursuant to Section 71(2) of the PBR Law and enacted Regulations permitting breeders of *Orchedea* varieties, who are citizens of Taiwan, to request the registration of a PBR, despite Taiwan not being a member of UPOV.[1251]

The requirement that non-residents must appoint a representative seems to be discriminatory and is questionable as such. If a resident may apply for a PBR without being represented, a non-resident should be treated equally.

If a person intends to file an application for the registration of a PBR abroad before such application is filed in Israel, he must notify the Registrar in writing within thirty days before filing abroad. If such notification is not provided, the applicant will not be able to file an application in Israel unless he specifies certain details in his Israeli application relating to the foreign application.[1252]

For the purpose of examination of the application, the PBR Registrar is entitled to demand from the applicant propagation materials or any other material, or further details concerning the subject of the application.[1253] The PBR Registrar will review the application to determine whether it includes all of the requisite details and, if so, the PBR Registrar will transfer the application to the Council for deliberations and a final decision.[1254] If the application is lacking, an office action will ensue informing the applicant of the deficiencies and that the applicant is entitled to cure the deficiencies within a prescribed time. If the applicant does not cure the deficiencies within the prescribed time, the Registrar may reject the PBR application *in limine*.[1255]

The PBR Registrar's decision to transfer the application to the Council for consideration and final ruling will be published in the *Official Gazette* and in a professional agricultural magazine within sixty days[1256] for third-party opposition.[1257] The details of the publication include: (1) the name of the applicant; (2) the denomination proposed by the applicant; (3) the description of the variety and the details of its characteristics, as submitted by the applicant; and (4) any other detail deemed worthy of publication in the opinion of the Registrar.[1258] Note that the publication refers to all characteristics and not to the '*basic characteristics*' which will be registered in the PBR Register (see below).

1249. Section 71(1)of the PBR Law.
1250. Section 71(2) of the PBR Law.
1251. Plant Varieties Rights Regulations (The Registration in Israel of *Orchedea* Varieties Cultivated in Taiwan), 2011.
1252. See Rule 2 of the PBR Regulations.
1253. Section 21(b) of the PBR Law.
1254. Section 15(c) of the PBR Law.
1255. Section 15(d) of the PBR Law.
1256. Section 22(a) of the PBR Law; note that this provision was revised in the 1996 Amendment. This revision shall apply also to applications filed prior to the date said amendment went into effect.
1257. Section 23(a) of the PBR Law.
1258. Subject to the provisions of the PBR Law (s. 22 of the PBR Law).

III. Examination

368. The PBR Council is required to examine applications, which the PBR Registrar transfers to the Council.

The Council enjoys wide discretion in regards to the means for conducting such examination. It may take '*measures it deems fit*'[1259] including, *inter alia*, (i) inviting examiners or other experts to give their opinions on professional questions; (ii) perform, whether by itself or by examiners, research works, trials or examinations that are necessary in order to adopt a decision; (iii) transfer the application details to an international institution in order to search material which would facilitate examination.[1260]

The applicant bears the cost of examination, as determined by the Registrar who may also require payment in advance. The Registrar is entitled to defer the examination of an examination pending compliance with payment requirements, and he may cancel an application thirty days after giving the applicant an advance notice.[1261] The applicant is entitled to follow the conduct of field trials, if he so requests in writing and upon conditions that may be prescribed thereto by the Council.[1262] However, an applicant is not entitled to actively participate in the field trials, but merely observe them.[1263] In addition, the Council is required to allow the applicant to testify before it, prior to issuing its decision.[1264]

In practice, the examination in the field is executed by the Council's examiners, which are employees of the Ministry of Agriculture. Their field examinations are concluded into examination reports which are forwarded to the Council, along with all of the additional documents and data of the application for examination. According to current practice, the PBR Registrar allows applicants to request a copy of the examination reports after the varieties and reports were discussed in the subcommittee(s), prior to the convening of the Council.

The Council's examiners may also rely on the results of the examination of the variety by a foreign PBR office. There is no formal policy concerning the circumstances and conditions for such examination.

If the Council finds reasonable grounds to assume that an application is tainted with fraud, it will suspend the proceedings before it and resort to a special proceeding as set out in the Law.[1265] Following publication of the transfer of an application to the Council, opposition proceedings may be initiated. The Law is not sufficiently clear in regards to the effect of such opposition on the examination process.

1259. Section 16(a) of the PBR Law.
1260. Subsections (1)–(3) of s. 16(a) of the PBR Law, respectively.
1261. Section 16(b) of the PBR Law.
1262. Section 16(a)(2) of the PBR Law. See also Rule 6 of the PBR Regulations.
1263. CC 2056/03 (Jerusalem) *Danzinger Flower Farm v. Shmuel Mor et al.*, Dinim-District 2008 (9) 1978, s. 30.
1264. Section 17 of the PBR Law.
1265. Section 25(b) of the PBR Law.

IV. Opposition

369. Within ninety days of publication of the transfer of a PBR application by the Registrar to the Council, any person may lodge an opposition to the grant of the PBR.[1266] Note that there are no special standing requirements and such an opposition may be lodged by 'any person'. The Israeli oppositions are pre-grant proceedings, thereby deferring the grant of a PBR to the final ruling in the opposition proceeding.

An opposition may only be based on two grounds: (a) that the opponent's right to be registered as the proprietor of the PBR is superior over that of the applicant; and (b) that the variety does not meet the eligibility requirements set out in section 6 of the PBR Law. An opposition that is not based on one of these two grounds will be dismissed *in limine.*[1267] Literal reading of the Law suggests that if an opposition is based on any ground other than the two statutory grounds, the entire opposition should be dismissed *in limine.*[1268] It stands to reason, however, that the PBR Registrar will either dismiss the inadmissible ground or allow the opponent to amend its opposition by deleting the inadmissible ground to avoid dismissing the opposition *in toto.*[1269]

If the Opponent raises the ground of entitlement to the PBR, the Council will suspend the opposition proceedings before it and allow the opponent to submit an appropriate action to the competent court. However, before suspending the opposition proceedings, the Council will determine whether the variety is eligible for registration. Following judgment of the court, the Council will issue a final decision in the application in accordance with said judgment.[1270]

In principle, oppositions (and other *inter partes* proceedings) may be a more effective and extensive means of ensuring that only eligible varieties are registered, as compared with *ex parte* examination. This is because the opponent, often being a competitor, may be willing to invest considerably more effort than an administrative public body.[1271] However, in practice, very few PBR oppositions have been lodged over the years. In view of the above, the PBR Registrar is inclined to authorize an extension of the period granted by law to lodge an opposition (i.e., beyond the ninety days), the PBR Registrar is empowered by section 91 of the PBR Law to extend any period prescribed by the PBR Law (with few exceptions with respect to the payment of fees and priority right).[1272]

1266. Section 23(a) of the PBR Law.
1267. Section 23 of the PBR Law.
1268. This was the conclusion of the PBR Registrar in its decision in opposition to PBR applications 3922/06, 3923/06, 3924/06, 3925/06 *Danzinger 'Dan' Flower Farm v. Shmuel Mor et al.* (2007).
1269. Section 23(c) of the PBR Law.
1270. Section 25(a) and (c) of the PBR Law.
1271. Cf. HCJ 665/84 *Sanofi Ltd v. Unipharm Ltd,* P.D. 41(4) 729, s. 4 (addressing similar issues with respect to utility patents).
1272. Opposition to PBR application 3681/04 *Danzinger Flower Farm v. Shmuel Mor* (PBR Registrar, 2005), Opposition to PBR application 3572/03 *Shmuel Mor v. Beit Haemek Biological Industries* (PBR Registrar, 2005).

In addition, it was held that an opponent may follow field trials in the same manner that an applicant is entitled to follow the conduct of field trials, if he so requests in writing and upon conditions that may be prescribed thereto by the Council.[1273]

In an appeal filed on the Council's decision to refuse an opposition, a district court ruled that it is not only limited to discuss 'administrative issues' of the Council in an appeal, but also the merits of the Council's decision. Nevertheless, the district court ruled that since the Council is a professional and scientific body, the appellate court will rarely intervene with the Council's conclusions. The court also ruled that although the adducing of evidence in an appeal is allowed under PBR Law (section 88 of the PBR Law[1274]), it should not be used to extend the scope of discussion in the appeal to a completely new discussion or to abuse the proceeding in an attempt to conduct a 're-trial'.[1275]

V. Grant

370. If the Council finds that the variety was examined, that it meets the DUS eligibility requirements, that all materials and professional literature concerning the variety which were lawfully submitted to the Council were considered, and that any opposition filed is to be dismissed, the Council will instruct the PBR Registrar to register the PBR in the PBR Register in the name of the applicant, and the grant will be published in the *Official Gazette*.[1276] The PBR becomes effective upon its registration in the Register, and the publication is therefore of a declaratory nature.[1277]

VI. Breeders' Rights Register

371. According to section 5 of the PBR Law and the PBR Regulations, a Breeders' Rights Register shall be maintained for the registration of breeders' rights, and it shall include, *inter alia*, the name of the holder of the right, the denomination of the variety, a concise description and specification of the variety's basic characteristics and the claims, as specified in section 20(a)(5) of the Law, which were accepted for the purpose of registration.

As explained above, the applicant is not required to specify in his application the basic characteristics of the variety, but rather the variety's characteristics in their entirety. However, when the Council examines the variety, it is required to do so with respect to the variety's basic characteristics and it is these basic characteristics that are to be registered in the PBR Register. Thus, there is a 'missing link' between

---

1273. CC 2056/03 (Jerusalem) *Danzinger Flower Farm v. Shmuel Mor et al.*, Dinim-District 2008 (9) 1978, s. 30.
1274. See para. 366 above.
1275. CC 253/09 (Jerusalem) *Danzinger Flower Farm v. Shmuel Mor et al.*, Nevo Pub. (2012).
1276. Section 24 of the PBR Law.
1277. Section 4 of the PBR Law. The renewal fees are determined in s. 9(b) of the PBR Regulations and shall be paid yearly post registration in January.

the variety's 'characteristics' that the applicant is required to specify, and the variety's 'basic characteristics' that are subsequently registered,[1278] and as a result, there is some ambiguity as to the significance and scope of the 'basic characteristics' under the PBR Law.[1279]

VII. Priority Right

372. The PBR Law defines the priority right similarly to the respective provisions of the UPOV Convention. Accordingly, an applicant may claim the benefit of priority of a foreign application filed by the applicant or his predecessor not more than twelve months before the filing date of the application in Israel, for the purpose of determinations pursuant to sections 7 and 9 of the Law, provided that other conditions prescribed by the PBR Regulations are fulfilled.[1280]

Upon an applicant's request, he may be granted a two-year extension after the expiration of the period of priority in order to furnish additional data that may be requested by the PBR Registrar in connection with the Israeli PBR Application.[1281] This provision was introduced to the PBR Law as part of the 1996 Amendment to meet the requirements of the corresponding provision in the UPOV Convention.[1282]

VIII. The Actual Breeder

373. The person who actually bred the variety[1283] (referred to in the PBR Law as the 'Actual Breeder'), and the Actual Breeder's survivors are entitled to apply to have the name of the Actual Breeder recorded in the PBR Register.[1284] Although not discussed specifically in relation to breeders, it seems that this right cannot be waived.[1285] The mere registration of the Actual Breeder's name does not entitle the latter to any right to the variety and the PBR.[1286]

1278. This is exacerbated by the fact that, in practice, when Registration excerpts are issued by the Council, the 'basic characteristics' are not identified.

1279. It is also not sufficiently clear what the relationship is, if any, between the PBR Law's 'basic characteristics' and the term 'relevant characteristics' appearing in the UPOV Convention (e.g., Arts 8 and 9).

1280. To date, no such conditions have been prescribed.

1281. Section 72(b) of the Law. As to the authority of the PBR Registrar to request additional data, see ss 15 and 21 to the PBR Law.

1282. Article 11 to the UPOV Convention.

1283. As distinguished from the Actual Breeder's successor (such as, for example, his employer).

1284. Section 55 of the Law.

1285. Section 59 of the Law. Cf. Opposition to the registration of the inventor's name in Patent Application no. 146776 (an inventor's right to be registered in the Patents Register cannot be waived). This issue was affirmed by the Court of Appeal in CA 49328-10-10 *Shahal Telerefua Ltd v. Eli Oren* (2011).

1286. Section 60 of the Law.

IX. Amendment

374. The holder of a PBR may apply for the amendment of any detail or description of the variety registered in the PBR Register, if such amendment is necessary in order to clarify claims by the PBR owner or to remove an error (except a mere clerical error[1287]) in the application as it was filed. The clarification or removal of error may not broaden the scope of the claims and may not add any detail that was not mentioned in essence in the application as it was filed.[1288]

The request for amendment will be published in the *Official Gazette* by the PBR Registrar within sixty days of the date of filing of an application and will then be forwarded to the Council for consideration.[1289] Any person may file an opposition to the amendment within sixty days from the date of publication on the ground that the amendment does not achieve the purpose for which it was requested.[1290] The Council will issue its decision after allowing the parties an opportunity to present their arguments before it.[1291] The resolution of the amendments proceeding is recorded in the PBR Register and allowed amendments will be published in the *Official Gazette*.[1292]

Where an application for an amendment is filed while a proceeding for an infringement or cancellation of a PBR is pending in Court, the Council is not entitled to consider it without the Court's permission. If an amendment application is filed prior to infringement or cancellation of a PBR in Court, the Council is entitled to consider it unless ordered otherwise by the Court.[1293]

X. Nullity and Cancellation of a PBR

A. Nullity of a PBR

375. The Council may declare a PBR null and void, *sua sponte* or upon an application by an interested person, on one of the following grounds: (1) the variety did not meet the Distinctness, Uniformity and Stability (DUS) conditions stated in section 6 to the PBR Law at the time the PBR was granted; or (2) the PBR was granted to a person who was not entitled to it, unless the PBR was transferred to the person entitled to it.[1294] The initiation of the nullity proceedings is published in the *Official Gazette*. The Council will issue its decision only after allowing the PBR holder and the applicant an opportunity to present their arguments.[1295]

1287. A Clerical Error may be amended by way of a simpler procedure; see s. 99 of the PBR Law.
1288. Section 26(a) of the PBR Law.
1289. Section 26(b) of the PBR Law. This provision was revised in the 1996 Amendment. The revision applies also to applications filed prior to the date of the 1996 Amendment.
1290. Section 27 of the PBR Law.
1291. Section 26(d) of the PBR Law.
1292. Section 28 of the PBR Law.
1293. Section 29 of the PBR Law.
1294. Section 29A(a) of the PBR Law. Cf. Art. 21 of the UPOV Convention.
1295. Section 29(c) of the PBR Law.

Where the PBR is declared null and void, such declaration is registered in the PBR Register and the PBR is deemed as never having been granted.[1296]

The principles of resolution of priorities between the courts and the Council that apply to amendment proceedings apply to nullity proceedings.

B. *Cancellation of a PBR*

376. The Council may *sua sponte* or upon an application by an interested person cancel the PBR on one of the following grounds:[1297] (1) the variety no longer meets the DUS conditions stated in section 6 to the PBR Law; (2) certain data and materials requested by the Council;[1298] (3) the applicant has not permitted an examination of the measures taken by him for the preservation of the variety; or (4) a Court decided that the right of another to be registered as the holder of a PBR is superior to the right of the registered holder. The initiation of the cancellation proceedings is published in the *Official Gazette*.

The provisions of the PBR Law regarding cancellation of a PBR differ from the corresponding provisions in the UPOV Convention.[1299] Primarily, the Convention permits cancellation of a PBR if the Uniformity and Stability requirements are no longer met; however, the PBR Law allows cancellation with respect to all DUS requirements. Of note here is Article 22(2) of the UPOV Convention that provides that no breeder's right shall be cancelled for reasons other than those referred to in paragraph (1) of Article 22. Second, the UPOV Convention provides that all other cancellation grounds[1300] may be decided upon application filed within a prescribed period; however, the PBR Law permits *sua sponte* cancellation on all grounds.[1301] Third, the Convention entails one ground which is not specified in the PBR Law, namely, the failure to propose an alternative denomination. The Council will issue its decision after allowing the PBR holder and the applicant, if applicable, an opportunity to present their arguments.

Where the PBR is cancelled, such declaration is registered in the PBR Register and the PBR is deemed cancelled as of the date of the cancellation decision.[1302]

1296. Section 30 of the PBR Law.

1297. Section 29(a) of the PBR Law.

1298. The language of the relevant provision of the Law (s. 29(a)(2)) is:

> the breeder did not provide the Council, upon its request and within the time it prescribed therefore, which will not be shorter than one growing season, the propagating material of the variety – and in respect of a hybrid variety, propagating material of its parents – the basic characteristics of which are the same as the characteristics specified in the PBR Register, in the quantity requested by the Council, as well as documents and information, all for the purpose of the re-examination of the variety.

1299. Article 22 of the UPOV Convention.

1300. The ground of cancellation of a PBR due to non-payment of maintenance fees is dealt with in the PBR Law separately.

1301. This is in accordance with the policy of the Patents law, which provides that the Statute of Limitation will not apply in cancellation proceedings.

1302. Section 30 of the PBR Law.

The principles of resolution of priorities between the courts and the Council that apply to amendment proceedings apply to cancellation proceedings as well.

If the court finds that the right of a third party to be registered as the PBR proprietor is superior to that of the PBR proprietor of record, the right of the former shall be registered in the PBR Register, effective as of the date of registration of the PBR.[1303] The Law and Regulations are silent on the effect of this provision on the rights of third parties who may have transacted with the former proprietor of the PBR.

XI. Maintenance Fees and Restoration of Term

377. Maintenance of a PBR requires payment of annual renewal fees. Failure to make timely payment of the fees results in expiry of the PBR on the due date for payment. However, the PBR Law provides for a grace period of six months, during which the renewal fees may be paid and if paid, the PBR is deemed as if it did not expire.[1304] Even where the maintenance fees were paid within the grace period, the court has power to deny compensation for infringement that occurred during the period between the due date for payment of the fees and the actual date of payment, if the court finds that there was no justified reason for the late payment, with the burden of showing a justified reason lying with the plaintiff.[1305]

If the fees are not paid within the aforesaid six-month period, the expiration of the PBR is published in the *Official Gazette*.

A PBR proprietor may petition the PBR Registrar to restore the term of an expired PBR. The grounds for a petition for reinstatement are if the holder of the breeder's right did not pay the fee for reasonable reasons, was unaware of the expired right and did not desire its expiration and that the petition for restoration was filed as soon as the holder of the breeder's right, or a person on his behalf, became aware that the fee had not been paid.[1306] The decision of the Registrar to restore the term is subject to opposition by any member of the public. If no opposition is filed within the time prescribed, or if the opposition is dismissed, the Registrar may restore the PBR term, and may set conditions for such reinstatement, including, *inter alia*, compensation payments to any person adversely affected by the restoration order and the right to continue using the registered variety in the course of business in the conditions set forth by the PBR Registrar.[1307]

Notably, grant of prior user rights is discretionary and these rights may not be howsoever transferred, other than together with the business that used the registered variety.[1308]

1303. Rule 10 of the PBR Regulations.

1304. Sections 74 and 75 of the PBR Law. The rate of the fees is subject to change from time to time (s. 104 of the PBR Law) and is linked to the consumer price index and is amended yearly, on 1 July (Agriculture Fees Regulations (Index Linkage), 5741-1981).

1305. Section 68 of the PBR Law.

1306. Section 78 of the PBR Law.

1307. Sections 79 and 80 of the PBR Law.

1308. Section 81 of the PBR Law.

XII. Appeal

378. Any person aggrieved[1309] by the decision of the Council or the PBR Registrar, which is not subject to opposition or contestable (including the Council's decision in proceedings of oppositions, cancellation and nullity) may lodge an appeal on it to the District Court of Jerusalem within thirty days from the day on which the decision was brought to his knowledge as prescribed. A decision of the PBR Committee (Tribunal) may also be appealed in the same manner.[1310]

An appeal on refusal of a PBR application by the Registrar *in limine* (i.e., before the application is transferred to the Council and published, according to section 15(d) of the PBR Law) is heard *in camera* so as to preserve the secrecy of the information concerning the variety.[1311]

Notably, the PBR Law stipulates that a court which hears an appeal may accept evidence, either evidence already accepted by the Registrar or the Council or other evidence, and may demand that evidence be presented by affidavit or in any other manner it deems appropriate; where the evidence is presented by affidavit, the court may permit, upon request, the affiant to be cross-examined, unless it sees reasonable cause not to permit it.[1312]

§5. Ownership and Transfer: Licenses

I. Ownership and Transfer

379. A 'breeder' is defined in the PBR Law as '*a person who bred a new variety within its meaning in section 7, including his successors by process of Law, by transfer or by agreement*'.

The Plant Breeder's Right becomes effective upon its registration in the PBR Register in the name of its proprietor.[1313] In the event where several breeders apply for the registration of breeders' rights to a single variety, the right shall be registered in the name of the person who first lawfully applied for its registration.[1314]

A PBR and the right to apply for the PBR registration are transferable in writing as well as by the operation of law. However, a transfer of a PBR is not valid *vis-à-vis* third parties, unless registered in the PBR Register. It will, however, be enforceable as between the transferor and transferee.[1315] The writing requirement in the Israeli Patents Law was held to be an evidentiary requirement (as distinguished

1309. As was held by the District Court, a person or entity that failed to lodge an opposition to a PBR application may not file an appeal on the Council decision to register the PBR, although such person is 'aggrieved' by the decision (CA 324/91 *Yuval Totzeret Haklait Ltd et al. v. Pepiniere Et Roseraise George Belard* (1991)). Of course, such person may initiate revocation proceedings.
1310. Section 86 of the PBR Law.
1311. Section 87 of the PBR Law.
1312. Section 88 of the PBR Law.
1313. Section 4 of the PBR Law.
1314. Section 9 of the PBR Law.
1315. Section 43 of the PBR Law.

from a mandatory constitutive requirement). The writing requirement pursuant to the PBR Law is evidentiary as well.

The transferee of a PBR, either with respect to a registered variety or an application to register a variety,[1316] may apply to the PBR Registrar and have his right recorded in the PBR Register or the PBR application wrapper, as the case may be.[1317]

The PBR Registrar is also required to register, in accordance with procedure to be prescribed by the Minister of Justice, transfer of rights as determined in judgments of the courts. According to the PBR Regulations, subsequent to said judgment, the right of the transferee will commence from the date of the PBR registration in the PBR Register.[1318]

II. Ownership of Service Varieties

380. The Minister of Justice shall appoint a PBR Committee, which is constituted of three members, a district court judge, the PBR Registrar and a professional expert in the field of cultivating plant varieties. The Committee's main roles in respect of granting licenses and service cultivation inventions will be explained hereunder.

An additional tribunal (*Breeders Committee*), appointed by the Minister of Agriculture pursuant to the State Service Employment Regulations (*Takshir*) as detailed below, determines the rate of remuneration awarded to State Employees for the variety cultivated during their employment with the State.

An employee must notify his employer in writing of any variety cultivated by the employee during the service (employment) term or in consequence of his employment, as soon as possible after the conclusion of the cultivation, but prior to the filing of a PBR application thereon. In addition, an employee must notify his employer of any PBR application the employee has filed (*Employee Notification*).[1319]

In principle, a variety cultivated by an employee *in consequence* of his employment is the employer's property, unless otherwise agreed amongst them, or unless the employer waives its right within six months from the Employee's Notification. If an Employee's Notification specifies that in the absence of the employer's response the PBR shall be owned by the employee, and such response was not obtained within the six-month time frame, the PBR shall be the employee's

1316. The transferee of the right to apply for a PBR where the PBR application had not yet been filed is entitled to apply for the PBR in his name.

1317. Section 97(a) of the Law.

1318. Section 97(b) of the PBR Law and Rule 10 of the PBR Regulation. In accordance with Regulation 11 of the PBR Regulations, the transferee must pay fees as described by the PBR Regulations, file an application to the PBR Registrar accompanied with all of the material submitted in the framework of the opposition, file any other document requested by the PBR Registrar and pay the expenses to additional examinations if requested by the Council.

1319. Section 45 of the PBR Law.

property.[1320] Literal reading of the PBR Law allows for the conclusion that an employer showing a causal connection (*in consequence*) may claim rights in a variety cultivated by the employee, even if the cultivation was made (in whole or in part) after the termination of the employment. In contrast, the Patents Law provides that an employer will own an employee's invention only if the invention was made both during the employment term and in consequence of it.

Absent an agreement between the employer and the employee concerning the employee's entitlement to remuneration for a variety cultivated in consequence of the employment, the employee's entitlement to such remuneration, if any, may be determined, from time to time, by the Committee.[1321]

The employee has to do all in his power to assist his employer to attain a PBR,[1322] including the maintaining of confidentiality in regard to all information concerning the variety prior to the submission of the application thereon.[1323]

Additional and more specific rules apply to State Employees.[1324] The Agricultural Research Organization (ARO), the research arm of the Ministry of Agriculture and Rural Development is responsible for most of the governmental agricultural research conducted in Israel. The practice of submission of requests for remuneration to the Breeders Committee,[1325] State-employed breeders, is quite common. The rate of remuneration awarded by the Breeders Committee is often set at 33%.[1326] The remuneration that may be awarded by the Breeders Committee will not exceed the ARO's recommendations.[1327] The decision of the Breeders Committee may be appealed to a special tribunal.[1328] In a decision granted by the tribunal, the panel held that the stronger the connection between the position of the State Employee and the cultivation of a variety is, the lower the remuneration the State Employee may obtain (one rationalization to this ruling is that the State Employee's salary, *inter alia*, provides adequate compensation). Another principle that guided the tribunal was the need to take into consideration the governmental budget in determining the reasonable remuneration.[1329]

1320. Section 46 of the PBR Law. According to s. 48 to the PBR Law, where an employee has cultivated a variety during the employment term, it is presumed that he cultivated the variety in consequence of his employment, unless proven otherwise.

1321. Section 49 of the PBR Law. Among the factors that the Committee may take into consideration, the Law lists, '(1) the position that the employee held; and (5) expenses which under the circumstances, were reasonably incurred by the employee to secure protection of the variety in Israel.'

1322. Section 53 of the PBR Law.

1323. See, e.g., s. 73.17 of the State Service Employment Regulations (*Takshir*).

1324. Pursuant to the State Service Employment Regulations (*Takshir*). In addition, State Employees and employees of certain entities may not submit a PBR application outside of Israel, unless certain conditions are met.

1325. Appointed by the Minister of Agriculture pursuant to the State Service Employment Regulations (*Takshir*), s. 73.11.

1326. Up to a certain ceiling (cap).

1327. The State Service Articles Regulations (*Takshir*), s. 73.153.

1328. Comprising a district court judge, the PBR Registrar and a third member.

1329. CA 380/00 *Yilon Shori v. the State of Israel*, Dinim-District (10) 1299 (2006).

III. Licenses and Their Registration

381. The PBR Law does not refer explicitly to voluntary licenses of PBRs.[1330] Thus, a PBR license need not be registered. However, it seems that the licensee does not have standing to sue for PBR infringement in his name.[1331] In at least one case, the PBR Registrar agreed to record a PBR license, notwithstanding the absence of explicit reference to the power to record such right.[1332] In the authors' opinion, this is a correct result. Because the PBR proprietor is entitled to license his rights, the PBR Register should reflect such transactions, if only to prevent third parties from acquiring ownership of the PBR in ignorance of the license.

IV. Compulsory Licenses

A. General Note

382. Most legal systems that acknowledge intellectual property rights also acknowledge the need to limit their boundaries and their influence, and do so by developing the concept of compulsory licenses, as it represents the other aspect of the grant of an exclusive right.

In the UPOV Acts, the rights of the breeder are ensured to the extent that the State is not allowed to restrict the breeder from exercising his right, except in cases of public interest. When the breeder is forced to license out his variety, he will receive an equitable remuneration.[1333] The Convention's provisions, however, are ambiguous since they do not define the concept of 'public interest'.[1334] It is debatable whether or not the Israeli PBR compulsory license provision should be interpreted as having regard to the provisions of TRIPS.[1335]

Israel, as well as other countries, which adopted the provisions of the UPOV Convention, has implemented compulsory licenses into its PBR Law enabling two types

1330. In one case, the Court held that a party to a voluntary license is estopped from challenging the validity of a PBR, even after the license agreement was terminated (notably, the court did not address the 'license estoppel' doctrine, yet it seemingly applied same, albeit in the context of proceedings for a temporary injunction (C.C. 1227/01 M.C.A. 2426/01 *Taasiot Biological Beit Haemek Limited Partnership v. Danziger Flower Farm,* Dinim District (20) 571 (2001)).
1331. This is the author's opinion, based, *inter alia*, on the decision in CA 650/80 *Empisal Israel Ltd v. Naimi*, 37(3) P.D. 780 [1983] that reached a similar conclusion with respect to trademarks licensees (see para. 324 above). However, the issue had not yet been decided by the courts. In addition, see para. 393 below.
1332. Section 97 of the PBR Law allows the 'transferee of rights in the variety' to request that the transferee be registered as the proprietor of such rights. Narrow interpretation of this Section will limit its application to assignments of ownership interest. The more appropriate interpretation will encompass other rights, such as a license.
1333. Article 9 of the 1978 UPOV Convention and Art. 9 of the 1961 UPOV Convention.
1334. See Art. 17 to the UPOV Convention.
1335. As noted below, the Israeli legislator elected not to amend the PBR Law when it adapted Israeli intellectual property legislation to the requirement of TRIPs. Therefore, it is not clear whether the requirements of TRIPs concerning compulsory license of patents (e.g., Art. 31) apply where a member chooses, as in Israel, to protect plant varieties by means of an *effective sui generis* system.

of compulsory licenses: a compulsory pharmaceutical license and a compulsory agricultural license. However, in practice, this mechanism is not resorted to.

B. Compulsory Pharmaceutical License

383. The Council may permit the use of a PBR after consulting with the Committee without the holder's consent if it finds it necessary to do so in order to supply the public with means of treatment in reasonable quantities and prices. This sort of compulsory license may be granted only to a person or entity that is capable of utilizing the registered variety under the conditions set by the Council.[1336]

C. Compulsory Agricultural License

384. The Council may also permit the use of a registered PBR after consulting with the Committee without the holder's consent, setting conditions it finds necessary, if the PBR holder did not exploit the registered right or exploited it under circumstances and conditions which did not benefit the public.[1337] This provision was amended and extended in the 1996 Amendment, adding as an additional ground for a compulsory license the refusal to allow exploitation of an Essentially Derived Variety (EDV).[1338] The power to grant such compulsory license may not be exercised during the first two years following the registration of the PBR unless the Council finds special reasons to do so. The Council may not exercise its power of permitting the use under this provision within two years of the PBR's registration.[1339] In addition,[1340] the Council may cancel the right of a PBR holder if it demands the PBR holder to deliver and provide propagating material of the variety, and in respect of a hybrid variety, the propagating material of its parents, and said holder does not prove that he has delivered these accordingly. In this regard, the Council may prescribe to whom the propagating material is to be delivered and determine the conditions, quantity and time period during which these should delivered.[1341] The Council may not exercise its power of permitting the use under the provision within two years of the PBR's registration.[1342]

1336. Section 40 of the PBR Law. A similar provision of a compulsory pharmaceutical license in the Israeli Patents Law was cancelled as part of the adaptation in the year 1999 of the Israeli Intellectual Property legislation to the provisions of TRIPS (cf., *inter alia*, TRIPS, Art. 27(a), requiring that patent protection shall be enjoyed without discrimination in the field of technology).
1337. Section 41(a) of the PBR Law.
1338. The definition of an EDV is provided in *infra* n. 1367.
1339. Section 41(c) of the PBR Law. The Council may grant the permission of use before the two-year time limit expires if it has special reasons for doing so.
1340. In accordance with s. 41(b) of the PBR Law.
1341. Section 41(b) of the PBR Law; the time periods no less than one growing period may be extended determined by the Council at its discretion.
1342. Section 41(c) of the PBR Law; the Council may grant the permission of use before the two-year time limit expires if it has special reasons for doing so.

D. Prior User Rights

385. A person who proves to the satisfaction of the PBR Registrar that for at least three years before the application date (or, if relevant, the priority date)[1343] he exploited a registered PBR in Israel, in good faith, will be entitled to exploit the variety personally, and in the course of his business alone. If such a use was permitted by the PBR Registrar, the Committee may, upon request of the PBR holder, prescribe remuneration payable by such user to the PBR proprietor.[1344] The PBR Law is silent on the timing of such petition to the PBR Registrar.[1345]

The scheme of Prior User Rights pursuant to the PBR Law differs from the corresponding scheme pursuant to the Patents Law in several respects. The rights under the Patents Law apply by operation of law, whereas the benefit of the rights under the PBR Law require petition to the PBR Registrar. In addition, the PBR user may be required to pay the PBR proprietor for such use, whereas an exempt prior user of a patented invention may not be so required.

Notably, grant of prior user rights is discretionary,[1346] and these rights may not be howsoever transferred, other than together with the business that used the registered variety.[1347]

§6. Scope of the Exclusive Rights

386. As we will explain in more detail below, the proprietor of a PBR is entitled to prevent unauthorized 'exploitation' of any of: (i) the variety (i.e., the variety's propagating material);[1348] (ii) the variety's harvested material;[1349] and (iii) a variety that is essentially derived from the registered variety.[1350] Such unauthorized 'exploitation' is defined as an 'infringement' of the PBR.[1351]

This part of the Israeli PBR Law underwent a major revision during the 1996 Amendment, as part of the implementation of the 1991 Act of UPOV. In dealing with this issue, we will also explain which law, the former law (namely, the pre-1996 Amendment) or the current Law (namely, the post-1996 Amendment), applies.

1343. The determining date is defined by the Law as the date on which the application for the registration of a breeder's right is filed in Israel or where priority is claimed for that application, the date on which that application was submitted, in respect of which the priority is claimed.
1344. Section 44(a) and (b) of the PBR Law.
1345. For example, the law is silent on the question of whether such petition may be made after commencement of PBR infringement proceedings.
1346. Compare ss 53–54 of the Patents Law, 5727-1967, under which prior user rights are granted as a matter of law in the case of restoration of an expired term of a patent.
1347. Section 44(c) of the PBR Law.
1348. In contrast to Art. 14 of the UPOV Convention, which distinguishes between the exclusive rights with respect to 'propagating material' (Art. 14(1)) and with respect to 'harvested material' (Art. 14(2), the Israel PBR Law distinguishes between Plant Breeders' Right with respect to 'the variety' (s. 36(a)) and with respect to 'harvested material' (s. 36(c)). Notably, at least as of the 1996 Amendment, the reference to 'a variety' in s. 36(a) of the PBR Law should be construed as reference to the variety's propagating material.
1349. Part II below.
1350. Part III below.
1351. Section 36(a) and (b) of the PBR Law.

The role of the claims, as detailed above (§4 Part VI), remains unclear in respect of the scope of rights.

I. The Exclusive Rights in Respect of a Propagating Material

387. Both before and after the commencement of the 1996 Amendment, the proprietor of a registered variety was entitled to prevent any person from 'exploiting' the registered variety (i.e., the variety's propagating material) without the proprietor's consent, or unlawfully, such unauthorized 'exploitation' being defined as an 'infringement' of the PBR.

As part of the 1996 Amendment was broadened so as to comply with the provisions of the UPOV Convention,[1352] the current definition of 'exploitation' of a variety[1353] now includes the list of the following acts:[1354]

> (1) the Variety's cultivation or propagation; (2) preparation for its propagation; (3) offer for its sale; (4) its sale, export, import or marketing in any other manner; (5) its stocking for purposes of one of the acts enumerated in this definition; (6) other acts, prescribed by the Minister with approval by the Knesset Economics Committee.[1355]

The new broadened definition of 'exploitation' applies to all varieties, registered both before and after the commencement of the 1996 Amendment.[1356]

II. The Exclusive Rights in Respect of a Harvested Material

388. Similar to Article 14(2) of the UPOV Convention,[1357] section 36(c) of the PBR Law[1358] provides that the rights of the PBR's proprietor will also extend to:

1352. In particular, Art. 14 thereof.
1353. Section 1 of the PBR Law.
1354. In conformity with Art. 14 of the 1996 Amendment.
1355. As of 2010, the Minister did not prescribe such additional acts.
1356. Thus, the significance of the former definition of 'exploitation' is practically non-existent. It stands to reason that the former law continues to apply to acts that occurred prior to the commencement of the 1996 Amendment. However, the causes of action in connection with such acts are most likely time-barred by the Statute of Limitation. For the sake of those interested, we note that the definition of 'exploitation' prior to the 1996 Amendment included cultivation, propagation and marketing of a variety and any derivation of benefit therefrom in any other manner prescribed in Regulations. We also note that the former definition did not conform to Art. 5 of the 1978 Act of the UPOV Convention, where the acts enumerated were restricted to the production for purposes of commercial marketing, the offering for sale and marketing.
1357. Which provides that the acts enumerated in Art. 14(1) with respect propagating material will require the authorization of the breeder also with respect to harvested material.
1358. Introduced as a part of the 1996 Amendment. In at least one case decided in accordance with the PBR Law as it was before the 1996 Amendment, the Court interpreted the term 'variety' rather broadly, holding that any part of the plant *capable* of being used for reproduction constitutes a 'propagation material' (regardless of actual use of the plant material). Thus, the court held that the marketing of Gerbera flowers constitutes PBR infringement, as marketing of the 'variety'

> Harvested Material, including entire plants and parts of plants, which was [*sic!*] obtained by the unauthorized use of propagating material of the Protected Variety,[1359] unless the proprietor of a PBR was given an adequate opportunity to exercise his rights in relation to the propagating material'. A 'Harvested Material' is defined[1360] as 'a plant, and any part thereof, including its fruit that is not intended for vegetation[1361] or propagation'.

Article 14(3) of the UPOV Convention provides that each contracting party may provide that the acts referred to in Article 14(1) with respect to propagating materials, when made in respect of products made directly from harvested material of the protected variety falling within the provisions of Article 14(2) through the unauthorized use of said harvested material shall require the authorization of the breeder, unless the breeder has had reasonable opportunity to exercise his right in relation to said harvested material. The Israeli PBR Law empowers the Minister, upon approval of the *Knesset* Economics Committee, to promulgate regulation to that effect.[1362] However, such regulations were not promulgated.

The protection of the PBR Law with respect to harvested material applies only to PBRs, which were registered after the commencement date of the 1996 Amendment.

III. The Exclusive Rights in Respect of an Essentially Derived Variety and Certain Other Varieties

389. The scope of PBR protection was broadened, in the 1991 Act of UPOV, to apply to essentially derived varieties (EDVs) and to certain other varieties. These concepts were introduced to the Israeli PBR Law by means of the 1996 Amendment. Similar to the language and structure of the UPOV Convention,[1363] the PBR Law[1364] extended the protection afforded by a PBR registration to: (1) EDVs,[1365]

(O.M. 917/96 *Interselect Graberferking B.V. et al. v. The Council to Produce and Market Ornamental Plants*, District Dinim 401(6) (1997)).

1359. The Registered Variety is defined (in s. 36(b) of the PBR Law) as 'the variety in respect of which the (Plant Breeders) Right was registered'.

1360. In s. 1 of the PBR Law.

1361. The word 'Hebrew' in the original literally translate as 'growth'.

1362. Section 36(d) of the PBR Law.

1363. Art. 14(5).

1364. Section 36(e) of the PBR Law.

1365. The PBR Law defines an EDV similar to the Convention (s. 36(e)(1)(a)–(c) of the PBR Law, cf. Art. 14(b)–(c) of the Convention):for this purpose, a variety shall be deemed essentially derived from another variety if all the following hold true for it: (a) it is predominantly derived from the original variety or from a variety which itself is predominantly derived from the original variety, while retaining the expression of essential characteristics that result from the genotype or combination of genotypes of the original variety; an essentially derived variety may have been obtained by the selection of a natural or induced mutant or of a somaclonal variant, by the selection of a variant individual from plants of the original variety, by backcrossing, by a transformation by genetic engineering, or by any other similar method it is clearly distinguishable from the initial variety; by backcrossing, by a transformation by genetic engineering, or by any other similar method; (b) it is not clearly distinguishable from the original variety; (c) except for differences where the protected variety itself is not an EDV; (2) varieties which are not clearly distinguishable from the protected variety; and (3) a variety whose production requires the repeated use of the protected variety.[1366]

In proceedings of PBR infringement, where the accused variety is alleged to be an EDV, the PBR Law includes a special provision that may shift the burden of proof to the defendant.[1367] If the plaintiff proves one of the following, the onus will shift to the defendant to prove that his variety is not an EDV: (1) there is a genetic conformity between the original protected variety and the variety which is claimed to be an EDV, or (2) if the variety claimed to be an EDV maintains, except for minor differences, the expression of the essential characteristics that arise from the genotype or from the combination of genotypes of the original protected variety.

As noted above, the provisions of the 1996 Amendment with respect to harvested material apply only to varieties registered after the commencement date of the Amendment. In contrast, all varieties, whether registered before or after the commencement date, are eligible to the extended protection *vis-à-vis* EDVs. However, either varieties registered before the commencement date or a PBR applied for before the commencement date are immune from claims under the EDV provisions of the Law.[1368]

IV. The Relevance of DNA Evidence

390. Israeli courts have had the opportunity to explore the question of relevance of DNA evidence to the finding of PBR infringement.

Israeli courts held several times that DNA similarity may be relied upon in showing a *prima facie* case of infringement for the purpose of issuing a temporary[1369] injunction. In one early case,[1370] decided before the 1996 Amendment, the court refused an application for a temporary injunction, where 96% similarity was deemed insufficient to establish a *prima facie* case of infringement in view of morphological differences. In another case,[1371] in which the plaintiff argued that the defendant's variety infringes, *inter alia*, as an EDV, the court issued a temporary injunction on the basis of a 99.6% DNA similarity. The sole basis for the injunction

which result from the act of derivation, it conforms to the original variety in the essential characteristics that result from the genotype or combination of genotypes of the original variety.

1366. Subsections (1), (2) and (3) of s. 36(e), of the PBR Law, respectively.

1367. Section 62A of the PBR Law, also introduced as part of the 1996 Amendment, although not required by the UPOV Convention.

1368. Thus, even if it is shown that variety A was derived from variety B, if the breeder of variety A applied for a PBR prior to the commencement date, the proprietor of the PBR in respect of variety B will not have claim against variety A. In contrast, if the breeder of variety A did not apply for PBR prior to the commencement date, exploitation of variety A will infringe the PBR in respect of variety B, even though the derivation occurred prior to the commencement date.

1369. As to temporary remedies in general, see *infra* n. 1393.

1370. CC 1403/94 MCA 1091/94 *Hazera (1939) Ltd v. A.B. Zeraim Ltd et al.* (1995); application for leave to appeal refused – ALA 2762/95 *Hazera (1939) Ltd v. A.B. Zeraim Ltd et al.* Dinim Supreme (2) 1012 (1996).

1371. CC 2512/02 MCA 22337/02 *Shmuel Mor v. Danzinger Flower Farm* (2003); application for leave to appeal refused – ALA CA 3377/03 *Shmuel Mor v. Danzinger Flower Farm*, Dinim Supreme (23) 327 (2003).

was the DNA evidence, and the injunction was issued notwithstanding the registration of the defendant's variety in the PBR register. In yet another decision,[1372] a district court issued a temporary injunction having concluded that the defendant's variety was created by means of chromosomal duplication. The court held, albeit within the framework of temporary remedies proceedings, that a variety so created will constitute 'at least an essentially derived variety', regardless of whether the duplication occurred naturally or through artificial manipulation,[1373] and regardless of certain morphological differences.[1374]

It thus seems that, at least where it is argued that the infringing variety is essentially derived from the original protected variety, an Israeli court may be willing to issue a temporary injunction based on DNA evidence.

In a detailed and thorough decision,[1375] a district court issued a final judgment finding that the defendant's variety is an EDV based on DNA evidence. However, the court noted that while DNA evidence may be sufficient to establish the presumption that the accused variety is an EDV, the final determination whether or not the accused variety is an EDV will be based on morphological evidence.[1376] In discussing the parties' expert evidence concerning the morphological characteristics of the protected variety and the infringing variety, the court agreed that the morphological differences resulted from the act of derivation, and hence could not preclude the finding that the defendant's variety is an EDV.

V. Exceptions to the Scope of Protection

A. *Exhaustion of Rights*

391. Section 36A of the PBR Law, introduced by the 1996 Amendment, introduced a new statutory exception to the PBR Protection, namely, exhaustion of rights. In particular, it provides that the right of a proprietor of the PBR shall not apply to the exploitation of '*a protected variety*' and '*of a variety essentially derived from it*' if the variety was sold or otherwise marketed by the proprietor of the PBR or with his consent within the territory of the State of Israel.[1377] This exception will not apply if exploitation involves one of the following: (1) the repeated propagation of the variety; or (2) exportation of propagating material or of harvested material of the variety, which enables propagation thereof in a country that does not protect

1372. CC 2002/05 MCA 16462/05 *Danzinger Flower Farm v. Shmuel Mor*, Dinim District (58) 899 (2005); application for leave to appeal refused – ALA 10192/05 *Shmuel Mor v. Danzinger Flower Farm*, Dinim Supreme (3) 149 (2006).

1373. This is consistent with Art. 14(c) of the UPOV Convention.

1374. Unfortunately, the Court did not elaborate on those differences.

1375. CC 1228/03 *Danzinger Flower Farm v. Hanania Azulai and Astee Flowers B.V.*, Dinim District (26), 225 (2009); the defendant, Astee Flowers B.V. appealed to the Israeli Supreme Court. No decision has been issued yet.

1376. In the case at hand, the defendants did not succeed in proving that the allegedly infringing variety is not an EDV.

1377. It remains unclear whether the concept of international exhaustion may still apply based on general principles.

varieties of the genus or species to which the protected variety belongs, except such exportation for purposes of consumption.

The transition provisions of the 1996 Amendment are silent on the application of the new section 36A. Accordingly, it apparently[1378] applies to varieties registered before the commencement date of the Amendment. This is an odd result, having regard to the fact that the provisions of the 1996 Amendment with respect to protection of harvested material do not apply to old varieties.

As noted above, one exception to the exception of the exhaustion of rights is '*exploitation involv[ing] the repeated propagation of the variety*'. This exception to the exception was broadly interpreted in the Supreme Court decision in the matter of *Florist De Kwakel* handed down in 2013.[1379] The Supreme Court held that where a plant was obtained as a result of an unauthorized repeated propagation, all acts of exploitation (as defined in the PBR Law) of such plant or its harvested material infringe, and not only the repeated propagation of it.[1380]

Furthermore, the Supreme Court ruled that the remedy of an injunction could be granted in cases where actions of infringers are found outside the scope of exhaustion. Nevertheless, the injunction is to be limited to the prevention of exploitation of a variety, for commercial reason, *which relate to the repeated propagation of the variety only.*

B. Permitted Exploitation of a Registered Variety

392. Notwithstanding the exclusive rights afforded by section 36 of the PBR Law, a person may, without the consent of the proprietor of the PBR, exploit the propagation material of a registered variety for experimentation towards the development of a new variety. However, one may not exploit the propagation material repeatedly for the commercial production of another variety.[1381] In addition, a person may, without the consent of the proprietor of the PBR, exploit the propagation material of a registered variety for the purpose of research, science or laboratory testing, or for any act performed privately and for non-commercial purposes.[1382]

The foregoing two exceptions are mandated by Article 15(1) of the UPOV Convention. It is noteworthy that Israel elected not to legislate a 'farmer's exception',[1383] as it was entitled to do pursuant to Article 15(2) of the Convention.

1378. This conclusion is not free from doubt. However, discussion of this question exceeds the scope of this work.

1379. CA 10717/05 *Florist De Kwakel et al. v. Baruch Hajaj et al.*, Nevo Pub. (2013).

1380. In the *Florist De Kwakel case*, the defendant acquired from the breeder's distributor plants of a protected variety of the genus Gerbera which produces flowers for one (or two at the most) annual flowering seasons and then resorted to repeated propagation to grow flowers for additional flowering seasons.

1381. Section 37(1) of the PBR Law. Cf. Art. 15(1)(iii) of the Convention.

1382. Section 37(2) of the PBR Law. Cf. Art. 15(1)(i)-(ii) of the Convention.

1383. The Farmers' Exception enables a farmer to use for propagating purposes the product of harvesting which he has obtained by planting on his premises outside the right scope of protection of the PBR.

In addition, where a plant material[1384] is lawfully confiscated, its utilization shall not constitute infringement, except if it constitutes repeated propagation.[1385]

§7. Infringement and Remedies: Procedural and Criminal Aspects

I. The Right to Bring Suit

393. Only the PBR Proprietor and his agents are entitled to file an action of PBR infringement.[1386] The Law does not define who qualifies as an 'agent' and whether the 'agent' is entitled to file action in his name, or only in the name of the proprietor. This may raise some interesting questions, particularly with respect to licensees (with respect to which the Law is silent as well).

An action for infringement may not be filed until after the PBR is registered. However, a successful plaintiff will be entitled to retroactive remedies for infringement that occurred after publication of transfer of the application to the Council.[1387] These provisions closely follow similar provisions of the Israeli Patents Law. With respect to the latter, there are conflicting decisions of district courts whether suit may be brought prior to publication based on the cause of action of Unjust Enrichment (unfair competition).[1388]

II. Defences

394. Any grounds for opposition to the registration of a PBR and some of the grounds for cancellation and nullity of a PBR registration[1389] may be used as a defence in an infringement action. Thus, it seems that applications for cancellation and nullity of a PBR on other grounds should be filed with the Council. If the court allows such a defence, it shall order the amendment of the particulars of the registration in the PBR Register or the cancellation of the PBR, as the case may be.[1390]

III. The Remedies Available

395. The PBR Law provides that a plaintiff is entitled to the remedies of (permanent) injunction[1391] and compensation.[1392]

1384. A 'product of a variety'.
1385. Section 63 of the PBR Law.
1386. Section 61 of the PBR Law.
1387. Section 62 of the PBR Law.
1388. See Ch. 2.
1389. Namely, the cancellation grounds pursuant to s. 29(a)(1) of the Law and pursuant to s. 29A(a)(1) of the Law.
1390. Section 64 of the PBR Law.
1391. In addition to permanent injunction that is awarded after trial, a court may award temporary (interlocutory) remedies, pending final judgment, upon showing of a *prima facie* case, and having regard to the balance of convenience and other equitable factors. The decision of the court does

Prior to deciding the plaintiff's entitlement to compensation, the court may order the defendant to deliver a report as to the extent of the infringement; however, the court shall not be bound by the report when it determines the amount of compensation, but may set the amount in accordance with the circumstances of the case.[1393] In setting the amount of compensation, the court may take into consideration the defendant's act of infringement, as well as the plaintiff's position in consequence thereof, and it may also take into consideration, *inter alia,* the direct damage suffered by the plaintiff, the extent of the infringement, the profits which the infringer derived from the act of infringement and the reasonable royalties, which the infringer would have had to pay, had he been given a license to exploit the PBR in the scope of the infringement.[1394] An identical provision in the Israeli Patents Law was interpreted as granting the court a very wide discretion in awarding damages.[1395] Thus, a court may base the award of compensation both on calculation of the damage suffered by the plaintiff and on restitution of benefits derived by the defendant, provided that the award of compensation does not result in double compensation.[1396] In addition to compensation, the court may award the plaintiff with punitive damages, in an additional amount that may not exceed the award of actual compensation, if the infringement was committed after the plaintiff has warned the infringer.[1397]

Lastly, in the Supreme Court decision in the matter of *Florist De Kwakel,*[1398] it was also decided that if infringement of a PBR was proved, the holder of the right will be denied of the remedies under the law only in rare and exceptional circumstances, where the lack of faith and abuse of the plaintiff is extreme and apparent.[1399]

IV. Declaratory Judgment of Non-infringement

396. A person who intends to exploit a registered variety may request from the court a declaratory judgment that such exploitation will not constitute an infringement of a specified PBR and the proprietor of the PBR will be named as a respondent to such a request. The court shall make a declaratory statement only if the

---

not constitute a final resolution of the parties' rights. In at least one case, the court refused to consider arguments of invalidity within the framework of an application for temporary injunction (CC 1227/01 M.C.A. 2426/01 *Taasiot Biological Beit Haemek Limited Partnership v. Danzinger Flower Farm* (20) 2001) 571.

1392. As the Israeli Supreme Court held in another context, the statutory list of remedies is not exhaustive (*Ubi Jus Ibi Remedium*).

1393. Section 65(D) of the PBR Law.

1394. Section 65(A) and 65(B) of the PBR Law.

1395. CA 3400/03 *Ruahama Rubinstein et al. v. Ein Tal et al. (1983) Ltd,* P.D. 52(6) 490 (2005).

1396. This part of the PBR Law was drafted practically verbatim from the provisions of the Patents Law. Among the provisions copied are ss 66 and 67 of the PBR Law, which deal with limitation of the right to compensation where the claims of the PBR were amended, and where the PBR was revoked in part, respectively. The practical significance of these provisions, if any, is not clear.

1397. Section 65(C) of the PBR Law.

1398. CA 10717/05 *Florist De Kwakel et al. v. Baruch Hajaj et al.,* Nevo Pub. (2013).

1399. Which did not apply for the matter *Florist De Kwakel.*

applicant delivered to the holder of the PBR full particulars of the planned exploitation or of the variety in respect of which he applied the request to court, and the latter refused such a request or did not grant his permission within a reasonable amount of time. However, it should be noted that the court may not reject a request merely because it was filed before the expiration of such reasonable time. In such a proceeding, the costs will be borne by the applicant and no plea in which the PBR is invalid may be claimed and the court's judgment will affect the determination of the PBR's validity.[1400]

V. Criminal Aspects of PBR Infringement

397. Knowingly infringing a PBR constitutes a criminal offence, which may result in imprisonment or fine.[1401] Moreover, knowingly committing an act with regard to a variety, the period between the publication and the registration of the PBR, which would have constituted an infringement if the PBR had been registered, is likewise a criminal offence.[1402]

VI. Duration of the PBR

398. The duration of the registered PBR is, in conformity with UPOV Convention, twenty years from the date of registration, except for vines, fruit trees, forest trees and any other perennial plants,[1403] which enjoy a duration of protection of twenty-five years from the date of their registration.[1404]

Prior to the 1996 Amendment, the duration of PBRs in Israel was shorter.[1405] The extended duration introduced in 1996 Amendment applied to PBRs of varieties registered before the commencement date that had not yet expired at such time, thereby extending the duration of such PBRs.

The PBR Law empowers the Minister to prescribe, for a particular plant or for a particular genus of plants, a longer duration of protection.[1406] The Law does not specify, however, the criteria for issuing an extension order. The PBR Regulations (Extension of Term), 5753-1993, prescribe a period of protection of twenty years from the registration for the genera of melon and cotton.

§8. Trademarks and Denominations

399. As noted above, a PBR applicant is required to propose a denomination for his variety. The proposed denomination will not be registered in the PBR Register

1400. Section 69 of the PBR Law.
1401. Section 82 of the PBR Law.
1402. Section 83 of the PBR Law.
1403. Extended protection for perennial plants is not required, but permitted, by Art. 19 of the UPOV Convention.
1404. Section 38(a) of the PBR Law.
1405. Fifteen and eighteen years, respectively.
1406. Section 38(b) of the PBR Law.

if, in respect of agricultural crops of the same species, name or class, an identical or similar denomination or description is registered in the Trademarks Register.[1407] The PBR Law also provides that no denomination shall be registered under the Trademarks Ordinance in respect of aforesaid crops if an identical or similar denomination of a variety was registered at any time in the PBR Register.[1408]

This provision is quite unclear as to what is meant by *'agricultural crops ... of identical or similar class'*. For example, would the registration of Trademark XXX® with respect to apples (rather than fruit in general) prevent registration on denomination XXX with respect to avocado? Should the reference to *'description'* be understood as reference to *species*, having regard to Article 20 of the UPOV Convention,[1409] which refers to denominations that will differ for the same or similar species?

In one case that went all the way to the Supreme Court, the appellant filed with the trademark office an application to register the trademark 'More Stars' in class 31. An opposition was lodged by another breeder who holds registration of the 'Million Stars' and 'Lucky Stars', also in class 31. Both parties used their trademarks with respect to different PBR-protected varieties of the gypsophila genus.

The Supreme Court held that the opposition should be allowed[1410] since the requested mark of the respondent was found to be confusingly similar to the registered trademarks of the appellant. Notably, the Court did not take into consideration any provision or factor relating to PBR Law and based its analysis solely on provisions of the Trademark Ordinance and legal tests derived from them.[1411]

In addition, a denomination of a variety shall not be registered under the PBR Law if:[1412] (1) it is identical with the denomination of a registered variety of the same species or misleadingly similar to it; (2) it is identical with the denomination of another variety of the same species which is mentioned in an enactment within the scope of the Minister's authority; (3) it is identical with the denomination of a variety of the same species registered in a Paris Union State, or it is similar enough to an aforesaid denomination of a variety to be misleading; (4) it is identical with the denomination of a variety of the same species registered in a Union State or misleadingly similar to it; (5) it is liable to violate the *ordre public* or morality or mislead the public; (6) it is liable to mislead the public in respect of the variety or its characteristics, or in respect of its differentiation from other varieties of the same species; (7) it does not comply with accepted international standards on variety denominations.

The PBR Law requires the use of a registered denomination in respect of such variety, whether or not a trademark is attached to the denomination. The Law allows use of a covert denomination upon an application submitted to the PBR Registrar and decided by a person appointed by the Minister. In order to avoid confusion

1407. Maintained pursuant to the Trademarks Ordinance (New Version) 5732-1972; see Ch. 3.
1408. Section 31(a) of the PBR Law.
1409. Section 20 to the UPOC Convention reads as follows: ' ... in particular, it must be different from every denomination which designates, in any member States of the Union, existing varieties of the same or a closely related botanical species'.
1410. The Supreme Court reversed the Deputy Registrar's decision in the opposition.
1411. CA 1611/07 *Micha Danzinger v. Shmuel Mor*, Nevo Pub., (2012).
1412. Section 31(b) of the PBR Law.

between varieties' denominations, the PBR Law forbids the use of denomination identical or misleadingly similar to a denomination that was registered at any time.[1413]

The variety's denomination is published together with the Council's decision allowing registration of the PBR. The denomination may be contested by way of an application to the PBR Registrar, which is to be filed prior to the expiration of one year from the date of publication.[1414]

1413. Section 34 of the PBR Law.
1414. Section 33 of the PBR Law.

Chapter 6. Chip Protection

§1. Sources: Legislation

400. Protection of the topographies, or layouts, of integrated circuits in Israel is governed by the Integrated Circuits (Protection) Law, 5760-1999 (the '*Law*'). The Law was enacted in order to implement Israel's undertakings in respect of circuit protection under the TRIPS Agreement. The TRIPS Agreement[1415] in turn partially incorporates the undertakings under the Washington Treaty on Intellectual Property in Respect of Integrated Circuits of 1989 (the '*IPIC Treaty*'), to which Israel is not a party.

The Minister of Justice, who has the power, under section 14 of the Law, to promulgate regulations under the Law, issued an order in furtherance of the Law in respect of the national treatment of original topographies protected in the WTO member countries, namely the Integrated Circuits (Protection) (TRIPS Agreement) Order, 5760 – 1999 (the '*Order*').

The provisions of the Law are yet to come before the courts in Israel.

§2. Subject Matter of Protection

401. The Law affords protection to a layout-design, or topography, of integrated circuits which meet the conditions of protection (discussed in section §3 'Conditions of Protection' below).

In line with the definition of an integrated circuit in the IPIC Treaty, an 'integrated circuit' is defined in section 1 of the Law as a product in its final form or in an intermediate form which meets two cumulative conditions: (i) its elements, at least one of them being an active element, and some or all of the interconnections are integrally formed in or on a layer or layers of material; and (ii) such product is intended to perform an electronic function. A 'layout-design', or 'topography', is defined as the three-dimensional disposition of an integrated circuit or such three-dimensional disposition prepared for the manufacture of an integrated circuit, however expressed.

§3. Conditions of Protection

I. Formal Requirements

402. There is no registration requirement in Israeli law in order to obtain protection for a layout-design or integrated circuit under the Law. A layout-design is entitled to protection if it meets the substantive conditions discussed below.

1415. Section 6, Arts 35–38 of the TRIPS Agreement.

II. Substantive Requirements

403. Originality. The provisions of this Law shall apply to an original topography.[1416] A topography is considered original either if: (1) it is the result of its creator's independent development, and on the date of its creation was not a commonplace amongst creators of topographies or manufacturers of integrated circuits; or (2) it consists of a combination of elements and interconnections that are commonplace, provided that the combination as a whole fulfils the condition of originality (i.e., the result of its creator's independent development and on the date of its creation was not commonplace).[1417]

Territoriality – Attachment and National Treatment. Protection under the Law is afforded to topographies the creator of which was, on the date of creation, an Israeli national or domiciliary,[1418] and to topographies the creator of which is a person or corporation, which has, on the date of creation of such topographies, an effective establishment for the creation of topographies or for the manufacture of integrated circuits in Israel.[1419]

In addition, the Law confers on the Minister of Justice the power to make orders in order to make the provisions of the Law applicable, in whole or in part, to other original topographies, to which the foregoing points of attachment to Israel do not apply, if such is set out in an international treaty to which Israel is a party.[1420]

The Order, which commenced on 1 January 2000, makes the provisions of the Law applicable to an eligible foreign topography, that is, an original topography which does not have a point of attachment to Israel under section 2(a) of the Law and the creator of which was, on the date of creation, a citizen or resident of a WTO Member State, or had, on the date of creation, an effective establishment in an WTO Member State for the creation of topographies or for the manufacture of integrated circuits.[1421]

Commencement of protection under the Law. The Law came into effect on 1 January 2000;[1422] however, its provisions also apply to topographies created prior to its commencement of this Law, but do not apply to acts performed in respect of topographies prior to the commencement of the Law.[1423]

§4. Formalities: Procedure for Obtaining Protection

404. As discussed in section §3 'Conditions of Protection' above, Israel adopted no registration mechanism for the protection of the topography of integrated circuits, so that no formal procedure needs to be followed for obtaining protection for an eligible topography.

1416. The Law, s. 2(a).
1417. The Law, s. 3.
1418. The Law, s. 2(a)(1).
1419. The Law, s. 2(a)(2).
1420. The Law, s. 2(b).
1421. The Order, s. 2.
1422. The Law, s. 15.
1423. The Law, s. 16.

§5. OWNERSHIP AND TRANSFER

I. Ownership

A. *First Owner of a Layout-Design*

405. Under section 4(a) of the Law, the creator of a layout-design is the first owner of it.

B. *Layout-Designs Created by Employees*

406. In respect of a layout-design created by an employee in consequence of his employment and during the term of his employment, the employer is deemed to be the creator of the layout-design, unless an agreement between them differently provides.[1424]

II. Transfer and Licenses

A. *Transfer*

407. Under section 5 of the Law, an agreement for the transfer of rights in a topography shall be in writing. Although there is no case law in this respect, the common understanding of such prerequisite in intellectual property legislation is that the writing demand is evidentiary.

B. *License*

408. Under section 5 of the Law, an agreement for the grant of a license to use exclusive rights in a topography shall be in writing.

§6. SCOPE OF EXCLUSIVE RIGHTS

409. Section 6 of the Law sets forth the two types of acts that fall within the scope of the owner's exclusive right in respect of the protected topography – namely, reproduction of a protected topography, and commercial distribution of a protected topography or an integrated circuit incorporating such topography or articles containing such circuit.

1424. The Law, s. 4(b).

I. Reproduction

410. The owner of a topography has the exclusive right, in respect of such topography, to copy, or to authorize others to copy, the topography or part thereof, including by incorporation into an integrated circuit.[1425]

II. Commercial Distribution

411. The owner has the exclusive right, in respect of a topography, to import, sell or otherwise distribute for commercial purposes: (a) the topography; (b) an integrated circuit in which the topography is incorporated; (c) any article containing an integrated circuit that incorporates the layout-design, only if such article contains a copy of the topography made in breach of the owner's exclusive right to control copying.[1426]

§7. Limitations of the Scope of Protection

I. Other Original Topographies

412. The owner of a protected topography has no rights in respect of any other original topography created on the basis of analysis or evaluation of such protected topography.[1427] The owner of a protected topography has no rights in respect of an identical original topography created independently.[1428]

II. Exhaustion of Rights

413. The exclusive right of a topography owner, under section 6(2)(b) and (c) of the Law, to control commercial distribution of an integrated circuit in which a protected topography is incorporated or of articles containing an integrated circuit that incorporates the layout-design copied in breach of the owner's exclusive right to control copying, does not apply to an integrated circuit sold or distributed by the topography owner or with his authorization in Israel or outside Israel.[1429]

III. Compulsory Licenses

A. Compulsory Licenses due to Abuse of Monopoly

414. Similarly to the mechanisms existing under the Patents Law, 5727 – 1967, the Law in section 13 confers the power on the Patents Registrar to grant a license

1425. The Law, s. 6(1).
1426. The Law, s. 6(2).
1427. The Law, s. 7.
1428. The Law, s. 7.
1429. The Law, s. 8.

compelling the exploitation of a protected topography and makes the relevant provisions of the Patents Law applicable, *mutatis mutandis,* to topographies. For this purpose, a topography is viewed as a patented invention and the date of its creation is viewed as the date of patent grant. The provisions of the Patents Law governing the grant of compulsory licenses for the exploitation of a patent for the benefit of the public (due to the proprietor's abuse of monopoly) are discussed in Chapter 2 'Patents' in section 7 'Limitations and Exceptions to the Scope of Patent Protection; Compulsory Licenses' in section III.

B. *No Compulsory Licenses to Exploit a Later Invention*

415. The provisions of section 121 of the Patents Law that deal with the license to exploit a patent in order to exploit a later invention do not apply to topographies.[1430]

C. *Compulsory Licenses to Exploit a Later Invention*

416. The designated government minister[1431] may authorize the exploitation of a topography for the benefit of the State, and for this purpose, the provisions of the Patents Law shall apply, *mutatis mutandis*. The provisions of the Patents Law governing the grant of compulsory licenses for the exploitation of a patent for the benefit of the State are discussed in Chapter 2 'Patents' in section §7 'Limitations and Exceptions to the Scope of Patent Protection; Compulsory Licenses' in section III.

IV. Non-infringing Acts

417. Section 11 of the Law provides for an exception of the fair use type, permitting the performance, without the authorization of the owner of the layout-design (topography) and without payment, of certain acts (listed as an exhaustive list). Statutorily exempted acts are: (1) any act relating to non-original parts of the topography; (2) copying for private purposes; (3) copying for the purpose of evaluation, analysis, research or instruction; (4) creation of another original topography based on the analysis or evaluation of the topography.

1430. The Law, s. 13.
1431. The Patents Law, s. 112.

§8. DURATION OF PROTECTION

I. Duration of Protection for National Topographies

418. Under the Law, the exclusive right in a topography commences on the date of creation of the topography.[1432] The 'date of creation' of a topography is defined in the Law as the date on which the topography is expressed in writing or is set in a tangible form.[1433]

In line with Article 38 of the TRIPS Agreement, protection of a topography expires on the earlier of: (1) the end of ten years from the date on which the topography or an integrated circuit in which the layout-design (topography) is incorporated were first lawfully sold or distributed commercially in Israel or outside of Israel; or (2) the end of fifteen years from the date of creation of the layout-design (topography)[1434] (the date of creation, as noted above, being its expression in writing or in tangible form).

§9. INFRINGEMENT AND REMEDIES

I. Infringement

419. The performance of any of the acts falling within the scope of the topography owner's exclusive right (as set out in section 6 of the Law and discussed in section §6 'Scope of Exclusive Rights' above) – namely, reproduction of a protected topography or commercial distribution of a protected topography, an integrated circuit incorporating a protected topography, or an article containing such circuit where the topography was copied in breach of the owner's right – without his authorization constitutes an infringement of the owner's exclusive right.[1435] The infringement of the exclusive right is a tort to which the provisions of the Civil Wrongs Ordinance [New Version] apply.[1436]

II. Innocent Infringement

420. Where a person purchases or orders an integrated circuit or an article containing an integrated circuit without knowing and without being expected to know at the time of such purchase or order that the integrated circuit constituted an infringing copy of a protected topography, such person may commercially distribute an integrated circuit incorporating the protected topography and articles containing such integrated circuits and shall not be liable for infringement of the

1432. The Law, s. 9(a).
1433. The Law, s. 1.
1434. The Law, s. 9(b)(2).
1435. The Law, s. 10(a).
1436. The Law, s. 10(b).

exclusive right;[1437] however, such acts of permissible distribution by an innocent infringer are subject to the payment of reasonable royalties to the topography owner from the date of receipt of reasonable notice that the integrated circuit constitutes an infringing copy.[1438]

§10. Overlapping and Relation to Other Intellectual Property Laws

421. There are no provisions in the Law regarding its interrelationship with protection under copyright laws, and the issue has not yet come before the courts.

Because an integrated circuit oftentimes embodies a computer program that has been permanently transferred onto it, a question may arise as to whether integrated circuit protection excludes the copyright protection conferred upon the computer program transferred onto it. In our opinion, integrated circuit protection is not exclusive of the protection of the computer program by copyright, and thus there exist separate layers of protection for the computer program and for its physical embodiment in the integrated circuit.

1437. The Law, s. 12(a).
1438. The Law, s. 12(b).

Chapter 7. Unjust Enrichment

§1. Sources: Legislation

422. In 1979, the Unjust Enrichment Act was enacted in Israel.[1439] The Act establishes the grounds for financial restitution in situations in which a person unlawfully received a service or any other benefit from another person.[1440] The substance of the Act draws from the Continental system of law and Jewish Law, and is without parallel in the Common Law systems. Three elements are required to establish grounds for claim under the Unjust Enrichment Act: (a) obtaining of enrichment (b) another person is the source of enrichment (c) the enrichment is without legal cause. The President of the Supreme Court (retired) Justice Aharon Barak coined the following phrase in describing the effect of the laws of unjust enrichment: 'the wings of an eagle hovering over the entirety of the civil law'.[1441] However, in a famous article of Supreme Court Justice (retired) Yitzchak Englard, he coined another phrase in criticism of the excessive reliance on the Unjust Enrichment Act, 'the wings of a predatory eagle threatening to devour the civil law'.[1442] This dispute pertaining to the role of the laws of unjust enrichment reached its peak in the context of the laws protecting intellectual property.

§2. The Protection of Intellectual Property through Unjust Enrichment

423. The principle of unjust enrichment as grounds for claim was developed extensively in Israeli case law. In a district court decision of 1989 regarding the use of goodwill, the court ruled that unjust enrichment may be grounds for a permanent injunction and not only restitution.[1443] In a Supreme Court decision of 1990 concerning the parallel importing of merchandise marketed under protected commercial brand name (the 'parker' pen), the Court decided that the third foundation of the Act – the requirement that the enrichment be 'without lawful cause' – may be established in accordance with the question of whether the enrichment was unjust. In other words, it need not be shown that the enrichment is in defiance of any law other than the Unjust Enrichment Law, such as the Trade Marks Ordinance, and it is sufficient if the court rules that the enrichment is unjust, for example having been accompanied by conduct in bad faith, or some other form of illegitimate conduct.[1444]

This broad interpretation of the grounds of unjust enrichment paved the way for numerous claims in situations in which products were copied and in which there was no possibility to sue for violation of established intellectual property rights,

1439. Unjust Enrichment Act, 5739-1979.
1440. Article 1 of the Unjust Enrichment Act.
1441. FH 20/82 *Adders Building Materials Ltd v. Harlow and Jones GMBH*, IsrSC 42(1) 221.
1442. Yitzchak Englard, *The Wings of a Predatory Eagle Threatening to Devour the Civil Law*, Gad Tedeschi Memorial Volume, Studies in Civil Law 37 (1996).
1443. CF 1769/83 *Boeing Corp. v. Boeing Travel and Tourism Ltd*, P.M. 5749 (3) 108 (1989).
1444. LCA 371/89 *Leibovitz v. A & Y. Eliyahu Ltd, et al.*, IsrSC 44(2) 309 (1990).

such as the Designs Law, Patents Law or Copyright Law. For example, many claims based on unjust enrichment were filed by reason of copying of fashion products which were not officially registered as designs, for various reasons, such as the short shelf life, etc. In the Tel Aviv District Court (the largest district in the State), the tendency was to accept these claims.[1445] However, in the Northern District Court, the tendency was not to accept claims based on unjust enrichment pertaining to intellectual property in the absence of a violation of any other institutionalized intellectual property right.[1446] This anomaly had negative consequences, such as 'forum shopping', and there was a need for a binding ruling of the Supreme Court.

In 1998, the leading judgment was given by the Supreme Court in the *A.S.I.R. case,*[1447] which concerned an industrial design that had not been registered and an invention for which no patent had been registered. The question was whether the copying of these products, which were not registered as official and institutionalized intellectual property, created grounds for a claim on the residual grounds of unjust enrichment (which as mentioned above, entitles the plaintiff both to financial restitution and to injunctive relief). The Supreme Court considered the question of principle – whether the law of intellectual property is regulated exclusively by the laws dealing with intellectual property, or whether other grounds of claim may also be enlisted in the protection of intellectual property interests. The decision in the *A.S.I.R* case was convoluted and the variety of opinions among the Supreme Court justices left some uncertainty. At the same time, the majority (five against four) holding was that the grounds of unjust enrichment may be resorted to in cases in which the institutionalized laws of intellectual property do not provide protection, albeit subject to certain conditions. The main condition referred to by most of the majority justices is that a residual grounds of action based on unjust enrichment may be recognized in cases featuring an 'additional element', variously referred to as 'unfair competition' or 'unfairness'.[1448] Apart from the definition of the additional element, the justices considered a list of guiding considerations, in accordance to which it would be determined whether the act of copying involved 'unfair competition' or 'unfairness'. The conditions mentioned included the following: the degree of innovation and uniqueness of the product, the degree of effort invested by the creator; the intensiveness of the copying; the mental foundation of the copier (awareness of the act of copying); the alternatives for copying; the reason for the non-registration of the right, and whether it was possible to register the right.

The courts in various forums frequently cite the *A.S.I.R* judgment, but the complexity of the judgment and the multiplicity of views and considerations cited in it make it difficult to view it as a source of unequivocal guidelines for the exercise of judicial discretion in the subjects it deals with.

In the field of designs, there have been many cases in which claims based on unjust enrichment were accepted, even though no design had been registered, given

---

1445. CF 1572/93 *Anima Fashion Ltd v. Reuven Ballan* (not reported).
1446. CF 1572/90 *Ronit Sadeh Schwartz v. Yehoshua Mauzner* (not reported).
1447. LCA 5768/94 *A.S.I.R Import, Manufacture, and Distribution v. Accessories and Products Ltd*, IsrSC 52(4) 289.
1448. LCA 5768/94 *A.S.I.R Import, Manufacture, and Distribution v. Accessories and Products Ltd*, IsrSC 52(4) 289.

that the registration of a design for a seasonal product was not economic.[1449] Occasionally, even in cases concerning the copying of a non-seasonal design, claims based on unjust enrichment were accepted.[1450] All the same, there were cases in which the actions grounded on unjust enrichment were dismissed where they related to industrial design for a number of reasons, such as the absence of the 'additional element'.[1451] It bears note that it was specifically the Supreme Court that dismissed two claims for the copying of fashion designs, which had not been registered.[1452]

In the area of patents, the courts are more cautious in their application of the *A.S.I.R* ruling. In a case where no patent had been registered for a medicine, the court dismissed a claim for copying based on unjust enrichment.[1453] The question that arose was whether in cases where an application for registration of a patent had been registered, but not yet approved, it was possible to prevent the copying of an invention during the interim period, on the grounds of unjust enrichment. The Supreme Court confirmed the decision of a district court and held that the Patents Law determines unequivocally that copying cannot be prevented during the interim period and that this rule cannot be circumvented by the grounds of unjust enrichment. In explaining its decision, the Court stated that the Patents Law establishes a

---

1449. For example, in Capp (T.A) 17647/01 *Remtax Ltd v. Erotax Ltd* (not reported) (temporary injunction against the publication of a catalogue that included copies of samples of cloth); CF 671/05 *Subahi Nahala v. Shivuk Kafe Almocatar Ltd* (not reported) (injunction against imitation of the design for jug used for marketing of spices); CF 860/02 *Impla Shoe Fashion v. Meir Daniel Josef and Sons Ltd* (not reported) (monetary relief due to imitation of a shoe sole); Capp (T.A) 23905/ 04 *Sigal Dekel v. Zip Hop Ltd* (not reported) (temporary injunction against the produce and sale of trousers).

1450. For example, CF 2085/01 *Avganim v. Beriah* (not reported) (temporary injunction against the copying of a locking device for which no patent had been registered); CF 2303/03 *Dialet Ltd v. Diamond Company Ltd* (not reported) (temporary injunction against the copying of a machine for polishing diamonds (the design of which was not registered); CF 97/16218 *Single Fashion Design 1994 Ltd v. Moses Ben Isaac Kuba* (not reported) (injunction against imitation of the design for trousers (the design of which was not registered)); CF 06/1439 *Simanda Andrei v. A.G.A.S.A Jewelry Ltd* (injunction against imitation of the design for jewelry (the design of which was not registered)); CF 03/1561, *Plasto-Wok 1990 Ltd v. M.A.G. Plastic Ltd* (not reported) (accounting relief against imitation of design for disposable plastic container); CA 3894/ 03 Doitch v. Isra-flowers Ltd (injunction against imitation of the design for jewelry, which was not registered).

1451. For example, CF 7361/05 *Maizlik v. Karshi International Ltd* (not reported) (dismissal of a claim for copying of Judaica products that were not registered as a design); CF 2108/06 *Ozgom Ltd v. Traplex Pal-Yam Ltd* (not reported) (dismissal of a claim for copying of bathroom products); CF 1510/04*New- Light Lasri – Manufacture of Lighting Devices Ltd v. Or-Ad Importing and marketing of Electric and Lighting Devices Ltd* (not reported) (dismissal of a claim for copying of lighting device); CF (Jerusalem) 03/11080 *Click Ltd v. Ro-Dan Fashion Ltd* (not reported) (dismissal of a claim for copying of fashion designs).

1452. CA 502/04 *Buffalo Boots GMBH v. Galli Shoe Stores Chain, Gali Tashlum Ltd,* IsrSC 58(5) 487 (2004) (dismissal of application to receive leave for appeal decision to grant injunction for copying of design of shoes, the design for which was not registered); CA 9568/05 *Shimoni v. Mobi Birenbaum Ltd* (published 2007) (dismissal of application for injunction for copying of breast-feeding bra, the design for which was not registered); CA 10/9070 *Tali Dadon Yfrach v. A.T. Snap Ltd* (published 12 Mar. 2012) (dismissal of application for injunction for copying of fashion design, for which the design was not registered).

1453. CF 2417/00 *smithkline Beecham plc v.Unifarm Ltd* (not reported).

delicate balance of interests, which should not be interfered with, and that in the current case the law should be viewed as exclusive.[1454]

In the field of copyright, the application of the *A.S.I.R* decision has not been uniform. Regarding the broadcasting of the sporting events 'in real time', a decision on an application for a temporary injunction held that the sports games as such are not a subject for copyright protection, but that the *A.S.I.R* holding was that the rules of intellectual property do not deny the protection of the subject matter by way of unjust enrichment laws in suitable cases. The court ruled that the broadcasting of sport in real-time should be regarded as the intellectual property of the body that organizes the game. Football games are a mass entertainment event, and the Football Association is therefore entitled to derive maximum economic benefit from them.[1455] In other cases, the grounds of unjust enrichment was recognized for purposes of protecting the 'narrative structure'[1456] or as a tool for granting an injunction in a case in which the front of house was photographed and used for marketing purposes.[1457]

In 2010, the Supreme Court handed down a judgment that restricted the scope of the *A.S.I.R.* decision with respect to the matters protected by copyright law.[1458] The question was whether the game boards of the football league in England have copyright protection in Israel. An affirmative answer to this question would have meant that the Israel Sports Betting Board (the body exclusively responsible by law for conduct of betting in sports in Israel) is in violation of copyright when using the information on those boards in framework of the betting forms. The Court answered the question in the negative, because the test of creativity is not fulfilled, and the game boards are therefore not a creation protected by copyright. This being the case, the question arose as to whether using the game boards provides grounds for a claim based on unjust enrichment. The Supreme Court ruled that the additional element required under the *A.S.I.R* ruling – unfair competition – does not exist in this case, given the nature of the Israel Sports Betting Boards as the sole body in Israel authorized to conduct sports betting. As such, there was no relevant commercial competition. The conduct of betting does not in any way impinge upon the profits of the English League. Moreover, the Court further held that even if the Board had not been the sole body authorized to conduct sports betting in Israel, the information used was available to all, for no charge, and as such could not be regarded as unfair competition. The Court also expressed its view on the broadening of the use of the unjust enrichment laws in the area of copyright. The Court held that the *A.S.I.R* ruling applies to intellectual property in products, which from a technical perspective cannot be protected by the classical laws for protection of industrial property, such as patents and designs. This situation differs from cases in which copyright protection is not given because of a specific balance of interests, which justifies the

1454. LCA 6025/05 *Merck & Co. Inc. v. Teva Industries Premtzmbauit Ltd*, IsrSC (published 19 May 2011).

1455. CF 2235/01 (Dis – T.A.) *Ongoing Radio Ltd et al. v. Broadcasting Authority* (not reported).

1456. CF (Dis – Jer) 6157/04 *David (the best) Davash v. Adler, Homski and Wershuski* (not reported).

1457. CF (Dis – Jer) 7236/05 *Levin v. Avni Ravid* (not reported).

1458. CA 8485/08 *The FA Premier League v. Israel Sports Betting Board*, IsrSC (published 14 Mar. 2010).

negation of the protection. The broad use made of the laws of unjust enrichment in these cases is undesirable and should be restricted.

The restrictive approach regarding the application of the laws of unjust enrichment in cases governed by copyright law was implemented by a district court in a case concerning the copying of data from 'job wanted' advertisements in the press. The court ruled that these data are not protected by copyright, and copyright protection cannot be extended to the entirety of 'job wanted' advertisements by way of unjust enrichment laws.[1459]

Alongside the role played by unjust enrichment law as a ground of action, parallel to the institutionalized laws of intellectual property, the laws of unjust enrichment also serve to expand the protection of intellectual property fields that are not regulated at all in Israeli law. One example of this is a Supreme Court decision that recognized in principle the possibility of protecting the 'Publicity Right' of celebrities, a right that involves the protection of commercial value of personality-related traits such as name, appearance, or voice, by way of the laws of unjust enrichment, in the absence of any specific legislation in that field in Israel.[1460]

1459. CF 1074/05 Capp. 2018/05 (Dis. T.A.) *Ma'ariv –Modi'in Publication Ltd v. All You Need Ltd* (not reported).

1460. CA 8483/02 *Aloniel Ltd et al. v. Ariel Macdonald*, P.D. 58 (4) 314 (2004) (s. 56 of the judgment).

Chapter 8. Trade Secrets/Confidential Information

Conventions:

The Agreement on TRIPS, Marrakesh 1994.

§1. SOURCES: LEGISLATION

424. The protection of trade secrets under Israeli law is anchored in the Commercial Torts Law 5759-1999. Prior to the enactment of the Commercial Torts Law, trade secrets had been protected by case law on the basis of various legal doctrines such as contract law, unjust enrichment, property law and the general obligation to act in good faith.

§2. THE PROTECTION OF TRADE SECRETS/CONFIDENTIAL INFORMATION

425. A trade secret is defined as business information of any type whose secrecy affords its owner a business advantage and that is not in the public domain and is not easily discoverable by others through lawful means, provided that the owner of the secret implements reasonable measures to maintain its secrecy. Also, a person who lawfully controls the trade secret would be considered an owner thereof:

(1) the law prohibits a person from converting a trade secret of another. A trade secret conversion includes: the taking of a trade secret without the owner's consent, by improper means, or the using of the secret by the taker, regardless of whether the secret was obtained from its owner or from another person who possesses knowledge of the secret;
(2) the use of a trade secret without the owner's consent, where such use is contrary to a contractual obligation or to a duty of trust that is imposed on the user with respect to the secret's owner;
(3) the receiving of a trade secret or the use thereof without the owner's consent, where the receiving party or the user is aware or where it is self-evident at the time of receipt or use that the secret was transferred to him or her in a manner prohibited according to (1) and (2) above, or that the secret was transferred to another person in a prohibited manner as aforesaid before reaching the receiving person/user.

The term 'use' in the Law is defined in a broad manner so as to also encompass the transfer of a trade secret to another. Where the user of a trade secret makes changes therein, such user will also be regarded as a user of the trade secret, provided that substantial similarity exists between the trade secret and the information actually used. There is a presumption in the law that a defendant is deemed to have used the plaintiff's trade secret if the following two conditions have been met: (i) the trade secret reached the knowledge of the defendant or he had access to it; and (ii) the information used by the defendant bears substantial similarity to the information subject of the trade secret.

Reverse-Engineering:

The discovering of a trade secret by means of reverse-engineering would not be considered, by itself, improper according to (1) above. The term 'reverse-engineering' addresses the disintegration or analysis of a product or process with the aim of deciphering a trade secret in reverse.

Limitations to Liability:

A person would not be liable for trade secret conversion in the event that: (i) the information embedded in the trade secret reached said person in the course of his employment with the owner of the trade secret and such trade secret has become part of the general professional capacities of said person, and (ii) the use of the trade secret is justified for reasons of *ordre public*. Nonetheless, when the use by a person of another's trade secret is justified by *ordre public*, and such person has gained benefit from the use, the court is empowered in proper cases to oblige such person to return the benefit to the secret's owner entirely or partially.

A person who received or used a trade secret without the consent of its owner in circumstances where the user was aware or was supposed to be aware of the conversion shall nevertheless not be liable for any use made of the trade secret if such person has purchased and received the trade secret in good faith and for consideration, unless the court holds that for the purpose of rendering justice between the parties, liability should be imposed on such person for trade secret conversion. In the event that the court does impose such liability, it may exempt the person responsible for the conversion from all or part of the remedies that the secret's owner is entitled to.

Remedies:

The law provides, in addition to the remedies of injunction and damages, for specific remedies, such as compensation, without proof of damage, of up to ISL 100,000 for each tort, order for accounts, receivership, *Anton Piller*-type order and destruction of goods.

Jurisdiction:

Where the conversion of a trade secret emanates from an employer-employee relationship, the district labour court has exclusive jurisdiction over the case. When the cause of action is mixed in with other causes of action, the action will be separated such that the claim of trade secret conversion by the employee will be divested to the labour court while the other claims will remain with the general court.

Chapter 9. Appellations of Origin and Geographical Indications

Primary Legislation:

Protection of Appellations of Origin and Geographical Indications Law, 5725 – 1965.

Secondary Legislation:

Protection of Appellations of Origin (Procedure before Appeal Boards) Regulations, 5726 – 1966.
Appellations of Origin (Procedure for Registration of Appellations of Origin Originating in Israel) Regulations, 5726 – 1966.
Appellations of Origin (Procedure for Registration of Appellations of Origin Originating in a Foreign Country) Regulations, 5727 – 1967.

Conventions:

The Paris Convention for the Protection of Industrial Property, 1883.
The Madrid Agreement for the Repression of False or Deceptive Indications of Source on Goods, 1891.
The Lisbon Agreement for the Protection of Appellations of Origin and their International Registration, 1958.
The Agreement on TRIPS, Marrakesh 1994.

§1. Sources: Legislation

426. Israel's obligations as a signatory to the Lisbon Agreement for the Protection of Appellations of Origin and their International Registration are reflected in the Protection of Appellations of Origin and Geographical Indications Law, 5725 – 1965 (the 'Law'). The Law has been further amended in 1999 to incorporate the protection of geographical indications as introduced by the TRIPS Agreement.

The Law affords protection against unlawful use of appellations of origin duly registered in Israel and against unlawful use of geographical indications within the meaning of the Law. Furthermore, according to the Law, unauthorized use of appellations of origin constitutes an offence in contravention of the Merchandise Marks Ordinance.

Further protection for geographical indications and other use of geographical names in trade is afforded through trademark legislation (discussed in more detail in Chapter 4 'Trademarks' at §3 Conditions for Protection), in particular barring from registration trademarks containing misleading geographical indications with regard to wines and spirits under the Trade Marks Ordinance [New Version], 5732 – 1972.[1461]

1461. The Trade Marks Ordinance [New Version], 5732 – 1972, ss 11(11) and 11(12).

§2. The Protection of Appellations of Origin and Geographical Indications

I. Appellations of Origin

A. *Overview of Protection: Definition of an Appellation of Origin*

427. Definition. An 'appellation of origin' in the sense of the Law means the geographical name of a country, region or locality contained in the name of a product and intended to convey that such product has its origin there and that its quality or its characteristics are mainly due to that geographical area, including its nature and people.[1462]

Civil liability – protection from infringement. Under the Law, unlawful use of a registered appellation of origin constitutes infringement of the rights of the holder of such registered appellation of origin. It is not required that infringing use be misleading.

Criminal liability. Unlawful use of an appellation of origin is regarded as use of a false trade description under the Merchandise Marks Ordinance.[1463] Thus a person who unlawfully uses an appellation of origin, unless such person proves that the use was made without intent to defraud, would be guilty of an offence and would be liable to imprisonment for one year or a fine. A specific protection is afforded under the Merchandise Marks Ordinance to the only Israeli appellation of origin 'Jaffa' (for citrus fruit), whereby merchandise other than citrus fruit cannot be designated with the appellation Jaffa and other variants of this registered appellation of origin and such designation is deemed to be a false trade description.[1464]

B. *Obtaining and Maintaining Registration of Appellations of Origin*

1. Appellations of Origin Originating in Israel

428. Registration of appellations of origin originating in Israel. Any person interested in protection for an appellation of origin may apply for registration.[1465] The application to register an appellation of origin must demonstrate to the Registrar's satisfaction that the designation applied for is an appellation of origin and not merely an indication of provenance or type.[1466] Upon formal examination of compliance with application requirements as to provided details[1467] and substantive

1462. The Law, s. 1.
1463. The Law, s. 24.
1464. The Merchandise Marks Ordinance, s. 2A. A recent IPTO decision disallowed registration of trademarks 'Old Jaffa' in respect of dried fruit, preserves, coffee and other goods in classes 29 and 30, holding that registration in violation of s. 2A of the Merchandise Marks Ordinance would violate public policy (*Citrus Fruit Marketing Board v. Malchi*, Opposition to registration of marks 220541, 220542, Application to cancel registration 220581 'Old Jaffa' [2015]).
1465. The Law, s. 3.
1466. The Law, ss 4 and 5.
1467. The Law, s. 5.

examination as to whether the designation applied for is an appellation of origin,[1468] the Registrar, upon being satisfied that the designation is *prima facie* an appellation of origin, shall accept the application.[1469]

The substantive examination for registration purposes is conducted according to the criteria of an appellation of origin as defined in the Law, namely, that it contains a geographical name, which indicates that the product originates in such locality, and that the quality or feature of the product is primarily due to the geographical environment, nature or people of such locality.[1470] An accepted application is advertised in the *Official Gazette* for oppositions.[1471]

Homonymous appellations of origin for wine. In implementation of the provision of Article 23(3) of the TRIPS Agreement, the Law provides that the Registrar may accept more than one application, by different applicants, for the registration of homonymous appellations of origin for wine which indicate different geographical areas, provided that the Registrar prescribes a distinction between them, taking into account the need to ensure equal treatment to manufacturers involved and the need to prevent consumer confusion.[1472] The Law defines 'homonymous' appellations as those having identical spelling or identical pronunciation but different in their meaning.[1473]

Two grounds for opposing the registration of an appellation of origin may be invoked: (a) that the designation is not an appellation of origin, but an indication of provenance or type,[1474] or (b) that the person claiming to be entitled to the appellation is not so entitled.[1475]

Appellate review. A person who considers himself aggrieved by a decision of the Registrar may lodge opposition to it with a ministerially appointed board of appeal presided by a judge,[1476] which may, at its discretion, confirm, vary or rescind the decision of the Registrar.[1477]

Term of protection; conditions of renewal. Registration is granted for ten years and may be extended, on application of the owner, for additional ten-year terms,[1478]

1468. The Law, s. 5.
1469. The Law, s. 7.
1470. See ACH 376/90 *Anheuser-Busch Inc v. Budejovicky Budvar Narodni Podnik et al* 46 P.D. (4) 843 [1992]('Budweiser 1992') at 860 regarding the substantive nature of the examination. See also Appeal (Jerusalem) 1011/05 *Citrus Fruit Growing and Marketing Council v. the Registrar of Patents, Designs and Trademarks* [Nevo, 2007] (the *Jaffa* matter) where the board of appeals presided by a district court judge reversed the Registrar's decision not to renew the registration of the Israeli appellation of origin 'Jaffa' for citrus fruit, holding that the designation continues to meet the statutory criteria for an appellation of origin and that licensing the use of a designation protected in Israel as an appellation of origin in a country not party to the Lisbon Agreement where such designation is protected as a trademark/brand name does not prejudice its status as an appellation of origin in Israel.
1471. The Law, s. 8.
1472. The Law, s. 7A(a).
1473. The Law, s. 7A(b).
1474. The Law, s. 10.
1475. The Law, s. 10.
1476. The Law, s. 30(a).
1477. The Law, s. 30(c).
1478. The Law, s. 13(a).

subject to the Registrar's ascertaining that the designation continues to be an appellation of origin and subject to advertisement of the application for extension.[1479] The renewal proceeding is designed for a substantive examination as to whether the registration reflects the legal status of an appellation as such.[1480]

Reversing the Registrar's refusal to renew the registration of the Israeli 'Jaffa' appellation on the grounds of it having ceased to be an appellation of origin, the board of appeal has ruled that where the registrant of the 'Jaffa' appellation licensed an identical trade name, accompanied with know-how, in countries which are not members of the Lisbon Convention and which therefore do not recognize appellations of origin, such licensing did not render the registration vulnerable to cancellation.[1481]

Removal of registration. In accordance with section 14(a) of the Law, any interested person may apply for the removal of a registration of an Israeli appellation of origin if the appellation has become a mere indication of type or provenance or if the conditions, which served as the basis for the registration, had ceased to exist.[1482] Such application may be made at any time. The Registrar has the power to remove a registration on such grounds on his own initiative.[1483] An application to strike is treated as an opposition and follows a similar procedure.[1484]

2. Foreign Appellation of Origin

429. Registration of foreign appellations of origin under the Lisbon Agreement. A foreign appellation of origin, registered with the International Bureau and notified to the Registrar by the International Bureau under the Lisbon Arrangement, is examined as if it were an Israeli appellation of origin, and may be opposed in the same manner on the same grounds (namely, that the designation is not an appellation of origin, but an indication of provenance or type,[1485] or that the person

1479. The Law, s. 13(b).
1480. The *Jaffa* matter.
1481. The *Jaffa* matter.
1482. In the *Budweiser* matter, where a declaration of invalidity of a foreign appellation of origin was sought in court proceedings, the Supreme Court in a *dictum* observed that with regard to an Israeli appellation of origin, in accordance with s. 14(a) an existing registration cannot be directly attacked (before the Registrar) on the basis that the designation was not eligible for registration from the outset but only on the basis of subsequent loss of eligibility (CA 784/88 *Budejovicky Budvar Narodni Podnik et al v. Anheuser-Busch Inc.*, 44 P.D. 44(2) 531 [1990] ('Budweiser 1990') at 541–543). The Supreme Court in the additional hearing (Budweiser 1992 at 861–862), held that an appellation of origin may not be attacked, either directly or indirectly at court, on the ground that registration should not have been granted in the first place (except where it is shown that the Registrar decision was made through breach of administrative duties, e.g., failure to exercise any discretion whatsoever) and that the lists of grounds of attack are exhaustive. It remains to be seen whether the subsequent enactment of a broadly worded defence in s. 33A in the wake of the TRIPS Agreement (see below) would affect the interpretation of the grounds for revocation under s. 14.
1483. The Law, s. 14(a)).
1484. The Law, s. 14(b).
1485. The Law, s. 10.

claiming to be entitled to the appellation is not so entitled).[1486] If the Registrar is satisfied that the foreign appellation of origin is eligible for protection in Israel, such appellation shall be registered in the register;[1487] if the Registrar is satisfied that it is not eligible for protection, he shall notify the International Bureau within one year.[1488]

Effect of foreign registrations. The validity of a foreign appellation of origin registered in Israel will be the same as in its country of origin,[1489] without need for a renewal of registration.

Removal of registration of a foreign appellation of origin. Any interested person may apply for the removal of the registration of a foreign appellation of origin on the ground that the appellation of origin is not protected in its country of origin or that it ceased to be so protected.[1490] The Registrar has the power to remove a registration on such grounds on its own initiative.[1491]

C. Infringement of an Appellation of Origin

1. The scope of Infringement

430. Under the Law, use of a registered appellation of origin amounts to an infringement thereof even if the true origin of the goods is indicated besides the appellation of origin and even if the appellation appears in translation or accompanied by expressions such as 'kind', 'type', class', 'imitation' or the like.[1492]

As implied in the Lisbon Agreement, the protection for a registered appellation is absolute in the sense that misappropriation or imitation constitutes infringement even if it is neither false nor confusing.[1493]

1486. The Law, s. 17.
1487. The Law, s. 18.
1488. The Law, s. 19(a).
1489. The Law, s. 20.
1490. The Law, s. 21(a). See Budweiser 1990 at 541–543 and Budweiser 1992 at 861–862 where the Supreme Court read s. 21(a) to say that the revocation grounds are limited to loss of protection in the country of origin. It remains to be seen whether the subsequent enactment of a broadly worded defence in s. 33A in the wake of the TRIPS Agreement (see below) would affect the interpretation of the grounds for revocation under s. 21(a).
1491. The Law, s. 21(a).
1492. The Law, s. 22.
1493. Budweiser 1990 at 537–538. In a recent case involving an appellation of origin, a local manufacturer's long-term (and non-confusing) use of the marketing slogan 'Water of Eden - The Champagne of Nature' (in Hebrew, accompanied with logo and/or the manufacturer's name) used in respect of mineral water was held to constitute unlawful use of an appellation of origin; the word 'champagne' was held not to have become generic for sparkling wines or general laudatory term, and the court opined that the protection of the Law was not limited to products of the same kind (CC (TA Distr.) 22286-03-11 *Comité Interprofessionnel du Vin de Champagne v. Eden Springs Ltd* [Nevo, 2015] ('Eden Springs')).

2. Limitations to the Scope of Infringement

431. Defence of non-validity of the registration. Following the amendment of the Law in 1999 in the wake of the TRIPS Agreement, it has become a defence against a claim based on a registered appellation of origin that the appellation of origin is not an appellation of origin.[1494]

Legitimate use defences

Continued use of trademark. An exception permits continued use of a trademark registered or applied for in good faith, or of a trademark in which rights had been acquired through use in good faith; the relevant section provides that the registrability or continued validity of the mark are not affected by the fact that the mark is identical or similar to an appellation of origin, if the mark was applied for, registered or acquired prior to 1 January 2000 or prior to the time when the appellation of origin was awarded protection in the country of origin.[1495]

Good faith. Another exception permits use of one's name in good faith. The registration of an appellation of origin shall not prevent the use of one's own name or that of one's predecessors in a business, provided that such use is in good faith and in such a way so as not to mislead the public.[1496]

3. Relief for Infringement

432. The court may order the infringer to refrain from infringing an appellation of origin and prescribe conditions for such order or stay its execution for up to six months on conditions it may prescribe.[1497]

In line with case law laid down by the Supreme Court, the court may prescribe other remedies such as compensation, albeit not provided for in the Law.[1498]

1494. The Law, s. 33B. The district court in a procedural motion in the *Budweiser* matter (OM (TA Distr.) 8654/97 (in CC 1819/87) *Budejovicky Budvar Narodni Podnik v. Anheuser Busch Inc*, 5763 (2) P.M. 1 [2004] at 12) noted that this defence, which was not available under prior law as interpreted by the Supreme Court in Budweiser 1990 (at 541–543) and Budweiser 1992 (at 864) (which held that, unlike a domestic appellation of origin, a foreign appellation of origin may be attacked solely on the basis of its loss of validity in its country of origin, in parallel to the revocation ground in s. 21(a).), has become available under the amendment and has changed the legal environment of the Budweiser proceedings.

1495. The Law, s. 33A. In the *Eden Springs* matter, the defence did not avail the defendant, as it was held not to have acted in good faith in adopting the slogan involving the word 'champagne'.

1496. The Law, s. 22A.

1497. The Law, s. 23.

1498. MCM (TA Distr.) 14458/01 (in CC 1819/87) *Anheuser Busch Inc et al v. Budejovicky Budvar Narodni Podnik* [Nevo, 2002].

II. Geographical Indications

A. *Overview of Protection: Definition of a Geographical Indication*

433. Under the Law, geographical indications are protected from improper use, which is unlawful. The protection of geographical indications pursuant to the TRIPS Agreement has been introduced in Israel in 2000 by way of amendment of the Law. In contradistinction to appellations of origin, a geographical indication need not be registered to be accorded protection but a likelihood of confusion as to geographical origin must be shown.

A 'geographical indication' in the sense of the Law is an indication that identifies in Israel goods as originating in a given geographical area which is a Member State, or a region or locality therein, where a given quality, characteristic or reputation of the good is essentially attributable to its geographical origin.[1499]

B. *Unlawful Use of a Geographical Indication*

1. Scope of Infringement of a Geographical Indication

434. Use of a geographical indication in respect of a product, the origin of which is other than the geographical region indicated therein, is unlawful use of a geographical indication if the geographical indication is misleading as to the true geographical origin of the good, and shall be regarded as an infringement of an appellation of origin.[1500] The Law provides additional protection for geographical indications for wines and spirits, and prescribes that the use of such expressions as 'sort', 'type', 'kind', 'imitation' or similar expressions in any language does not derogate from the use of a geographical indication being unlawful.[1501]

2. Limitations to the Scope of Infringement of a Geographical Indication

435. Defence of non-validity of a geographical indication. The amendment of the Law in 1999 in the wake of the TRIPS Agreement set a defence against a claim based on a geographical indication, where the geographical indication does not constitute a geographical indication[1502] according to the Law.

The Law deems lawful a use in respect of a product of a geographical indication that is not protected (or has ceased to be protected) in the geographical region indicated therein, or has ceased to be used in such geographical region.[1503]

1499. The Law, s. 1.
1500. The Law, s. 21A.
1501. The Law, s. 21B(a).
1502. The Law, s. 33B.
1503. The Law, s. 21C(2).

Legitimate use defences

Commonly used name and name devoid of indication of origin. It is lawful to use, in respect of a product, a geographical indication that is identical to a linguistic expression commonly used in Israel as the name for the product.[1504]

As noted above, it is also allowed to use, with respect to a product, a geographical indication that is not (or ceased to be) protected, or ceased to be used, in the designated geographic area.[1505]

Homonyms. It is lawful to use, in respect of wine, homonymous geographical indications that indicate various separate geographical regions which can be differentiated from each other.[1506] 'Homonymous' indications in the sense of the Law are indications having identical spelling or identical pronunciation but differing in their meaning.[1507] Where the defence of a homonymous geographical indication for wine is invoked, the court, when determining whether there is differentiation between the homonymous geographical indications, shall take into consideration, *inter alia*, the need to ensure equitable treatment as between the various producers involved and the need to ensure that consumers will not be misled.[1508]

Good faith. Another exception permits use of one's name in good faith. The lawful use of a geographical indication under this Law shall not prevent the use of one's own name or that of one's predecessors in a business, provided that such use is in good faith and in such a way so as not to mislead the public.[1509]

Defences based on prior use

Wine / spirit beverage. A person who has continuously used the geographical indication of a Member State for identifying a wine or spirit beverage, may continue to use such geographical indication in respect of wine or spirit beverages or in respect of any related product if it was used for a period of at least ten years prior to 15 April 1994 (the date of the WTO Agreement) or if the use of it was made in good faith and commenced prior to 15 April 1994.[1510]

Grape species name. It is lawful to use, in respect of a grape product, of a geographical indication that is identical to a commonly used expression of a species of grape, if such term for the species of grape was commonly used prior to 15 April 1994 (the date of the WTO Agreement).[1511]

Continued use of trademark. An exception permits continued use of a trademark registered or applied for in good faith, or of a trademark in which rights had been acquired through use in good faith; the relevant section provides that the registrability or continued validity of the mark are not affected by the fact that the mark is identical or similar to a geographical indication if the mark was applied for, registered or acquired prior to 1 January 2000 or prior to the time when geographical

1504. The Law, s. 21C(1).
1505. The Law, s. 21C(2).
1506. The Law, s. 21C(4)(a).
1507. The Law, s. 21C(4)(c).
1508. The Law, s. 21C(4)(b).
1509. The Law, s. 22A.
1510. The Law, s. 21B(b).
1511. The Law, s. 21C(3).

indication was awarded protection in the Member State in which the geographical region indicated in the geographical indication is situated.[1512]

3. Relief for infringement.

436. The court may order the infringer to refrain from infringing a geographical indication and prescribe conditions for such order or stay its execution for up to six months on conditions it may prescribe.[1513]

In line with case law laid down by the Supreme Court, the court may prescribe other remedies such as compensation, albeit not provided for in the Law.[1514]

1512. The Law, s. 33A; cf. the Trade Marks Ordinance, s. 52A.
1513. The Law, ss 21A and 23.
1514. MCM (TA Distr.) 14458/01 (in CC 1819/87) *Anheuser Busch Inc et al v. Budejovicky Budvar Narodni Podnik* [Nevo, 2002] (in respect of appellations of origin, but the reasoning holds true for geographical indications).

Selected Bibliography

§1. Copyright and Neighbouring Rights

I. Primary Legislation

Copyright Act, 5768-2007.
Copyright Act, 1911 (repealed; continued application in certain aspects).
Copyright Ordinance, 1924 (repealed; continued application in certain aspects).
Performers' and Broadcasters' Rights Act, 5744-1984.
Customs Ordinance [New Version].

II. Secondary Legislation

Copyright Regulations (Libraries and Archives), 5769-2008.
Copyright Regulations (Public Performance in Educational Institutions), 5770-2010.
Designs Rules, 1925 (Rule 72 addresses designs excluded from protection by virtue of section 22 of the Copyright Act of 1911).
Copyright Order (Berne Convention), 1953.
Copyright Order (United States of America), 1953.
Copyright Order (International Convention), 1955.
Copyright Order (Convention for Protection of Producers of Phonograms), 1978.
Copyright Order (TRIPS Agreement), 1999.
Performers and Broadcasters Rights Order (TRIPS Agreement), 1999.
Copyright, Performers and Broadcasters Rights Order (Rome Convention), 2002.

III. Books and Articles

Afori, T. *Copyright Act* (Nevo Pub. 2012) (*in Hebrew*).
Elkin-Koren, N. 'Users' Rights under Copyright'. In *Creating Rights – Essays on the New Copyright Act in Israel* (Nevo Pub., Editors Michael Birnhack and Guy Pessach, 2009), 327 (*in Hebrew*).
Fischman Afori, O. *The Right to Prepare Derivative Works in Copyright Law* (Nevo Pub. 2005) (*in Hebrew*).
Fischman Afori, O. 'Employees' Moral Rights: The Israeli Solution to an Ongoing Dilemma'. E.I.P.R 30 (2008): 521.
Fischman Afori, O. 'An Open Standard "Fair Use" Doctrine: A Welcome Israeli Initiative', E.I.P.R. 30 (2008): 85.

Selected Bibliography

Fischman Afori, O. 'The Silent Revolution: Judicial Discretion In Granting Injunctive Relief'. In *Creating Rights – Essays on the New Copyright Act in Israel* (Nevo Pub., Editors Michael Birnhack and Guy Pessach, 2009), 529 (*in Hebrew*).

Netanel, N. 'Israeli Fair Use from an American Perspective'. In *Creating Rights – Essays on the New Copyright Act in Israel* (Nevo Pub., Editors Michael Birnhack and Guy Pessach, 2009), 377 (*in Hebrew*).

Weisman, J. 'The Personal Right in Copyright Law'. Mechkarey Mishpat 7 (1989): 51 (*in Hebrew*).

§2. Patents

I. Primary Legislation

Patents Law, 5727-1967 (as amended).

II. Secondary Legislation

Patents Regulations (Office Practice, Procedures, Documents and Fees), 5728-1968 (as amended).

Patents Regulations (Extension of Patent Term – Application for Order, Opposition and Cancellation Procedure), 5758-1998 (as amended).

Patents Regulations (Implementation of the Patent Cooperation Treaty), 5756-1996 (as amended).

Patents Regulations (Notification of a Patent Invention by State Employee), 5730-1969.

Patents Regulations (Notification of a Patent Invention by Employees of Defence Forces and Soldiers), 5729-1969.

III. Books and Articles

Gilat, D. 'Experimental Use and Patents', IIC Studies 16 (1995): 1.

§3. Trademarks

I. Primary Legislation

Trade Marks Ordinance (New Version), 5732-1972 (as amended).
Merchandise Marks Ordinance of 1929 (as amended).
Customs Ordinance (New Version) of 1957 (as amended).
Commercial Torts Law, 5759-1999.
Civil Wrongs Ordinance [New Version] of 1968 (as amended).
Unjust Enrichment Law, 5739-1979.
Consumer Protection Law, 5741-1981.

II. Secondary Legislation

Trade Marks Regulations, 1940 (as amended).
Trade Marks Regulations (Appeal before the Supreme Court), 5748-1987.
Trade Marks Regulations (Implementation of the Madrid Protocol), 5767-2007.

III. Books and Articles

Seligsohn, E. *The Law of Trade Marks and Neighbouring Laws* (Tel Aviv, 1972).

§4. Industrial Designs

I. Primary Legislation

Patents and Designs Ordinance (1924).
Copyright Act 5768-2007.
Unjust Enrichment Act, 5739-1979.

II. Secondary Legislation

Design Regulation, 1925.

III. Books and Articles

Fischman Afori, O. 'Reconceptualizing Property in Designs'. *Cardozo Arts & Entertainment Law Journal* 25 (2008): 1105.
Fischman Afori, O. 'The Role of the Non-functionality Requirement in Design Law'. *Fordham Intellectual Property, Media & Entertainment Law Journal* 20 (2010): 841.
Noam, M. 'Protection of Architectural Works as Designs in Israel'. *Eyuney Mishpat (Tel- Aviv University Law Review)* 15, no. 2 (1990): 343 (Hebrew).
Seligsohn, A.H. *Fundamentals in Copyright, Trademark, Patent and Design Laws* (1963) (Hebrew).

§5. Plant Variety Protection

I. Primary Legislation

Plants Breeders' Rights Law, 5733-1973.

II. Secondary Legislation

Plants Breeders' Rights Regulations, 5734-1974.

Selected Bibliography

§6. CHIP PROTECTION

I. Primary Legislation

The Integrated Circuits (Protection) Law, 5760-1999.

II. Secondary Legislation

The Integrated Circuits (Protection) (TRIPS Agreement) Order, 5760-1999.

§7. UNJUST ENRICHMENT

I. Primary Legislation

Unjust Enrichment Act, 5739-1979.

II. Books and Articles

Englard, Y. 'The Wings of a Predatory Eagle Threatening to Devour the Civil Law'. Gad Tedeschi Memorial Volume – Studies in Civil Law 37.

Index

The numbers here refer to paragraph numbers.

Index

www.ingramcontent.com/pod-product-compliance
Lightning Source LLC
Chambersburg PA
CBHW071430230926
51846CB00001B/175
9789041168580